# Books by F. Lee Bailey

---

For the Defense                           *(1975)*
The Defense Never Rests              *(1971)*

SERIES

The Criminal Law Library
*(with Henry B. Rothblatt)*   *(1968–1974)*

# FOR THE DEFENSE

# F. Lee Bailey

# FOR THE DEFENSE

---

WITH JOHN GREENYA

New York

## ATHENEUM

1975

———————————————

I was writing a dedication for this book to my wife, Lynda, who asks very little and gives a great deal, when she said, "No . . . Dedicate this book to those whom justice has eluded."

And so it is.

———————————————

# "Together"

---

HEAVY trials make me thirsty. When you've spent the entire day in court, arguing to protect your client's life or freedom, a quiet drink with friends can work wonders. Sometimes it almost makes you feel human again.

A couple of years back I was trying a particularly heavy case, and when we came to the close of the week, one of the lawyers in my firm suggested we stop for a drink. I had to see the judge's clerk briefly, so I told the others to go ahead—I'd meet them shortly in the bar.

When I got to the cocktail lounge, I noticed with no great surprise that one of the younger lawyers was talking to an unusually pretty girl. Dressed in a white knit dress, she sat back in her chair almost defensively. Her long hair was blond, not really streaked but layered with different shades, and her eyes were green and amazingly clear. But what really caught my attention was the wide mouth and the slow, startling smile.

As I moved in shamelessly on my junior colleague, I learned that the girl's name was Lynda Hart, and that she worked for a large charter airline as a supervisor of stewardesses. I noticed her delightful accent, not clearly British, but similar.

On top of her handbag was a paperback copy of a popular novel that she had apparently been reading before my associates moved in on her and bullied her into having a drink with them. Instinctively, I opened my briefcase and took out a copy of my own book, *The Defense Never Rests.*

"Here," I said, pushing it toward her, "forget that trash and read something worthwhile."

She made a few polite comments, and I could tell she hadn't the foggiest notion of who F. Lee Bailey was. What's more, as the conversation progressed and I monopolized it, I got the strong feeling that she had no interest in filling that particular gap in her general knowledge.

I was quite right. Later, just before the group broke up, I said something, and then turned to check her response. She smiled that same dazzling smile and said, "You remind me very much of a captain I used to fly for. He was a proper cocky bastard, too."

If Lynda Hart had been a witness, I would have lost the entire jury with that line. Even in casual conversation, criminal lawyers do not like to lose. But there was no doubt that this beautiful young girl with the intriguing accent had just put me down.

Eventually I got the last word. On August 26, 1972, in a small wedding ceremony in Iowa attended by a handful of close friends, Lynda Hart of New Zealand became Lynda Hart Bailey of Marshfield, Massachusetts.

Since the day of our marriage, Lynda has been with me through every trial, every skull session, and every one of those long, horrible minutes while the jury is out. I've been told by a number of longtime friends that, because of Lynda, the "proper cocky bastard" is easier to get along with. All I know for sure is that he is a far happier man.

My marriage to Lynda marked a personal turning point, not so much in my career, but in my ability to roll with the punches that any successful criminal lawyer must take. A few of the cases in this book took place before I met Lynda, some of them overlap, and most of them are of recent vintage.

When Lynda came into my life I had been married twice before, once at twenty and again when I was almost thirty. Although both marriages were to lovely women and produced three wonderful sons, the manner and pace of my professional life meant too many nights away from home. Mine is a life style guaranteed to strain any relationship between two people.

Since our marriage, Lynda and I have been apart for no more than ten or twelve nights. It's the only way that a man like me can make a marriage work. It's also what I want most.

*The Defense Never Rests,* which came out four years ago, told of the half-dozen or so cases that brought my clients, and eventually me, to public attention in the swirling sixties.

The freeing of Dr. Sam Sheppard, a case that involved everything from the simplest legal forms to oral argument before the Supreme Court of the United States, was an all-out attempt to find the last shreds of justice for a man who'd already served ten years in jail for a murder he didn't commit. The Supreme Court's decision went a long way toward ensuring that others would not suffer the same fate, and it opened the gates of the prison by ordering a new trial for Dr. Sam. But no one could give him back those ten years. He tasted freedom for a few years and then he died, much before his time. Somehow, a cog had slipped in the machinery of the American criminal justice system; once it was repaired, it was too late for Sam Sheppard.

Dr. Carl Coppolino, another medical man accused of murder, was both more and less fortunate. He was tried for two different murders, one in New Jersey, where he was set free, and one in Florida, where he was convicted. His appeal failed, and he is still in prison. As far as I am concerned, his greatest crime was to spurn a woman who later turned up as his chief accuser.

Hands down, my most unusual case during the 1960s was that of Albert DeSalvo, otherwise known as the Boston Strangler. When I learned, and was finally able to prove outside of court, that Albert was the man who had terrorized Boston with an incredible string of rapes and murders, I thought for once society had a chance to study this strange, twisted man who epitomized violence. I was wrong. In its fight for revenge and a perverse kind of glory, the state of Massachusetts rushed Albert to judgment, and by its haste ensured that he would spend the rest of his life in a prison—not a hospital. In late 1973 DeSalvo was found in his cell. He'd been stabbed to death during the night. No one ever really studied him, and society learned little or nothing about how to spot the early warning signs of this horrible kind of madness.

Not all the cases in my first book were unsettling. There was the account of the Great Plymouth Mail Robbery, the largest cash heist in the nation's history. Not only wasn't it solved, but the spectacular ineptitude of the postal inspectors all but guaranteed the acquittal of my clients, several of whom were about as capable of pulling that gigantic job as they were of building a nuclear reactor. Normally, a lawyer might say about such a case that "if it weren't so serious, it would be funny." This case was so funny that eventually it wasn't even serious.

The other cases in the book illustrated one facet or another of the profession I entered officially on November 16, 1960. I wrote the book (with the expert help of Harvey Aronson) to explain what it had been like to be on the inside of cases that were headline news for months, cases so fascinating to me that I was sure others would

enjoy reading about them, cases I simply couldn't get out of my
mind until I had them down on paper.

Life, and the law, goes on. Fortunately, the cases have continued
to come into my office. As the sixties became the seventies, I found
myself involved with several clients whose stories I felt were every
bit as interesting in their own ways as those that eventually made
their way into the pages of my first book.

First and foremost, there was Ernie Medina. From all appearances
the Army wanted to go just so far—and no farther—in its investigation of the massacre at Mylai 4. When it began to lose all of its cases
(with one spectacular exception), it zeroed in on Ernie Medina. I had
the privilege of defending Captain Medina, who is perhaps the most
decent man I have ever met. Medina stood trial twice: once in his
own mind; and again in that hot, stuffy courtroom at Fort McPherson, Georgia. I can only guess at what happened the first time, and
I'm sure it wasn't pleasant. I know all of what happened the second
time, and that story is in this book.

Glenn Wesley Turner. He's in this book, too. And on the surface
you couldn't find a man more different from Ernie Medina than
Glenn Turner. Medina is quiet, polite, reserved, and conservative to
the core; Turner is loud, gregarious, purposely outrageous, and
wildly liberal. Medina was a career military man, and Glenn Turner
was the hottest cosmetic salesman since Eve talked Adam into a fig-
leaf. Yet there are similarities.

Glenn Turner ran into trouble with the government, too. And he
decided to fight for the same reason Ernie did—he didn't think he
had done what the government said he had. I was part of that fight,
and it is in this book.

A criminal lawyer can not always actually *admire* the people he
defends. Take, for example, my client Billy Phillips. Certainly he
was charming, but you had to consider the record—Billy had been
one of the most successful crooked cops in all of New York City,
which is saying something. His downfall came when he met no less
a personage than Xaviera Hollander, soon to be known as the Happy
Hooker. "Love," however, had nothing to do with it. She was paying
*him,* to do a few illegal favors that would keep her in business, and
he got caught by the Knapp Commission, the official body that was
investigating police corruption in New York City. Billy became the
Commission's star witness, and he performed very well. In fact, he
performed too well. He was indicted, several years after the fact, and
charged with murder and assault to murder of a pimp, a prostitute,

and a "john." I may not have really admired Billy, but I couldn't help liking him—and I never thought he was a murderer.

The other cases in this book run the gamut of citizens known and unknown. All shared the odious distinction of having been indicted for a serious crime. All experienced the crushing weight of a major criminal trial.

Finally, there is my own case. My own turn as a criminal defendant. Almost without exception, from Clarence Darrow on down, defense lawyers in this country who've achieved some degree of national fame had been indicted at some point in their careers. I've known that fact for years, but never really believed I would join that fraternity. Yet it happened. In May of 1973 I was indicted for mail fraud, along with my former client Glenn Turner, eight of his past and present officials, and three of his corporations. It turned out to be the longest trial I have ever been a part of, in any capacity. And that most definitely is part of this book.

As of this writing, F. Lee Bailey is alive and well in Boston and Marshfield, Massachusetts. The seventies have not been exactly serene thus far, but I am rolling with the punches and looking forward to each new day.

There are a number of sustaining factors. Lynda is first and foremost, then there is the fact that the phone keeps ringing, the tower keeps clearing me for takeoff, and the sun keeps rising.

Each year, fewer and fewer lawyers go into the criminal law. Potentially fine advocates are lured away by the safety of private practice or the security of government service. A few admit that they are scared away from the criminal law by the risks, and the comparative lack of "respectability." The pendulum, however, will have to shift, for the times demand it. In my experience there is nothing on earth —well, almost nothing—to compare with the special joys of being a criminal lawyer.

Once in a while, if you're lucky, you get a special compliment, the kind that makes everything worthwhile.

A few years back I was defending a poor, frightened backwoods girl in the bayou country of Louisiana. All the law had to do was show her the portable electric chair that was then in use and she promptly confessed to two murders—even though she had been in jail on a minor charge when the killings took place.

The trial, such as it was, was conducted in a decrepit county office building, or "parish hall," as they are called in that state. The judge was an unusual man. He didn't care for what he called "lawyers' talk," so I soon learned to echo the prosecutor. Instead of "I object," we said, "Hey, Judge, that ain't right." After the first day, we all wore boots, put our feet up on the table, and used the spittoons.

But we practiced law, in the best sense of all that the term should mean. As the judge spoke the words ordering my client released from jail, I felt a large lump in my throat.

When the trial was over, the judge called me aside and told me that it had been an honor for him to have me in his courtroom. I thanked him and returned the compliment. Then he said something I will never forget. He said, "Mr. Bailey, I want you to know one thing. You're the furst Yankee lawyer ever come down here what didn't try to *smartass* me."

# Contents

# FOR THE DEFENSE

# The Road
# to Marshfield

---

T H E first few months of our marriage were hectic, filled with work and fun and the small joys of getting to know a loved one. They were also very tiring. My office was handling a large number of cases, and Lynda and I had been crisscrossing the United States almost nonstop. I was used to the pace, but it was beginning to tell on her.

The occasional weekend at home in Marshfield, near the South Shore below Boston, was a special pleasure, but it had to be squeezed into the heavy trial schedule. One Sunday night in late September I found her asleep on the couch in the living room. She had made her usual excellent dinner, and also as usual she'd worked too hard. Her blond hair was caught behind her, and she looked even younger than her twenty-four years. I started to pick her up and carry her to the bedroom, but decided to let her sleep where she was for a while.

I stood and looked at her. She really did resemble her favorite expression for herself—"this little kid."

An hour later I came back and picked her up. Halfway down the hall she opened her big eyes. "Where are you taking me, Lee?"

"To bed."

She grinned her most mischievous grin. "You fast-talking lawyers get me every time."

I woke early the next morning and felt like a swim. There was packing to do, and a briefcaseful of documents to gather before we took off, but I felt the urge to get in the water.

I went through the sliding glass door that connects our bedroom with the sun deck. It was going to be a fine day, but the air was far too chilly for an outdoor swim.

One of the trade-offs of a life like mine is that money *can* buy a certain amount of happiness, in the form of extras such as an indoor swimming pool. I went downstairs and dove in, not bothering with trunks. A few laps later I was wide awake.

After a fast semicold shower I went upstairs to the kitchen to make coffee. Lynda usually leaves the fixings out the night before, but she'd conked out right after dinner, so I had to rummage around, trying not to make too much noise.

I put the kettle on for instant coffee, lit a Pall Mall, and stared out the kitchen window. I could see the steam rising from the warm water of the pool. Kyp, Lynda's German shepherd puppy, was nosing around the driveway grass, sniffing the new day. It was a pleasant moment.

I bought the house in 1966. Over the years I had put a great deal of money into expanding and improving it, and the acreage that came with it.

It sits on a level lot, except for the long lawn that runs down the hill in front, across the road from a stand of tall birches. There is a winding drive leading up from the road, but most of the traffic uses the wide rear driveway that separates the house from the pool and the two-story cabana. The sliding doors that face the rear of the house are really the main doors, for they open onto the foyer of the living room.

Set into the small hillside, the house is a long, greenish-gray rambling ranch of simple contemporary design. Each of the far ends of the rectangular house are of the same height, but a thirty-foot peak extends above the living room and the foyer, which are separated by a gigantic, double-facing fireplace. The living room side of the fireplace is finished in huge fieldstones. On the foyer side the builder used a light-colored marble.

The north end of the main floor contains the kitchen and the dining room. Below is a good-sized den with couches, another fireplace, a television set against one wall, plus a huge recreation room—with an artificial Christmas tree still standing because Lynda likes to feel the Christmas spirit all year long—and a long, curved bar with ten stools.

The other end of the lower level contains the swimming pool, a long, narrow room with seldom-used pool and Ping-Pong tables (I'd like to convert it into a conference room), the laundry, and a storage room. The last room is a bedroom. A guest dubbed it "the womb" after we installed a separate window air conditioner and blocked out the only window, giving the room a timeless quality. With no light to bother them, guests have been known to sleep around the clock.

On the main level, the south wing contains our bedroom, one guest bedroom, and two others that I have converted to office use. I have a good-sized private office and my secretary has one almost as large. There is also a den equipped with video-tape equipment. All in all, about sixteen rooms.

Each end of the house has an attached garage. The one on the north holds two cars, and the one on the south is actually a hangar, for it holds a helicopter.

The helicopter facility is my newest acquisition, the one I find most functional. There is a landing pad on the back lawn in the middle of the circular drive, but the hangar itself has a mechanized device consisting of long metal tracks and a huge steel dolly in the center. The helicopter is landed on the dolly, facing the direction of the wind. Then, at the press of a button, the whole assembly retracts into the garage and the doors keep out the Massachusetts weather. With a shedful of snow removal equipment, even the worst storm is no deterrent to using the helicopter.

It's a big house, but there isn't a room that doesn't get used when we're home. When we're not home, even the room with the pool and Ping-Pong tables sees some action from the people who drop in to make sure everything is all right.

After we were married I asked Lynda if she wanted to hire a maid to help with the cleaning, or perhaps someone to cook. She said no. Her answer was, "If I need help with this house then it's too big for us." I couldn't exactly see the logic, but when Lynda makes up her mind, that's that.

The kettle was starting to sing, so I made some coffee and took it out to the cabana. I looked at the telephone. All four outside lines were blessedly still. They wouldn't start ringing for another hour or so, about the time that my secretary arrived for work. It was too late for bugs, so I left the screen door open and sat down to sip my coffee and stare at the pool.

I looked over at the house, still and large in the earliest sun. Kyp trotted up for a nuzzle, got it, and went off to sprawl under a table. In a moment we were both lost in thought, or so it must have looked.

I was born and raised in Waltham, Massachusetts, once the largest watch and clock manufacturing city in the United States. I suppose there might be some deep psychological mark left by spending one's childhood in a city whose chief industry is time, but if there is it has not yet surfaced.

All I remember about time in those early days is that my friends and I always made the most of it. And we hated its inexorable demands—lunchtime, suppertime, bedtime, and especially time to get up.

My mother founded a nursery school shortly after I was born, and when I was eight we moved onto the grounds. There was a small lake for boating in the summer and hockey—my lifelong avocation—in winter. It was as close to an idyllic situation as I've ever been in.

What was a grand time for me was a quite different period for my parents. My father, an advertising salesman, and my mother, an unusually hardworking and single-minded woman, were trying to hold their marriage together for the sake of myself and my younger brother and sister. If it is true that opposites attract, then theirs was the exception that proved the rule. I was ten when they separated.

My years in the public school system of Waltham were not happy ones. I was eager to learn, perhaps too eager, but I wanted to learn on my own terms. The school wasn't having any. I'll never forget the eighth-grade shop teacher who told my mother that he'd keep me sanding a block of wood until I learned to do it his way if it took all year. It took all year, but I still did it my way.

Then, when I was thirteen, and my unhappiness with the public school was becoming more obvious, something happened that changed the course of my life. My mother read an advertisement for a new school in the mountains of New Hampshire. Since we hadn't enough money for the tuition, they offered me a working scholarship. Everything about that school, Cardigan Mountain, was as different as it could be from the rigidity I'd known. I loved it.

When Cardigan Mountain opened in 1946 there were but twenty-five to thirty students in the four grades, sixth through ninth. I was a ninth-grader, newly freed from the constant rules and regulations of Waltham's North Junior High and transported, by the magic of my mother's persuasiveness, into a school that advertised itself as offering flexibility and freedom.

Of course there were problems, problems with the students and problems endemic to any new venture. But the small staff, most of whom were married couples, was involved in a labor of love. And it rubbed off on all of us, like the contagion of laughter, as we pitched in to serve—and even prepare—meals, mend the cranky old furnaces, and keep the buildings and grounds in something like repair.

And the only rule in shop class was: "Show me you know how to use these tools and you can do anything you want with them."

The basic curriculum included English, math, science, French, history, and Latin, but the broader course of studies encompassed the way of life chosen by the teachers and the staff—experienced, motivated people who cared about what they were doing. These people were not concerned with security, with building up years toward a pension. They wanted something more out of life. It was a lesson I never forgot.

One of my working assignments, one for which I gladly volunteered, was to help in the kitchen. There I met Clancy, Richard J. Clancy, a former cook at the Vermont State Prison in Windsor County. Among the many things he taught me was a glimmer of what it must have felt like to live your life out behind bars for a moment's error in judgment—or the almost unimaginable anguish of spending even a day in prison for a crime you did not commit.

I can't remember if Clancy was the first person who ever told me anything about Clarence Darrow, the country's most famous criminal lawyer, but his stories about Darrow are still clear in my mind. Darrow had defended Johnny Winters back in the 1920s and saved him from execution. Winters was serving his term of life in the Vermont State Prison when Clancy worked there, and the cook knew the details of the trial better than most of the reporters who had covered it at the time.

Clancy had other stories to tell about the men behind bars, some of them still claiming innocence after twenty and thirty years in prison, and stories of the men who had defended them. But my interest at the time was in the lives of the prisoners, not the lawyers, for I had just begun to think I might become a writer. What kind of emotions drove a person to take the life of another, to hold up a bank or break into someone else's home? What happened to a man or woman falsely accused of such crimes? What kind of people had they been, and how did they change as a result of such an injustice?

I won't pretend the course of my life was set because of those talks in the warm kitchen of Cardigan Mountain School or even that it was strongly influenced. Yet I find it interesting today that one of my earliest sources of what life was like in a prison came from a man who worked in one, a man who could go home at the end of his working day.

The year at Cardigan Mountain changed my attitude toward school. When I went on to Kimball Union, a prep school in Meriden, New Hampshire, I was more receptive to learning—and to regulations. And again it was a very good school.

At Kimball Union my interest in writing became stronger. I wrote for the yearbook, edited the school paper (even trying my hand at editorials), and relished the short story assignments in English class. Encouraged by my teachers to try all forms, I wrote some credible science fiction (for a fifteen-year-old) and some very imaginative bad poetry.

My three years at Kimball Union were generally happy. I couldn't say the same for my first two years of college.

From the time I left for Cardigan Mountain and returned with my diploma from Kimball Union, I had rarely lived at home. I was sixteen. I had changed, and so had my home.

In 1948 my mother had remarried (she and my father having divorced two years earlier) and I had given her away, a curious experience for a fifteen-year-old. Our new stepfather was a kind, quiet, educated man named Donald Mitchell. It would be wrong to say that my brother Bill, my sister Nancy, and I accepted him immediately. We didn't, being like most kids whose own father is replaced. We were young, not very tolerant, and still somewhat puzzled by the whole thing. But Don Mitchell is a man so fundamentally decent and kind that you can't hold anything against him for long, especially something that wasn't his fault. By the time my first precollege summer was over, Don Mitchell had forged his own unique place in the family. We loved him. We still do.

In May of 1950, a month before my seventeenth birthday, I was accepted by Harvard College. The headmaster at Kimball Union had suggested a smaller, less prestigious school, but everyone I had talked to said Harvard was the best. To me there seemed to be no real choice—if you can get into the best school, why go anywhere else? It was a decision I would come to regret.

Harvard engenders a certain awe in many students, but I was a bit too young and unprepared by life for that. Instead, I felt a growing uneasiness, in part brought on by the amount of work, in part because I wasn't so sure after all that I wanted to be there. My grades were too often the so-called "gentleman's grade"—the C, or as one of my friends called it, "the Hook."

When I say that I would come to regret that decision, I don't mean to say that it was the fault of Harvard; I simply wasn't ready for it at the time. Nor do I say that it was a two-year period of unhappy drudgery. There were many high points.

There were the courses in literature through which I was introduced to the two poets whose work has stayed with me the longest —T. S. Eliot and William Butler Yeats. (And of the two, although I love the language of Eliot and his supreme ability to capture pieces of life in a single startling line, Yeats has probably had the greater influence. It seemed to me then, and still does, that while Eliot bemoaned the human condition he nonetheless accepted his fate, whereas Yeats cursed it, and fought against it, all of his life.)

And there was the English course I took from Professor Alfred in 1952. I spent more time researching the papers I wrote for that course than for anything else that year. And they brought me the most satisfaction.

Another high point was rather unusual. In 1950 my mother had returned to college to finish her degree in fine arts. Suddenly we had four students in the house at the same time. We kidded her unmercifully, which she loved, and we helped her with her homework, which we loved.

My mother, with her strong sense of knowing just what she wanted, kept after that college degree. I didn't. By the end of my sophomore year at Harvard I wanted out. I knew I'd probably have to come back, but I wasn't doing well enough and I wasn't happy. I needed to get out for a while.

Technically, Harvard held the door open for me by granting me a leave of absence. I enlisted in the Navy while still in the second semester of my second year, and I finished the year and a summer school course before I was sworn in.

I chose the Navy because it offered a program that would teach me to fly jet airplanes. There was still a chance I could see action in Korea; and there was a better chance that I could settle my life down, at least for a while.

When I arrived in Pensacola, Florida, on November 11, 1952, for pre-flight training. I left Harvard and my family behind, but only temporarily. My mother's nursery school was by then a successful business, and she hired Dolly Gott, the girl I had been dating for more than a year, the girl who would become my first wife and the mother of my sons Bendrix and Brian.

Dolly and I were married in December of 1953. We were both twenty years old. After I graduated from pre-flight school, the Navy sent me down to Corpus Christi, Texas, for advanced training in jet flight. A few months later I transferred from the Navy to the Marine Corps and Dolly and I took a small apartment near the base, at Cherry Point, North Carolina. It had become clear that I wouldn't get to Korea, and the marines offered a better chance to fly fighters rather than transports.

One of the axioms of military life is "Never volunteer." Not being too fond of axioms, I volunteered for the unpopular duty of second assistant legal officer of Marine Fighter Squadron 334.

It changed my life.

I have said many times that the decision to follow the law, rather than writing, came as a result of reading one book, *The Art of Advocacy*, by Lloyd Paul Stryker, a book that claimed criminal lawyers were an endangered species. Yet I have to admit that fate—and my volunteering for the legal aide post at Cherry Point—played a large part in the way my life has worked out.

There were almost five hundred men in the squadron when I took that extra duty. Like any group of servicemen anywhere, they were adept at getting into all the usual, and some of the unusual, forms of trouble. We had a few thieves, many brawlers, very many men with domestic problems and a host of other legal snarls. And then we had a number who were accused of crimes and infractions but were in fact innocent.

Within weeks I was fascinated by the many challenges of my new position, for in the military an officer plays all the roles—prosecutor, defense counsel, juror, and even judge.

I continued to fly, and by this time I had picked up a commercial pilot's license and been introduced to that magnificent world of seat-of-the-pants flying, but the legal assistant duty offered me something brand new. And it began to look more intriguing each day.

Then fate stepped in. The first assistant legal officer of the squadron was killed in a tragic crash. The post of chief legal officer became vacant immediately after, as the lieutenant next in line was unnerved by the crash and turned in his wings.

By attrition, then, I became the chief legal officer. Not only wasn't I a lawyer, but I hadn't even finished college.

For the next two and a half years I tried, defended, judged, and reviewed just about every type of legal action known to military man. In all there must have been two hundred different cases. It was experience that a lawyer-to-be could not have gained anywhere else, no matter how wealthy he was or how good his connections were. I learned a legal system, that of the military, and came to respect it. And I laid the groundwork for learning the legal system that would be my life's work.

I had another bit of great luck. I was unusually fortunate to meet a civilian lawyer by the name of Harvey Hamilton. He was in private practice in Morehead City, North Carolina, the same small town where Dolly and I had an off-the-base apartment.

After we had met through a case, I asked Harvey if I could act as a troubleshooter on some of his cases. He agreed, and my first real apprenticeship began. For the next year, until I got out of the marines in late 1956, I did everything a nonlawyer can do for a lawyer. And Harvey was a busy trial lawyer. Those months were an exciting and highly valuable education.

I left the service at a run and all but galloped through law school. Boston University Law School still had a "three and three" program, which meant you could enter law school after your third year of college if you qualified on the basis of tests and other criteria. I didn't have a full three years, but did manage to get a waiver based on my legal experience in the service and with Harvey Hamilton.

On the day I began law school I opened my own investigative service. I wasn't interested in trailing deadbeats or spying on adulterers; I wanted to work for lawyers. My recent experience had taught me the importance of—in fact, the absolute necessity of—thorough pretrial preparation.

I wasn't a lawyer yet, but I already knew what some lawyers apparently never learn, that cases are seldom if ever won in court. They are won by the side that comes into court fully prepared because it has slaved to find the facts of the case before trial ever begins.

The investigation service was a success—financially because it paid my way through law school, and personally because it taught me things about the law and about myself that I could never have learned otherwise.

Law school. The memory is blurred, perhaps intentionally. I remember the work, the school work and the investigative work, and the many nights without sleep, and the cramming to get through an exam. There was hockey whenever I could steal the hours, and flying whenever I could borrow the money. And there was always the tension.

It was not a good time for Dolly, my wife, and by my second year of law school it was clear that we were not going to make it.

I'd been a lawyer for eight months when we were divorced, in July of 1961.

Dolly tried as hard as anyone could to make it work, but I was setting a pace that only I could understand. Even today, I'm not sure why I worked that hard. I guess I was driven. After the divorce, odd as it may sound, things were easier for both of us. Thanks to her innate goodness and decency, we were able to remain friends. Our sons, Ben and Brian, live with their mother, and visit with me often.

Once I had my ticket, I was off and running. I wonder if I've ever really stopped since.


The house in Marshfield, a suburb twenty miles south of Boston, is not far from where I had grown up, fifty miles at most. But the house on the grounds of the Green Acres School in Waltham was light-years away from my present life style. I don't mean to paint my early years as a period of hunger and longing in the Great Depression. Things were never really bad for us. But there was a lot of stretching to make ends meet.

Here in Marshfield I own a house two or three times more expensive than the one I grew up in—and I'm lucky if I use it more than three months of the year.

When I was sixteen I bought my first car, a 1932 Chrysler, for fifty dollars. Now, at forty-one, I have two cars out in the garage—a Mercedes 350 SL and a Citroën Maserati—and I couldn't buy a spare tire for either one of them for less than fifty dollars. And I own two beautiful airplanes and a company in Michigan that makes helicopters.

My law offices in Boston are located in the penthouse suite of one of the newest buildings in the renewed downtown area. There are several people on the payroll there, and another half dozen or more work for me as pilots, mechanics, and secretaries in Marshfield.

In the last decade, I've been the host of a television program produced by David Susskind (who probably should have been the star, too, considering the program's short run), and authored books both for criminal lawyers and the general public (*The Defense Never Rests*, written with Harvey Aronson, which chronicled my defense of such famous clients and cases as Dr. Sam Sheppard, the Boston Strangler, the Great Plymouth Mail Robbery, and Dr. Carl Coppolino, among others). I've probably made more speeches than even Hubert Humphrey.

The boy from Waltham who'd gone off to boarding school on a working scholarship had become a criminal lawyer whose face was on the cover of national magazines. It has been—as my teen-aged sons would say—"quite a trip."

The trip began to pick up speed as soon as I passed the bar examination. When I opened my own office in November of 1960, my friends told me I was long on guts and short on good sense. In truth, I had a lot more fingers than cases. But that same month I fell right into the middle of the most highly publicized murder trial in recent Boston history. The defendant's name was George Edgerly.

His trial was in its third week when I got a call from Charlie Zimmerman, an expert polygraph examiner whom I'd hired to test a client in another case. Charlie was calling to ask if I might be able, on very brief notice, to assist Edgerly's lawyer in preparing the cross-examination of a polygraph examiner the government had sprung on the defense as a surprise witness.

It was a particularly unsavory case, the kind that newspapers love. George and Betty Edgerly were hardly model citizens. Although George was a skilled and dependable auto mechanic, praised by his boss, his private life was something else. Fidelity was an unknown word in the Edgerly household, but though George's record was bad, Betty's was worse. Also, she had once served time. Her specialty was to pick up a man, usually a serviceman, and suggest they get better acquainted in her car. Unfortunately, her car was already occupied by her cohorts, who would beat and rob Betty's new friend.

Somehow the marriage held together, until the night of December 27, 1959, when Betty and George were driving home and he got stuck in the snow. He left on foot to find help; when he returned, Betty was gone.

The following May, she turned up in the Merrimac River, but not entirely. When the grappling chains brought up her body, in pieces, it was short one arm and a head. The papers immediately tagged it the Torso Murder Case. And after many months George Edgerly was picked up and charged with the murder of his wife.

In the spring of 1960, while I was studying for the bar exam, I read the newspaper accounts of the arrest with great interest and considerable envy of John Tobin, Edgerly's lawyer. Then past seventy, Tobin had a well-deserved reputation for excellence in the practice of criminal law.

My interest and envy were rekindled that winter when I read the accounts of the first few days of trial. One story that I read several times said the police gave George Edgerly three lie-detector tests. According to the newspaper, although two were inconclusive, the third indicated that he was not telling the truth when he denied killing his wife.

It was this last test that brought me into the case. While in the service I had gained a good deal of experience in the use of the polygraph (which is not a lie detector but actually a truth verifier: It is considered accurate in recording honest answers; the presence of stress reactions to certain important questions *may* show dishonesty).

In the investigative service for lawyers I had run when I got out of the service and began law school at Boston University, one of our chief services was to encourage the use of polygraph tests. So, even though I had been a lawyer for less than a month when Charlie Zimmerman called me, I was one of the few attorneys in the entire state of Massachusetts who knew anything at all about the polygraph. For one thing, the question of the tests' admissibility as evidence was still being tested on a case-by-case basis.

As Zimmerman explained over the phone, the prosecutor had neatly sandbagged John Tobin on the polygraph issue. Knowing that his client had been given two tests by the police, and that the results were not positive one way or the other, Tobin moved to admit the tests into evidence when he heard one of the investigating officers testify about certain "test results." What Tobin didn't know, because his client had forgotten to tell him, was that there had been a third test. And this one, as the headlines proclaimed, showed EDGERLY FLUNKS LIE DETECTOR TEST.

The third examination had been administered by Augustine Lawlor, a local druggist who was gaining experience in his hobby of polygraph testing by conducting free tests for law enforcement groups in and around Lowell, Massachusetts. When he tested George Edgerly, he told him it was a freebie, which caused Edgerly to forget about it. Tobin asked Zimmerman to find a lawyer who knew something about this polygraph device, and to find him fast. Lawlor was scheduled to testify the next day.

Zimmerman explained that the test results were not particularly clear and asked if I knew enough about the polygraph to take apart a self-styled expert in front of the jury. This rocked me. Until then all my experience had been in showing the reliability and accuracy of the machine. I had no idea how to go about showing the opposite, but I did know that a test is only as good as the person who administers it, so I accepted.

When I met with John Tobin less than an hour later, I could see he was not a well man. In fact, he told me that he was on his

way home to bed under doctor's orders. We talked the afternoon away. He told me that until the government had surprised him with the Lawlor test, the case was going Edgerly's way. (There were several witnesses who had testified to seeing Betty on the street after the date George had allegedly killed her.) But the Lawlor surprise had turned things around. If Lawlor's testimony stood up under cross-examination, Edgerly was in big trouble.

Tobin was too sick to absorb the immense complexities of the polygraph technique in a few hours, and too sick to cross-examine even if he knew the technique cold. He asked if I would pinch-hit for him. He had no need to twist my arm.

That night I sat down in my apartment with a pound of coffee, two close friends (one my chief investigator and the other a lawyer I'd gone to school with), and all the books on the polygraph I could find. What I didn't read, the others summarized for me, and when morning came I was ready.

John Tobin was not in court when I got there. His doctor had ordered him to remain in bed.

George Edgerly was there, though. You couldn't miss him. At that time the state of Massachusetts still clung to the barbaric practice of putting defendants in a gigantic wire cage directly across from the jury box. To my surprise, Edgerly was confident and alert. "Do you think you can tear this lie detector guy apart?" he asked.

I told him I couldn't guarantee it, but I was sure going to give it my best shot.

Lawlor was not an easy mark. Some witnesses who appear positive on direct examination begin to weaken at the first sign of a vigorous cross-examination. Not Augustine Lawlor.

But I had an advantage—he was an honest man. He would not shape his answers to protect himself or the state's case. And he had not expected to face a lawyer who knew anything more than the dictionary definition of the polygraph.

When it was all over, two hours later, he had admitted that although both the institute where he had studied (the justly respected Keeler Polygraph Institute) and the handbook that came with the Keeler machine he'd used to test Edgerly recommended against it, he had used only two of the usual three methods of recording the subject's physical responses.

He also admitted that he noticed the subject was not in the best physical condition—George, out on bail, had in fact tied one on the night before the test and had a good-sized hangover—even though he knew that the best examiners will not test a man unless the subject is well rested and in apparent good health. He also said he knew Edgerly had been interrogated by police officials for four hours just before the test.

The jury had appeared impressed with Lawlor's credentials when he'd testified on direct, but when they heard that he did the tests for nothing while others charged for the same work, their faces began to change. Later, as I questioned the witness on the actual test records, the polygrams, which I'd had pinned to a large board near the jury box, the jurors heard a man who was no longer so sure that his results were conclusive.

There was no dramatic reversal, no sudden breakdown on the part of the witness in the manner to which Perry Mason has made us accustomed. But when I finished, the witness no longer appeared to be an expert.

George Edgerly motioned me over to his cage. "That was pretty good. How about sticking around 'til the case is over?"

I explained to George that it was John Tobin's case and that he couldn't be in better hands. When you are a defendant in the most famous murder case of the day, you need all the experience and wisdom you can hire.

That afternoon John Tobin called and invited me into the case personally. For a young Boston trial lawyer in his first year of practice, there could not have been a more valuable offer. I have lectured ever since then about the fundamental importance of hard work and thorough preparation, but I've never discounted the *x* factor. You wouldn't want to make book on being in the right place at the right time, but it happens. I know.

Edgerly's defense hung on the credibility of two most reluctant witnesses. The first was a former accomplice of Betty Edgerly's in her pick-'em-up-and-roll-'em days who had served time for the same offense that had sent her away. Unlike Betty, he'd mended his ways. When we found him he was a model citizen, understandably hesitant to have his family and neighbors learn of his past.

The second witness was a man who knew that the bloodstains found in the back of George Edgerly's car were not necessarily those of the deceased. He knew because he had borrowed the car from George and used it for a back-seat tryst. His reluctance to testify stemmed from the fact that his partner on that amorous occasion was a girl who'd been engaged to marry someone else. He didn't want to bring her name into it.

I sympathized with their problems, but I called them both to the stand. When a man is on trial for his life, that problem takes precedence.

Fortunately, it was not necessary to mention the name of the girl who had been in the back seat of George's car on the night he lent it to his friend. The testimony was most helpful.

We almost lost the benefit of the testimony of the second man. He testified that he'd seen Betty on a downtown Lowell street six weeks after the date that George had allegedly killed her. But the prosecutor surprised us by confronting the witness with a signed statement he'd given a policeman, saying he wasn't sure it was really Betty. The witness claimed the police lieutenant had forced him to sign by threatening to expose the man's past if he insisted on testifying.

Our hopes were rekindled when I was able to bring out, on cross-examination, that there had been a third party present when the witness talked with the lieutenant. And that third party, whom the witness had asked to be present for moral support, was a Roman Catholic priest.

Today, there are many cities around the country where the word of a priest carries little more weight than that of, say, a television personality. But in Boston, Massachusetts, in February of 1961, a week or so after the inauguration of John F. Kennedy as President of the United States, we could not have asked for better corroboration. Unless, of course, we could have gotten Cardinal Cushing.

The priest, however, was nowhere to be found. He had been transferred out of state, and all efforts to contact him had failed. The police lieutenant took the stand and admitted he knew the priest, but claimed the clergyman had not been present at the meeting. Without the priest we were in a real box, and it wasn't a confessional, though as it turned out it amounted to the same thing.

We finally made phone contact with the priest in upstate New York. But he had a problem of his own; he viewed his contact with the witness as part of a priest-penitent relationship and would not discuss it over the phone, perhaps not even in court. However, he would come to Boston the next day.

The waiting was terrible. We had no idea whose testimony he would corroborate, our witness's or that of the policeman.

At the suggestion of both the prosecutor and the defense lawyers, the priest met alone with the judge in his chambers. An hour later the judge informed us that not only had the priest said the policeman was lying and the version given by our witness was completely true, but that the priest had also related that the policeman had called him the day before and asked him to stay away. The next morning the judge informed the jury that if the priest had taken the stand he would have corroborated the story of our witness.

It was time for final argument. John Tobin made me another offer: Would I like to make the final argument to the jury?

It was not the easiest proposition. For one thing, although I had read all the testimony in the four-week case, I had heard less than half of it myself. For another, I would have to attack the government's polygraph "expert," Mr. Lawlor, at a time when I was working on a case that could turn on the legality of using polygraph evidence. And finally, there was the defendant to consider. He had hired one of the ablest and most experienced criminal lawyers in Boston and was now faced with having a twenty-seven-year-old neophyte make his final plea.

I looked at John Tobin. He was seventy-two years old. He was recovering, but not too quickly under this pressure, from a recent heart attack. George Edgerly was looking at him, too.

Finally, the defendant said, "Look, Mr. Tobin, you're my lawyer. But I don't want you to kill yourself. If you think the kid can do it, that's okay with me."

I argued to the jury for two hours. It was a rambling, impassioned indictment of lying police officials, politically ambitious prosecutors who weren't above getting a false indictment and riding the publicity to reelection, and just about anything else I could think of, including unlicensed "experts" who practice on their patients.

I was exhausted when it was over. The jury left at four o'clock in the afternoon. At two in the morning we were summoned from the bar across the street by a call from the clerk's office. The jury had reached a verdict.

"Mr. Foreman, how say you? Is the defendant guilty or not guilty?"

"We find the defendant, George Edgerly, not guilty."

The win in that case brought a flood of stories in the Boston press that guaranteed new clients. And some of these clients, unlike George Edgerly, had money for lawyers' fees. When they didn't, the notoriety of the case was enough to start the phone ringing with another batch of prospective clients. For a criminal lawyer it was a winning circle.

Most of the clients who came into my office as a result of the Edgerly publicity were something less than solid citizens. There were a number of ex-convicts, small-time hoods, and people who worked some small hustle on the fringes of the mob. Many of them hadn't committed the crimes they had been charged with, but they very well might have. It was in their line of work, so to speak.

The exception was Dr. Joseph Kreplick. His line of work was psychiatry, and he'd done very well at it. He had a large practice, a beautiful wife and family, and a large home in the prestigious Boston suburb of Arlington. Though not a blueblood from one of the founding families, he was by all standards a solid Bostonian professional man.

When he walked into my office in early 1962 he looked as if he'd been sent over by Central Casting. A graduate of Tufts medical school, Joseph Kreplick was tall, decidedly handsome, polite but reserved. And he was in big trouble.

Dr. Kreplick was charged with raping a patient. The alleged victim was an attractive young woman, aged twenty-nine, who said the doctor had treated her with sodium pentathol to lower her resistance and then took advantage of her.

Recent newspaper stories have informed us that as many as 7 percent of all practicing psychiatrists use sexual intercourse as a method of treating patients. But in the early sixties such a form of treatment was most definitely banned in Boston.

Nor, for that matter, did the woman contend that the act was in any way part of the treatment or that the doctor represented it as such. What she called it was rape.

Conviction would have ruined Dr. Kreplick's practice and probably also his life. Even if he were acquitted of rape by the jury's finding that the act of intercourse was not forced upon the woman, he would still have to face the disciplinary action of the medical society.

I had to prove his complete innocence.

The woman testified that the act had occurred on her twenty-fourth visit to Dr. Kreplick, whose office was in his home, that she was a virgin at the time, and that she had been seeing him because of a nerve problem.

I had some doubts whether a woman that attractive had been a virgin at the age of twenty-nine, but there was no doubt about her having a nerve problem.

When the case began—and the woman was thirty, married, and a mother—it was clear that she had trouble breathing when she became nervous. She suffered from hyperventilation, a condition caused by taking too much air into the lungs, particularly during moments of stress. The jury was clearly sympathetic to the state's chief witness.

Unlike some of my other early clients, Dr. Kreplick had money, which meant we were able to do a thorough investigation. The digging turned up two important pieces of information. The first was that George, the woman's husband, had been her boy friend during the time she saw Dr. Kreplick, and the second was that she had seen another psychiatrist prior to being a patient of the defendant.

I couldn't put the husband on the stand and ask him if he and his wife had been lovers prior to their marriage (because of the husband-wife privilege), but the witness herself gave us the opportunity to pursue the issue.

On direct examination, she made a statement that sent all the reporters in the packed courtroom scrambling for the telephones. She testified that when the doctor first suggested intercourse he told her that his "equipment was bigger than George's."

Once George had been so colorfully introduced we had the testimony we needed, so we could ask her if she and George had ever had sexual intercourse prior to marriage and prior to the date of the alleged rape. Her answer to both questions was yes, but she said that Dr. Kreplick had encouraged her to have relations with George in order to "relieve tension."

That took care of her virginity—no jury will accept postdated virginity—but we were still left with the charges of rape and adultery.

My investigation had brought out several interesting facts. First of all, the complaining witness had seen another psychiatrist for years before she ever went to see Dr. Kreplick, and because the state of Massachusetts does not have a law prohibiting doctors from testifying as to professional relationships, we could call her first psychiatrist as a defense witness. Secondly, the woman was no longer receiving psychiatric care, which allowed the presumption that she considered herself to be cured. Third, a doctor who had examined her hours after the alleged rape had not reported indications of forcible entry. And finally, she and other members of her family had pooled funds to hire a lawyer and bring a $50,000 malpractice suit against Dr. Kreplick.

It was a difficult cross-examination. No jury likes to see an aggressive defense lawyer hammering away at a lay witness, especially a shy, attractive young woman who was so nervous she had trouble getting her breath. But there were inconsistencies in her direct testimony that I had to go into.

As carefully as I could, I established that she had not stopped the doctor, or even tried to, when he removed her underpants: "I assumed he knew what he was doing." Also, I brought out that she had testified to his hands being on her legs, her shoulders, and her stomach, all at the same time. She told the jury that although he stood while performing the alleged act, his hands were "all over the place." The jurors were confronted with a mental image of a male figure with six arms.

Finally, she had testified that she knew the house was empty, Mrs. Kreplick being away, yet the doctor had attacked her on the examining table in his office. In itself, this was not such startling testimony, even though it cast some doubt. But I had an ace to play. The examination table stood three feet four inches off the floor—half a foot higher than Dr. Kreplick's crotch. Even a contortionist on tiptoes could not have done the deed on that table.

What doubt remained in the jurors' minds was wiped away by the testimony of the psychiatrist who had seen her before she went to Dr. Kreplick. He said she had visited him sixty-seven times under a free public health program, stopping the treatment when he told her she should begin to pay for her visits. He related that she had told him numerous times of a fantasy in which she was approached by a strange "faceless man" and pushed up against a wall and attacked, each time imagining severe pains "in the genital region." This dovetailed neatly with her direct testimony about the alleged attack by Dr. Kreplick.

After two hours of deliberation, the jury came back with an acquittal.

Dr. Kreplick's troubles were far from over. As I had suspected from the beginning, and had learned by way of an anonymous phone call early in the first trial, another indictment awaited him.

Several months after the verdict in Kreplick I, a sealed indictment was handed down against him, accusing him of rape, five counts of adultery, and abortion.

This time the complaining witness was a single woman, aged twenty-seven, who said she had been forced to have intercourse with the doctor over a four-month period.

A petite woman, weighing less than a hundred pounds, the state's witness was a fledgling writer who had gone to Dr. Kreplick to relieve her recurring bouts of depression. She testified that she had been seeing Dr. Kreplick for a month when he forced her to undress, and within three hours had relations with her four times. According to her story, which I felt was rooted in impure fantasy, the semireluctant affair continued until January when she found she was pregnant.

The witness, demure and initially calm, testified that Dr. Kreplick came to her home in February of 1960 and performed an abortion. It was shortly thereafter, she said, that she went to the authorities and swore out a complaint against the doctor.

We had a strong witness for the defense in another psychiatrist, whom the witness had consulted during her alleged rape-adultery-abortion affair with Dr. Kreplick. On the stand, he said that the witness was "mentally ill" when he treated her, and that she had difficulty distinguishing reality from fantasy.

The prosecutor, John Irwin, was an able lawyer and a strong cross-examiner. He managed to poke some holes in the defense witness—and to goad me into several outbursts—but I felt we had managed to put considerable doubt in the minds of several jurors.

Then the defendant took the stand. Dr. Kreplick was an impressive witness. Tall, like the prosecutor, patrician, and confident without being cocky, he stood up well under Irwin's questions. But he made a classic mistake, one of the kind that cause defense attorneys to wake up screaming in the middle of the night.

It was not an important point, in the sense that it would show guilt or innocence, but it jolted Dr. Kreplick's credibility.

The complaining witness testified that Dr. Kreplick had treated her for a vaginal infection during the time the alleged adulterous acts had taken place. The doctor denied it, emphatically, when I questioned him about it, and his denial on the stand was equally firm. I took my client's word for it. And I learned a lesson.

The night before Dr. Kreplick took the stand, John Irwin sent a law clerk to the pharmacy where the woman claimed to have taken the prescription. In the druggist's files he found a three-year-old prescription for the witness-patient signed by . . . Dr. Kreplick.

On the stand the next day, the defendant denied ever having written a prescription for a vaginal infection for the complaining witness. Irwin then produced the small piece of paper. Kreplick identified the exhibit as one of his own prescriptions, and when Irwin asked him to read it to the jury, the doctor was forced to tell them that it was a prescription for Tritheon, a drug used to combat vaginal infection.

The second Kreplick trial was extremely emotional, with both Irwin and me showing flashes of anger. He was upset with me for keeping the witness on the stand for three days of intense cross-examination during which she lost her veneer of calm maturity. I had objected strongly to the manner in which he ridiculed the older and highly respected psychiatrist I had put on as a defense witness.

Finally it came to a head. During my examination of another defense witness I told the court that Irwin had intimidated the witness. Irwin stood up and shouted, "The witness is a liar."

I blew, and called Irwin a liar.

He wasted no time in losing his own temper: "Call me a liar again and I'll knock you over the jury rail."

"You'll what?" I shouted back.

The judge got into the act by ordering us "Into the lobby! Into the lobby!"

Out we went. But after a few moments of heavy glowering, we both began to cool down. It was the closest I'd ever come to a fist fight in open court. I can just imagine what the Boston Bar Association would have done with that.

The jury in the second Kreplick case was out for nine hours. It acquitted the defendant on the rape charge and two counts of adultery and found him guilty of three counts of adultery and the one count of abortion. He served several months of an up-to-five-year indeterminate sentence before he was paroled. When he got out, both his practice and his marriage were long gone.

Kreplick and Edgerly were but two of the early cases I tried in Massachusetts. I remembered the names of some of the others: *Commonwealth* v. *Page, Commonwealth* v. *Bonomi, Commonwealth* v. *Martin, Commonwealth* v. *Kadra,* and *Commonwealth* v. *Fatalo.*

The names brought back a rush of memories from those early days. Nights without sleep, the little office I shared with Bob Barton across from my apartment in Boston, and the time I insisted my kid brother Bill skip the dinner his Harvard fraternity house was giving for Nathan Pusey, the University president, so we could play hockey. (I told Bill no one would miss him, because they always made him sit way in the back of the hall anyway; later he learned his seat had been directly across from the president's and a variety of lame excuses had been made for him.)

They weren't very flush times, but they were good ones. And it was good to remember them.

Kyp's friendly bark brought me back to the present. I looked up from my coffee to see Gerry Gibson pull a battered tennis ball from the dog's mouth and throw it toward the road.

"Morning, Lee."

"Hi, Gerry. Oh, tell your mother we won't be able to make it for dinner on Saturday. We'll be in Michigan for the weekend. Tell her maybe the weekend after that, okay?"

"Sure," Gerry grinned. A big husky nineteen-year-old, Gerry had been in charge of cutting the grass, and other general chores, for almost as long as I'd lived next door to his family. Now that he was halfway through college, his younger brothers would soon inherit his job.

I watched Gerry drive the large tractor-mower out of the shed, listened to hear if the engine was running the way it should, and got up. I noticed how much he was beginning to resemble his father, "Chewy" Gibson, my neighbor and friend. Time passes. Amen.

When I got to the house, Lynda was setting the table for breakfast.

"Morning, hon. The eggs are almost ready. Remember, you have to call Ernie at the helicopter factory this morning. Something about the shafts, I think."

I grinned back at her. "Shafts?"

She grinned back. "Shut up and eat your eggs."

Any time a criminal lawyer with some years of experience sits down to write a book, and a surprising number of them have done so, there is a process of elimination that has to be followed. Sometimes, a truly fascinating case cannot be used because it might further damage an innocent man or woman who, quite rightly, wants only to forget a horrible experience.

In *The Defense Never Rests*, there was one case that I could not use because it hadn't quite finished, and it bothered me greatly to have to leave it out. It was the case of the *United States Army* v. *Captain Ernest Medina*. Medina had been Lt. William Calley's company commander in Vietnam, generally, and in Mylai 4, specifically. If ever the inside story of a case deserved to be told, this is the one. Therefore, the first of the recent cases in this book is that of Ernest L. Medina, Capt. U.S.A., *retired*.

# "Oh, My God, What Happened?"

*The briefing that I conducted for my company was that C Company had been selected to conduct a combat assault operation onto the village of Mylai 4 beginning with LZ time 0730 hours on the morning of the 16th of March of 1968. I gave them the enemy situation, intelligence reports. Good intelligence reports were that the 48th VC Battalion was located at the village of Mylai 4. I told them that the VC Battalion was approximately— numbered approximately—250 to 280 men and that we would be outnumbered approximately two to one and that we could expect to—a hell of a good fight and that we would probably be heavily engaged.*

*. . . I told the people that this would give them a chance to engage the 48th VC Battalion; that the 48th VC Battalion is the one that we had been chasing around the Task Force Barker area of operation, and we would finally get a chance to engage them in combat. And we would be able to destroy the 48th VC Battalion.*

*. . . My company had closed into the night defensive position where we were going to marry up with the Bravo Company, 4th of the 3rd Infantry. We were to establish our night defensive position in his graveyard. We arrived there sometime approximately between 1530, 1630 hours on the 16th of March. . . . Also, at this time, I had an indication that the 48th VC Battalion which was supposed to have been in the village of Mylai 4, had not been there. That there had been a number of noncombatants killed.*

*At that time Maj. Calhoun had instructed me to try to deter-*
*mine the number of innocent civilians that had been killed at*
*the village of Mylai 4. I got my platoon leaders together and I*
*asked them for a body count of innocent civilians that had been*
*killed.*

*The 1st Platoon leader, Lt. Calley, told me in excess of 50.*
*Lt. Brooks, the 2nd Platoon leader, told me the like number.*
*He says, "I believe the like number of 50 or more." Lt. LaCross,*
*the 3rd Platoon leader, gave me a body count of six.*

*At that time, I said, "Oh, my God, what happened?"*

> Capt. Ernest L. Medina,
> testifying at the court-
> martial of Lt. William
> F. Calley, Jr.
> March 10, 1971

FORT Benning, Georgia, the home of the U.S. Infantry, is a city unto itself. Its miles of roads wind past homes, schools, chapels, athletic fields, and hundreds of classroom buildings. The clean streets and neat lawns are in sharp contrast to the rugged Georgia countryside, with its red clay and tall pine forests, where troops are schooled in the realities of hard terrain.

The guards at the main gate of Fort Benning wear a distinctive patch: a sword upon a shield, and the words, "Follow Me."

In early November of 1969, two young men sat across a desk in one of the many offices of the legal section, the Judge Advocate General's Corps. They were both captains, but there the resemblance ended. Edwin Richards had been an Army lawyer for six months. He had come in as a captain, exchanging four years' service for the privilege of not being drafted while he was in law school. The other man was Richards' service opposite; a fourteen-year veteran, the thirty-three-year-old career officer had come up through the ranks. His name was Ernest Medina.

Nineteen months earlier, Captain Medina had been the company commander of Charlie Company when its troops swept through an obscure South Vietnamese hamlet that would go down in history as Mylai 4. One of the platoon leaders was an inexperienced young second lieutenant by the name of William Calley.

Medina and Richards were discussing the likelihood of a court-martial against Medina, in light of the charges that had recently been brought against Lieutenant Calley.

Just weeks before their meeting, Medina was getting ready to move his family to Florida, where he was to attend the University of Tampa. The Army would pay for him to complete his undergraduate studies, an investment more than justified by his record. The day before he was to leave, he was called to the office of the battalion commander and told that he had been put on "administrative hold." He was informed that Captain Richards was to be his military counsel.

After they had talked for more than an hour, Medina said to the other captain, "With all due respect, I'm afraid that your two AWOL cases are just not going to be enough experience for what's ahead of me."

Richards repeated what they both knew so well, that no formal charges had been filed, but Medina was not satisfied. The dark-skinned Mexican-American had a feeling, almost a premonition. He felt he was headed for the fight of his life.

"Captain Richards, who are the best criminal lawyers in the United States today?"

Richards' eyes widened. "Are you serious?" Medina did not bother to answer, so Richards said, "Well, I guess Percy Foreman, F. Lee Bailey, and Edward Bennett Williams."

Medina nodded. "Okay. I never heard of two of them, so tell me— how do I get in touch with F. Lee Bailey?"

As it happened, I was in my Boston office when Captain Richards called. After listening for a few minutes, I told him that I read the situation much the way Captain Medina did. The papers were filled with news of the charges against Calley, and that, plus the "administrative hold" on Medina's orders, sounded ominous to me. I said I'd be happy to talk with them if they could come up to Boston.

I prefer to meet prospective clients in my own office—probably because it is such a pleasant contrast from meeting them in a state or federal prison—and I looked forward to sitting down with them. But as it turned out, it was a few weeks before we got together.

For one thing, the Army refused to pay Captain Richards' air fare to Boston. Then it took several more days to clear the paperwork so Richards could accompany Medina (at Medina's expense) to meet with me in Columbus, Ohio, where I was in the middle of a trial.

My client was a heavy by the name of Frank Baldasarro, who was on trial, along with the eight policemen he was accused of bribing, for conspiracy to violate the gambling laws, mainly in regard to the numbers racket.

Because I had not yet decided to take the case, I was concerned as to how the press would react if I was seen talking to Medina in the courthouse, and later turned the case down. So I went to the airport myself to meet them.

I had told Captain Richards where I'd be, and when I saw an olive-skinned young man of medium height and build hurrying toward me, I thought it had to be Medina. But he went hurriedly past me and disappeared through the men's room door.

As it turned out, it *was* Medina. By the time he came back from the toilet, Captain Richards had already introduced himself, and we were standing there talking. Embarrassed, Medina explained that he thought he had recognized me, but he was in no condition to stop— it was a question of first things first.

Back at my hotel, we sat down and talked for a long time. Richards did the talking for Medina, and one of the points he mentioned intrigued me: when Medina learned that his orders had been changed, that he had been put on "administrative hold," he reacted angrily and insisted that the battalion commander read him his rights (under Article 31 of the Uniform Code of Military Justice) then and there.

This meant that Medina was insisting that he be charged with a crime. He wanted the trouble out in the open. I took this as a sign of character.

As I listened to Richards, I watched Medina. You can learn a lot about a man by the way he reacts while a lawyer is talking for him. Does he nod too often in agreement? Does he look uncomfortable as the alleged facts are laid out? Or does he, in exasperation, finally take over the narrative himself?

For a while, as Richards explained the chances of a court-martial against Medina, the latter sat quietly, an impassive figure behind a mask of military bearing. But as points were ticked off he began to react, ever so slightly at first, and then more visibly. After fifteen minutes, he couldn't hold himself back. The first thing he said was prefaced by, "Mr. Bailey, sir," a form of address he was never to abandon.

Medina began to speak, haltingly at first, his words tumbling out in all their military clumsiness, and then suddenly he stopped.

"Mr. Bailey, I have to talk about money."

I raised my hand to let him know that I would hear his full story before any discussion of fees was necessary, but he plunged on. "I don't have much money. But if I sell my car, and take a loan on my furniture, I can raise almost five thousand dollars. If you would accept that as—"

I finally got him to shut up. My office takes a number of worthy cases each year for no fee, and I had almost made up my mind that this would be one of them. But I wanted to hear Medina's defense, his own story of what role he played in the Mylai tragedy. It took considerable persuasion to get him off the topic of my fee.

"Well—" he looked at me uncertainly—"what happened is this."

An hour and a half later, I knew what I had to know. Either this young Army captain was innocent of any killings or I was listening to a pathological liar. I had one last point.

"Captain Medina, if it should become necessary, because of conflicting stories that others might tell about you, will you take a polygraph test?"

Medina looked confused. After a moment he said, "A what?"

I had to grin. "A lie-detector test. To see if you are telling the truth."

"Oh." His face brightened. "Yes, I will. Of course."

I had all that I needed to know for the moment. There was no doubt, as far as I was concerned, that I was talking to an innocent man. I told Medina to be quiet while I explained that I did, on occasion, take cases for nothing, and that his would be one of those. I told him to keep his car and his furniture, and to consider our agreement binding.

I wasn't being totally altruistic. For one thing, I owed a debt to the military. It had given me my first legal training, and in fact, had it not been for the military, I would not have become a lawyer in the first place. The training I had gotten in the military made it possible for me to step out initially as an experienced lawyer. I liked the military system of justice and had frequently praised it.

In this case I wanted to see it work, and wanted to help make it work. I thought—and this was of great importance—the military forum was the proper place for Medina to be charged and tried.

To pacify Medina, I finally agreed that the fee for legal services would be no more than one thousand dollars. For the first time in two hours, he looked relieved.

I suggested that since we all needed to eat something, we should go across the street and have dinner. We had just sat down, and I had ordered drinks, when I saw Medina was looking nervous again.

He was reading the large, two-sided menu that had the descriptions on one side and the prices on the other. Medina was looking at the prices.

I told him to relax, that this dinner was on me. And finally he did. But he ordered the least expensive dinner on the menu.

Alone in the hotel room, I made myself a drink and thought about this man Medina. I'd formed a strong horseback opinion of him as an honest man. But what did I really know about him? In the next few weeks I received more pieces of his story. And the more I learned, the more I liked.

Ernest L. Medina was born in late August of 1936 in Springer, a foothills town in northern New Mexico. His father was a ranch hand. Within a year of his birth, Medina's mother died of cancer, and the infant and his ten-year-old sister were sent to live with their grandparents in Montrose, Colorado. The boy's father became a sheepherder.

Life with his grandparents was simple, hard, and loving. Only Spanish was spoken in the home, and children were expected to perform all tasks quietly and without complaint. At one point Medina mentioned, "If my grandfather wanted a glass of water, I was to get it for him, bring it to him, and then stand there silently until he'd finished so I could then carry it back to the kitchen." It was a thoroughly regimented life, probably an ideal atmosphere for a young boy who would one day become a noncommissioned officer in the United States Army.

In the grandparents' home there was love and respect, exactly what the people of Montrose felt and displayed toward their country. Patriotism was real and vibrant during the years of World War II and the conflict in Korea while Ernie Medina was growing up in Colorado. He told me, as he would tell so many other "interviewers" in the months to come, that one of the clearest memories of his early teen-age years was that of serving as an altar boy for the funerals of soldiers who had been shipped home for burial. The playing of taps, and the simple dignity of the flag-draped coffin, had made a deep impression on the serious young boy.

There was never any doubt that Ernie Medina would enter the military. For one thing, he could not afford to go to college, and the handicap of speaking Spanish at home and English in school during his early years had made him less than confident about meeting the challenge of higher education. In 1954, when Medina graduated from high school, he had been in the Colorado National Guard for four years, rising to the rank of sergeant first class. He could have joined the Army at that same rank, but, typically, he felt he was not ready, and instead enlisted as a private.

This same careful self-appraisal led him, two years later when he was a sergeant stationed in Germany, to decline his first chance at Officers Candidate School. Bothered by his lack of a college degree—which he felt was a prerequisite for a good officer—he turned it down. Several years later he accepted, but by then he was a married man and a father, having wed a German girl whose parents were East German refugees. He graduated fourth in his class of two hundred.

He stayed at Fort Benning, Georgia, for ranger and airborne schools, and then, to his disappointment, was assigned as an instructor for two years. Medina longed for "command time," but knew that it went first to West Pointers, then to ROTC officers, and finally to officers like himself who had come up through the ranks.

He finally got his chance in 1966, when he was sent to Hawaii, where he was assigned to a battalion of the Eleventh Light Infantry Brigade. When he took it over, Charlie Company was something less than a disciplined, cohesive unit; by the time it was sent to Vietnam, in 1967, it had developed both pride and discipline. It would never have a great deal of combat skill. There wasn't enough time for that.

Earlier that evening, Medina had described the events of February 25, 1968, the day on which Charlie Company suffered its heaviest losses, and still another day on which it never saw the enemy. He began with an account of the night before, when a soldier came to him with a problem:

" 'Sir . . . I don't know how to go about . . . I don't want you to think I am running out on you or that I am chicken or that I want to leave the people here, but I have a brother that is serving in Vietnam.' [Army regulations forbade two members of the same family serving in Vietnam at the same time.] And I told him, 'Why didn't you tell me before? I could have put you on the resupply ship that just brought in the resupplies, gotten you back to Chulai and we could have checked your story out.' He says, 'No, sir, that is not what I wanted . . . I will wait until we get back in.' "

Medina's way of expressing himself is pure Army. There is a striving for accuracy that often results in awkward, ungrammatical constructions. And there is the tendency, all too familiar to those who remember military accounts of the progress of the fighting in Vietnam, to depersonalize—a man, a woman, a soldier, even a child becomes simply "the individual."

On the morning of February 25, Charlie Company began to move through a large field. Three men went first, carrying minesweepers.

"We were moving rather slow trying to clear the area when the lead element detonated a mine. First I thought it was incoming artillery. Another one went off and another one. Immediately the cry started going up for, 'Medic! Medic!' In the mine field incident, I lost a number of people. My senior medic who had moved through the mine field very courageously also was—had given a lot of medical assistance, was trying to get to the third platoon leader when he detonated a mine and blew his foot off.

"We started sweeping the area as best we could with mine detectors, taking pieces of toilet paper and marking the mines that we found. We had one individual that we could not evacuate that was dead; it was the individual that had talked to me the night before about wanting to leave South Vietnam because he had a brother that was serving there. I took the medic that was with me, the platoon medic from the first platoon, and he and I moved through the mine field to where the individual was laying. He was split as if somebody had taken a cleaver and right up from his crotch all the way up to his chest cavity. I have never seen anything that looked so unreal in my entire life; the intestines, the liver, and the stomach and the blood looked just like plastic. We took a poncho and we spread it out and the medic started to pick him up by the legs. I reached underneath his arms to place him on top of the poncho and we set him on top of another mine. The concussion blew me back. I fell backwards, as I got up the medic was starting to go to pieces on me. He started to come out of the ditch and I looked at him as if he had stood behind the screen and somebody had taken a paint brush with red paint and splattered it through the screen. He was—had blood all over him. I grabbed him as he started to pass me and I shook him and I said, 'My God, don't go to pieces on me. You are the only medic I have got. I have got people that are hurt.' I hit him. I slapped him. I knocked him to the ground and I helped him get back up, and I seen on his religious medal a piece of liver and I tried to get it off the individual before he seen it. The individual was very shook up.

"We lost approximately sixteen wounded in the mine field, and four—three—that were killed by mines and booby traps. As we were moving back, Lieutenant Brooks's platoon was—point man—was moving through a hedgerow, detonated a fifteen or 105 artillery shell killing him and wounding a couple of others."

For his courage and heroism in leading his men out of that mine field on February 25, Captain Medina earned the army's third highest decoration, the Silver Star.

Everything I learned about Medina, during that first conversation and in the weeks and months that followed, led me to the certainty that the man who had sat across from me in my hotel suite in Columbus did not look, act, or sound like the kind of man who would order—or even tolerate—the massacre of old men, women, and children.

Still I did not minimize the danger that Ernie Medina was facing. Calley had been charged with multiple murders, and if Medina was to be charged, it was a good bet that the charges against him would be similar. For one thing, there was a growing clamor in the country to get to the truth of that fateful day in March of 1968. Were Calley to be the only soldier seriously charged, there would be a tremendous hue and cry. It was a good deal like sitting on a time bomb.

I was pleased that Medina would most likely be tried, if he were to be tried at all, by a military court. Many people disagreed with me in those early days of the case, for they believed that the Army wanted several lower-level scapegoats, and that Calley and Medina appeared to fill the bill.

I felt just the opposite. As far as I was concerned, Medina's chances would be potentially far worse with a civil jury, where an emotional juror who violently opposed the war in Vietnam might well equate Ernie Medina with the entire war effort, and see a vote of guilty as a way of objectifying his or her strong antiwar position. To my mind, Medina's best chance was with a jury of his own people, military officers, who knew what it was like to get hit with that "red paintbrush."

Another reason why I felt more comfortable with a military jury and judge was that I expected we would one day be faced with a direct conflict in testimony. If and when it came down to Medina's word against that of another soldier or officer, I wanted that conflict to be resolved by a panel that knew something about military relationships.

Finally, I had the reassurance, based on personal knowledge, that the military placed a great deal of weight upon the results of the polygraph. In my experience, there was never a case of the military bringing a man to trial after he'd passed a polygraph examination. All things considered, we had a lot going for us.

The strongest factor, however, was the impression I had formed, almost from the first instant, that Ernie Medina was a good man. When I told him, in our first meeting, that I would treat his case as

a sort of pro bono matter, for no fee, he was not entirely happy. He
didn't say it, but I could tell he didn't like the idea of being a charity
case. That's why I told him that I would take the case for a fee "not
to exceed one thousand dollars." And that's when his face broke into
the wide, open smile I would get to know so well. I had the feeling
that he fought down the urge to salute.

Although there are similarities to the civilian system, the military's
criminal justice procedure differs in important particulars from our
state and federal systems. There are three levels of courts-martial,
just as there are lower and higher courts, but the only one with jurisdiction to try offenses as severe as those involved in Mylai 4 was the
general court-martial, which could impose the death penalty for murder in the first degree or treason.

A general court-martial is composed of a minimum of five and a
maximum of eleven officers, all of whom are superior in rank to the
accused, and presided over by a military judge who is usually a full
colonel but who has power and stature similar to that of a federal
district judge. His is the final word on matters of law, and the military
jury—sometimes called "the court"—has the final word on matters of
fact.

Unlike civilian systems, where almost always a unanimous vote is
required either to convict or acquit, a military jury looks for a two-
thirds majority. If two-thirds or more vote to convict, that is a conviction; if less than two-thirds vote to convict, that is an automatic
acquittal. This is, in my mind, a far superior system, eliminating in
almost every case the "hung jury" that causes justice to spin its
wheels so frequently in civilian courts, especially in these times of
widely differing viewpoints among individual jurors.

Perhaps equally important, the military jury itself may summon
witnesses that neither lawyer has cared to call, and to put questions
to those witnesses by submitting them in writing to the military
judge. If the questions are not patently improper, or if the judge can
reword them so that they will fit the rules of courtroom propriety, the
judge puts the questions. If the answers are unsatisfactory, the military jury can modify or resubmit the questions.

Basically, a military jury is a strong cut above any civilian jury
that is ever likely to be assembled. All the jurors are officers—except
in the case of an accused enlisted man who demands enlisted participation—and almost always each military officer has a good education
and some pretty good common sense. The shenanigans in which
counsel usually indulge in order to mislead some jury of mediocre

intellectual powers, are senseless tactics in a military court, because they are quickly perceived by military jurors and almost always rejected as an insincere attitude on the part of counsel, and ultimately his client.

In my opinion, the single greatest attribute of the military system is its painstakingly careful pretrial screening procedure—which does, in fact, eliminate most innocent men from ever going to a full-fledged court-martial. What this involves is the presentation of charges, written up in formal fashion, and signed by someone having personal knowledge sufficient to make the charge in the first place. These are then sent to the convening authority, that is, the ranking officer with the power to assemble a general court-martial by appointing its members—judge, jury, and counsel—and submitting those charges to it for trial. That convening authority is the first party to review the result of the trial if there is a conviction, and unlike any civilian appellate court, has the power to disagree with the court in its findings of fact, and order an acquittal where a conviction has taken place. (An acquittal, of course, can never be reviewed.) The convening authority also has the power to lower the sentence, if he believes it has been too harshly imposed.

Prior to trial, however, he must convene what is called an Article 32 investigation by appointing an officer senior in rank to the accused to act as investigating officer (and he need not be a lawyer), and in the case of a general court-martial, by appointing certified military lawyers to act for both the prosecution and the defense.

Unlike the secret and too often clearly unfair grand jury proceedings in the civilian sector, the Article 32 investigation, although not open to the public and the press, nonetheless requires the presence of the accused and his counsel at every stage of the proceedings. And counsel is permitted to cross-examine the government witnesses. If he elects to do so, the accused can present witnesses of his own in an effort to persuade the investigating officer that no trial should be recommended.

As a result of this system, there is very little excuse for counsel to be unprepared, or to be swinging in the dark, as is too often our lot in civilian courts.

It is ironic that many people criticize the military system of justice as inferior and unfair, principally, I suppose, because it lacks the "jury selected at random," which is supposed to be a mainstay of our due process system.

The fact is, if I were innocent, I would far prefer to stand trial before a military tribunal governed by the Uniform Code of Military Justice than by any court, state or federal. I suppose that if I were guilty and hoping to deceive a court into an acquittal or to create a reasonable doubt in the face of muddled evidence, I would be fearful of a military court because their accuracy in coming to the "correct" result (in fact and not simply a legally correct result, which means only a fair trial, and not that guilty men are found guilty or that innocent men are acquitted) has a far better accuracy rate than any civilian court has ever approached.

This is not to say that the military system is without abuses or possible abuses. There is no question but that a venal commanding officer can exercise a certain degree of control over the appointment of his military court, one that might tend to shape the result. In the olden days, it used to be popular to suspect that military jurors would say to themselves, "Well, the commanding officer knows more than we do about his case, so we'll convict the accused and give him the maximum sentence, and then the commanding officer can see that justice is done at his first level of review."

I personally never encountered that attitude in three years of trying, defending, reviewing, and sitting as a juror in the Marine Corps. And I do not believe that it was a factor in any of the Mylai trials.

One exception that I have to my admiration for the military system lies in the enforcement of purely military laws. There is no such thing (except in contempt of court charges for disrespect in open court) in civilian life that is tantamount to disobedience of an order, or unmilitary conduct. And I think that military courts sometimes lean a little too strongly toward conviction when charges of this nature are at issue, simply to provide reinforcement of the supremacy of discipline. But in the case of any so-called civilian offense, a regular felony such as robbery, rape, or murder, I think that a man with a defense—that is, a man who is not facing an open-and-shut case—is generally far better off in a military court than he would be in any civilian court.

Some of the disrepute into which military courts have been thrown lately resulted from the 1970 trial of Capt. Howard Levy, an Army doctor who refused to give training to Green Beret troops because he claimed to have personally known that they were committing atrocities. He was then charged, among other things, with disobedience of orders, and was defended on the grounds that no one had the right to order him to assist men in the perpetration of atrocities, which was exactly what his training would have done.

Perhaps if Captain Levy had been tried after the military had to face up to Mylai 4, he would have had a better opportunity. But in all probability, given the way that the charge was drawn and the way that the law was given to the military court that convicted him, they had very little choice in the matter.

Captain Levy's is one of those rare cases where the defendant might have been better off before a sympathetic civilian jury, some of whose members might have disregarded the instructions of the court and voted for acquittal out of sympathy—something that is not very likely to happen in a military trial.

However, in my opinion, the most salient feature of injecting a military attitude into due process of law is that military people are by their nature disciplined—that is, they are equipped to follow orders and instructions that they might not like very much personally. A jury is given the terrible and uncomfortable task of freeing everybody in whose favor a reasonable doubt remains, and to my mind this takes a high degree of discipline, especially when the jury as a whole feel that a defendant is "probably" guilty, and yet the government has failed to quite prove a case beyond "a reasonable doubt."

In this gray area (and I think that many trials wind up with the total factual picture landing in the gray area between a "probability" and "beyond a reasonable doubt") a military jury is, by way of its own mental attitude, far better equipped to follow the hard rule of law than to attempt to mix social and value judgments together with the judge's charge, and see that "justice" is done. I think that a military juror feels far less discomfort than his civilian counterpart at simply saying to himself, "This is not proof beyond a reasonable doubt. The charge is not proven, and therefore my verdict is 'not guilty.' "

At the time I met Ernie Medina, all our talk of the differences between the civil and military systems of justice was just that—talk. The only hard fact clear in his mind was that things had gone terribly wrong at Mylai 4.

Charlie Company was nothing to be proud of when Captain Medina took it over in Hawaii in 1966. But after months of small victories—getting a new mess sergeant, printing company stationery, and begging sports equipment—it was shaping up. But "shaping up" is a relative term, and when the company was finally shipped to Vietnam in the last month of 1967, the troops were still green.

At 1530 hours on March 15, 1968, Medina gave his company a final, and ultimately notorious, briefing. Morale may or may not have been high, but the adrenalin level was. February 25 was still clear in everyone's mind. For two months the men of Charlie Company had moved under the specter of the famed 48th VC Battalion, a force they were told was 250 to 280 men strong.

Medina told his troops that they would finally be engaging the enemy that had caused the death of so many of their number, the silent and deadly 48th. It was the company's first real chance to meet the enemy. He attempted to inspire his men, drawing on all that he had learned about the new and confusing way that war was fought in Southeast Asia. He did not have to tell his men about the dangers of civilians who appeared to be noncombatants; they already knew all about that—a week earlier they had passed an old woman on the road, and asked her if there were mines on the trail ahead. She shook her head no. When they found the first one, so obviously in their path, they knew she had to have just walked around it.

If Medina said anything special to, or even looked directly at, Lt. William Calley, he doesn't remember it today. Calley was not his most trusted lieutenant.

And there was another problem. On February 25, the day of the mine field tragedies, Lieutenant Calley had been on leave—or "R and R," for rest and recuperation—and the death of his buddies had shocked and angered him. Medina knew Calley wanted "revenge."

The captain told his troops to destroy the village.

Someone asked if that meant poisoning the wells, and Medina said no. He explained that the wells should be closed by filling them with bamboo stalks, but that the men should not go so far as to poison them.

Someone else asked if they were to shoot women and children. In that context, it was not a startling question. Medina said no, again, and carefully explained that they should "use common sense." If the civilians presented no visible threat, they were to be rounded up for evacuation.

The next morning, at 0720 hours, the artillery started laying down a barrage of protection so that Charlie Company could move into the hamlet. Helicopter gunships strafed the village. Ten minutes later they started in.

Back in the command post, Medina waited for reports. Not long after, a helicopter pilot reported that the LZ (landing zone) was "cold," which meant that no enemy fire was being drawn. Seconds later another chopper pilot cut in to say, "Negative, the LZ is hot." Medina sent the "hot" message forward, and the platoons moved in toward the village itself.

At some point during the next three hours, for reasons no one has ever been able to explain fully, Captain Ernest Medina lost control of his troops.

Shortly after 1030 hours, Medina and his command group of almost ten soldiers moved toward the village. Still under the impression that they would meet the feared VCs at any moment, they moved quickly. Yet Medina saw things that shook him to his core.

And he shot a human being for the first time in his life.

By the time he had moved down the trail and almost out of the village, Medina had seen bodies. And he knew they were not the bodies of VC soldiers. As he reported later, "I estimated the number of dead noncombatants at twenty to twenty-eight."

When it was all over, he would have to revise that estimate.

The next day, with the rumors of a massacre of civilians reaching upward through the chain of command, Medina was ordered by Major Calhoun to go back into Mylai 4. He resisted. He was ordered again, but suddenly a voice cut in through the radio channel to proclaim, "Negative. That [body count] sounds about right. Don't send him back in there." It was General Koster, the division commander. Captain Medina never went back.

When it came time to make out the report, Medina asked for the estimates of civilian deaths. Each platoon leader gave his report, Calley, Brooks, and LaCross. All but one gave figures that shocked Medina. Yet he filed a most conservative report, using a number he feared might have been far too low.

Almost a year later, a former soldier from another company wrestled with his conscience and lost. Ronald Ridenhour wrote a letter to several congressmen. It set in motion a chain of events that would eventually culminate in the trials of six soldiers, including Lieutenant Calley and Captain Medina.

Nineteen seventy was a long, hard year for Medina. It was a year of hopes raised, only to be dashed, a year of frequent testimony and extensive preparation, and a year of terrible, unavoidable soul-searching. Most of all it was a year of uncertainty, for although it always appeared that formal charges were to be announced, they were never made.

On the first of March 1970, while he was still stationed at Fort Benning, and trying to act busy at a make-work job, Medina took a telephone call from a party who apparently had the wrong number. Medina found the right extension and had the caller transferred. Moments later, the phone rang again. It was the same person, but this time he asked for Captain Medina.

To Medina's orderly, military mind, such small confusions and inefficiencies meant time wasted. It was a minor example of sloppy soldiering, something he deplored.

"Captain Medina? This is Captain Mark Kadish at Fort McPherson. I've just been appointed your defense counsel."

"What?"

"I said I'm your new defense counsel. I'd like to come up and see you this afternoon . . ."

"Just a minute, Captain," Medina interrupted bluntly, "unless you know something I don't know, I'm not aware that I need a military defense counsel yet. Captain Richards is my military counsel, and no charges have come down against me. Also, I have civilian counsel."

"Yes, I understand you have retained F. Lee Bailey."

By now the wheels were turning in Medina's mind. He knew that the appointment of a defense counsel meant only one thing. "Captain Kadish, I assume that you've been around long enough to know that if you've been appointed my defense counsel, I'm going to be charged. Now just what do you know?"

"Well," Kadish answered, "they're investigating the whole thing, and we don't know exactly . . ."

"Don't give me that bullshit," Medina cut in again. "You either know I'm going to be charged or you don't."

Yet Kadish didn't know; all he knew was what he had told Medina. But Kadish had been a military lawyer for two years, and he knew one thing for sure, as he said later, that "Ernie Medina was in very hot water."

Kadish asked Medina for my law firm's number in Boston so he could talk to me about the all-but-certain case. Medina told him not to bother, that he would make the call himself and get back in touch with Kadish. It was definitely a "don't call us, we'll call you" situation.

And there were a few questions that Medina wanted Kadish to answer. He asked Kadish where he had gone to college, what law school he'd graduated from, how long he'd been in the Army, and what legal experience he'd had.

A few minutes later he knew that Kadish was twenty-eight years old, a graduate of Lafayette College (an excellent liberal arts school in Easton, Pennsylvania) with a law degree from New York University, and that he had worked for a Wall Street firm for eight months before taking a commission in the Judge Advocate General's Corps. He had been in ROTC in college. Medina also learned that for the first year and a half Kadish had been a "collections lawyer" for the Army, but that he had worked solely as a defense lawyer for the last six months, and had successfully defended a soldier charged with rape.

Although he'd hoped for a defense lawyer with more experience in courts-martial, Medina was impressed with Kadish's educational background and with the fact that he had been married since his junior year in college. To Medina, this last fact meant that Kadish had to be able to apply himself to his studies, for—like Medina—Kadish was a father (one child to Medina's three).

Whatever budding confidence Medina might have had in his new military lawyer was almost destroyed the next day, when the two captains met for the first time. As Medina later reported to me, "He drove down to Fort Benning in a motor pool car, and when he got out, he looked like almost every other JAG corps officer I'd ever seen —long hair, his brass wasn't shined, his jacket was unbuttoned, and his shoes were dusty. He wasn't very impressive at all, in fact he was a mess, a complete mess."

Kadish wanted to go over and meet Captain Richards, Medina's first military counsel, but Medina had a few things he wanted taken care of first. "Now look, Captain," he said to Kadish, "before we go anywhere, you're going to get yourself straightened out. Button up your jacket. The next time I see you I want your hair cut and your brass polished, and you shine those shoes." As Medina would tell people later, in a classic understatement, "We really didn't hit it off too well."

A week later, Medina was in Kadish's office in Fort McPherson when the phone rang. Kadish took the call, and after a moment looked over at Medina with raised eyebrows. "The colonel wants to talk with you."

Medina sighed. "I'm sure he doesn't want to welcome me to the post. I imagine this is it."

Kadish said, "Look, when you go over there, if he starts to read you your rights under Article Thirty-one of the Uniform Code of Military Justice, tell him you want your military counsel present."

Medina nodded and took the phone. But instead of a request that he come to the colonel's office, Medina heard a Colonel West begin to read the charges against him—over the telephone.

Medina was stunned. By the time his short phone conversation was finished he had been charged with the overall responsibility for the murder of one hundred unnamed civilians, the murder of a woman, the murder of a young boy, and two counts of assault with a dangerous weapon. A week later, another charge was added, almost as an afterthought: attempting to cover up the massacre at Mylai 4.

By the end of March 1970, two things had changed. The military side of Medina's defense was functioning well, and Medina and Kadish were getting on famously.

On the day after their first meeting, Medina had told Kadish he should get started organizing the material, categorizing it, and putting things into books. To his surprise, when he came back the next morning Kadish had already made an impressive start. Medina was beginning to see that under Mark Kadish's less-than-military exterior there was a first-rate legal mind, and a commitment to neatness and order that even Medina would come to envy.

The importance of good organization would soon become apparent. Before Colonel West concluded his phone call to Medina he informed the captain that he would be referring the charges for an Article 32 investigation, and that it would probably get under way quite soon.

Apparently, the Army had made the charges against Medina public, for the phone in Kadish's office suddenly began ringing, almost nonstop. The young captain found himself being questioned by Chet Huntley and David Brinkley, and other calls came in from the major wire services, even the European Reuters News Service.

All of the callers wanted a statement from Medina. Mark called my office but they couldn't reach me, so Kadish had to make a quick decision. He made it: Medina would hold a brief press conference that same day at FortMcPherson.

That evening Medina faced more cameras, photographers, microphones, and interrogators than he'd ever seen before in his life. Kadish handled things well, and Captain Ernest Medina told the world that he was innocent of the charges, and that he fully expected that the upcoming Article 32 investigation would not recommend a court-martial.

For his part in arranging the press conference, Kadish earned a sharp rebuke from Colonel Taylor, the man who had appointed Kadish to defend Medina. It was the beginning of a rift between the Army and Medina's military defense lawyers that would widen as the case progressed.

The Article 32 investigation got under way with the naming of Col. James Mobley as chief investigating officer. An engineer rather than a lawyer, Mobley was a solid, experienced officer with a lot of time in the Army. His job was to conduct the hearings and direct the Army investigators, who were interviewing all the present and past members of Charlie Company with any knowledge of the Mylai affair.

Laymen, and even lawyers with little knowledge of the military system, often compare an Article 32 investigation to the civilian grand jury. But the two are as different as day and night, or Scotch and soda. The most important differences are that in a 32 investigation the accused is constantly represented by counsel, and the defense has the right both to cross-examine witnesses and to call its own.

My partner Gerry Alch, Kadish, and Ed Richards were at Medina's side for the first phases of the investigation, and watched, with some surprise, as a number of witnesses gave testimony harmful to Medina. (My own role, initially, was that of legal strategist. I planned the moves that were carried out by Gerry and the Army defense lawyers.)

Prior to the appearance of any of his former men, Medina would sit down with Kadish and Richards and give them some background on the witness. Because of these briefings, and the fact that the defense had most of the prior statements made by the witnesses (which might have been given to Army CID investigators, the Peers Committee, or before congressional hearings), they were able to cross-examine a number of the witnesses effectively. By so doing, they were able to either contradict earlier statements or at least cast some doubt on the truthfulness of the person on the stand.

As the number of witnesses passed thirty, Alch reported the first signs of a change in Medina's attitude. One day Ernie said to me, "At the beginning, I felt that I could put my trust in the military judicial system because I grew up with it, and I've been led to believe it was good and very fair. And I've always tried to be very fair when I sat in on courts-martial boards or when I had somebody court-martialed. So I felt the system would be fair to me. But the way this is going, I'm starting to have second thoughts. It doesn't seem to me that they're really interested in investigating this thing, but just in compiling a record so they can charge me formally."

Toward the end of the Article 32 proceedings, the Army called a witness who could have done great damage to Medina's cause. Instead, he provided ammunition for the defense—and one of the few light moments in the entire proceedings.

At the time of the attack on Mylai 4, Herbert Carter was a private in Charlie Company. A young, eager black man, Carter had always been rated a good soldier by Medina. In the treacherous territory of

South Vietnam, Carter was always one of the first to check out a tunnel or a hootch. He even volunteered for the duties of a "tunnel rat." Medina had liked him as much as any member of his company.

But Carter had given damaging testimony against Medina in both the Peers Committee hearings and to the Army's CID investigator. Reading over the file, Medina said, "This just doesn't sound like Carter."

The defense knew that Carter was now a civilian, but it hadn't been able to locate and interview him prior to his appearance before Colonel Mobley's 32 hearing. We had heard that Carter was now managing an up-and-coming rock group known as Sly and the Family Stone, and when he walked into the hearing, he definitely looked the part. He acted it, too.

Dressed in brilliant red bell-bottomed slacks and a shirt to match, Carter had a huge medallion hanging around his neck, and his long hair was plastered to his head. As he came down the aisle, all but strutting, he was every inch a "with-it dude."

Incredibly, when he was sworn in, he turned to Colonel Mobley and said, "How you doing, baby?" Then he attempted to give the startled colonel the "brothers' salute," an open-palmed slap.

Neither Colonel Mobley or Major Eckhardt, the quiet, pipe-smoking officer who would be the chief prosecutor, was able to get anywhere with Carter. They just didn't speak the same language. I had somewhat better luck, probably because I was a civilian. After a few minutes Carter and I were getting on just fine.

When I asked him if he had testified truthfully about Captain Medina before the Peers Committee and when he talked to the CID investigator, he said he had "probably" not.

"Why do you say that?"

" 'Cause I was stoned on heroin."

"You were what?"

"I was stoned out of my head on heroin. I didn't know what those cats wanted, but I said whatever I thought they wanted to hear."

"Were you a heroin addict after your tour of duty in South Vietnam?"

"I would use it now and then. Today I'm clean. But when they interviewed me, I was on the stuff."

With all the stories in the papers about drug use by the troops overseas, no one on the other side appeared to be particularly anxious to open that can of worms, so the Army let Carter go.

His appearance had been one very light moment in an otherwise too-serious affair, but Carter had one more "scene" before he left. I had come to Fort McPherson from the Northeast, carrying a three-quarter-length mink coat that a client had given me as a Christmas present. The coat was a beautiful thing, and I noticed that Carter stopped to admire it as he passed the defense table. I said, "Do you like that coat, Mr. Carter?"

Carter stopped, looked at me, and broke into a magnificent smile. He walked over and gave me an elaborate slap on the palm, saying loudly, "I love that coat to death, baby!"

With that he turned and left the room, followed by every pair of eyes.

Medina was right in his appraisal of the Article 32 investigation. At the conclusion of the hearings, Colonel Mobley recommended to Gen. Albert O. Conner, the general court-martial convening authority at Fort McPherson, that Captain Ernest L. Medina be court-martialed on all the original charges, and that General Conner name the military judge and set a date for trial.

For quite some time I had been saying, publicly as well as privately, that Medina would never come to trial. But after mid-1970 I no longer was so sure.

For one thing, during the Article 32 proceedings and over my strong objection, Colonel Mobley allowed into evidence a number of statements that had not been made under oath, statements harmful to Medina. When we pressed the issue, insisting that only sworn statements be allowed, he denied our claim. Also, Colonel Mobley read into evidence several written statements, damaging to Medina, without attempting to produce the authors of the statements for verification or cross-examination.

In the fall of 1970 the Article 32 investigation was still going on, and although I couldn't really call it a "railroading," I had to agree with Medina's earlier appraisal that it looked like the Army was only interested in compiling a record so it could charge him.

All year long, the press had been having a field day. In December of 1969 *Time* magazine showed its penchant for not letting facts get in the way of a good story. It quoted one of Medina's former troops as saying he had seen Medina shoot a small boy while the child was surrounded by numerous civilian bodies, including that of the child's mother. The same issue also carried this extremely damaging statement: ". . . the biggest mystery so far is why no charges have been placed against Captain Medina, who played an important role in the slaughter by the accounts of a number of his men, though exactly what orders he issued is disputed."

Within days, Medina's children began to have trouble in school. His son had to be disciplined for fighting with a classmate who shouted at him, one day at recess, "Your father shoots babies! Your father's a murderer!"

I filed suit against *Time* for libeling my client, charging:

Said statements hereinabove referred to were false and were published by the Defendant maliciously, wantonly and in reckless indifference to the Plaintiff's rights, feelings, and reputation. . . . Said false statements, published and circulated by Defendant as hereinabove stated, did hold out and represent to the subscribers and readers of Defendant's magazine that the Plaintiff was a murderer of mothers and children and should be legally charged as such. . . . By reason whereof, the Plaintiff was held up to public and national hatred and contempt, was brought to scorn and ridicule, and was further thereby greatly injured in feelings and reputation.

We sued for ten million dollars in compensatory damages—and a hundred million in punitive or exemplary damages.

Shortly thereafter, I got a call from Henry Anatole Grunwald, *Time*'s managing editor. He told me he thought our suit wasn't worth much, but he had a question: he said he could understand the ten-million-dollar figure, but not the "incredible" amount we were demanding in punitive damages. I explained that we added the larger amount as part of a plan; knowing that *Time* was in some financial trouble, we hoped to recover the hundred million dollars and use it to buy the magazine. And we planned to rename it, *The Medina Newsweekly*.

He said he "failed to see the humor." Unfortunately, he got the last laugh. The court threw out the suit on the grounds that we could make no showing of actual malice. That is the now the prevailing legal view (according to the case of *Sullivan* v. *The New York Times*); you can libel a person all you want as long as you don't do it out of a mean spirit. Or, at least as long as no one can prove it was malicious. Interestingly, *Time* was able to claim that Medina was a public figure through *Time*'s own efforts—and therefore fair game.

The *Time* episode was one of several instances during the ordeal of Ernie Medina when I was reminded of the press coverage of one of my former clients, the late Dr. Sam Sheppard. In fairness to the press, however, I had to admit the uniqueness of the situation: the country was fighting a war that only a few people still looked upon as a "noble effort." There was deep division in the nation, and each day the antiwar ranks gained in size and influence. This, too, was a hard fact for Medina to face.

Still, Medina was holding up fairly well. He went through a long struggle with the military to get housing on the base at Fort Mc-Pherson (he wanted to move there as soon as he could; he was spending half his time driving the two hundred-mile round trip from Fort Benning to aid Kadish and Richards in organizing the material for his defense). It was a losing battle. The Army appreciated Medina's situation, acknowledged that his family would be safer on the post, but couldn't bump the senior officers already in line ahead of him. In June of 1970 he rented a house in Atlanta, five miles from the base.

One of the things that helped to buoy up the young captain was his mail. As the investigation dragged on, he got more and more letters from people he had never met, and all but a tiny fraction were messages of support.

What particularly pleased him was that the mail reflected a cross-section of Americans, not just a rabid superpatriotic fringe.

One of the letters that most touched him was from a lawyer in the South who explained that he could offer nothing more than moral support, but that he and his wife had some idea of what it must have been like over in Vietnam because their only son had been killed there. The couple was troubled by the change they had seen—through their son's letters—in a boy who had always been decent to everyone of all races and creeds; but his letters from Vietnam revealed a young mind growing more and more ambivalent toward the people he was supposed to be helping. The lawyer didn't spell it out, perhaps he couldn't, but he felt that this had something to do with the tragedy at Mylai.

Another factor that helped Medina keep things in balance was Mark Kadish's offbeat sense of humor. Often, after a twelve- or four-teen-hour day, when both men were too tired to read another CID statement or another newspaper account for possible adverse pretrial publicity, Kadish would put his feet up on the desk and dig into the mail bag. After a minute or two he would find what he was looking for, and read loudly, " 'Dear Captain Medina: Don't let it get you down. I know what you are going through. I have been a prisoner for years, but don't let them do it to you.' Signed" . . . and then Kadish would wait until he had Medina's full attention, " 'Napoleon Bonaparte.' "

What had begun as something less than a mutual admiration so-

ciety between Medina and his military defense counsel had changed
into a strong friendship. Medina had learned that although there
were a number of surface differences, he and Kadish were both hard
workers and essentially serious young men. They were developing
into a good team.

Under Medina's unrelenting scrutiny, Kadish had changed some
of his unmilitary habits, but not to the point of giving in entirely.
Even in front of newsmen, who were becoming frequent visitors to
Fort McPherson as 1970 wore on, Medina would look at Kadish and
suddenly snap, in all seriousness, "Captain Kadish, you're a miserable
excuse for a soldier. Button that jacket!" Kadish would snap a salute,
and respond, "Yes sir," but the jacket would stay as it was.

Life was not easy for Ernie Medina and his family, but it was
beginning to fit a pattern. And Medina was used to patterns.

As the year dragged on, it became more and more clear that Ernie
Medina was headed for a confrontation with a troubled young man
by the name of William Calley.

We had heard that Calley had signed a book contract with Viking
Press, and that former *Esquire* editor John Sack was to help him
write it. Their advance was reportedly $150,000. Word began to filter
back that Calley was not at all harsh on Medina in the tapes he had
done so far, and there was an underlying tone to the Calley "Confessions" (as they were labeled in *Esquire*) that expressed his own
ineptness as an officer.

This worried us because we also knew that Calley had refused the
out offered him by the report of one of the congressional subcom-
mittees that had held hearings on Mylai. The report stated that the
atrocities were so grave as to suggest that the American soldiers who
had perpetrated them must have been temporarily insane. Rusty
Calley was not buying it; no one was going to call him insane. (In
fact, I later learned that Ed Bennett Williams had turned down the
chance to defend Calley because he would not have full control of
how the defense was to be run.) For better or worse, Calley was going
to call the shots in his own trial.

The tone of the "Confessions," plus Calley's refusal to consider
an insanity defense, meant only one thing to me: he was going to lay
it all on Medina.

Whatever doubt about the issue of whether or not Medina had
ordered his troops to kill noncombatants at the infamous March 15
briefing was erased—according to Calley's version—in the second

*Esquire* installment, February 1971, which hit the newstands right in the middle of the Calley trial.

By this time, everyone on Medina's defense team was thoroughly convinced that Ernie was innocent of all the charges that had been brought against him. But there was one factor we could not ignore— the Yamashita case.

Japanese General Tomouki Yamashita commanded all the Japanese troops in the Philippines during the last months of World War II. In those final days of fighting, with the empire's defeat all but certain, Yamashita's troops lost contact with their commander. They ran amok, slaughtering thousands of Philippine civilians. Although it was clear, and not disputed, that Yamashita was totally unaware of the atrocities committed by the troops far down the line of his command, the United States brought him to trial.

Based on the legal theory that a war commander is responsible for the crimes committed by his troops—whether he knew of them or not—General Yamashita was tried and convicted. An appeal was taken to the Supreme Court of the United States, which refused to overturn the conviction. President Truman would not grant clemency. General Douglas MacArthur was quoted as saying that the Japanese general had "failed utterly his soldiers' faith." On the fourth anniversary of Pearl Harbor, Yamashita was sentenced to be hanged to death.

In one sense, it made little or no difference what Lieutenant Calley said; the Army prosecutors had all the precedent they needed. Still, it was our strong feeling that we had more to fear from Calley than Yamashita. We felt that way for one simple reason—if the Army pushed the precedent of the Yamashita case, the chain of responsibility would not stop with Capt. Ernest L. Medina. It could go all the way up to the top, to the commander of all the U.S. forces, the President of the United States. We didn't think the Army wanted that. We thought the Army wanted the buck to stop with our client.

The Army's own investigation into the Mylai massacre had several phases, but the most important was the hearings held in the fall and the winter of 1969–70 in a cavernous room in the bowels of the Pentagon in Washington, D.C. It was known as the Peers Committee hearings, because its chief officer was Lt. General William R. Peers. It called hundreds of witnesses. When it was finally satisfied that it had as much of the truth as it was liable to get, the committee wrote its report.

Released on March 17, 1970, the report stated what everyone already knew—that "a tragedy of major proportions occurred"—and divided the blame between those who killed and those who tried to cover it up. The alleged cover-up was the subject of the Peers Committee investigation. Recommendations for courts-martial were part of the committee's report, and twenty-five soldiers, including Captain Medina, were named. Thirteen were charged with murder and other crimes; twelve were charged with a cover-up. Some were officers, some were not.

On October 6, 1970, the first soldier went on trial. David Mitchell, a staff sergeant from Louisiana, a member of Lieutenant Calley's platoon, was charged with "about thirty" murders.

After telling the court that he would call thirteen witnesses or more, the prosecutor surprised everyone by resting his case after the testimony of three witnesses. If they were believed, he said, then he had proven his case against Sergeant Mitchell.

A few days later, after deliberating for six hours and fifty minutes, the military jury returned its verdict—"not guilty."

No one on our team had wanted to see a guilty verdict; nonetheless a chill went down our collective spine for one reason—Sergeant Mitchell's successful defense had been that he was merely "following orders." It was not a good omen.

If Mitchell had simply been following orders, it could be argued that Calley was also following orders. As an officer, that would be a harder defense for Calley to use, but it would not be implausible. Then finally, the buck could stop—as far as those on the scene at Mylai 4 were concerned—with the officer who gave the orders, Captain Ernest Medina.

Quite soon, though, there was no time to think about Sergeant Mitchell. The big one was beginning, the trial of Lt. William F. Calley, Jr.

The trial would be a long one. That was evident from the slow, careful, and extremely skillful way that the Army prosecutor, a quiet, reflective young captain named Aubrey Daniel, was building his case. It was like watching someone paint a picture of a crime by the numbers method—and leaving the most important figure for last.

Through the testimony of scores of credible witnesses, the bodies of the many dead were shockingly clear by the time Daniel got ready to paint in the face of Rusty Calley.

Then, on February 22, 1971, in the fouth month of a trial that had become the longest in military history, the defense called its final witness—Lieutenant Calley.

(By this time, one other Mylai trial had taken place: earlier that same month Sgt. Charles Hutto had been found not guilty. Again, the successful defense was "following orders.")

Early in his testimony—which lasted for nine hours over a period of two and a half days—Calley made it clear, in response to questions from his defense attorney, George Latimer of Salt Lake City, that he had been taught to obey orders.

He added that he had never been taught that he had either the right or the duty of deciding whether or not an order was legal. When Latimer asked him what he thought he should do if he had doubts about the legality of an order, Calley replied, ". . . I was supposed to carry the order out and then come back and make my complaint."

It didn't take a genius to see what he was building up to. He did more than pass the buck. He tried to tighten the noose.

Q. [Mr. Latimer] There has been some information disclosed that you heard before the court that you stood there at the ditch for a considerable period of time; that you waited and had your troops organized, groups of Vietnamese people thrown in the ditch and knocked them down in the ditch or pushed them in the ditch and that you fired there for approximately an hour and a half as those groups were marched up. Did you participate in any such shooting or any such event?

A. [Lt. Calley] No, sir, I did not.

Q. Did you at any time direct anybody to push people in the ditch?

A. Like I said, I gave the order to take those people through the ditch and had also told Meadlo if he couldn't move them, to waste them, and I directly—other than that, there was only that one incident. I never stood up there for any period of time. The main mission was to get my men on the other side of the ditch and get in that defensive position, and that is what I did, sir.

Q. Now, why did you give Meadlo a message or the order that if he couldn't get rid of them to waste them?

A. Because that was my order, sir. That was the order of the day, sir.

Q. Who gave you that order?

A. My commanding officer, sir.

Q. He was?

A. Captain Medina, sir.

Q. And stated in that posture, in substantially those words, how many times did you receive such an order from Captain Medina?

A. The night before in the company briefing, platoon leaders' briefing, the following morning before we lifted off and twice there in the village.

Calley's testimony was no surprise. From mid-December the news media had been reporting the testimony of other witnesses who had said parts of the whole that Calley gave. And the reports were head-line-blunt in the implication that it was Medina, not Calley, who was responsible.

On January 15, 1971, the *Washington Post* ran an account, under the bold heading CALLEY LAWYERS TAG MEDINA AS MYLAI BAD GUY:

FT. BENNING, Ga. Jan. 14—The battle-tempered commander of Charlie Company has not gone on trial yet for his role in the affair, but defense lawyers for Lt. William F. Calley point to Capt. Ernest Medina as the bad guy of Mylai. Calley is the pla-toon leader on trial here for 102 murders.

Medina—if the jury believes Calley's defense witnesses—or-dered everyone killed in the village, saw the bodies of civilians scattered through the hamlet and did nothing to stop it for hours.

Two ex-GI's who accompanied the commander through Mylai described today what they saw and, by inference, what Medina may have seen.

"To be very general," said Louis B. Martin, a 24-year-old policeman from Modesto, Calif., "I would say 20 to 100 bodies—definitely more than 20 and possibly more than 100."

James Errol Flynn, 22, a pipefitter from Rochester, Minn., said he not only saw lots of bodies, but saw Medina order one child killed.

"I took my radio off my back," Flynn remembered. "As I was making a call, Capt. Medina gave the order, 'Get him, get him.' There were two shots fired and I looked up and seen a little boy fall down."

According to Flynn, the boy, four or five years old, clad in the black shirt of the Vietnamese peasantry, fell in the same trail-side area where Calley allegedly murdered 30 people a short while earlier.

In a bizarre moment of the Calley court-martial, Flynn ex-amined the prosecution's color photograph of Mylai victims—

dead people charged to Calley—and picked out a small figure he
he said was the same dead boy.

The captain, a 35-year-old career officer who denied any "responsibility" for a "massacre" at Mylai, will get his own day in
court if the Army decides to go ahead with his court-martial at
Fort McPherson, Ga. But, according to corridor gossip, Medina
might even volunteer to testify in this trial, as a rebuttal witness
for the prosecution, in order to refute the damaging statements
made about him. . . .

The reporter was quite right about the rumor, for Medina was
getting more and more agitated. He had given his story to the press
in several conferences, but now that Calley had put it on the line,
he wanted the chance to pit his credibility against that of his lieutenant.

For a while, though, it looked like he wouldn't get that chance.
The Army did not want him to testify. We knew that the prosecutor
in the Calley case, Captain Daniel, wanted to call Medina as a government rebuttal witness to testify that he had not given the orders Calley claimed he had. One might think that in a proceeding that was,
in theory at least, a search for truth, fairness would prevail. One
would be wrong.

The Army found itself in a bind: it knew that if Captain Daniel
called Medina as a witness for the prosecution, then the Army would
be vouching for his truthfulness. Yet how could it claim Medina was
telling the truth—and Calley not—and then turn around and prosecute Medina?

It was, as the King of Siam used to tell Anna, "a puzzlement." The
Army solved it by refusing Daniel the permission to call Medina.

When Ernie heard this he was furious. There was little that anyone could say to him that seemed to reduce his anger. The rest of us
were hardly calm, but as lawyers we knew all too well that the sides
in any trial do not always conduct themselves in a manner that the
man on the street would call "fair."

In early March of 1971 we filed suit against the Army in the
Military Court of Appeals in Washington, D.C., to force the Army
to let Medina testify. Technically, our suit was a petition for "a writ
of mandamus and/or prohibition and/or other appropriate extraor-
dinary relief." As the respondents, we named the Secretary of the
Army, the Judge Advocate General of the Army, the Commanding
General of the Third Army, the staff Judge Advocate of the Third
Army, the major who was probably going to be Medina's prosecutor

(William Eckhardt), and the two Army prosecutors in the Calley trial, Col. Robert Lathrop and Capt. Aubrey Daniel.

In addition to alleging violation of due process and the lack of an impartial Article 32 investigation, we also spelled out other charges:

### VII.

In the trial of *United States* v. *Lieutenant William Calley,* that defendant has claimed that his alleged criminal conduct was occasioned by the direct order of Petitioner. Your Petitioner is ready, willing, and able to testify on behalf of the Army in direct refutation of Lieutenant Calley's testimony.

### VIII.

Respondent Daniel, your Petitioner believes and therefore alleges, wished to call your Petitioner to testify as a rebuttal witness in the court-martial of *United States* v. *Lieutenant Calley.* He has, however, been directed by respondents not to do so.

### IX.

There exists a written directive dated on or about 26 February 1971 from Respondent Lathrop to Respondent Daniel reflecting the prohibitive order negating Respondent Daniel's desire to call your Petitioner in rebuttal as aforesaid.

### X.

There exists a special reason which substantiates Respondent Daniel's belief in Petitioner's credibility and his desire to utilize the available testimony of Petitioner in rebuttal.

We didn't expect an immediate decision by the Court of Military Appeals, but we did expect a timely one, probably a week or so. There were, however, a couple of surprises in store for us before the court would rule.

Daniel was blocked from calling Medina. But—and here again one of the advantages of the military system worked in our favor—the Calley judge, Col. Reid W. Kennedy, advised the jury that it had the right and perhaps also the duty to call certain witnesses itself. He limited just how far "up" the chain of command the jury could go, but everyone on the panel knew he meant it could call Capt. Ernest Medina. And the jury did so.

That was the good news. The bad news came one day before Medina was slated to testify.

On March 8, 1971, the United States Army formally charged Capt. Medina with: "The murder of an unknown number of unidentified Vietnamese persons, not less than 100, by means of shooting with machine guns, rifles and other weapons," with two separate counts of murder, and two counts of assault with a dangerous weapon.

If Medina was angry before, at the Army's refusal to allow him to take the stand at the Calley trial and tell his side of the story, now he was all but stunned. He had never expected that the Army would play the game this way. We were deluged with press requests for a statement from Medina, and I asked Ernie what he thought.

Now that he was finally charged formally, with his court-martial a certainty, he had somewhat different rights and obligations. As did the defense team. But none of us had any desire to muzzle Ernie Medina; that was the Army's game.

Medina was in Washington that day, and he released a statement to the press. In part, it said:

> I am surprised and dismayed that the Army has taken this action. My trust in the military has caused me to consistently resort to proper military channels in seeking justice. Now pending before the U.S. Court of Military Appeals is a petition to bar this [court-martial], a petition upon which that Court was not given the opportunity to act. The Army, by its precipitous action today, has pre-empted its own highest court.

He finished by saying, "I am innocent of the charges against me."

Most of the legal work during the Article 32 investigation had been done by my partner Gerry Alch, Mark Kadish, and Ed Richards. I appeared for a number of key sessions, such as the Peers Commission and the congressional hearings, but Gerry and the others were the ones who saw Medina at first hand. They knew his day-to-day moods. And everything they felt was summed up by Gerry one day in late winter of 1971: "Ernie Medina, as a client, is an absolute delight. I don't know how long it's been since I've had such a strong feeling of pride, and really honor, to be associated with someone's defense."

I couldn't have agreed more. I remembered the day I appeared with Ernie before the subcommittee of the House of Representatives that was chaired by the late Congressman Mendel Rivers. When the committee had finished its interrogation, and Medina had told his side of the story of Mylai 4, he was asked if he cared to make any statement.

I was a bit surprised when he said yes. Then, for the next ten to fifteen minutes, he explained in careful, impassioned words, how no dishonor should be done to the memory of his own commanding officer, Colonel Barker, the man who had briefed Medina before he in turn had briefed Charlie Company. Medina had felt tremendous respect for Colonel Barker, who was killed in a helicopter crash a few weeks after the assault on the village, and he had been disturbed by the media's implications that Barker had been implicated in the tragedy.

When Medina finished his statement, the entire subcommittee rose, as one man, and began to applaud. It was a most moving scene. Then the congressmen stood at the door, and as we left, each one shook Ernie's hand.

I thought of that day, and of Gerry's comment, on the night before Medina was to take the stand, at the jury's request, to be a witness in the Calley trial. And I felt a tinge of momentary regret at what I was about to do.

Ernie had the right, now that he was finally charged and slated for his own court-martial, to plead the Fifth Amendment, as Calley had done several times. But that was not Medina's way. Still, his defense team had to debate, for some time, the relative merits of his taking the stand. It was probably a foregone conclusion, but we had to make sure he understood that he was running a decided risk. It is one thing to appear as a witness before a committee; it is quite another to appear as a witness in court, where one side or another stands to lose because of what you say—not to mention what you stand to lose if your testimony comes off badly.

And that was the basis of my tinge of regret. I was about to give Ernie Medina an object lesson in what it feels like to be cross-examined by someone who knows the facts and shows no mercy. It was to be a practice session—not to "coach" the witness, but to let him know what might happen the next day.

For the better part of three hours I raked Medina over the coals. The minute he even blinked, I hit him with a harder question than the one that had caused the blink. And if he seemed to forget a fact, no matter how small or seemingly unrelated, I shouted at him, banged him back in his chair, verbally. If he became tongue-tied, I smothered him with scarcasm. After a while he began to get the hang of it (it is not something you ever get "used to").

I glanced at Kadish a few times, and he looked a bit white. He started to raise his hand, to signal me to let up a bit, but his lawyerly instincts outweighed his compassion for Medina's feelings, and he let the hand drop.

Lawyers, especially criminal trial lawyers, have a crude but accurate expression for the kind of cross-examination I was putting

Medina through; we say that we are going to "tear the witness a new asshole." By the time I called a halt to the "test," Ernie knew exactly what the expression meant. More to the point, he knew what it felt like.

Medina is a strong man, emotionally as well as physically, but most of all his character is strong. Before he left the room that night, he thanked me. And then he shook his head and said, "I can't imagine tomorrow will be *anything* like that."

There are, however, all kinds of hells, and Medina entered one the next day. It is one thing to undergo a vicious "practice session" in the quiet of an empty office. It is quite another to face a courtroom filled with press, prosecution, and maybe a few friends and attempt to undo the harm that you truly believe another man has done to you and yours. There are some things you can not prepare a client for in advance.

When Captain Ernest L. Medina took the stand at Fort Benning, Georgia, at 9:00 A.M. on March 10, 1971, he was very close to being Rusty Calley's last hope. Aubrey Daniel had produced a parade of witnesses who testified that Calley had killed unarmed and unresisting civilians. Yet Calley denied all.

Then his defense swung in the opposite direction, and he testified that whatever he had done, he had done under direct and specific orders from Medina. It was as if he were saying, "No, I didn't kill anybody. But anybody I killed, I killed because Captain Medina ordered me to kill them."

This change in tactics did not sit well with the military jury, whose six members had been hearing gruesome testimony for more than three months. Still, they wanted to see and hear Captain Medina for themselves. They had a lot of questions.

He didn't get off the stand until close to eight o'clock that night. Minus the breaks, he was on the stand for more than six hours. His voice was almost gone. But he had done very, very well.

I doubted if there was a person in the courtroom who still believed Calley over Medina.

There were so many contrasts between the two men. Medina was alert, sharp, and specific to the point of being too "military," because his reliance on the phraseology of the Army was so ingrained. In direct contrast to Lieutenant Calley, Medina knew dates, places, and times. He knew where he had been—and more importantly, where he had not been.

Medina was questioned by the military judge, by the jury through the judge, and then by the prosecutor. Finally, both before and after the dinner hour, he was harshly questioned by Calley's defense lawyer. Near the end, he showed the fatigue he had to be feeling. But as George Latimer got more and more insistent, shrill, and obviously disbelieving, Medina seemed to catch a second wind.

Toward the very end, Latimer asked him the hardest question. He asked him why he had covered up. All of us at the defense table tried not to look at one another. This was the question we knew would come, but did not want to hear, for Ernie had never—even to us—articulated his exact reasons.

I watched, and listened, as he cleared his tired throat. And I wondered anew how he would answer it, for George Latimer had phrased it for maximum drama. It was an almost perfect defense question.

Q. Why—when you first shot the woman, Captain Medina, you felt so horrified and sick about it, why, when you saw the small boy running by and you saw somebody kill him, and why, when you saw that body there, you didn't call somebody and notify them what you had seen and make it positive that you had seen it and reported it to higher headquarters?

I thought I knew what Ernie's answer would be. But he surprised me.

A. There were four reasons, sir.
Q. Let's have them. [In snapping the question so brusquely, Latimer may have made a tactical error, because the answer that followed was slowly and carefully worded, and in a tone of deep seriousness.]
A. Number one, sir, I did not expect to find any noncombatants in that area; I expected to go in and do combat with the 48th VC Battalion. The woman—I was shocked. It was the first human being that I had shot and I assumed that I did kill her. The four reasons that I did not report the shooting of any innocents or noncombatants at the village of My Lai 4 and the reason that I suppressed the information from the brigade commander when I was questioned are as follows: Number one, I realized that instead of going in and doing combat with an armed enemy, the intelligence information was faulty and we found nothing but women and children in the village of My Lai 4, and seeing what had happened, I realized exactly the disgrace that was being brought upon the Army uniform that I am very proud to wear. Number two, I also realized the repercussions

that it would have against the United States of America. Three, my family, and number four, lastly, myself, sir.

I looked at my client with respect and a feeling of pride. Not I, nor anyone else on the defense team, had anything to do with Medina's answer. There had been no coaching, no suggestion of how he should answer that crucial question. It was heartfelt, sincere, and undoubtedly the result of much introspection. I should have remembered that, as a Catholic, Ernie Medina knew all about examining his conscience. Catholics must do that before they can go to confession. And Ernie had just gone to confession.

He would get no absolution from George Latimer, but I could see that the military jury was impressed. As for the members of the news media, some of whom I talked with later (and off the record), for the most part they felt that Medina had answered from the heart. Some of them even wrote it that way.

That answer was one of the highlights of Medina's day on the witness stand during the trial of Lieutenant Calley. But we felt that there had been an even more important, a more telling moment. It came when Colonel Kennedy, the military judge, asked him the most important question of all:

"Now, did you at any time on the fifteenth of March or at any time on the sixteenth of March order or direct Lieutenant Calley to kill or waste any Vietnamese people?"

Medina's answer was immediate. His voice was loud and firm as he said, "No, sir." And as he said it he raised his glance and looked —for the first time—directly at his accuser, Lt. William Calley.

Calley would not meet his captain's gaze. He kept his eyes on the floor.

Less than a week later, the military jury found Lieutenant Calley guilty.

An immediate firestorm of protest swept the country, and it raged for months, finally engulfing President Nixon—and then Capt. Aubrey Daniel, Calley's prosecutor, who wrote an open letter to the President criticizing him for interrupting the orderly process of the law.

It was an ugly, unpleasant time, a time when hundreds of thousands of citizens claimed that the army had made a scapegoat of Calley, and that it had persecuted him for nothing more than following orders.

Thousands screamed, in letters to the media, that the Army had taught Calley to kill and then punished him for doing his job. Hundreds of ex-soldiers wrote to admit that they had committed atrocities during earlier wars—and nobody had convicted them. On the contrary, they claimed, they had been called heroes.

It was a bitter, divisive time, and it mirrored the nation's attitude toward the war in Vietnam.

Yet for us it was simply a time of hard, hard work. Now we knew for sure that Medina would face a court-martial, and even though no date had been set for trial, there was no longer any doubt. Even if the Army, after hearing his testimony at the Calley trial (testimony that had apparently convinced the military jury of six combat veterans that Medina was telling the truth and that Calley was not), had wanted to drop the charges against Medina, it could not have done so without setting off an even greater storm of sympathy for Calley.

Unfortunately, I think that for quite some time the Army would have liked to drop the charges against Medina. But it had been the consensus of the defense team that this was a case that the Army intended to send to trial even if the evidence looked ridiculous. Because to announce that Captain Medina had been exonerated in some secret pretrial proceeding would certainly have set up a tremendous hue and cry that the fix was in, that the Army was protecting its own, and that the military system was a joke.

In a sense, I was in sympathy with this. And although I firmly believe that unless a strong pretrial case is made out a trial should not ensue, because of the tragic consequences that attach to any trial proceedings, there are rare and unusual circumstances where perhaps it is best that a trial be had in the public view, so that the result can be laid to some impartial body like a jury, instead of to bureaucratic or other manipulations.

The prior military case that comes to mind involved two white men, twin brothers, who'd been in a fight with six blacks in Germany. One of them had killed three of the blacks in thirty seconds, and I will never forget the report of the Article 32 investigating officer, who said, "There is strong doubt as to the guilt of this man for any of the homicides involved. It looks to me like a solid case of self-defense in two instances, and a legitimate defense of a third person, the twin brother, in the third instance. I recommend trial nonetheless."

He was taking a nonlegal approach, but I think it was an immensely practical one. He said, "There was nearly a race riot when these homicides occurred." (A rumor had spread immediately that the blacks had been the victims of a white conspiracy.) If the convening officer did not recommend a trial, he felt, "the blacks in the military community in West Germany would conjure up all sorts of unflattering reasons for that recommendation and would allege, not implausibly, that when 'whitey kills blackie it's not homicide.' Therefore I recommend, so that the matter be handled in public view, a trial of this man."

There was a trial. Over the objection of everybody in the courtroom, including the defendant, I left a black major on the jury. After two hours of deliberation, the white soldier was acquitted, and the first vote for acquittal was cast by the black major.

I felt, and I think Gerry and Mark agreed, that the same result would obtain in the case of Ernie Medina.

Because of the tremendous uproar that had arisen from the Calley prosecution, and the resentment for pinning "a poor lieutenant" for a massacre that Calley's supporters felt must have come from no less than the Secretary of the Army, any attempt by the Army to cut off responsibility, through its own machinery and without resort to the judicial process, was probably going to cause enough public uproar to deter the Army from taking that route, no matter how badly it might have wanted to do so.

And I suspected that in this case it wanted to do so rather badly. Medina was really the model of what the Army was losing on a daily basis, and that was a dedicated man whose whole upbringing had pointed him toward the military way of life, toward respect for the flag and rank—a respect that was disintegrating rapidly toward the end of the 1960s and certainly by the early 1970s.

If the Army could have picked a model to attract new men, Medina would have been ideal.

But the Army was put in a position where it had to prosecute Medina. And that was where we found ourselves in March of 1971.

In January of 1971 we had added a new member to the defense team. Because of family hardships caused by the press of the work following his transfer from Fort Benning to Fort McPherson along with Medina, Captain Ed Richards had to bow out. It was an amicable parting, and he and Ernie shook hands as friends.

There were numerous suggestions as to who should replace him. Kadish had several names in mind, but hesitated to mention one of them because he was a close personal friend. Then Medina surprised Kadish by saying, "Why don't we get Captain John Truman?" Truman was Kadish's friend.

In his late twenties, John Truman was tall, thin, and sarcastic to the point of acerbity. He had a quick mind, and his loyalty to his client was all but tangible from the first day. His intelligence was a strong plus—and we did not think it would hurt us that he happened to be the grandnephew of former President Harry S Truman.

While Kadish had the extroverted sense of humor of the talkative New Yorker, laced with updated vaudevillian overtones, Truman was a master of the sardonic comment. His leaning was more toward the intellectual, but his vocabulary had the same saltiness that on occasion brought his granduncle some unwanted headlines. My partner Gerry Alch, who in addition to being one of the finest trial lawyers I've ever seen is an extremely funny man, immediately dubbed Kadish and Truman "the odd couple." It fit and it stuck.

By the time Truman joined the defense team, the Army had been preparing its case against Medina for well over a year. This is not to say that the entire Army investigation had been centered on Medina, but that by interviewing all the members of Charlie Company, it was inevitable that a large portion of the reports and documents dealt with the company commander.

In most trials, the prosecution's sources of information and investigation—although distinctly greater than that of the defense—are limited to the traditional areas (such as the police or the FBI). But in the Medina case, some of the members of the company had been interviewed as many as eleven times. There had been an original "in-house" investigation while the troops were still in Vietnam (though it was skimpy), there was the Peers Committee investigation held at the Pentagon, and there had been separate congressional committee hearings. Also, the Army had conducted extensive interviews through its CID (Central Intelligence Division) branch, and had added and duplicated many more during the Article 32 investigation.

When the various members of Charlie Company appeared before Colonel Mobley, Medina would give Kadish and Truman a "backgrounder" on each man. This became the beginning of our own interview files, a set of books and records that eventually filled a whole room and more than six large filing cabinets. The point was that we had to have our own file on each man—and that meant each and every one had to be interviewed.

Truman saw what we were up against when he read the testimony from the Peers Committee. He read a few excerpts, and then put the volume down, shaking his head. "Jesus, it's just what I was afraid of.

When you've got a general questioning a private, it's not hard to guess which one is crapping in his pants."

In the last months before the actual trial of Captain Medina, Mark Kadish and John Truman interviewed 115 witnesses. They were gone so often and for so long that their spouses began to feel like Navy wives. In order to interview every member of the 1968 complement of Charlie Company—most of whom were back in civilian life—they held interviews in ghettos, in factories, in farm kitchens, and on college campuses. At the Army's expense they visited thirty-seven states, covering the nation from coast to coast and border to border. The trip took almost eighteen weeks.

According to Kadish, they interviewed "every extant, more-or-less living member of Charlie Company." The value of the trip is apparent in one statistic: they got 80 percent of the men they talked to to repudiate the statements they had given the CID investigators.

It was fortunate that Truman, only recently married, had no children. Kadish was close to becoming a stranger to his two small girls.

They took a weekend off when they returned, and then began to work on a series of difficult pretrial motions that I was afraid we were going to have to file. The Army was not giving us an inch, especially after the Calley decision, and we had to prepare for a battle royal.

Until the time that the formal charges were filed against Medina, I was feeling just a bit smug. I had an ace up my sleeve, and I believed it would be the winning card.

It is my normal practice, as I indicated earlier, when I have any doubt about the defendant's candor in telling me his or her side of the story, to suggest (in either polite or harsh fashion as the circumstances may require) a polygraph test. I make it quite clear that I have no control whatsoever over the outcome.

If the defendant is telling the truth, I can fairly promise that that will be demonstrated. If he is telling anything less than the complete truth, say even one little white lie, he can expect to flunk the test and have to make a further explanation before he can pass it.

Once I was convinced, by the regular reports of Gerry Alch and Mark Kadish, that Medina was slated for trial no matter what, I decided to take one final shot at prohibiting such a trial by resort to the polygraph.

My foundation for such an attempt was far stronger in the military system than in any civilian system. Although federal and state investigators rely on the results of polygraph tests daily, to determine who should be indicted and who should not, they are not exactly straight shooters when it comes to making public statements.

A prosecutor is very apt to say, "X is not being prosecuted because he passed the polygraph test with 'flying colors' "—the trite phrase that has unfortunately dominated the industry. On the other hand, if a defendant accused of a crime demands that *he* be subjected to a polygraph, the same prosecutor is very apt to say, "I'm sorry—we don't give polygraph tests in criminal cases where an indictment has been returned."

This is an inequity at best, but it has prevailed for the twenty years that I have been aware of the law. In the military, however, this is not the rule. The military has a long history of reliance on the results of polygraph tests, and I was banking on that the day I requested a conference with Colonel Freeman (the staff judge advocate to the general who was the convening authority for the court-martial) to propose for the first time that Medina be given a polygraph examination.

I wrote the colonel a letter and suggested two methods of selecting an appropriate polygraph examiner, for it is a truism within the field that a test is only as good as the examiner who gives it. One method was to go to the American Polygraph Association, which is to that profession much as the American Bar Association or the American Medical Association is to those professions. And to have them select a team of the most qualified examiners and have that team administer the test to Medina, with questions based on the charges that were then pending against him. The other method was that the Army would select an examiner, any examiner, that I would select an examiner, and that those two would select a third examiner who would actually run the test, in consultation with the first two.

What I knew—and I suspect that Colonel Freeman did not—was that it really doesn't make that much difference, once you reach the top shelf of examiners, whom you select. For one thing, they are scrupulously concerned about any fear or favoritism involved in polygraph tests, or about any slanting of the results toward the party paying the bill. Usually they will bend over backwards not to pass a man for a defense attorney who has hired them, or not to flunk a man for a prosecutor who has hired them. Because they are in the business of telling the truth, like no other people on the face of the earth, they are downright rigid about administering polygraph tests, especially in highly publicized cases.

I had a conference with Colonel Freeman, who demurred by saying he would have to take up my request with his superiors and his staff. Finally I got the Army's answer, which was in essence, that if you want a polygraph test in the Army ("And we do admit, Mr. Bailey, that you're correct—any defendant who wants a polygraph test is usually given one") it must be given by an examiner of the Army's choice, and there will be no impartial associations or panels. "And, to save you the trouble of agonizing over whom that might be, our examiner will be the chief examiner of the United States Army, Robert Brisentine." It was a take-it-or-leave-it proposition.

I am sure that this rather arbitrary approach was meant to be, in the view of Colonel Freeman and his associates, an end to the matter. It would be extremely unusual for a competent lawyer to let the other side select an expert, especially in view of the fact that expert testimony, in general, too often aligns itself with the man who is paying the bill. But I knew, much better than Colonel Freeman or anybody else in the Army, that in the polygraph industry this simply isn't so.

I picked up the phone and began to call my many good friends who are on the top shelf of the polygraph profession, and quickly learned a number of things. First of all, I learned that Robert Brisentine had an impeccable reputation. Second, he had done some of his training in Germany under a man I was privileged to call a very good friend, a man named Charlie Zimmerman, who happens to be one of the very best polygraph examiners in the entire world.

Zimmerman's testimonial to Brisentine's ability and integrity was all that I needed. I sat down and wrote the army a letter that said, "Mr. Brisentine is acceptable to us. When will the tests be run?"

I wish I could have seen Colonel Freeman's expression when he read that letter. He must have looked like the classic, egg-on-the-face recipient of the totally unexpected. At that point, having committed himself in writing to the selection of Brisentine, he could hardly reject my acceptance of the man. The tests were scheduled.

I've been involved in thousands of polygraph tests, but the tests of Ernie Medina, done in Washington, D.C., in November of 1970, were the most difficult.

The polygraph is essentially a simple instrument that attempts to learn, through physiological reactions to stimuli in the form of questions ("Did you do this? Did you do that? Are you telling me the truth when you say this?" etc.) whether or not the individual being tested is suffering any change in blood pressure, in breathing, or in the other significant physiological criteria over which he has no voluntary control, changes that are inconsistent with deception, or inconsistent with telling the truth.

Still, we had a special problem that made the tests very difficult. The problem was that the charges against Medina were so vague and nebulous. And to get clear-cut results you had to be able to ask clear-cut questions. The charge of "being responsible for the deaths of one hundred or more Vietnamese citizens," for example, didn't really lend itself to any specific question. The charge of having shot the woman "deliberately and with malice aforethought," which would constitute the crime of murder, hardly addressed itself to the circumstance under which Medina had confronted the woman. (According to his own story and that of several other witnesses, she was dressed as a warrior, and in Ernie's mind at least, she conducted herself like one for long enough to get shot.) The charge of having shot a small boy was even harder to handle, because no one knew the identity of the boy, or even which of several small boys might have been involved.

Nonetheless, having asked for the test, we could hardly walk away from it.

Charlie Zimmerman went with me to Washington, and for almost four days we ran what I think was probably the most difficult polygraph examination in history.

The results were not crystal clear. But we were very pleased, because the results relating to all the serious charges were more than clear. And to his everlasting credit, Robert Brisentine wrote a report that would warm the cockles of the heart of any criminal defendant.

What he said in essence was, "I represent the Army; I have tested Captain Ernest Medina; Captain Ernest Medina is telling the truth when he denies the charges that have been placed before me."

I suppose I should have been less naïve than to think that Colonel Freeman would have the guts to recommend that the test results be highly publicized and that this be the termination of the case against Medina. Indeed, knowing the ignorance of the public, and knowing the many wrongful stories that circulate about the polygraph, I suppose—in his shoes—I might not have done that either. Nonetheless, Robert Brisentine was prepared to testify that of the fifty thousand examinations he had run for the Army, not a one of those who had passed had ever been prosecuted in a military court.

The Army let us use Brisentine as a witness before Colonel Mobley's Article 32 investigation. Brisentine took the stand and testified that his examination showed Ernest Medina was telling the truth when he denied the Army's charges. Colonel Mobley allowed us to enter the testimony as evidence, but he apparently did not give it much if any weight—and I doubt if he actually understood just what it meant.

So I was not too surprised, when Medina entered the courtroom of Colonel Kennedy during the Calley trial, to hear the colonel say to him, "Now I don't want any slips. I don't want to hear a word in here about any polygraph tests."

The ace up my sleeve turned out to be a low hole card—of the wrong suit.

By the spring of 1971 there had been four Mylai trials. Staff Sergeant Mitchell had been found not guilty. Sergeant Hutto had been found not guilty. Lieutenant Calley had been convicted, and in April Capt. Eugene Kotouc was acquitted. Of the original twenty-five men that the Peers Committee said should be court-martialed for crimes of varying degree relating to Mylai, the charges had been dropped against all of the enlisted men and nine of the eleven officers.

Two men remained to be tried, Captain Medina and Colonel Oran Henderson.

If it were true, as some commentators were saying, that the American people and the United States Army had lost the desire to follow up the other Mylai cases after the conviction of Lieutenant Calley, you couldn't prove it by us.

Every day we had new indications that we were in for a hard fight. And one of the strongest indications was that the Army was not exactly playing by the rules.

Very early on in the investigation, Kadish got the impression that someone might be listening in on his phone. One of the things that worried him was that a room very near the old BOQ quarters that now served as the Medina defense room had a new tenant, a man reported to be a CID investigator. Someone told Mark that the officer had a great deal of "sophisticated electronic equipment," and that he stayed in his room almost all day.

Kadish called the Army office in charge of the phone installations, and together with a repairman they walked to the rear of the building. At the juncture box, which contained the wiring for more than fifty phones, they found two wires hanging loose. They had been connected to Kadish's phone.

As an indication of the kind of suspicion that was developing, sometime later someone told Mark that this might have been a red herring—a plant that they were supposed to find so they wouldn't look for any more. That was the atmosphere that was developing as we got closer and closer to trial.

On June 15, 1971, John Truman checked the typing job on the last of a thick sheaf of legal motions that lay in front of him on the desk. Satisfied, he pushed them away, lit a cigarette, and said to Kadish, "The shit is about to hit the fan."

He was exactly right. In another all-but-last-ditch effort to head off the trial, Mark and John, under my direction, had done all the legal research and the writing of twenty motions.

Of these motions, the one that made the biggest hit was the motion for dismissal based on allegations of improper command influence. Ernie's boys weren't kidding around.

If either Kadish or Truman had held any deep-seated desire for a career in the military, they were in the process of kissing it good-bye. Within days it was known that several of the higher-ranking officers referred to them, in private of course, as "the twin scourges of Fort McPherson."

Late in the day, on June 15, 1971, I put the wheels of the Lear Jet down, and applied myself to the business of landing the airplane. Once on the ground I left my chief pilot, Andy Crane, to take care of the paperwork. I had other paperwork to go over, and Truman and Kadish were waiting in a military staff car.

Back at Fort McPherson I read over the motions that I would argue before Col. Kenneth Howard, the military judge named to preside over the case of *U.S.* v. *Medina.*

I couldn't have been more pleased. The legal quality of the work was excellent—and perhaps even more of a pleasure—the motions were unusually well written. Even a layman would have no trouble understanding what they said. Not only were Kadish and Truman good young lawyers, but unlike so many lawyers of all ages, they could use the English language. I marveled at the amount and quality of the work they had plunged into right after their long stint on the road.

Of the twenty motions in the thick file, most could be filed without accompanying argument, but there were several that I planned to support orally.

The main one was the motion to dismiss the charges against Medina because of improper command influence. As we had expected, it caused a tremendous flap. Judge Howard announced that he was not "going to allow a fishing expedition," and ordered a separate hearing for the following Monday, the twenty-first.

Clearly distressed by our motion, though not because he had in any way prejudged it but only because of the gravity of the charges, Judge Howard said, "We will go into whether there was undue command influence, whether there was impartial and fair judgment by officials, and whether they abandoned their official demeanor in a nonjudicial way."

The motion was based on two central charges: (1) that Colonel Freeman had actively discouraged Mark Kadish and John Truman from a full and fair defense of their military client; and (2) that a Charlie Company sergeant now stationed in Colorado was threatened with a murder charge himself unless he revised his testimony, given before the Peers Committee, to make it more damaging to Medina.

There had been hours and hours of talk before the command influence motion was even drafted. No one wants to make the Army mad at them when they are going to be tried in an Army court, but Kadish and Truman were nearing the end of their rope. They knew that Medina's affection for the Army would give him second and third thoughts about taking this particular tack, but they also knew that he was about to go on trial for his life.

As they began to explore the grounds of this motion, they were met with strong opposition from their superior officers at Fort Mc-Pherson. In fairness to the higher-ups, it should be mentioned that what they were doing was almost unprecedented.

In order to interview these higher officers, they felt it only proper to warn them officially and legally, because "command influence" is a crime. And this meant reading them their rights under the Uniform Code of Military Justice. One of the superior officers got very upset when Mark began reading him the warning, and pounded his fist on his desk, ordering them out of his office. He shouted, "No captain is going to read me my rights!"

Kadish and Truman had begun to worry after a March 17 meeting with Colonel Freeman's deputy, during which they discussed the possibility of raising the issue of command influence. To their great surprise the colonel's deputy stated that even if they were successful with such a motion, it could be overruled by General Connor, the convening authority. What so shocked them was the idea that the very parties found guilty of command influence would be able to overturn the court's decision and take Medina to trial anyway.

There was no doubt in the minds of the two young captains that their colonel was doing a little arm-twisting.

Another bothersome point was that John Truman had received a low mark for "loyalty" on his latest Army fitness report, and that when he questioned the colonel about it, Freeman asked him where he thought his loyalty lay. Truman answered, "with Captain Medina," and Freeman corrected him, saying, "No, it should be with the United States Army."

Both Truman and Kadish felt that their strong defense efforts on Medina's behalf were resented by the senior legal officers.

Another bothersome point was that Freeman had been quite critical of the conduct of Aubrey Daniel, Calley's Army prosecutor, stating that Daniel should have asked him before attempting to call Medina as a rebuttal witness for the Army. During the course of the March 17 meeting, Colonel Freeman told Kadish and Truman that he felt Captain Daniel "had a complete disregard for the feelings of higher authority."

The second major issue behind the command influence motion was based on what we had learned from a Sergeant LaCroix, who had been a member of Charlie Company. He told us that after he had testified before the Peers Committee—and had given testimony that was favorable to Medina—he was taken aside by several high-ranking officers (both in Washington and at Fort Carson, Colorado, where he was then stationed) and warned that he might find himself charged with murder if he didn't begin to cooperate with the prosecution of Captain Medina.

Judge Howard was visibly upset throughout the three days of hearings. Finally, I had no choice but to put everyone concerned on the witness stand and ask them for their versions of what had happened.

Truman and Kadish related their story of the March 17 meeting. Colonel Freeman then testified that they were all wrong, that they had misinterpreted his words. He said that his comment about General Conner's authority to supervene a dismissal based on command influence was mentioned as nothing more than a "possibility," one that he had mentioned simply to "inform" them. He denied that it was in any sense a prediction or a warning.

Similarly, the three colonels who LaCroix claimed had tried to pressure him denied the charges.

Included in our motion was the charge, also supported by testimony during the hearing, that the Army had deliberately tried to undermine the effectiveness of Medina's appearance before the jury in the Calley case by announcing the formal charges against him on the day before he was to testify.

Late Wednesday afternoon, after the last man had testified, Colonel Howard denied all our motions. From the bench, he said that during the course of the hearings he had heard a number of things that he hadn't liked, and some of them had "distressed" him. He said that clearly there had been poor judgment on the part of "certain staff officers . . . but it did not rise to the level of command influence."

We were convinced that he was referring to one Col. Wilson Freeman, but there was no way of being sure. The defense team was disappointed in the outcome, but we were heartened somewhat by the obvious fairness and concern of Colonel Howard, the military judge. Still, the Army had won another round.

On Sunday, June 27, 1971, the *New York Times* ran an article entitled "Medina's Turn," which began:

> "I've been waiting almost two and a half years for this," said Captain Ernest L. Medina last Friday, and there was relief in his voice that the waiting was almost over. He had just been told by Col. Kenneth Howard, the military judge at Fort McPherson, Ga., that his court martial for the murders of at least 102 Vietnamese civilians at Mylai 4 would finally begin with the selection of a jury on July 26.
>
> Captain Medina had gone before Judge Howard last week with a pre-trial motion to dismiss the charges on the grounds that higher officers had exerted "command influence" on subordinates and potential witnesses that prejudiced the possibility of a fair trial, and that they had dictated that he be tried to protect the Army's image even though the evidence against him was skimpy. Judge Howard refused to dismiss the charges and ordered the captain to stand trial.

At the time it was written, the account was quite right, but in keeping with the history of the Medina trial, there was one more delay in store for us.

Major Eckhardt, the Army prosecutor assigned to the Medina case as well as to several other previous cases, wanted to take testimony from two South Vietnamese soldiers who had worked for the United States Army as civilian interpreters. The defense was

equally interested in their testimony because they had been with
Medina the day after the killings, when the captain had interrogated a suspected Vietcong.

Given the long and tortuous history of the war in Southeast
Asia, perhaps we shouldn't have been surprised when the Republic
of Vietnam refused to allow the two men to come to the United
States and testify, but we were. I guess we felt that since our government had been their employer, they would be allowed to come.
But they were barred. The Vietnamese officials said that we could
come over there and take their depositions. Without any hard information as to what they would say, and recognizing the inherent
danger in letting "the other side" conduct the deposition, we decided that the defense team—and the defendant—had better be
present.

So on July 4, 1971, Captains Kadish, Truman, and Medina
boarded a Seaboard Airlines charter flight in San Francisco, bound
for Vietnam. Aside from the obviousness of its being Independence
Day, there were other ironies crowding Ernie's mind. For one thing,
although it was not a military plane, the flight was in essence a
troop transport. The uniform of the day was battle fatigues. Most
of the passengers were "first-timers," new troops on their way to
South Vietnam for their first tour of duty. Exactly what thoughts
went through Medina's mind I do not know, but he must have
been reminded of the company of 180 men that took a similar
flight in December of 1967, a few short months before it was to
play the major role in a tragedy.

Although the captains were dressed in fatigues like everyone else,
they were going to Vietnam for several days; the troops were going
for a year.

Also of interest was that the military prosecutors were on the
same plane. Medina, with the savvy born of experience, told Truman and Kadish to wait until the prosecutors had boarded—in fact,
to wait until the end of the line. "That way," he explained, "we'll
be seated up front, closer to the stewardesses; we'll be able to stretch
our legs, and we'll get better service."

The flight was barely in the air when word was passed around
that "Captain Medina" was on the plane—"and so are those bastards who are prosecuting him." By this time, most enlisted men
and lower-ranking officers were very sympathetic to Medina, and
while the two defense lawyers and their client were feted in the
front of the plane, Major Eckhardt and his first assistant, Captain
Wurtzell, were getting something less than polite treatment by the

troops in the middle. (As Ernie told me later, "No one was being disrespectful, but . . . anything they could do not to make it nice for them, well . . .")

There are times in life when small victories are the sweetest.

The first stop was Anchorage, Alaska. The defense trio had begun their trip in Atlanta, and when they found there was to be an hour's layover in Alaska, they made straight for the closest bar. They ordered drinks and relaxed. In a few minutes one of the GIs from the plane came up and told them that the prosecutors, who were also thirsty, didn't want to be seen in the same bar with the defendant and his lawyers, so they were drinking soft drinks in the lobby.

The time for reboarding came too soon, of course. Kadish, who drinks only moderately, didn't seem to mind, but Medina and Truman wanted one more. Ernie suggested that they buy Cokes from a machine and spike them with bourbon. They did so, and waited, sipping happily, as the rest of the plane boarded. But the Seaboard Airlines stewardess, who had no intention of breaking the rules, or passing out barf bags unless it was absolutely necessary, stopped the two captains halfway up the ramp.

"Is that alcohol in those cups?"

"No, of course not," said Medina, smiling. But the girl had had too much experience with Army types. She grabbed Truman's cup, took a drink, and made a face. Then she smiled. "You'd better finish these on the ground."

After a quick, not too pleasant chug-a-lug, the captains boarded. A laughing Kadish said, "Did you enjoy your cocktail, gentlemen?"

The next stop was in Yahota, Japan, where an electrical failure caused an eight-hour delay, and from there it was a direct flight to Bien Hoa Air Force Base in South Vietnam. The trip had taken twenty hours. When they arrived it was six in the morning, Vietnam time. According to their watches it was four in Atlanta—of the following day.

Captain Medina's return to Vietnam was definitely "news," and the three captains were greeted by a mob of reporters and photographers. Neither Truman nor Kadish had been to Vietnam before, and they were startled by a shouting mob and the strange, singsong cadence of the language they were hearing for the first time. Truman said later that he was "downright shook. For all I knew we were in the middle of an anti-Mylai demonstration or an enemy raid." It turned out to be a prophetic comment.

On the way to their quarters, Medina ran into a warrant officer

who greeted him happily. It turned out to be his former food officer at Fort McPherson, a soldier with whom he'd shared many
good times. The warrant officer saw to it that the defense team had
whatever it needed, and even though the prosecutors' quarters down
the road were better quarters, Kadish, Truman, and Medina got
what Ernie called "a much better deal."

*Stars and Stripes*, the Army newspaper, had run several stories
about Medina's impending visit, and word swiftly passed throughout the base that he had arrived. In July of 1971 it was more than
a year since the charges had come down against Medina, and four
months since his well-publicized testimony in the Calley trial. Almost to a man, the base supported Medina, and so the troops did
whatever they could to make his stay easier.

On the second day Medina told an Associated Press reporter
how surprised he was at all the changes he'd found. He described
the situation when his troops first moved into the countryside, in
1967. "There we were, digging in a hole you had dug yourself,
trying to keep dry with a poncho. And when you came back to a
base camp, all you'd have was a bunker you constructed yourself.

"Now, at Long Binh, they have refrigerators, tennis courts, bas-
ketball courts, massage parlors, sauna baths, Chinese restaurants,
swimming pools—and even ice cream trucks."

The point of the trip, the deposition, with Kadish conducting
the cross-examinations, was almost an anticlimax. Truman could
not get over the fact that the interpreters could barely speak English. He kept saying to Kadish, "Jesus, they're supposed to be interpreters, interpreters!" Kadish and Truman had an opportunity
to interview the two Vietnamese, and came away with good notes
that would be helpful if it ever became necessary to use them.

Once the deposition was over, there was a general sigh of relief. As it was to be their last night in Vietnam, Medina took his
two defense lawyers to the base officers club, where the two neo-
phytes marveled at hearing a Filipino band play American mu-
sic and sing American songs. Kadish, with his penchant for the
unusual, was enthralled.

They had been in the club but a few minutes when it seemed
that everyone there knew of Medina's presence. Soon the free
drinks were coming at an incredible rate. It went on for hours.

Medina found himself, late in the evening, with thirty-eight
Scotches lined up in front of him. Kadish had not been able to
discourage the friendly offers, and had almost as many untouched
drinks. Knowing it would be a long night, Truman thought it

would be wiser to drink beer; he stopped counting how many he'd had when he realized that there were more than fifty bottles on the table.

There were a few more surprises in store. Back at the barracks, Truman was taking a therapeutic shower when one of the Vietnamese cleaning women walked casually into the bathroom. Medina laughed while Truman shouted for him to get the woman out of there; Ernie knew it was commonplace. Before the woman left, she went into the toilet area and handed a roll of toilet paper to a very startled Kadish, who was reposing on a stool.

Just as the three were about to turn in, the air lit up with flares and tracers, and the sound of bombs and gunfire was everywhere. The base was being attacked.

Out on the porch, Medina spent half an hour pointing out the various types of gunfire and heavy ammunition that the American veterans early on began to call "fireworks." Having seen it so often, he decided to go to bed.

"Go to bed?" said Kadish. "What if something happens?"

Medina answered, "If they're going to get you, they're going to get you. There's nothing you can do about it."

Truman and Kadish stayed on. After a particularly loud burst, they were joined on the porch by a young officer who had been sleeping. "What's going on?"

"It's an attack."

"Oh, my God, I've been here a year and this is the first one I ever saw. And I'm going home tomorrow. Why do you think they're doing it?"

Kadish couldn't resist. "Didn't you hear that Captain Medina's on the base?"

"Yeah, I read it in the paper. Do you know where he's staying?"

Truman pointed to the room behind them. With that, the officer went back to his room, got his blanket and pillow, and sprinted down the road to the nearest bunker, cursing and yelling as he ran.

The next morning they took a flight home. Ernie Medina had gone back to Vietnam. Now he was ready for trial, and there were to be no more delays. The ordeal was entering its final and most important stage.

The colonel was trim, not too tall, and very military. He was a decorated combat veteran of three wars—Vietnam, Korea, and World War II. In Korea and Vietnam he had been a helicopter pilot; in World War II he had commanded a company of infantry.

His name was William Proctor. Forty-seven years old, Colonel Proctor would be—if we chose him for the jury—the likely "president" of the panel, because he outranked the other nine officers from whose number we would choose the five-man jury.

Major Eckhardt, the chief prosecutor, had a question for Colonel Proctor. "Based on the massive publicity in this case, have you formed an opinion that illegal acts occurred at Mylai?" The colonel answered, "Yes, undoubtedly something illegal occurred at Mylai."

I looked at Proctor and liked what I saw, despite his answer. There was something "straight" about him. I had a question or two of my own to ask.

But Judge Howard did, too. "Could you listen to the testimony in this case," he asked, "and decide on that basis alone this case on its merits?"

"Absolutely," said Col. Proctor.

I asked the colonel if, based on his belief that something illegal had happened in Mylai, he would necessarily saddle Captain Medina with the responsibility. He responded, "If I have a soldier who goes AWOL, I'm not responsible for his going AWOL."

That was the kind of answer I'd been hoping for. I indicated no objection to Col. William Proctor, nor did the prosecutor, and he was seated on the panel.

Three days later we had our jury. It was composed of six officers, all of whom outranked Medina. There were three colonels, two lieutenant colonels, and one major. On the last day of jury selection the Army exercised one of its peremptory challenges and struck one member. The remaining five, our jury, were all veterans of the war in Vietnam.

It was July 28. The prosecution told Judge Howard that it planned to call some fifty witnesses, so the judge, who knew that subpoenas had to be made out and travel arrangements made, declared an eighteen-day recess. He set the first day of trial for August 16.

The press was waiting when we left the courtroom. They wanted to know if the trial would last four months or more, like the Calley trial. Major Eckhardt, his ever-present meerschaum pipe bobbing up and down in his mouth, told them he thought it probably would. I said two weeks, adding that I wasn't even sure if I would call any defense witnesses. Mark Kadish told them, "four to six weeks. This is definitely not going to be a replay of the Calley trial."

Over the next few weeks I was pleased, though not greatly surprised, to see how well Ernie was holding up. The Army had been working on his case for over two years, and during that time he had lived under a cloud that grew progressively darker. Yet he appeared genuinely relieved and even anxious now that we were finally going to trial.

Several months back Medina had called me and said he was getting a lot of questions from the media about his future plans. Should he answer them? I had seen him conduct himself in so many news conferences by that time that I had no reservations. "Tell them whatever you want!"

And he did. He told them that whatever happened, his days in the Army were numbered. Medina had been in the service for sixteen years, and had more than fulfilled his early promise. But in that time he'd learned what happens to an officer with a blot on his record, acquittal or no acquittal.

He knew that if he stayed in the Army he would be buried behind a desk at some out-of-the-way post. He had embarrassed the Army, and that would stay with him.

Knowing all that I did about Medina, I was still very touched by something he said to a reporter for the Associated Press just before the trial began. He'd been asked what his plans had been before he was charged, and Ernie explained how he had wanted to finish college, and then, some day in the future, teach in an elementary school. "But," he told the reporter, "after all this, who is going to want Captain Medina teaching their kids?"

It was almost the saddest thing I ever heard him say; the saddest was his account of what happened in Mylai 4 on March 16, 1968.

By trial eve Medina had told his story in detail at least four times. He had told it to the Peers Committee; to congressional hearings chaired by Mendel Rivers and by F. Edward Hebert; to the jury in the trial of Lieutenant Calley; and way back at the beginning of our relationship, to me.

Pared down to its essentials, his story was this:

On March 15, 1968, he had attended a briefing given to the company commanders by Colonels Barker and Henderson. Based on the best intelligence, he told his men, that same night, that the Forty-eighth VC Battalion would be in Mylai 4 the next day; that the women and children would leave for the market by seven each morning, as they did every day; that anyone found in the village would be VC or their sympathizers; and that Charlie Company was to destroy the village.

Sometime later Medina received the last of several calls that the helicopters had seen VC troops with weapons and that the pilots had dropped smoke bombs to indicate the locations. As he had no one else to send to check out the last report, Medina and his command group answered it themselves. He found no VC with weapons, but he did see people who had been hit by either shrapnel or gunship rockets.

His group moved up an incline toward the village, and there Medina shot the woman who was lying in the rice paddy. There was hardly time to think about the incident when a call came through informing Medina that Private Carter had shot himself in the foot.

On his way to see to Carter, who was "medivaced" or airlifted out—medical evacuation—Medina crossed the north-south trail and saw what he later reported as the bodies of "twenty to twenty-eight civilians." Here, too, was where he saw a small boy, who had apparently been shot just minutes before.

At this point the first platoon, Calley's, was somewhere up ahead, and Medina, stunned by the number of bodies he had seen, radioed a message to cease fire. Later he could still hear firing, so he sent another, stronger message, "Damn it, what is going on up there? I want all this firing stopped."

Then he passed east of the village itself, and finally encountered Lieutenant Calley. At this point, Medina still believed that the dead civilians he'd seen had been VC, killed by rocket or artillery fire. Nothing that Calley told him changed his mind. After a brief discussion regarding a helicopter pilot who had landed and questioned Calley about the operation, Medina told his troops to break for lunch. He went off and ate by himself.

After lunch he gave his company orders to move on. The troops moved off, heading to the northeast. That was the end of Charlie Company's "revenge" on the Forty-eighth VC Battalion.

Major Eckhardt stood quietly in front of the panel, seldom gesturing, a picture of seriousness. It was Monday, August 16, 1971, and at 9:00 A.M. the trial of Ernest Medina began.

In his opening statement, Eckhardt told the military jurors, "When Captain Medina got on the ground, he knew his orders were being misconstrued and that his men were committing murder and he did nothing to stop them. . . . His nonintervention was intended by him to give comfort to and encouragement to his men."

Before he finished he had accused Medina of shooting the woman in the rice paddy and also shooting the small boy. And he claimed that on the next day, the seventeenth, Medina had violated the rules of war by shooting at a VC suspect in an attempt to coerce him into talking.

My own opening was relatively brief. The central point was simple: there was no evidence that Captain Medina had ordered, or even been aware of, a massacre.

Rather than change the way it had been treating Medina from the outset, the Army had made still another noose-tightening move just days before the trial began. It changed the charge of personally killing the 102 Vietnamese civilians to one of being "responsible for them." As Eckhardt put it, Medina was being tried as a "principal," one who "is as guilty of the crime as if he had committed it. The government does not intend to say that he pulled the trigger."

Perhaps in the hope it would make a conviction easier to get, the Army had dropped its request for the death penalty, asking instead for life imprisonment, and—surprisingly—it also dropped the misprision of a felony charge that was based on the alleged cover-up.

John Truman spoke for all of us when he said how happy he was to see the government drop the misprision count. "I think the government's getting greedy. It wants the whole loaf or nothing!" Whatever the prosecutors' reasons, they were clearly trying hard to narrow down the charges in keeping with what they thought they could prove.

And they thought they could prove that Medina knew about the killings, did nothing to stop them, and was therefore guilty of murder. I had strong doubts that they could prove anything close to that, but we weren't about to get overconfident. Some of the former members of Charlie Company had given sharply conflicting testimony about their commander's actual role.

Also, we had to consider the attitude of the Army. Prior to the Medina trial it had lost or dropped every Mylai case except Calley's. Major Eckhardt, who'd lost the two previous cases he'd prosecuted (Hutto and Kotouc) was certain to be going all out on this one. If the Army pulled its punches, there would be strong voices raised that it did so to shield the higher-ups, the chain of command that some said was as responsible as any soldier at the scene.

The Army was not in an easy spot, and I was certain it would prosecute hard.

Shortly before 11:00 A.M. on July 16, the Army called its first witness against Medina.

Ron Haeberle, along with Ron Ridenhour, had been one of the media heroes. It was Haeberle's photographs, which *Life* Magazine had printed in horrible, vivid color, that had shocked and sickened the world.

Haeberle had taken shots of what had happened before Medina got to the village, and they were horribly vivid accounts of the carnage; I wasn't about to let the jury see them.

"Judge, these pictures relate to a period of time during which my client was not in the village. If these were indeed murders, they took place prior to Captain Medina's entry on the scene."

Judge Howard agreed. Leaning toward the jury, he asked that the panel take note of my observation.

Haeberle's testimony took up the rest of the morning. He recounted what he had seen. It was the grisly, unpleasant truth. But it did not really touch Medina—unless, of course, the specter of General Yamashita was somehow raised.

After that, things began to move. The prosecutors accelerated the pace, bringing witnesses to the stand for brief periods of questioning. I tried to figure the Army's strategy—but it didn't appear to have one.

The first witness to follow Haeberle was Charles Sledge, whose testimony had helped to convict Lieutenant Calley. Sledge said much the same thing before the Medina jury, but it had a different effect. After running down a litany of horrors that put Calley in the middle of all the shooting, Sledge testified that he had never seen Medina anywhere near the killings.

We knew that Sledge had been with Ernie later in the day, when Medina attempted to scare the truth out of a suspected VC soldier. But even that testimony was favorable.

A more experienced prosecutor would never have let it happen, but Major Eckhardt's aide, Captain Wurtzell, didn't see it coming in time. He had asked Sledge to describe the interrogation scene—in which Medina put the VC suspect up against a tree and fired a shot very near his head—which Sledge did, but then the witness said, voluntarily, "I would like to say that if he had wanted to shoot him he could have, because he was a pretty good shot [Medina was an expert rifleman]. So I think he just wanted to scare him."

We could hardly have asked for stronger pro-Medina testimony. Wurtzell looked slightly green as he excused the witness.

I questioned Sledge for only two or three minutes. My first question was, "Nothing was ever said by Captain Medina about harming noncombatants, was there?"

"No, sir."

"In fact, Captain Medina had told you not to harm them, hadn't he?"

"Yes, sir."

"And isn't it a fact that you were surprised when you saw Lieutenant Calley and the others shooting the noncombatants?"

"Yes, I was."

Robert Mauro was the next witness. I cross-examined him for less than two minutes. After he said that an Army CID investigator had "coerced" him, I asked him what he meant by coercion.

He said, "He was harassing me. He showed me his pistol a couple of times."

By the end of the second day, not a single witness had put Captain Medina even near the killings. I had told newsmen for weeks that I might not call any defense witnesses, and the more I heard of the government's case, the more I thought my statement might become a self-fulfilling prophecy. After the second day's testimony, the account in the *Atlanta Journal* was headlined NO ONE TAGS MEDINA A KILLER.

I was beginning to worry about what the prosecutors were doing. The first witnesses were testifying to the fact of a mass killing at Mylai 4. But no one was disputing that fact. Yet the Army seemed intent on showing that a massacre had taken place. By the end of the second day nine witnesses had testified, and not a one of them had imputed any on-the-scene responsibility to Ernest Medina. No one was denying that noncombatants had been killed, yet the Army seemed intent on proving that admitted fact. It began to look, to me, as if the prosecutors were trying to sneak the Yamashita precedent through the back door.

Either that, or they were trying to show that Medina *must* have known what was going on. The more I thought about it, the more it made sense. But there was no reason to complain. It was the prosecution's turn, not ours, and they were hardly making the most of it.

On Wednesday, the eighteenth, the *New York Times* ran an article by Homer Bigart, whose coverage of the trial was, in my opinion, the most accurate. He wrote:

What the Army prosecutors, Maj. William G. Eckhardt and Franklin R. Wurtzell, are attempting, at this initial stage of the presentation of the government's case, is to give a broad picture of the action at Mylai on the morning of March 16, 1968.

They are trying to prove that although Capt. Medina encountered no resistance in the sweep through the village, his men indiscriminately killed unarmed civilians, even babies, and that he must have been aware of the slayings but did nothing to halt them.

Except for the implication that Medina himself had moved through the village, Bigart's account was accurate. As he had reported, the Army was trying to show that Medina had known what was going on—and had let it happen. That was not true.

Unless the prosecution is using a particularly subtle tactic, the first witnesses in any case are among the heaviest, and their testimony usually dovetails neatly with the government's theory of its case. Also, early witnesses are normally hard to shake during cross-examination. For some reason, the Army was not exactly putting on a textbook case. I had a few theories, but there was no need to explore them as yet.

Not one of the first nine witnesses had placed Medina in or even very near the village; not one had heard him order the killing of civilian noncombatants; and not a one said he saw Medina shoot anybody, although a single witness testified that the captain was in a group when a child was killed nearby.

Frank Beardslee, a factory worker from Michigan, said that he saw Medina shoot into the tree to scare the suspect (who later turned out to be a colonel in the North Vienamese Army), but he added, "Then he walked up to him and told him the next one would be in the middle of his forehead, and the guy started talking." As that was the same way Medina told the story, I didn't worry about that testimony.

And then there was another former private, Leonard Gonsalez, who got mixed up about when certain things happened. On cross, I asked him, "In a matter of great importance, if you were confused, would you want to rely on your memory of the events at Mylai?"

Gonzalez's answer was "No."

My favorite among the first government witnesses had been Mr. Mauro, who told us that the Army CID man "harassed him for five hours" when he questioned him in the Brooklyn Army Terminal in 1969. I asked Mauro, "Did [he] try to get you to make a statement incriminating Captain Medina?"

"I would say so."

Thus, out of the first batch, we had one prosecution witness who felt the Army was trying to coerce him into giving anti-Medina testimony, one who volunteered exculpatory evidence bearing on one of the assault charges, and not a single witness who claimed to have seen Medina murder anybody. It wasn't a bad start.

On Wednesday, the nineteenth, I had the unique experience of being able to bring into court a group of men whose expertise in their field was so unquestionably high that we had to have established a record in the annals of expert testimony. I don't think a comparable group of experts, from any other field, had ever before been assembled in one courtroom.

Although we felt our chances were slim, we had decided to raise, and press, the question of Ernie's polygraph test results. And when I learned that the 1971 convention of the American Polygraph Association was to be held during the third week of August in Atlanta, Georgia, I viewed it as an unprecedented opportunity.

To me it seemed a perfect chance to argue for the admissibility of the polygraph test results, both as to Medina's case and on a test basis. Judge Howard excused the jury until Thursday noon, and for the next day and a half we thrashed the issue around.

During pretrial, after hearing our argument, Judge Howard had ruled out the polygraph evidence, stating that the clear prohibition of such evidence in the manual for court-martial proceedings used by the Army left him no choice.

Major Eckhardt, in attempting to clarify just why we were having this unusual session, claimed that I was accusing Judge Howard of Constitutional error, so I had to explain:

> It is my purpose to show, first, that the technique, as a science, is a reliable technique with a creditable history particularly in the military and that the use of such evidence would benefit the administration of justice and in this particular case render more likely the fact that the truth will emerge and justice will be done to this accused, and, of course, the United States.
>
> The second question presented is whether the particular examiner who ran the test is qualified. I suspect that we'll

have a stipulation on that, since the examiner was employed by the government and still is, but if not, he can stand on his own qualifications. That phase of it I won't go into until such time as for one purpose or another the evidence might become admissible. Today's hearing is to establish for Your Honor and for this record that the technique is venerable, well structured, and reliable to the extent that judicial admissibility should be granted, period.

With so many excellent examiners to choose from, I was a bit like the kid in the candy store. I chose Cleve Backster, a graduate of and former instructor at the Keeler Polygraph Institute (the nation's first, famous school) for fifteen years and the president of his own school in New York City. Mr. Backster had extensive experience in the U.S. Army, both as an examiner and a teacher.

The second witness was Mr. John Reid of Chicago, who also founded and still operates his own polygraph school, and has had more than thirty-five years of experience. Mr. Reid is co-author of one of the leading texts in the field. Next was Dr. LeMoyne Snyder, who identified himself as "a medical legal consultant," from Paradise, California. A graduate of the Harvard Medical College, Dr. Snyder was medical legal director of the Michigan State Police in the early 1930s when, as he put it, "I first rubbed shoulders with the polygraph," by virtue of meeting Leonard Keeler. The two men became close friends, and Dr. Snyder also became a leading authority in the field. When I asked him if he had ever written in the field of pathology, Dr. Snyder replied, with the simple modesty of a true authority, "I wrote a book called *Homicide Investigation,* and that came out first in 1944 in the English edition and has been reprinted ten times and revised."

The next expert was Claybourne Lowry, one of the Army's top polygraph examiners for almost a quarter century. He was followed on the stand by one of the country's best-known polygraph men, Leonard Harrelson, the president of the Keeler Institute since 1955. After him came Milton Berman, of Louisville, Kentucky, one of the charter members of the American Polygraph Association. (I asked Mr. Berman if he held any office with the association, and he said, quite seriously, "I did when I left there [Atlanta] this morning. I was a member of the board of directors. I know I have been renominated, I don't know how the election came out.") Mr. Berman testified, among many other things, to the fact that a good part of the membership of the association is made up of military examiners.

The final witness was the Army's own Robert Brisentine. His official position is "Chief Polygraph Advisor to the Commanding Officer, U.S. Army CID Agencies." Judge Howard noted that he was already quite familiar with Mr. Brisentine and his work.

Throughout the hearing, we discussed the polygraph from front to back. There was not a question that wasn't raised and answered. Several of the experts testified that some time ago they had opposed the use of polygraph evidence in criminal trials, but they were careful to explain that this was not due to any deficiencies in the machine itself, but rather with its human counterpart, the examiners. Their point was that in the years before the association grew to its present strength and influence, there was insufficient standardization of examiners' qualifications and training. Now, they testified, they felt no such qualms, and would allow polygraph evidence in any trial.

At one point I asked Mr. Lowry, the Army examiner, "If it were your responsibility to determine whether or not a witness, particularly an accused, were telling the truth, with all of the aids that we have—cross-examination and rebuttal evidence and so forth— would you think that your verdict as to who was telling the truth and who was not would be more or less accurate if you had the benefit of a polygraph examination to assist you?"

Without any hesitation, he said, "Much more accurate with the polygraph."

Leonard Harrelson, one of the "deans" of the profession, provided an interesting bit of testimony following one of my questions.

> Q. . . . to get to specifics, there is sometimes thought to be a danger that staleness in an individual, that is the lapse of time between an alleged criminal event and the test, will interfere with the accuracy of the result. Do you have any personal experience that would shed light on that proposition?
>
> A. Yes, sir.
>
> Q. Would you tell the court what it is?
>
> A. Well, we can start with one of your first cases when you were out of law school where you defended or you represented an individual by the name of Dominic Bonomi who had been in prison at that time, as I believe, for in excess of seven years. He was convicted of uxoricide [murdering his wife] in Boston and he wanted a polygraph examination and he convinced you that he didn't do it and I gave him a test and the polygraph test did not agree with him and he subsequently confessed that he had, in fact, killed his wife.

I was not exactly thrilled that he had remembered one of my
early losses, but I couldn't disagree with the facts.

Q. Yes, he did.

A. Then the other case, Mr. Bailey, is a case that took place in
the State of Maine. A man was convicted and sent to prison
in 1924. He was convicted of murder at that time. In 1958
everyone concerned officially had decided that they had made
a mistake and that they had this man in jail for all these years
and he was the wrong man. So, they decided they should free
the man and give him back a token check for the trouble
that they had put him through for $250,000 and the governor
agreed with this but he said he should take a polygraph examination. The test indicated that he was not telling the truth,
he had in fact committed the murder for which he had been
convicted and he confessed.

Q. And the lapse of time between the murder and the test?

A. Well, from '24 to '58.

Q. 34 years?

A. Yes.

A few minutes later, Mr. Harrelson gave us a history lesson
of a different sort. I had asked him if, based on his experience, he
felt the polygraph could make a substantial contribution to the
search for truth at a trial.

A. Mr. Bailey, I think it could make a substantial contribution. Sometimes the tests do not even have to be conducted.
I can remember when the President of the United States was
a congressman and there was a hearing called Alger Hiss [sic].
And Mr. Nixon had written to Keeler and asked him if he
could conduct a polygraph examination on Chambers and
Hiss, and Keeler agreed that he would do it. But, when the
two were asked by Mr. Nixon if they would take it, only Mr.
Chambers agreed.

There are some who would quarrel that this might not have been
the best example of a "search for truth," but Mr. Harrelson's example was nonetheless interesting.

Also of interest, but for a different reason, was a comment Judge
Howard made right after the following exchange between myself
and the witness.

Q. Can you think of any reason or any subterfuge or deliberate
effort on the part of knowing experts, should they in some way

become perverted as to their integrity, that is likely to be able to mislead, deceive, or otherwise jeopardize the judicial process —assuming competent counsel, a competent judge, and a half-way intelligent jury?

A. No, sir, I can't.

As I had no more questions for Mr. Harrelson, I thanked him. But Colonel Howard had something to say: "I'd like the record to reflect that when Mr. Bailey stated, 'a competent judge,' he pointed in my direction. I appreciated that, Mr. Bailey. True or not, I appreciate it."

And I appreciated the long and careful hearing that Judge Howard had given us. He stated he was still bound by the manual. Months later, the transcript would be printed in most of the polygraph journals. Nonetheless, the hearings brought no immediate benefit to one Ernest L. Medina.

Another oft-discussed element that had come up during the pre-trial phase arose in the first week of trial. And unlike the polygraph it was an element that could do nothing but harm to Medina. It was the Yamashita principle.

After the first ten or so witnesses had come and gone, I made a general objection to the redundant nature—and perhaps also the irrelevance—of their testimony. Then, to my great surprise, Judge Howard started to talk about the case of General Yamashita, and its possible connection.

Shocked, I said, and probably in a louder voice than I should have used, "Your honor, if you have even the slightest idea that you are going to give a Yamashita instruction, then you better tell me so I can try to put a stop to it."

Fortunately, the jury was not in the courtroom while we had our little go-round, because I was mad. The Yamashita principle had no place in our case.

In its decision, the military court that convicted Yamashita had said:

> It is absurd . . . to consider a commander a murderer or rapist because one of his soldiers commits a murder or a rape. Nonetheless, where murder and rape and vicious, revengeful actions are widespread offenses and there is no effective attempt by a commander to discover and control the criminal acts, such a commander may be held responsible, even criminally liable, for the criminal acts of his troops.

Not all the justices of the Supreme Court agreed with the majority's decision not to hear the appeal. One of them, Justice Frank Murphy, suggested that Yamashita's rights had been "grossly and openly violated without any justification." In a dissenting opinion, setting forth his reasons why he disagreed with the decision not to hear the appeal, he worried out loud, warning the nation about the danger of the precedent the case represented:

> The high feelings of the moment doubtless will be satisfied. But in the sober afterglow will come the realization of the boundless and dangerous implications of the procedure sanctioned today. No one in a position of command in an army, from sergeant to general, can escape those implications. . . . Indeed, the fate of some future president of the United States and his chiefs of staff and military advisors may well have been sealed by this decision.

I had no intention of letting Ernie Medina get involved in those "boundless and dangerous implications."

I could tell that the idea of Yamashita as a governing precedent scared the living hell out of Medina, even though he would not admit it. He could face the prospect of his word against Calley's, could deal with it intellectually and emotionally, but the idea that a general of the Japanese Imperial Army—a man whom *we*, the Americans, had tried, convicted, and hanged to death—could rise up from his grave and thereby send Medina to his own, was almost more than he could handle.

Colonel Howard's response to my outburst was that he was nowhere near a decision to allow the Yamashita precedent to be applied in this case, and in fact he planned to instruct the jury that it could not find Captain Medina "criminally responsible" for any killings unless it was convinced, by clear and irrefutable evidence, that Medina knew innocent noncombatants were being killed, and he did nothing to stop it.

To my mind, this meant that we no longer had to worry about General Yamashita. Instead, we could depend on the rule of law, as applied by Judge Howard.

In the heat of the argument I had made a statement that was something less than tactful. I had said, maybe even shouted, "I don't think that what is done to a Jap hanged in the heat of vengeance after a world war can be done to an American on an imputed theory of responsibility." My regret was in using the tired old epiphet "Jap," for I never use racial or ethnic slurs, but Colonel

Howard's mention of the Yamashita principle touched an old chord, and bundled me back into the past. But I make no real apology, for when I agree to defend a man's life, I do not promise to be tactful. Or even nice.

On Friday, August 20, the last day of the first week, we had our first conflict in the testimony. After two former members of Charlie Company had testified that they heard Medina give an angry cease-fire order as soon as he saw the first civilian bodies—in fact, one of them recounted Medina's shouting, "Cease fire, Goddamn it!"—another swore that he heard a slightly different order.

Thomas Kinch, of North Cape May, New Jersey, testified that Medina had received word from a helicopter crew that there were "bodies all over the place," so he gave the order, "That's enough shooting for the day. The party's over."

I looked at Ernie, and he was shaking his head from side to side, very slowly. He didn't even know I was looking at him. According to the defense "book" on Kinch, he had several AWOL and other disciplinary notations in his record. In fact, he had received a general, rather than an honorable, discharge.

I had not been spending much time in cross-examination of witnesses, mainly because they seemed to be on our side rather than the government's, but I had to go after Kinch. I could not imagine Ernie Medina saying, especially in the context of Mylai, "The party's over."

Kinch admitted his less-than-sterling record, but insisted that his memory of Medina's wording was accurate. Still, there was a small problem, from Kinch's standpoint, and that was that in his several interviews prior to taking the stand, he had only mentioned Medina's saying the party was over one other time.

I asked the witness why he had not mentioned it when he was interviewed by the Army, and he said, "I didn't remember it then; I've remembered it since." What bothered me was that the first time Kinch had described the order in such highly damaging words was when he was interviewed by *Life* Magazine. He admitted, "I might have said it in *Life*."

My point was that certain members of Charlie Company had learned that there was a flourishing market for quotes that made Calley, Medina, and other officers look bad. I couldn't prove that Kinch was one of these vultures, but I had my suspicions.

One of the next witnesses brought the pendulum back to our

side. And as a result of something he said, I made a remark that brought the wrath of the prosecutors down on me.

Jeffrey LaCross had been one of the three platoon leaders on March 16, 1968. When he testified, the former lieutenant was a student in Michigan.

On cross-examination, LaCross had testified that when Medina saw the group of twenty to twenty-eight dead civilians, he had already given an order to stop burning the huts. I asked him if men in his platoon had shot the people, and he said no.

Then I asked him if the people would have been shot if the cease-burning order had come sooner. (Medina had told me that all his men had orders to capture noncombatants.)

LaCross remembered Medina's order. His answer to my question was, "No, sir [meaning that prisoners were to have been captured rather than shot]. Everybody knew what was supposed to be done with noncombatants."

And I said, against almost instinctively, "Except a lieutenant named Calley."

The prosecutors shot out of their chairs, objecting loudly. Judge Howard looked less than pleased, but he accepted my explanation that my comment fit the defense theory that Lieutenant Calley was "acting on his own hook." Howard let my remark stay in the record.

Most of the reporters in the courtroom played up the argument my comment had precipitated, but LaCross had made a far more emotional comment. After testifying that he had seen the bodies of three small children who had been killed a short time before, the former lieutenant said, "I thought, 'They're no different from any other kids—like my brother and me.' They woke up this morning, and now they were dead. That's what really bothered me."

The trial moved into its second week after hearing nineteen witnesses, only one of whom had offered possibly damaging testimony. And that one was Kinch, with his "the party's over" comment. We were feeling rather pleased, especially because the prosecutors had backed off from their idea of using the Yamashita case as precedent. Major Eckhardt had told Judge Howard that he would not follow that line of argument, but that he intended to show, "with direct and circumstantial evidence," that Medina knew what was taking place—and had purposely allowed it to continue.

If the prosecutors really believed they could prove *that*, I wasn't too worried. We hadn't even put on a defense yet, and most of the witnesses sounded as if they were on our side.

As it turned out, there were other things to worry about. We were defending what had to be—thanks to Mark Kadish and John Truman, under the urging of Medina and the legal direction of Gerry Alch—the best-prepared case in the history of the military. Still, we were not immune to surprises. And we got one with the twenty-third witness.

Hugh Thompson was one of the few prosecution witnesses who was still in the Army. Thompson, a captain, had been piloting one of the helicopters that moved above and around the village on March 16. As he testified on direct examination, he had been in the air about 9:30 A.M. (0930 hours) when he saw "a captain" move toward a woman who was ". . . up on a dike, kinda moving, . . . on her stomach. He walked up, right up to her . . . I was hovering . . . thirty to forty yards away. It appeared that he walked up to her and nudged her and turned around and walked away, turned around and shot her."

At the Calley trial, Medina had explained why he had shot the woman:

"The first location we came to that had been marked with smoke, there was a man, a woman, and a South Vietnamese girl, I would estimate her age, I guess, to be around fourteen or fifteen, that had been hit by shrapnel from artillery or from rockets from the gunships. I could tell that it was not done by small arms fire because they were ripped up very badly. I looked in the immediate area; there were no weapons.

"As I came up the incline, there was a small trail, the VC was laying off the trail in the rice. I seen it was a woman. She was laying on her side, facing away from me. Her arm appeared to be under her. I did not see any weapon in the immediate area. I do not recall seeing any wounds on her whatever. I looked around the area. I didn't see a weapon. I started to turn away, my people were moving up behind me. And as I started to turn around, I caught movement from the corner of my eye. Her head started to move, her eyelid. She started—I could see her chest starting to move. And my immediate reaction was that the helicopter had marked a VC with weapon. 'She's got a weapon or hand grenade! My God, you have had it!' I just continued turning around and I fired twice, and I assumed that I killed her. I did not check her out. I did not turn her over. I assumed that I killed her."

Thompson's testimony suggested that it had been otherwise, that the captain had simply murdered the woman. From watching his testimony on direct examination, I had the feeling that Thompson was telling what he thought was the truth. But the "truth" is seldom what it appears to be.

On cross, I asked Captain Thompson a few questions about the mechanics of operating a helicopter. For once I didn't have to do any homework. I have been flying helicopters for fifteen years, and own a helicopter factory. I know what it takes to fly one.

I wasn't trying to sandbag Thompson. Hovering thirty or forty yards above the object of one's vision is not terribly difficult, in the sense of how many mechanical steps are necessary. But we were not talking about a simple helicopter flight; we were talking about flying a helicopter in Vietnam. There were two central points: one, it was a huge ship, not the sweet little three-passenger machines I manufacture; and, two, he knew he could have been shot out of the air at any moment.

"Wouldn't it have been flatly impossible," I asked, "for you to have any concentrated stare on anybody for any length of time?"

Answer: "Yes, sir."

"This woman could very well have made a sudden movement that 'the captain' a few feet away could have seen that you missed?"

"Yes."

My feeling that Captain Thompson's testimony had been neutralized was aided by something else he had said on the stand. He testified that he dropped smoke markers to indicate "the location of wounded Vietnamese." This was short of incredible, as the troops on the ground had been told, over and over again, that a smoke marker meant the location of a "VC with weapon."

What made this bit of testimony so important was that Thompson said he had dropped the smoke to mark the site of a woman in need of medical aid. I was sure the military jury could see the discrepancy, and its implications.

If they had any doubts, all they had to do was ask their president, Colonel Proctor, who had been a combat helicopter pilot in two different wars.

The prosecution got back on track with its twenty-sixth witness, Lewis Martin. In Vietnam Martin had been a radio operator. Now a civilian, he was a police officer in San Jose, California.

Martin testified that he had been in the line of troops, headed by the command group, that passed in a single column near the village. Martin said that he saw GIs shoot at eight to ten Vietnamese women and children. He had no doubt, he said, that some of the civilians were killed by the shots.

Martin's testimony was undoubtedly the most damaging thus far in the trial. There were two reasons for this: one, he said that Medina actually entered the village—which was the opposite of our contention that Ernie never went inside—and two, Martin was suggesting Medina had to know that his troops were killing noncombatants.

I got up to cross-examine Martin with the clear intention, to phrase it less crudely, of renovating his anal anatomy.

One of the first things I wanted to bring out was the makeup of that military column. Martin answered that there were more than a dozen soldiers, in single file, and they kept a distance from one another of ten to fifteen feet. I asked him if it was true that some of the members of the group were actually out of the sight of other members, because of the heavy vegetation and the huts.

"Yes."

I asked him where Medina was, and he said at the head of the column. "And where were you?"

"I was sixth in line." The commander was sixty to ninety feet ahead of him.

"Did you make any effort to report what you saw"—the alleged killings—"to your commander?"

"No, sir. I was with my commander . . . I assumed everyone in the line saw it."

As sometimes happens at the least expected moment in a dramatic bit of testimony, there was a moment of unplanned levity. Martin's explanation of who was in line caused me to make a remark that sent the courtroom into open laughter. He had said that one of the Vietnamese interpreters was followed by a soldier named Alaux—which was pronounced "Aloo"—and then came Martin himself. I said, without thinking how it would sound, "So it was Phu, Alaux, and you?"

The laughter was a good emotional release, and soon we were back to the serious business at hand. I pressed Martin by reminding him that Medina had already testified that he never entered the village. Could it be, I asked Martin, that he had made a mistake, and that he had never actually seen Medina at all that day?

"I just can't recall ever having been separated from the command group."

I asked, "If Captain Medina says he was not in the village, but went around the south end of the village, can you dispute it?"

Martin shook his head, wearily. "I guess that's true. I'm not very well oriented."

After a few more questions, I let up on Lewis Martin. He wasn't the type that you might enjoy skewering on the stand. Some witnesses come on so strong, are so cocky and positive, that even the jury can't wait to see them annihilated by the cross-examiner. But Martin was not that kind of witness. He was, as he himself had said, "not very well oriented." And I was sure the jury had already figured that out. Martin got off with his anatomy, but not his testimony, intact.

But if Lewis Martin was something less than a strong prosecution witness, he was a veritable rock in comparison with what the Army put up next.

On the twenty-sixth of August, the eleventh day of trial, the Army called former private Gerry Hemming. Clad in a brilliant shirt-length dashiki and sporting a black beret, Hemming took the stand and settled uneasily into the chair. He testified that he was with Medina in the village and that he saw three civilians shot in Medina's presence. He also said that Col. Oral Henderson arrived on the scene by helicopter and told Medina, "Some of these killings have got to stop." This was startling testimony; however, Hemming swore that Henderson was wearing the gold leaf, which is the insignia of a major.

Writing in the *Atlanta Constitution,* reporter Phil Gailey described Hemming's testimony as "the most confusing" of the day. Gailey's observation was probably based on the final series of questions and answers that occurred during my cross-examination. Kadish and Truman had done their work very well, as usual, and I had a folderful of dynamite in my hand.

I asked the witness, "Is it true that you are a user of hard drugs?"

"I've experimented with LSD, but I don't fool with hard drugs."

I knew from the file that Hemming's testimony here was not the same as he had given in earlier statements. So I asked him, "Have your 'experiments' given you any problems with your memory?"

"No."

"Have you changed your mind about some things?"

"Yes."

"Why?"

"Because I wanted to."

Later, I asked Hemming if he had been drinking the night before. In fact, I asked him specifically if he had, as the file said, drunk four quarts of wine the previous night.

"Yes. I do it every day."

I waited for a moment to make sure the jury got the full import of what four quarts of wine per day represented.

Finally, I asked the witness, "Have you been blowing any LSD lately?"

Hemming's answer, although it did little to restore his credibility, touched a responsive chord throughout the courtroom: "No, but I wish I could. Maybe it would make me forget this thing." Everyone knew he was talking about Mylai.

If Gerry Hemming had been a strange witness, Michael Bernhardt was downright bizarre.

When the government called Bernhardt as its next witness, I objected immediately. Judge Howard sent the jury out of the room. The previous night Kadish and Al Johnson, one of my legal associates, had talked to Bernhardt for over three hours. They reported, "This one is really weird."

Bernhardt had testified at the Calley trial that Medina had told him, and others, not to discuss the killings of noncombatants if asked by Army investigators, and that Ernie had dissuaded him from writing his congressman about the affair. Bernhardt had also testified that he, alone among the troops of Charlie Company, had not believed the intelligence report that they would find the Forty-eighth VC Battalion in the hamlet of Mylai 4. As he put it, "We never met the enemy head on, not if we could help it. Most of our casualties were from mine fields and booby traps. I didn't think it would pay the enemy to have a World War II battle. They were doing too well without it."

There was no doubt that Michael Bernhardt was bright; my concern was that he might have been disturbed. Short, no taller than Lieutenant Calley, he appeared at Fort McPherson with a full beard, casually dressed, and armed with an aggressively defensive attitude. Now a surveyor in Tarpon Springs, Florida, he was also a student and sometime boat maker.

The Army prosecutors planned to use Bernhardt's testimony to show that Medina had tried to cover up the massacre, which, by implication, would suggest he knew about it from the beginning, or soon after the killing began. But as it turned out, the Army had not bothered to check Mr. Bernhardt out. Based on what Johnson and Kadish had told me, he had some very unusual beliefs.

My first few questions brought firm, direct answers: No, he was not in any sense religious; yes, he belonged to an antiwar group, but as to whether or not that group might be called subversive, he would "take the Fifth"; and yes, he had knowingly withheld information during an Army investigation into the Mylai affair.

The prosecutors were not looking happy.

Then I shifted to some of the things that Bernhardt had told Kadish and Johnson during their long interview the night before.

"Didn't you say last night, 'I don't know whether I'll tell the truth tomorrow'?"

"I don't remember."

"Didn't you say you'd knowingly tell an untruth to preserve a principle—namely, justice?"

"I don't remember."

"Would you lie if you thought it would serve the ends of justice?"

"Okay. In answer to your question, yes, I could."

"When Captain Kadish asked you if you intended to exercise your prerogative today about telling or not telling the truth, did you reply, 'Be surprised'?"

"Yes."

Major Eckhardt, for once showing some cracks in his usual Germanic placidity, asked for a fifteen-minute recess. When the time was up, he told Colonel Howard that he had had no idea of Bernhardt's "personal views," and that in light of them, the Army wished to withdraw him as a witness.

The judge nodded in agreement.

August 26 was not turning out to be a good day for the Army, and it was going to get worse before it got better.

That afternoon we learned why the Army had so generously reduced the penalty from death to life imprisonment. In a capital case, one in which the convicted defendant could be sentenced to death, the Army can not use depositions. It has to produce each and every witness for live testimony—and cross-examination. By reducing the charge it could enter depositions into evidence, and the defense would have no crack at the witness on the stand.

The Army wanted to use the depositions of the two Vietnamese interpreters that had been taken in Vietnam in July.

We objected vigorously, but Eckhardt and Wurtzell, the prosecutors, claimed they had asked the State Department—"through the proper channels"—to produce the two men, but that the Republic of South Vietnam had refused.

Colonel Howard said he was satisfied that the government had done all it could to press the issue, but that didn't mean we, the defense, couldn't try.

I told the judge that we would call the White House and find out just how hard the government had pressed the issue. Howard looked at me with a slightly bemused expression and said, "I don't know the number at the White House. Do you?"

As a matter of fact, I did. I sent Mark Kadish to the nearest phone with instructions to call both the White House and the State Department and demand that the two interpreters be produced in court.

I was steaming. I said to the court, "It's a joke. If the United States, with all the military and economic aid we give that government, really wanted South Vietnam to produce two NCO interpreters, they'd be here."

Kadish came back in the room and reported the result of his phone calls. Judge Howard asked me what response we had gotten, and I told him: "The response was that a response would be forthcoming."

I continued my argument to the court: "If the President of United States really wants Captain Medina to have a fair trial, which means having these witnesses here, he can arrange it. And to do so would involve practical politics, not the red-tape garbage of the State Department."

I had read the depositions of the interpreters, and I knew that they could not hurt us too badly, but there were several potentially harmful statements—especially if the Army happened to dig up support, in the form of a witness or two with a grudge against his company commander (a not unlikely possibility, given the nature of armies and the war in Southeast Asia).

One of the interpreters, Sergeant Minh, had testified in the deposition that he had asked "a captain who looked Spanish"—he didn't know his name—"why we burn village and kill inhabitants?" And that "the captain's" response was something about "orders."

Even a cursory reading of the depositions was enough to find any number of ambiguities and possible contradictions. And there was also a serious language problem. Based on the depositions, we strongly suspected that at the time of the raid on Mylai 4, at least one of the "interpreters" could not really be said to understand English. To call him "bilingual," much less fluent in English, was to deny that words have meaning. One of the interpreters, who said he was a Buddhist, did not know the meaning of the word "oath."

Sergeant Minh, according to the deposition, could not even remember the name of the village or the date. And yet the army wanted us to agree to the use of his deposition, without the chance to question him or his partner on the stand.

We had a later answer to Mark's phone call—nothing more could be done because a "judicial determination" had already been made.

To his credit, on hearing this Judge Howard said, "If the President of the United States was to pick up a hot line to Saigon, to say we would love to have those witnesses, I would consider it an assist to this court."

No such assist ever came.

John Truman was talking to Medina, and I could see the flashes of anger in the young lawyer's eyes. Truman was reminding Medina that during the depositions in Vietnam, Sergeant Minh's language problem caused such difficulties that halfway through the proceedings the Army made the incredible suggestion that it needed an interpreter for the interpreter! And even more startling, the prosecutors (who were taking the deposition) asked if the defense would join them in that request. The defense had declined, and Truman, for one, had sat there trying not to laugh out loud as the remainder of the deposition was conducted through the "new" interpreter. (Several weeks later Mary McCarthy, a novelist whose excellence in that field does not extend into journalism, wrote in the *New Yorker* that my suggestion was frivolous, adding, "Aside from providing some Caucasian entertainment, Bailey's ploy was a gross waste of the court's time." Such "wisdom," in total disregard of the facts, has always sickened me. I've wondered, with her penchant for fault-finding and for searing the less intelligent with a few beautifully shaped sentences, what kind of defendant Mary McCarthy would make if she ever found herself on trial for her life or freedom.)

The issue of the interpreters' deposition was put off, and we moved to the next problem. The Army was calling Robert Brisentine, the polygraph expert who had tested Medina. Knowing full well that the results of the test could not be introduced, the prosecutors wanted to use Brisentine to show that Medina had made some incriminating statements in the pretest interviews. It was a clear case of having their cake and eating it, too. And they would have gotten away with it—if they had been better prepared, or even as well prepared as one would have expected in such an important case. Brisentine, as it turned out, sounded more like a defense witness.

The portions of the pretest interview that the Army wanted to use concerned questions and answers that had not been fully explored in the tests themselves. The Army claimed that the answers indicated Medina might have known about the killings earlier, and that he might not have done all he could to stop them. Even though the tests themselves did not support these contentions, and—far more importantly—despite the fact that the test results were fully favorable to Medina, the Army wanted to have Brisentine testify for that limited purpose. I told Judge Howard I thought it was "a classic example of sandbagging."

With the jury out of the room, Brisentine took the stand and we went over his potential testimony. Once Brisentine had been examined, we could see that his answers would not be as damaging as the

Army had led us to believe they would be. Our defense was simply that Medina did not learn of the killings until three hours after the attack on the village began, and that once he did learn, he immediately ordered a cease-fire.

According to Brisentine, Ernie had said, but not during the test, that when he had seen the first group of bodies he should have realized that mass killings were going on, and that he should have done more to stop them. He also told the examiner, and again this was during the pretest phase (which is designed to build confidence or rapport between the examiner and the subject so as to get a better test) that he lost control of his troops sometime after the first hour and a half. He expressed concern that he had not acted quickly and and decisively enough to stop the killings, but that he wanted "with all his heart" to believe the casualties were the result of rocket and artillery fire.

Very little, if any, of this was in conflict with the testimony Medina had given at the Calley trial, but there were harmful inferences that could be drawn from portions of the conversation if they were wrenched out of context.

Everyone on the defense team knew that for two years Ernie Medina had been through a real dark night of the soul, and there had been many nights when he couldn't fall asleep for thinking of all that testimony concerning the deaths of innocent people. Any moral human being would have had that response, especially after the notoriety that had ensued. And we felt that, given the chance to put everything back into context, we could explain any statement that appeared to differ from that of our basic line of defense.

Still, we thought it grossly unfair that the Army could use Brisentine but not the results of his test—especially because Brisentine had said that this was the first case in his experience with more than fifty thousand polygraph examinations for the army in which a defendant who had passed the test was later brought to trial. Nonetheless, Judge Howard ruled that the army could call Brisentine.

August 26 brought one last surprise that the Army had not counted on. When the prosecution called former private Frederick Widmer, they knew that an earlier witness had accused him of shooting the small boy—the one that Medina was charged with killing. But they felt that their grant of immunity would protect Widmer from the chance of any later prosecution for murder.

Widmer, quite naturally, was not so sure. And when he took the stand, he surprised the government by pleading the Fifth Amendment, with its protection against self-incrimination. Both the Army and Judge Howard were displeased. Carefully and clearly, the military judge explained the protection of the immunity. Still Widmer would not budge. Finally, Colonel Howard decided that he had no choice but to cite Widmer for contempt of court for his refusal to testify, and he referred the case to the U.S. District Court in Atlanta.

Not to be outdone, Widmer's lawyer brought suit in the same court to enjoin the Army from enforcing the contempt citation. This suit was successful, and Judge Howard was served with a restraining order. A hearing was set for the following Monday, a hearing that required Howard's presence, so on Friday, the twenty-seventh, a rather weary-sounding Judge Howard declared a recess in the case of *The United States* v. *Ernest Medina* until the eighth of September.

This, and other matters that had cropped up on the twenty-sixth, ruined the prosecution's plan to rest its case on Friday. Mark Kadish's prediction of a four- to six-week trial was looking better and better.

There was one more order of business before we left the courtroom, and considering the circumstances, it was rather unusual. The twenty-seventh was Medina's birthday, and suddenly a large cake appeared, complete with candles and the large number 35 stuck in the middle. Judge Howard, with his usual politeness, said, "At the risk of poor taste, we wish you a happy birthday."

Ernie smiled, his wife Barbara joined him, and the flash bulbs popped. Actually, and this says something about "news," the party was the idea of the photographers. Most of them, and the reporters as well, seemed to like Medina, but the cake was a "business deduction." One of the photographers said to John Truman as he snapped away, "This kind of thing is great for, you know, human interest."

Later the Medinas, the Trumans, and Mark Kadish relaxed over drinks. Barbara Medina, Ernie's German-born wife, whom he'd met at a castle-lighting ceremony in Heidelberg, looked momentarily relieved. She had attended every day of the trial and welcomed a respite in the constant worry about the outcome.

Kadish thought the time had come to read another of his special gleanings from the Medina mailbag. This crumbled letter, which he drew ceremoniously from his jacket pocket, was from an avid John Bircher, who warned Medina to "keep an eye out for any Jews around you."

Medina has a fine, low-keyed sense of humor, but he isn't usually the first one to retort. This time he was. In deadpan seriousness, he said, "Gee, Mark, with you on one side of me and Gerry Alch on the other, I'm afraid my eyes would fall out."

\*       \*       \*

That the case against Medina was not going well for the prosecution was being regularly reported in the media. Some ascribed the Army's lack of apparent success to the stilted, wooden manner of the chief prosecutor. (Major Eckhardt had the terrible habit of writing out all his questions for witnesses, and even if an answer surprised him, he plowed ahead with the next prepared question, to the occasional consternation of the listeners. Every once in a while Judge Howard would remark, wryly, "I believe that point has already been established." As the trial wore on, Capt. Wurtzell was handling more and more of the direct examination of witnesses.)

Some reporters gave me most of the credit for the way the case was going, which was simply not true. Kadish and Truman had laid everything out so beautifully that a green lawyer would have had little trouble. In the beginning Alch had showed them how to do it, but after a very short time it was entirely their baby. Nonetheless, I was getting—with the exception of Miss McCarthy—a great press. It reached a peak when *Newsweek* Magazine did an entire piece without once calling me "flamboyant." (They settled for "celebrity lawyer.")

There were even a few reporters who placed the blame on the judge. Unfortunately, they took him seriously when he referred to himself as "just a country lawyer," a frequent jesting remark common to many great lawyers and jurists from the South. (Sen. Sam Ervin is the most recent example.)

Like the others, Col. Kenneth Howard was anything but a country lawyer. Yet one of the journalists with the widest of audiences, Fred Briggs of NBC television, decided to take the judge at his word. And in a nationally televised broadcast on the weekend of Medina's birthday, Briggs reported that the case was being lost because the hotshot lawyer from Boston was waltzing the country-lawyer judge around the courtroom. Of course he did not use those exact words, but the effect was the same. And clearly that's what he meant.

Kadish and Truman got very worried when they heard the broadcast. For several days they had been warning me that they thought the judge, despite his obvious fairness on any number of issues, was ruling against us with increasing frequency—especially on the major points like the interpreters and the admissibility of Brisentine's testimony. They thought that Briggs's comments would make the judge harder to deal with, especially if he thought they were true.

We asked to see Judge Howard, and explained that we were extremely sorry about the televised comments. He said he understood that "these things sometimes happen in highly publicized trials," and assured us that it would not color his attitude toward us or our client.

Nonetheless, in the first week after the trial resumed, whether the judge was aware of it or not (and I truly believe it was mainly subconscious), we were losing almost all the rulings. As Truman put it, with his usual directness, "We aren't getting shit." By the end of the week, I agreed with Mark and John that something had to be done. I didn't want Medina to suffer on account of a bias that we had no part in creating. Like it or not, Judge Howard and I were on a collision course.

When the trial resumed after the recess, the Army called its highest-ranking witness yet, Maj. Charles Calhoun. It had been the major's responsibility to monitor all radio messages coming from Charlie and the other companies that made up what was designated as Task Force Barker (for Colonel Barker, who was in overall command of the ground troops).

We expected that the major, as a prosecution witness, would contradict Medina's explanation of his first reported body count and why he did not want to return for an additional count on the sixteenth. Instead, he backed up everything Medina had said. I made an on-the-spot decision and stated that we would call Major Calhoun as a defense witness when and if we had to put on a defense case.

The next "witness" was not so favorable to our side. After Major Calhoun had left the stand, the prosecutors offered the depositions of the Vietnamese interpreters.

After the readings, we felt that the impact was not quite as bad as we had originally feared, but it was hardly favorable.

Sergeant Phu, in his part of the deposition, had said that Medina told him "to talk to the people [in the village after Mylai] that the people can't stay in the village because that village unsecurity . . . and if the next time we come to the village, if the people are there, they be killed like the people in the other village."

Phu's colleague, Sergeant Minh, had said that he asked the "Spanish-looking captain" why we "kill everybody in hamlet and why we kill all animals and burn all hootches?" and that the answer was "orders."

I was still mad that a trial so important as that of Captain Medina was not considered important enough by the United States government to justify bringing the witnesses over in person. But my displeasure was somewhat mollified by looking at the military jurors. They did not appear unusually impressed by the depositions.

Still, it rankled. We should not have lost the fight over the depositions. I couldn't give Judge Howard a very high mark for that ruling.

We got a little bit back at the end of the day by announcing to the court and the prosecutors that we had decided to call, as a defense witness, Lieutenant William Calley. I was not kidding. We had evidence to prove that Calley might be ready to tell a new story.

The final day of the government's case against Ernie Medina began on September 9, 1971, with one last witness—Robert Brisentine.

But the witness had hardly taken his seat in front of the jury when we had a heated argument. Major Eckhardt's initial questions did not contain the single salient fact that this was the man who had conducted the Army's polygraph test of Captain Medina. Instead, he phrased it in such a way as to indicate that Ernie had been talking to Brisentine "voluntarily." Under the circumstances, that was not what the word meant to me.

When Medina was tested, in November of 1970, he had not been formally charged. If and when he *was* charged, he expected it would be for giving an illegal order to his troops to kill noncombatants. And on that basis, he discussed the events of March 16 with Robert Brisentine—and with my full encouragement.

But now, in early September of 1971, when he was on trial for being responsible for those deaths, the Army wanted to introduce evidence of that conversation against Medina. The whole thing smelled.

As I said to Judge Howard, in trying to block Brisentine's testimony, "Medina came to be tested on one thing and was secretly being tested on another. I think that verges on trickery, either intentional or otherwise—and not on the part of Mr. Brisentine. It seems to be ..."

Colonel Howard interrupted sharply. He wanted to know if I was accusing him of being party to a deception.

"The court," I said, "is not charged with being underhanded. The government—" and I meant the Army prosecutors—"has been charged from the outset with being underhanded about this."

It did us no good. Judge Howard allowed Brisentine to testify.

So Robert Brisentine, the Army's top polygraph examiner, who had tested Ernie Medina at the request of the defense, took the stand and told the jury that Medina had admitted to him that sometime during the morning of March 16 he had lost control of his troops.

As he put it, "Captain Medina stated to me that he did lose control of his men ... but that it was too late."

Eckhardt then asked, "What steps did he take to regain control?"

"He did not take any steps to regain control."

That was going too far. I objected, because Brisentine had already testified that Medina ordered a cease-fire right after he witnessed the death of the small boy on the outskirts of the village.

Brisentine then repeated his earlier statement that Medina had told him he shouted several contradictory commands ("Stop," "Shoot," "Don't shoot") when he saw the boy, but that someone in the company fired at the boy and he fell. According to Medina, through Brisentine, the soldier who fired was John Smail. (This complicated things, for Smail had testified that it was Widmer who shot the child; and Widmer's refusal to testify was still an issue before the District Court in Atlanta.)

Brisentine finished with a damaging statement. He said that after Medina had seen the twenty to twenty-eight bodies along the trail, he "was fairly confident in his own mind that it was Lieutenant Calley's people who had killed this particular group." Without a transcript of the pretest interview, and none had been made because of the special nature of that phase of the testing process, I couldn't very well object. But I had serious doubts that Ernie would ever have said he was "fairly confident" about that point. I think that was one of the big questions in his own mind that caused him so much anguish and guilt. I had to hope that the jury could properly weigh Medina's own testimony, which it would hear in a few days, against that of Brisentine's recollection of what Medina said nine or ten months ago.

I didn't blame Bob Brisentine for anything. But as he left the stand, I had to shake my head. Here was a man who made his living as an expert in the field of determining when someone is or is not telling the truth, a man who had tested Ernie Medina and found him to be telling the truth when he denied all the serious charges. And yet this man had been brought in to testify against Medina, and specifically warned not to say anything at all about the tests or the results. And they say, "The Army takes care of its own." What a laugh.

And with that the government rested its case.

As far as we could tell, all the Army had accomplished in its eleven trial days and its thirty-one witnesses was to prove everything we had admitted at the beginning.

Although the prosecutors had shifted their theory of the case to charge that Medina had known about the killings and did nothing to stop them, I still felt they had done a singularly inadequate job. And as I looked over at Ernie's "team," the odd couple of Kadish and Truman, I knew that we had simply outworked them. Most of the prosecution staff had treated the case as a nine-to-five job. But that was only part of why they had not been more effective; the main reason was that they were trying Medina for the wrong crime.

Just before the trial began, the government dropped the misprision of a felony charge, the "cover-up" charge, based on Medina's failure to report his suspicions. If they had not done that, we would very likely have been in trouble at the end of the government's case. But they had decided to go for the big one, the responsibility for the murder of 102 people, and in so doing guaranteed the slimness of their chances.

Truman's theory made the most sense: "Like so many prosecutors, civilian as well as military, they got greedy. They would rather put Ernie away for murder than for what they can prove."

On Friday, September 10, I argued to the court, the jury having been excused for the day, that Medina should be granted a directed verdict of acquittal.

Such verdicts are very rare in important cases, because they say, in essence, that the government has failed to prove its case and there is no question of fact for the jury to decide. I knew that the odds were not good (there had been several contradictions between witnesses, and the Widmer question had still not been decided), but as I joked with reporters that morning, "Considering the evidence in this case, I'm afraid I'd be disbarred if I didn't ask for a directed verdict of not guilty."

I argued for about forty-five minutes. Major Eckhardt took an hour in opposing my motions. Judge Howard ruled from the bench that the government had produced "some substantial evidence" in support of all its charges. He denied my motions.

I had one other important matter to take care of on the tenth. Now that we knew the trial would continue, I wanted one last shot at using the results of the polygraph tests. So I wrote to a man who had once publicly endorsed the machine's value, President Richard M. Nixon. My five-page request for aid began:

> I am writing this letter on behalf of my client, Captain Ernest L. Medina, but also on behalf of every American lawyer and citizen who believes that truth, and the ability to recognize and act upon it, is essential to our form of government.
>
> For more than twenty-two months now, I have been representing Captain Medina in connection with the massacre of Vietnamese noncombatants at Mylai 4 on March 16, 1968. During that period, he has testified under oath repeatedly and consistently as to his knowledge of the entire affair, in a conscientious effort to

help the United States reach the truth of what actually transpired. Never once, in hours of grueling examination by the Inspector-General of the Army, General Peers, the late Congressman Rivers, Congressman Hebert or the Court and counsel in the trial of Lt. William Calley did Captain Medina ever seek refuge in his absolute right to silence, or refuse answer to a question.

In pursuit of the only defense he has ever raised against allegations of his criminal responsibility—that is, the truth of his own recollections of what occurred on and just before that fateful day—Captain Medina sought to demonstrate his own candor of statement by submitting to a polygraphic truth verification test, commonly known by misnomer as a "lie-detector" test.

. . . Without troubling you with detail at this juncture, let me say that the results are favorable to Captain Medina, and would in all probability assist him in persuading the military jury now trying his case that his denial of the charges against him is the truth as he knows it. . . .

It will be a modern tragedy, Mr. President, if the United States Army succeeds in withholding from a military jury, appointed by a Lieutenant General of that Army, the truth. This is the risk we now confront. I, therefore, request that you instruct Military Judge Howard that he may, in the wisdom of his own judicial office, receive polygraphic evidence within the dictates of his own discretion. I make this request as an attorney petitioning a rule-making authority who has both the power and the duty to respond.

I realize, Mr. President, that some might suggest that this request be shelved unless and until Captain Medina is convicted, in the hope that the issue may never have to be confronted. But as practicing lawyers, we both know that shoving such questions to some possible appellate tribunal is a disservice to everyone concerned.

I earnestly hope that you will see fit to make the requested clarification in pursuit of simple justice.

I should have saved my time and postage. A few weeks later I received a reply. It stated that the White House did not have sufficient faith in the reliability of the polygraph to suggest a change in the courts-martial manual. The reply, by the way, did not come from the President. It was signed by John Dean. (Two years later, while watching the Watergate Committee hearings on television, I was surprised to hear the same John Dean offer to take a polygraph test to prove he was telling the truth about corruption in the Nixon White House. And I was startled to hear his description of the machine's worth—his words were taken all but verbatim from my letter of September 10, 1971.)

It struck me as ironic that President Nixon, who had seen fit to comment publicly about the Calley verdict, could not even be bothered to answer my letter personally. Also, it appears that the Hiss-Chambers controversy was more important than a man who was being tried for over a hundred murders.

As the Medina trial progressed, the audience had grown progressively slimmer. Even the working press did not attend all the sessions. Mary McCarthy, with characteristic insensitivity, had written of "the disgusted conviction that the Medina court-martial was a poor road show of the Calley hit." As usual, there was some truth in her observation, but none of the journalists I know and admire would have been so cruel as to phrase it that way in print.

The attendance picked up markedly on Monday, September 13, the first day of the defense case. The reason: our first announced defense witness was to be Lt. William Calley.

Our reason for calling Calley was to see if he would deny a story told us by a surprise witness who'd contacted us after the Calley conviction and explained that he had information "that could help Captain Medina." The witness turned out to be an Army captain who'd served in Vietnam, and although not a member of Charlie Company, had known both Medina and Calley. After we had interviewed him, and found his information to be very helpful, we asked why he hadn't come forth sooner, perhaps during the Calley trial. He said, "I thought Calley was in enough trouble already."

Therefore, we weren't too surprised when Calley's lawyer told us that his client would plead the Fifth Amendment. Nonetheless, on Monday morning Lt. William Calley, Jr., arrived at Fort McPherson in an army staff car, accompanied by George Latimer and a military policeman. He wore his dress uniform and dark glasses, and his brass was sparkling. The insignia on his sleeve read "Follow Me."

Calley did not appear in court. He waited in a room down the hall while his lawyer told the court that Lieutenant Calley would claim his Constitutional privilege. A few minutes later, when the jury was seated, Judge Howard allowed me to tell them that Lieutenant Calley would not appear as a witness. It did not hurt us, psychologically, that everyone knew Medina had testified at the Calley trial.

Our first witness was Robert Lee, a former member of Charlie Company. Lee had been the medic who helped Medina clear the dead and wounded from the mine field on February 25, 1968. For his valor on that occasion, he, too, had been awarded the Silver Star. Lee's testimony dovetailed perfectly with what Medina had told the Calley jury.

He told the crowded courtroom that, after he and Medina had set the body of a wounded soldier down on another mine and seen it blown away from them, ". . . I kind of went into hysterics." Medina then grabbed him by the collar and ". . . hit me a few times." "[He said to me] Bob, you're the only medic we have here, and you've got to pull yourself together."

Lee was followed on the stand by Michael Terry, now of Utah, who provided the link needed for the crucial testimony of the next witness, Gene Oliver. What made Oliver so important was that he had actually been the one who shot the small boy Medina was charged with killing.

Terry, a devout Mormon, said, "We'd just started to move out, and I spotted some motion in front of me. I heard a shot, and Gene Oliver had fired, and I looked and saw that it was a boy. I yelled, 'It's just a small boy.' "

I asked Terry what if anything Medina had said after the boy was shot, and the witness replied that because of his religious beliefs he could not repeat it exactly. Instead, he told the court, Medina's response was, "Blankity-blank, cease fire."

There was an odd quiet in the room.

On cross-examination, Captain Wurtzell tried to show that the defense had planted the story, or at least tried to suggest it, but Terry said simply that his memory had been refreshed by hearing Oliver discuss it with us out of court.

And then Oliver himself took the stand. A stocky young man in his mid-twenties, he was working as a carpet installer, trying to build a new life—and trying to forget that day in March of 1968 when he had shot and killed a small child. When Oliver read that his former commander was being tried for shooting that same child, it stunned him. He and his wife began to have talks that lasted far into the night. Finally they decided: Gene Oliver would come forward.

On the stand at last, he testified that as he was standing on the southern edge of the village, just after a soldier who had shot himself in the foot was evacuated by a medical helicopter, he "saw a movement, a human form, and I raised my weapon and fired."

But then he heard someone else yell, "It's only a child," and he knew what he had done. The next thing he heard was "Captain Medina yell, 'Goddamn it, cease fire.' "

I asked Oliver if it was something that Medina had said that caused him to fire. He replied, "No, sir. It was what I saw."

And there was one more question: "Why didn't you come forward before?"

"Because it was something I'd rather bury."

In my remarks to the jury at the opening of Medina's defense, I told them that I would present evidence of the kind of psychological stress that the troops of Charlie Company were under. And a statement by a lawyer in preface to his case, whether he is a defense lawyer or a prosecutor, is in reality a verbal promissory note. If he doesn't deliver on that promise, the jury has a duty to hold that failure against him.

I kept that promise on Monday afternoon, September 13, by calling Dr. Peter Bourne.

An Australian by birth, Peter Bourne is a psychiatrist with offices in Atlanta, Georgia, and the director of the state's antinarcotics program. The problem of human performance under stress had been a special interest of Dr. Bourne's for quite some time, and he spent a year in Vietnam studying soldiers in combat.

During that year, Bourne had traveled with a Special Forces Unit for several months, and gone on numerous combat missions to continue his study in the field under the most rigorous—and dangerous— conditions. Simply put, he knew what he was talking about.

Dr. Bourne testified that the war in Vietnam was so different a war, in terms of combat techniques, from all the other "modern" wars, that it produced unusual amounts and types of stress. He said that American soldiers in Vietnam feel an "enormous frustration, and tend to overreact to all Vietnamese." He talked about the growing fear of the "unseen enemy" that struck at night and disappeared during the day, obviously aided by sympathetic South Vietnamese civilians. (A not uncommon atrocity favored by the Vietcong was to capture and kill an American soldier—and then skin him, and leave him where his own men would find him.)

One of his personal accounts sounded very much like what might have happened at Mylai 4: "We were assaulting a village where there were suspected Viet Cong, and there was a thirty-minute fight before the commander entered the village. I went with him." Prior to going in, the Special Forces had surrounded the village and poured all kinds of weaponry into it.

"When we got into the village, we found several noncombatants who had been killed. The captain I was with was completely unaware of what had been going on. . . . The captain felt terrible about what had happened but at the time there was nothing he could do about it."

On cross-examination, Captain Wurtzell tried to belittle Dr. Bourne's field work by suggesting that a scientist was not likely to get very close to the action. He asked the witness if he had actually been at all close to the men while the fighting was going on.

Dr. Bourne, in his clipped, precise accent, said, "Part of my methodology was to take urine samples, and in order to do that, one has to get rather close to a chap." The roar of laughter that followed the psychiatrist's answer was the loudest and most spontaneous of the entire trial.

The rest of Monday was taken up by the character witnesses we had assembled to testify for Ernie. There were seven officers, all of whom were equal to or higher in rank than the jurors.

Obviously, no defense attorney in his right mind calls a character witness who has anything but the best to say about his client. Nonetheless, the military witnesses we called on behalf of Medina were men who had nothing to gain or lose, one way or another. And the word they used most often, in describing the record and character of Captain Medina, was "outstanding."

(FORT MCPHERSON) THE BIRTH OF A SEVEN-POUND, ELEVEN-OUNCE SON TO THE WIFE OF THE ARMY'S PROSECUTOR BROUGHT ABOUT A HALF-DAY DELAY IN CAPTAIN ERNEST MEDINA'S COURT-MARTIAL. THE DEFENSE WAS TO RESUME TESTIMONY THIS MORNING BUT THE BIRTH DELAYED THE TRIAL UNTIL EARLY THIS AFTERNOON. THE BABY WAS BORN TO MRS. MARGARET ECKHARDT, WIFE OF MAJOR WILLIAM ECKHARDT.

ASSOCIATED PRESS WIRE

14 SEPTEMBER 1971

After the celebration of life, we returned to the matter of death. We did not know it at the beginning of the afternoon session on Tuesday, but we had just about run out of road on the collision course between myself and Judge Howard.

When we announced that we wished to call two captains, Robert Hicks and Eugene Kotouc, the prosecution immediately objected. Our purpose was twofold: Hicks could provide the crucial information we were denied when Lieutenant Calley refused to testify; and Kotouc could show that Medina's interrogation of a VC prisoner did not include acts of physical violence.

The prosecutors argued that Captain Hicks's testimony would be hearsay, that Calley himself was the best witness, and that since Calley had refused to testify, we were simply stuck. They objected to Captain Kotouc's potential testimony on the basis of its not being germane to any of the charges against Medina.

The only way to test these issues was to hear what the witnesses would say, so Judge Howard excused the jury and Capt. Robert Hicks took the stand.

In July of 1968, four months after the killings at Mylai 4, Lieutenant Calley was still in Vietnam. One night, Hicks and a few other officers were sitting around his hut. Lieutenant Calley was in the group. According to Hicks, Calley started "telling war stories."

I asked Hicks to describe the tone of Calley's accounts. He said, "I guess you could call it bragging."

One of Calley's stories was about Mylai 4. As Hicks related it: "He said he didn't expect to find any civilians in the place . . . [when the American troops arrived] all the people came out and started to cheer, but they shut up real fast when someone shot a water buffalo and the rest of the men opened up."

The story didn't sit well with Captain Hicks. "Knowing Captain Medina as I do, I asked him where was Captain Medina at the time, and he said Captain Medina . . . was with the third platoon, and when he [Medina] came up, he said he was certainly surprised."

Hicks testified that he had considered Medina an "extremely professional commander," so he asked Calley another question: "I asked him if Captain Medina knew what they were doing. And he said, 'No.' "

There were two reason why Hicks's testimony was so vital to the defense: one, it indicated that Medina did *not* know about the killings until well after they had occurred; and two, he had never entered the village, as some witnesses had said. Also, by implication, he could hardly have ordered the massacre and then been "surprised" by it.

Judge Howard said that he would rule tomorrow, Wednesday, on whether or not Hicks and Kotouc could testify before the jury.

That evening I noticed that Medina was beginning to smile more often. I was pleased to see it, but I didn't tell him that we were still a long way from getting that testimony into evidence. Ever since the Briggs broadcast, Kadish and Truman had been telling me that we were, more often than not, on the losing end of the judge's rulings on important issues. Now I had to agree, even though I thought he would rule in our favor on Wednesday.

At 9:00 A.M., with the jury still out, Colonel Howard said he would rule later in the morning, so we put on a different witness. This time we were going to take a page from the prosecutor's book. We called Leonard Harrelson, a polygraph expert who had examined several of the government witnesses.

Harrelson testified that Lewis Martin, the policeman from California who had testified that Medina had witnessed the killings in the village, "registered a reaction"—which is examiner talk for a possible showing of deception—when he repeated that story to Harrelson. Martin also gave what Harrelson termed a "deceptive answer" when he said that he didn't want to "see Medina get in trouble."

Of greater importance was that during the examination Martin told Harrelson he "needed psychiatric treatment," adding that he had had "problems with delusions and illusions" throughout his life. Harrelson testified that Martin had told him he would not volunteer to take the stand and correct his testimony, but that he would do so if he were asked.

At this point the president of the jury, which was allowed to hear the "nonresult" testimony, stated the jury's desire to have Martin's three-week-old testimony read back to them as soon as it would be practical. Judge Howard said he would have the tape recording of Martin's testimony played for them the next afternoon.

Harrelson had made another test for us. Because Gene Oliver's testimony amounted to a complete defense against one of the charges of murder, it was imperative that the jury believe the former private who had admitted shooting the boy. Harrelson said, "In my opinion, he was telling the truth when he said he shot this little child."

Things were looking good—which should have been a sign to us that they would soon change. For change they did, and with dramatic suddenness.

The next defense witness was a tall, slim young man with a dark beard and a quiet manner. Roger Alaux had been an artillery officer in Medina's command group. He had been called by the Army to support the charge of Medina's killing the woman in the rice paddy, the woman Medina admitted shooting; but Alaux said Medina shot out of self-defense. Alaux, like so many of the government witnesses, turned out to be more helpful to the defense. We called him to repeat his account of the incident. He testified that the body moved, and *then* Medina turned and fired.

I followed with a question aimed at clarifying the matter even more. "Did something cause you to be in a state of apprehension the moment before the shots were fired?"

"Yes."

And one final, important question that we were not able to ask him on cross-examination when he was the Army's witness: "Did you see or hear Captain Medina say anything to indicate his acquiescence to the slaughter of civilians by his troops?"

Roger Alaux, who had been with Medina all morning long, said, "No, sir."

And then it happened, with all the force and fury of a Georgia thunderstorm. Judge Howard ruled that he would not allow the jury to hear our witnesses Hicks or Kotouc. And I blew up.

I shot to my feet and objected so loudly that heads snapped in the courtroom. I repeated my reasons why, in light of Calley's refusal to testify, Hicks was what the law calls "the next best witness." I could feel the skin on the back of my neck reddening, a sure sign of anger, so I finished my objection bluntly, by calling the ruling "completely erroneous."

Judge Howard didn't like that one little bit. He snapped back at me, in a tone almost as angry as mine, "I don't want you to repeat back to me that the judge is an idiot and doesn't know what he is doing!"

"I don't recall using those words," I said, "I believe that 'erroneous' is a respectable word."

We glared at each other. Truman, Kadish, and Medina were rigid in their chairs. Across the aisle the prosecutors sat, equally motionless. My mind was racing as I stood there, locked in a furious staring match. One thought kept intruding—that Mark and John were right, and that that damn Briggs television broadcast had marked the point at which all the major rulings began to go against the defense. I made a decision. I was not going to give an inch this time.

I asked Judge Howard if he would allow me to make further argument on the point at issue, and he said yes. I then told him that as I was about to make a motion of utmost gravity, I would like to request that it be done in private. He agreed, and the courtroom was cleared of both the jury and the spectators. As the room was emptied, I sat down for a moment, still seething.

I cursed Fred Briggs, mentally, as I sat there. His broadcast had been aired the Friday before last, and had been a six-minute, "wrap-up" account of the progress of the trial. It was shown at six o'clock and then again on the late news. As I was in the air at the time of the earleir broadcast, I missed it. But so many people mentioned it to me during the evening that I saw it on the late news. In fact, I had called Kadish and told him and Truman not to miss it.

Unlike Bruce Morton of CBS, who had covered the trial most assiduously, Briggs was one of those commentators who popped in and out. I was worried that his less-than-regular attendance might have given him an inaccurate picture of the trial.

As it turned out, I had good reason to be worried. Briggs's "quasi-special" was his own interpretation of the events of the trial to date, and he presented his analysis in a light most unflattering to the military judge and to the prosecutors. He described the latter as "bumbling," "unprepared," and "completely 'outgunned.' " As for Judge Howard, Briggs implied that he was so taken in by the sharp-ster from Boston that he was making all his rulings in favor of the defense. He made it sound as if Colonel Howard was all but mes-merized by the defense tactics.

The next day, acting on my instructions, Mark Kadish visited with Judge Howard to convey my personal resentment at the treat-ment the judge had received over national television, and to ask if this kind of publicity might incline him to toughen up his rul-ings in regard to the defense, simply to disprove what Briggs had reported.

Judge Howard admitted to Mark that he was less than thrilled by what had been described, especially because, as he correctly pointed out, he had actually overruled the defense more often than the prosecution, at that point. But he said he did not believe that his objectivity would be colored by this sort of public embarrass-ment, and that he would continue to rule as he thought proper under the law.

During the following week, it seemed to me that we were headed downhill. Although it wouldn't have been readily apparent to the untrained observer, as an experienced lawyer I felt that the judge was making a subconscious effort to demonstrate impartiality, and in so doing was actually causing the opposite effect. Because he had been accused of being partial to Medina, his rulings were tend-ing to slant in the other direction more often than I felt was jus-tified.

Truman and Kadish had felt that way even before I did, and

when Judge Howard ruled that Hicks could not testify, I joined them with fervor.

Once the courtroom was cleared, I asked Judge Howard to remove himself from the case. Technically, this is known as a motion to recuse. It is an unusual motion, and one that is rarely granted. In effect, such a motion accuses the judge of no longer being fit—for some reason of passion or prejudice—to hear the case before him. It is a motion that is made in only the most grave circumstances.

My motion to recuse was coupled with a motion for mistrial.

The reason for this drastic step was dramatically simple: the Army's final theory of the case was that Medina knew of the massacre and failed to stop it, but Captain Hicks's conversation with Calley (well before Mylai was ever publicized) proved just the opposite.

When I made the motion, I told Judge Howard that I was doing so with the greatest reluctance, because I felt that he was one of the finest judges that I had ever appeared before, and that he was handling an extremely complicated and difficult case with a great deal of professional and judicial acumen. Nonetheless, I sincerely felt that the unwarranted remarks made about his conduct by the press—and in particular by Mr. Briggs—had colored his judgment on some of the earlier rulings, and may have had some influence on his decision to prevent Medina's jury from hearing what Captain Hicks had to say.

There was a long discussion, highlighted by a good deal of give and take between counsel and the bench. When it was over, and I heard Judge Howard's point of view and his reasons for doing what he had done (and there is absolutely *no* rule of the court that says he must explain his rulings), which I thought to be quite candid, I made another decision. I withdrew the motion temporarily, and asked Judge Howard to declare a thirty-minute recess, during which time he would answer for himself two questions, if he should see fit to do so.

The first question was: "If you were in my shoes, as a defense counsel in a heavy case where his client had more than one hundred opportunities to get a life sentence, would you want to be before a judge in the frame of mind that you know you are in right now?"

The second question was: "If you were Ernest Medina, the one who would have to pay the penalty if he were convicted, and the chance of conviction might well rest on a discretionary ruling of the court (meaning one that couldn't be overturned on appeal), would you be content, within your knowledge of the system, to have a judge in the frame of mind of Colonel Kenneth Howard?"

Judge Howard said that this was a "reasonable request," and he declared a thirty-minute recess.

That half hour was very long. I've often said that I would like to base my fee in major criminal cases on the length of time that the jury is out, because the minutes are so horribly long and debilitating. That half hour was just like waiting for a jury verdict. And I have often wondered how Kenneth Howard, the man, spent that time: did he pace, did he read a law book, did he make a drink from a flask stashed away in a desk drawer, or did he simply put his feet up, his hands behind his head, and stare out the window at the scrub pines in the distance?

When Judge Howard returned, exactly thirty minutes later, the court was still closed to the press and the spectators, and the jury was still in its room. He said that, after reflecting on the matter, he could answer "yes" to both questions. And he could do so in all sincerity.

Based on those responses, I withdrew my motion to recuse, and asked if we could reargue the question of Captain Hicks's testimony.

Judge Howard said yes, and we began a lengthy reargument of the points of law. As before, I was aided greatly by an excellent legal brief that John Truman had drawn up, citing among others a recent California case that held that when a man makes "a declaration against a penal interest"—meaning, that when he makes a statement that could send him to jail—it is presumed to be true. And his unavailability as a witness for such reasons as death, insanity, or taking the Fifth, makes that statement an exception to the hearsay rule.

Colonel Howard then, in fact, reversed himself. And Captain Hicks was permitted to testify.

I know very few judges, indeed very few human beings, who would have been big enough to make that decision.

After all the intensity of Wednesday, September 15, it would have been fitting, and easier, to end the court session with Judge Howard's decision to allow Captain Hicks to testify. But that is not the way courts work, or trials progress.

Late in the day on Wednesday, the defense called its second-to-last witness, John Paul, who had been Medina's radio operator at Mylai, and was now a civilian living in Jupiter, Florida.

Paul testified—in direct contradiction to Lieutenant Calley—that one hour after the raid on the village began, Medina radioed Calley's platoon and said, "What is all the firing about?" According to Paul, there was no reply. Some time later, Medina, who had no information other than reports of firing, sent another message. This was a cease-fire. Paul said it was sent, "to save ammunition."

The ex-radio operator had other testimony to give. He said that he, too, saw the sudden movement by the woman in the rice paddy. As he put it, Medina had started to move away from the woman, but, suddenly, Medina said, "Oh my God, son of a bitch, she's got a grenade."

Paul testified that Medina then whirled around and shot twice.

The witness also testified that he was so startled that he dropped his radio receiver and reached for his rifle ". . . in case I needed it."

At 11:03 A.M. on Thursday, September 16, 1971, Capt. Ernest L. Medina took the stand in his own defense. As usual, he wore his full complement of ribbons and medals, and his captain's bars shone. He was very nervous, but unless you knew him well, you couldn't have seen it.

In the front row, Barbara Medina was in her usual seat, and again, if you didn't know her, you couldn't tell how terribly nervous she was. As John Truman had said, a few nights earlier, "You have to understand how it is for her. Her own parents were political refugees. And now her husband, the father of her children, who wouldn't harm anybody as far as she is concerned, is accused by his own government—*her* government, now—of killing people. She doesn't want to admit it, even to herself, but she fears one simple truth, and that is that if your government is after you, brother, your ass is grass. But at least in America you have a chance."

Ernie Medina would not have agreed with the first part of John Truman's statement. For he was ready, and this was what he had been waiting for. He would tell *his* story to *his* jury.

"I had intelligence reports that the women and children left the village every morning at seven, and that the man noncombatants would not be in the village."

His voice shook just a little at first, as I took him through the infamous briefing on the eve of the attack, but soon he had himself under control.

"I told them the Forty-eighth VC would be in the village and we could expect a good firefight. . . . And I told them we'd be out-numbered two to one, and I told them right frankly some of us wouldn't be coming back. This is going to give you a chance to go in there and make contact with these people. What I was doing was giving them a pep talk."

He explained, for perhaps the sixth time, that he had originally thought, right after the attack was launched, that the LZ, or land-ing zone, was "cold." But then he received a report from a helicop-ter pilot, "Negative, negative. You are receiving fire, the LZ is hot!"

I asked what the strength of Charlie Company was at the time he had told his men to expect 280 VC soldiers, and he answered, "It was down to one hundred and five people, due to small arms fire, mines, and booby traps."

He said that someone asked him what to do if they encountered women and children—were they to shoot them?—and Medina an-swered, "No, you don't shoot women and children. You use your common sense."

According to his testimony, while he waited outside the village with his command group of ten soldiers, he received no radio re-ports that the 48th VC Battalion was not in the village, but that he heard firing, so he thought his men had encountered at least some Vietcong. And while he waited, helicopters carrying su-perior officers were monitoring the area from above, and ". . . if there was something going on of that nature, they should have told me."

(Later, the jury questioned him on the point of his 8:30 cease-fire order. It wanted to know why, if he truly believed that the troops were encountering the VC, he ordered them to "conserve ammunition." Medina replied that he wanted them to save enough ammunition to kill the animals, one of the purposes of the mission. He said that later, when he heard sporadic firing, he thought the men were killing the animals.)

I asked him about the two specific murders with which he was charged, and his answers were brief.

As to the woman in the rice paddy, he said that he and the com-mand group had gone up to check on the smoke-marked "VC with weapon" that had been reported from one of the helicopters. He thought the woman was dead, but ". . . . she moved, and I thought, 'She's got a grenade. You've had it,' and I instinctively whirled around and fired twice and I assumed I killed her. . . . She was the first person I ever shot at and I just turned and walked away."

In answer to my question about the shooting of the child—whom Oliver had just testified he had killed—Medina said that they were walking up the trail when someone darted out from behind a hedgerow, and he shouted, "Get him, stop him, shoot, or don't shoot." But someone shot, and the child fell.

I asked him if he could remember exactly what he said, and he replied, " 'Goddamn it, I want this firing stopped,' or words to that effect."

Then I asked Medina to tell the jury what his opinion had been of Lieutenant Calley. (I saw no point in not addressing the issue head on, for if Medina had been the "unseen presence" at the Calley trial, surely the reverse was true at Fort McPherson.)

"Lieutenant Calley did not have the leadership ability to get along with his men. There were times when I had problems with his platoon." In fact, he said, he had transferred Calley from the second platoon to the first because the latter was made up of more experienced soldiers who would not need strong leadership.

Then I moved the questioning into an area that needed to be explored outside the presence of the jury. I asked Judge Howard if the jurors could be excused, and he agreed.

Medina then recounted what he did after he first began to suspect that a large number of civilians had been killed. He said that he called his platoon leaders together that evening and asked them for an accurate count.

Lieutenant Calley, he said, "hemmed and hawed" and didn't seem to want to answer.

Pressing him, Medina said, "I asked him, 'How many—one hundred, two hundred, how many was it?' "

According to Ernie, Calley finally answered, "More than fifty, maybe."

Then, two days after the attack, Medina was told by Colonel Barker (later killed in a helicopter crash) to find out how many noncombatants had been killed, and in particular to investigate a report that "a colored NCO was firing into a ditch."

Medina testified that he called Sergeant David Mitchell in for questioning, and that when Mitchell said, "Why are you picking on me? Because I'm colored?" Medina dropped the matter.

Lieutenant Calley had brought Mitchell in to talk with Medina, and after Mitchell left, Calley and Medina walked away together. They were discussing the shootings, and Calley said, "My God, I can still hear them screaming." With that, Medina whirled around and said, " 'Look, if something happened, I want to know about it.'

I told him that if he'd killed a lot of noncombatants he was in trouble."

But Calley assured him, " 'If there's an investigation, you don't have to worry about it. You had nothing to do with it, and I'll take the blame.' He said something about me having a family."

According to Medina's testimony, that was the last that was said about it until September of 1969, when Medina got a phone call from Calley. As Ernie testified, it went like this:

"Captain Medina?"

"Yes."

"This is Rusty."

"Oh, Lieutenant Calley. How are you? Where in the hell are you?"

"I'm somewhere near Hawaii."

"Has anybody been to see you?"

"Yes."

"Well, about Mylai?"

"Yes, the Inspector General."

After some minutes of general conversation, Lieutenant Calley got back to the point.

"Is there anything I should do?"

"Yes. You'd better get you a couple of good lawyers and you'd better tell the truth."

"Well, I just want you to know that our deal [the promise Calley made Medina in Vietnam] still stands."

Judge Howard ruled that it would be improper, under the rules of evidence, for the jury to hear that testimony.

My final question to Captain Medina in front of the jury was, "Did you have any awareness that your men were killing innocent civilians?"

His answer was a firm-voiced, "No, sir."

Eckhardt, the chief prosecutor, had been taking a back seat for the last few days, but he got up to cross-examine Medina when I indicated I was finished, after almost three hours. Eckhardt was not able to shake Ernie on any of the major points, but he did cause him to become flustered when he snapped at him, "Did you lose control of your company?"

Medina, his composure slipping for the only time, said, "I believe I did, sir."

By the time he left the stand, some of the starch had gone out of his uniform, but his story was as firm as ever. Unlike the Army, Ernest Medina had not changed it to fit the progress of the case.

At nine o'clock the next morning, we were very close to the end of the case for the defense. But there was one more matter that had to be cleared up. The prosecution had a complaint about one of the witnesses we had brought over to our side, Gene Oliver. Oliver had angered the prosecutors by blurting out, when he testified as a defense witness, that "They [the Army prosecutors] know he's innocent as well as I do!"

However, I was startled when Major Eckhardt stood up, and without asking that the jury be excused, said, "The witness Oliver has threatened to take my life and to take Captain Wurtzell's life . . . and I took steps to protect myself and my family."

There was an instant shouting match, but I finally got the judge to excuse the jury. I was damn mad, because I had an agreement with Eckhardt that the matter would be brought up only in the jury's absence, yet he had said, right in front of them, that Oliver (who had admitted to shooting the small boy) had told Len Harrelson that "he wanted to kill me."

The whole thing was simply ridiculous. Harrelson had reported, as I told Colonel Howard, that in his opinion Oliver "felt a tremendous hostility because he feels the government is prosecuting Captain Medina with malice." To make matters worse, Eckhardt said he had information that Oliver brought a gun with him to Fort McPherson.

As the argument heated up, Judge Howard surprised everyone when he said to Eckhardt, in a loud, stern voice, "I'll tell you right now, I'm going to grant a motion to direct a finding of not guilty as to this particular charge, so it's all irrelevant anyway." Eckhardt looked so embarrassed that I almost felt sorry for him—almost.

A few minutes later, I stood and said, "Your honor, the defense rests."

We then began to argue motions based on the two charges of premeditated murder that remained, the charge of killing the woman and the charge of being responsible for the premeditated murder of one hundred civilians.

I really didn't think we had a strong chance of winning our motions, but Judge Howard had apparently been giving the testimony a good deal of thought.

He stunned the courtroom by announcing that he had decided to instruct the jury that in regard to the charge of killing the one hundred civilians, it could only convict Medina of involuntary manslaughter.

He was thereby ruling out verdicts of first-degree murder, second-degree murder, and voluntary manslaughter, because he felt that the government had failed to prove that "Captain Medina intended for these people to be killed. In my mind, I do not feel that it would be fair to expose Captain Medina to a murder conviction when in my opinion there is insufficient evidence."

The maximum sentence Medina could be given under the reduced charge was three years.

With his earlier announcement that he would drop the charge of shooting the boy, the most serious charge that remained (in addition to the assault charge) was that of killing the woman. I had argued that it was a "justifiable battlefield homicide," but the judge disagreed, saying, "My conclusion is that if the government's evidence is believed, it is sufficient to show that Captain Medina shot an unresisting human being."

In an interview with the press that he granted later that day, Judge Howard explained why he had reduced the charges, and he explained why he had—once and for all—laid aside the Yamashita precedent:

"We are at the point now where there is no question that a new law will be made that will radically affect a field soldier in a battlefield situation.

"There is a big distinction between the commander at the scene as Medina was and a man like Yamashita, who was way off.

"If a commander on the ground becomes aware that his troops are misbehaving, does he have the duty to interfere, and if he doesn't, is he criminally responsible?"

That, of course, was what we would find out.

After a recess of two days, while the judge perfected his charge to the jury (his written instructions governing matters of law), we made final arguments on Wednesday, September 22, 1971.

Everyone on the defense team figured that Major Eckhardt would draw back on some reserve power and give a strong final argument. Everyone was wrong. He argued for only thirty minutes, and a good bit of that time was consumed by a labored reading of the charges.

If his delivery left something to be desired, his words were excessively strong, far beyond what I thought was either necessary or fair under the circumstances.

In arguing for a guilty verdict on all four of the remaining charges, Eckhardt said that Medina knew what was happening as soon as he discovered the bodies on the trail, and that he did not, as he claimed, issue a cease-fire order. He said that Medina should have made every effort to stop further killings, that "he should have turned the air blue" in order to do so.

He said that Medina "wrongfully failed to take corrective action," a failure that was "culpable negligence." What bothered me more than anything else was a statement that Eckhardt made in closing. He said, his deep, resonant, uninflected voice carrying throughout the small courtroom, "Captain Medina abrogated his responsibility as a commander—and like Pontius Pilate cannot wash the blood from his hands."

I was not the only one who didn't like the analogy. I could see several of the jurors narrow their eyes as they heard the Pontius Pilate reference.

I hadn't intended to speak for quite so long, but Eckhardt had made me mad. I went right after the biblical reference, calling it "righteous pomposity," and launched into a long statement that, boiled down, meant that the government had not come up with a single credible witness who "can demonstrate that he [Medina] saw or should have seen anybody killed at Mylai."

"He is no filthy felon who finally got caught by the law. . . . I am not going to defend Ernest Medina on the theory that war is war, and if people get killed, that's too bad."

I spent a long time explaining the legal concept of reasonable doubt, saying at one point, "If you are ninety percent sure that he is guilty, then you must acquit. You have no choice, for that's what reasonable doubt means."

Running down the nature of the war, the lack of training and experience that Charlie Company represented, and the clear mandate given to the troops in Vietnam by the Army ("Charlie Company set out to kill with a license from their government"), I stressed Ernie Medina's record and accomplishments, concluding by saying, "If Captain Medina were that kind of sadist, then how did his superior officers fail to see that flaw in his personality?"

As for the charges of killing the woman and assaulting the VC suspect, I said, simply, "Gentlemen, put yourself in his place." And I took a chance by warning the jury, "Do not impose on a man a finding of guilty unless you are sure—damn sure—that there is no hope for acquittal."

Finally, I made reference to what a guilty verdict on the murder charge would mean: "If you are prepared to hold Medina to this standard of conduct, then in the future you had better equip every battlefield soldier with a lawyer at his side—and you will surely see the machinery of warfare grind to a slow halt."

Colonel Howard took almost two hours to read his charges of law. Slowly, the jurors left the courtroom and walked to the jury room. It was all over but the waiting.

Although it was mid-afternoon, no one felt like eating. Instead we sat there, almost as if by our refusal to leave we could will the jury into returning quickly. Judge Howard did not lock up the jury, but told them that he was prepared to wait until the late evening, or longer if necessary, for their verdict.

Ernie was gulping water, and his wife Barbara could do nothing but stare at him, occasionally working up to a smile. Knowing, from the many times I had sat and waited for a jury to return, just how horrible it can be, I decided to tell Medina something that would make at least one small part of it shorter and less agonizing.

For some reason I have never been able to discern, the Army manual, unlike the procedure in civilian courts, has different wording for each verdict. If a defendant has been found guilty, the president of the court addresses the defendant by rank and name, and then says, ". . . it is my duty as president of this court to inform you that the court, in closed session and upon secret written ballot, has found you guilty of all specifications and charges." But if the verdict is "not guilty," the president of the court says, "it is my duty as president of this court to *advise* you . . ."

It may seem like a small difference, but when your life or freedom hangs in the balance, that wait for the end of the sentence can seem like an eternity.

Although everyone tried to change the mood, in an effort to get Ernie to think of anything else, no one was successful. Guesses were made as to how long the jury would be out. Someone said two hours, another said one, and a few said nothing at all.

Suddenly, Judge Howard was back on the bench, with the news that the jury had reached a verdict. Hearts didn't actually stop, but I'm sure a number of them slowed perceptively.

I looked at my watch. It had taken the jury fifty-seven minutes to come to a decision. That *had* to be a good sign.

People scrambled back into their seats, and the reporters had their pads out, as the jury filed in with no clear hints, one way or another, on their faces.

Colonel Proctor looked at Medina. Ernie stood, walked to the front of the courtroom, and braced. There was absolute silence in the room.

"Captain Ernest L. Medina, it is my duty as president of this court"—Medina was almost rigid, as if every muscle in his body had locked in place—"to advise"—I sensed an immediate release of the muscles, as Medina's body let go of him, an almost imperceptible relaxation of the tenseness—"you that the court, in closed session and upon secret written ballot, has found you not guilty of all specifications and charges."

Applause burst out behind me, and was quickly gaveled down by Judge Howard. Now Ernie slumped visibly, then pulled himself together long enough to make a weak salute toward Colonel Proctor, the president of the court. There was a quiet sound that continued; it was the sobbing of Barbara Medina, who had gasped once, and then leaned on the shoulder of a family friend sitting next to her.

Captain Ernest Medina, a free man, walked back to his seat and reached for a glass of water, not daring to look at his wife.

Back in the defense room, Ernie and Barbara embraced, as the rest of us stood around with silly grins on our faces. Then, in answer to the clamoring of the press outside the door, we all went out to make statements.

Ernie said that he had never lost his faith in the military system of justice; Barbara said that all she was thinking about while the jury was deliberating was "not guilty"; Truman and Kadish said something that no one could hear; and I said exactly what was on my mind: "I never got an acquittal for a nicer guy."

In the next few hours, days, and weeks, there was a flood of interviews. It seemed as if everyone in any way connected with the media got a hold of everyone in any way connected with the trial.

Col. Kenneth Howard said he was pleased with the verdict. Colonel Proctor gave newsmen a written statement that said, "We the jury, have done our job to the best of our ability." Another juror, Col. Robert Nelson, was effusive. He said he was "personally delighted. This jury began with the assumption that Captain Medina was innocent and we waited for the government to change our minds. It's apparent from the verdict that they didn't." Commenting on Ernie's several-week-old announcement that he would leave the Army no matter what the verdict, Colonel Nelson said, "I've never met him personally but I was impressed with him during the trial. I hope he changes his mind and stays in the Army."

I particularly enjoyed the frank interview Mark Kadish gave to a reporter from *Newsday,* the Long Island, New York, paper (Kadish grew up on Long Island). Admitting that he had become a close friend of his "client," something defense lawyers are warned not to do, Mark explained how unusual it was: "Here we were, two guys from practically opposite backgrounds, I come from a middle-class, New York, Jewish family. . . . We weren't what you call rich, but you could say we were comfortably well off, and here was Ernie, from a small town and a poor background. I had never known a person before who made the Army a career. Ernie was a whole, new, different person I had never known. He's a man who's devoted to his country, his family, his religion—not that I'm not—but he's the kind of man you think of when you talk about patriotism."

A few days after the acquittal, Ernie sat down for a long interview with Phil Gailey, an excellent reporter who had covered the trial for the *Atlanta Constitution.* Ernie had had some time to rest, and to reflect on what had happened. His answers to Gailey's questions proved what I had felt from the very beginning, from the day in November of 1969 when I first talked with Captain Medina, that he was a very special person:

Q. Captain Medina, your two-year ordeal is over and it ended the way you always said it would from the very beginning. How has it affected your life?

A. The last two, two and a half years have been something that had been almost unbelievable at times. My family and I have been unable to plan for the future or make any prior arrangements. It was more or less living day-to-day and week-to-week without actually being able to think ahead as to future plans and things of this type. It is quite a burden to live with, quite a burden to have your family subjected to this type of thing. It's very difficult for the children to understand comments by other children, comments by some adults and things of this type.

Q. You have said you plan to resign from the Army. Would you care to explain this decision?

A. Yes. This decision was reached quite some time ago prior to any decision by the jury. It was not made because of any coercion or threats by the Department of the Army, by the Pentagon or by any officers here at Fort McPherson. It was an independent decision which was reached by me. It was one that was rather shocking and surprised my wife because she's been a military wife for 13 years since we have been married. She's been part of the military community, and I think she was somewhat shocked and sorry about it. I had reached the independent decision myself and because of my involvement in this very unfortunate incident I just cannot represent myself as an officer to subordinates and superiors alike. I just don't think it would be fair to the U.S. Army, or fair to myself. It's a personal conviction and for that reason I must resign, and I'm going to do this.

Q. I believe you said that it was necessary for the Army to bring your case to trial. Would you elaborate?

A. Well, I think having been the commander of the unit involved in this particular incident and having been suspected and accused by various news media—two of the leading magazines in the country—of various crimes and having done various shootings myself, I think it was necessary that my particular case be brought to trial. I would have rather not . . . not have gone through the particular incident, because it was a very hard ordeal for myself, and my wife, and my family, but I think I would never have been able to have lived with myself as I will now after having been acquitted by a military jury. I think it will be accepted more by the public than if the Army had dropped charges against me a long time ago. . . . I think there would have been very much division as far as whether he was innocent or guilty. So I think it was very necessary. I'm glad it did happen and I'm glad it's over with.

# EPILOGUE

Not many criminal cases have happy endings. Even when a defendant is acquitted, he usually faces financial ruin and the continued suspicion of many of his neighbors that his lawyer "got him off." It is nice, therefore, to be able to report an exception to the rule. The Medina trial was the finest example I have ever encountered of the American criminal justice system working the way it was intended to work; but the aftermath of the case shines as well.

Ernie Medina knew the Army well enough to understand that even though he had been summarily and thumpingly acquitted, he was a marked man. He would have to resign the commission he loved.

On one hand I felt sorry for Ernie; and on the other hand I didn't at all. The character evidence that Mark Kadish and John Truman had produced for Medina convinced me that this wasn't just a bunch of friends saying nice things about a defendant. It was very clear that Medina had been a truly outstanding young officer. It was also clear that he had more potential than the United States Army would ever use.

The Enstrom Helicopter Corporation was just getting off the ground for the first time since I had bought it seven months before, and had a bright future. Ernie wasn't a helicopter expert, but he was intelligent, industrious, and an experienced administrator. I talked to him about coming to work for me. He was enthusiastic.

I was in Detroit when word of his new job began to spread, and Ernie happened to be with me. A reporter approached him and said, in a very caustic tone, "Isn't it true that this is just a publicity stunt, Mr. Medina, and that you don't know the first thing about helicopters?"

"How," Medina replied quietly, "do you think I got to Mylai 4?" He then proceeded to explain, in detail, what he knew about helicopters. When he had finished, the reporter said, "Thank you, sir."

Ernie moved his family to Marinette, Wisconsin, just across the state line from Menominee, Michigan, where the factory is located, and plunged in. Beginning as a staff aide, he set out to learn the business from top to bottom, and in the process earned a helicopter license from the FAA. It was immediately apparent that he would have the respect of the work force; he was the first to arrive at work, and usually the last to leave.

Since then, he has become vice-president of administration, vice-president of sales, and is now in charge of manufacturing. He has become an extremely valuable executive in a highly specialized field, as well as one of my most trusted friends. (He is also one of Lynda's honorary "uncles," an accolade not lightly bestowed.)

I hope that I will never again see this country at war with anybody, for any reason. But if ever the nation needs to be defended, I hope that Ernie Medina is around to help. Good men, as the saying goes, are hard to find—and this is a very good man.

# Con Man
# or Saint?

T H E color scheme of the motel room in Oklahoma City was standard bland, but you couldn't say the same for the outfit worn by the man coming through the door. His suit was a silky electric blue, the open coat revealing a double-breasted vest adorned with two rows of silver buttons. In one lapel he wore a jeweled American flag pin, and his pointed boots appeared to have a thin covering of animal fur.

He crossed the room in swift, confident strides, not about to wait for an introduction. The impression he gave was one of friendly self-assurance.

"Mr. Bailey, it's a great honor to meet you. I'm Glenn Turner."

It was October 9, 1969, and I was on my way from Norman, Oklahoma, where I had given a speech the night before, to Las Vegas for a board meeting of the Professional Air Traffic Controllers. That morning I had met with Mr. Don Long of the Interceptor Aircraft Corporation on some personal business in regard to an airplane I was interested in buying. The meeting with Turner had been arranged rather hurriedly, and I'd had very little briefing as to his problem—or, for that matter, the man himself.

I knew that his company, Koscot, manufactured and sold cosmetics and also sold the right to sell, to bring others into the company on a multilevel basis. I had been told that Turner's success with his company, which was just over two years old, had been phenomenal, but that he had recently encountered legal problems in numerous states. In effect, he'd been stopped from doing business in most of those states. Beyond that I knew nothing more.

Turner shook my hand with what felt like a weightlifter's grip. He was of medium height, but heavier and more muscular-looking than the average man. The colorful clothes were modish and noticeably expensive. His eyes were small, almost piercing, but of a striking blueness, almost China blue, and his nose was flat and rather broad. It was obvious that he wore a toupée, and even more obvious that he had a harelip.

When he began to speak, I had some difficulty understanding every word, but I was impressed by the flow of the words, the naturalness of pause and emphasis. Whatever impairments this man had, the strangely compelling pattern of his speech had to be considered an asset.

I asked him how many states had moved against him or were considering such action. He said, "At the moment it's me against the United States," and I kidded, "Good, I always liked a fair fight." We began to talk, and he explained that a number of state attorneys general had enjoined him from doing business in their states, but he couldn't determine their specific objections. Turner said, "Maybe I'm not doing everything right, but I'm convinced I have some legal rights, and I want to make sure they aren't being trampled on. All I want is what's coming to me, and nothing more. Perhaps I haven't had the best lawyers, I don't know, but if you'll take on my case I'm convinced that you can help me." That was the theme of the first meeting.

I told Turner that I would have to know a lot more about his legal problems before I could agree to represent him. What he was describing in general terms meant a sizeable undertaking. Because Turner already had a number of lawyers in the picture, I suggested that the first step would be for me to meet with them at his home offices in Orlando, Florida. I told him that after meeting with them I would have a better grasp of the situation and could decide if I could help him. He agreed to set up the meeting for the following week.

We had been talking for less than an hour, but I already found myself liking Glenn Turner. It wasn't the confidence, the straightforward manner, so much as it was the aura of sincerity. My impression of Turner was that he was a man earnestly seeking a legitimate way out. He wasn't the kind of potential client who says one thing but is really asking for some kind of deal; he had none of the mannerisms of that type of person. In fact, I had no negative reactions to him at all. I found him an unusually impressive person.

Our thirty- to forty-minute meeting had taken place in the Will Rogers Motel at the airport in Oklahoma City, so I walked Turner out to the field. When we got to his plane I had to smile. It was a ten-passenger "stretch" (or extended) Lear Jet. I then owned and flew the standard size model of the same airplane. We may not have had the same taste in clothes, but there were obviously other areas of agreement.

I told Turner I'd see him in Orlando the next week. He grinned, crushed my hand again, and bounded up the folding ramp of his Lear Jet.

Some unusual people have walked through the door of my law office in the last dozen years, and Glenn W. Turner was no exception. The son of a sharecropper in South Carolina, he'd dropped out of school in the ninth grade and forced himself to succeed as a salesman, a field that people had told him was impossible for someone with his physical defects.

I learned he had become a minor legend in the Southeast as a traveling sales representative for the Singer Sewing Machine Company. His business career had been marked by spectacular peaks and valleys until he decided to form his own multilevel company to sell cosmetics—after he'd worked with some success for Holiday Magic, a similar company. Reassuring the people he'd brought into Holiday Magic that his organization would live up to the promises of its recruiters, he put together a competitive line of products and a management team distinguished more by zeal (and a belief in Glenn Turner) than by experience.

Within two years Koscot was so successful at signing up investor-salesmen that, although it had impressive financial assets, certain state officials began to suspect that company was more concerned with selling the right to sell than it was with selling the product. A flurry of actions were brought or threatened, most of them in the form of injunctions that prohibited Turner's organization from conducting business in a particular state.

What so distressed Turner, as he had explained at our first meeting, was that the publicity of the legal actions caused the door-to-door sales force to become discouraged. Potential customers who had read about the legal problems doubted the value of the skin creams, the lipsticks, and everything else in the line. As Turner said to me, "Nobody, no judge or attorney general, has ever questioned the value of the product, but my salesgirls are running into people who act as if the face cream will turn their skin green!"

Turner's point was that, although he felt he could win all the legal battles eventually, he would go bankrupt in the meantime. I was familiar with the fact that justice delayed is often justice denied. I looked forward to the meeting with his lawyers.

On Monday, October 13, 1969, I arrived in Tampa, Florida, via National Airlines at 5:30 A.M. Turner's twin-engine Cessna 310 then flew us to Orlando, where I checked in at the Gold Key Inn. After a few hours' sleep I attended a meeting in Turner's offices with the lawyers who had been representing Koscot in the various states.

I asked the lawyers to review for me the problems in the states they'd been working in, and it soon became clear that many of the complaints brought by the law enforcement agencies bore a suspicious identity of language. Just what this meant was made clear by another man at the meeting, a former official of the Better Business Bureau, who explained that he had attended a meeting of assistant attorneys general in Arizona where the problems of consumer protection and pyramid (or multilevel) marketing plans were the main topic of discussion.

This man told me he'd heard one of the participants suggest to another that Glenn Turner would be a good target to use in putting down pyramid marketing plans.

I also learned from meeting with Turner's lawyers that one of the central problems was the vagueness of applicable laws governing these types of marketing plans. Turner was faced with a substantial legal problem, even without the "help" of the attorneys general who had apparently decided to make him a target.

The next step was for Turner and several of his top people to come to my office in Boston and explain to my legal staff the nature of their business operation. They did so on October 14, 1969. It was a lengthy meeting. After it was over I met with Glenn privately in my office to discuss the terms under which I could represent him.

I told him that if I took on the direction of his legal work it would mean literally dropping or rescheduling a great many commitments if I was to be truly effective, and that in all probability I would have to direct most of the lawyers in my office to do the same thing. Part of my reasoning was the vagueness of the law in the area under which he was attempting to operate. The other— and perhaps more difficult part—was that some of his past counsel had clearly antagonized a number of the state attorneys general. The job would be both difficult and delicate.

Turner understood what I was talking about. Then we turned to the question of my fee. In the early summer of the same year, 1969, Turner's business was booming. But the spate of legal actions in the fall had brought the operation to a near halt, and now he was very short of funds. The bad publicity stemming from the lawsuits had caused the retail sales force massive resistance in the field. When they identified themselves as Koscot representatives, they found doors slammed in their faces. The cash flow from the retail operation had all but stopped.

Turner had paid two million dollars in cash for his building in Orlando, the main building that housed the many facets of the operation, but he was having trouble getting a mortgage on it. Because he was so short of cash, he asked if I would consider a fee arrangement based on a retainer and a contingency. The retainer was to be twenty-five thousand, the cost of my office overhead for one month.

"What's the contingency?"

Turner said, "If you can solve the legal problems so that I can get this company back to the position it was in early this summer, before all the lawsuits hit us, then I'll pay you a substantial fee."

"And what would you consider a substantial fee?"

"Well," Turner smiled. He'd done his homework on me. Now it was time for him to play his hole card. "I know you had to sell part-ownership of that plane you like so much. I promise you this: You take care of our legal problems, and I'll buy you a new Lear Jet."

Anyone who has seen *The Godfather* knows what kind of offer that was. At that time a new Lear Jet sold for around $750,000. It was a fine offer, but still a bit too iffy.

"Tell you what. You pay all expenses, plus some fees, as they are incurred, and you underwrite the costs of operating my present Lear Jet while I travel mainly but not exclusively on your behalf. You do that and you've got yourself a deal."

It was Glenn's turn to ask a question. "What do you mean by 'mainly but not exclusively'?"

"I'll fly around the country for you, putting out what you call your brush fires, but if I make a quick stop for another client, I want to be able to do it without a lot of red tape."

Turner thought for only a moment. "Okay."

We shook hands on it.

Not everyone in my office was thrilled with the idea of our representing Glenn Turner. From a lawyer's standpoint he was a high-risk client. First of all, they pointed out, we had agreed to represent him at a time when his company was reeling under multiple legal attacks that drained income as soon as it was produced. Turner's companies didn't have profit, as such. What they had was cash flow. (In fact, cash didn't just flow; it flew. The paid-up legal bills for services prior to the time I agreed to represent Turner were staggering.)

Secondly, it became clear after very little investigation that, as far as Turner and his executives were concerned, management experience was conspicuous by its absence. With a few exceptions, these people had been—and at heart still were—salesmen. When their sales ability brought them success in the field as independent distributors they came to Turner's attention and he offered them salaried positions within the company. Even though this sometimes meant a hefty cut in income, very few refused the offer. Unfortunately, the talents that enabled them to succeed as salesmen did not always carry over to their new roles as administrators.

Finally there was the suggestion that we were straying a bit afield from our usual criminal law practice. I didn't buy that. Many of the states that had filed actions against Turner were talking fraud, as was the federal government, and that is decidedly a criminal matter. If Turner and his companies were going up against criminal charges, they needed the services of a criminal law firm. This was no place for a cautious civil lawyer who could afford to move slowly because "only money" was concerned.

And in the beginning there was a very basic question, seldom asked but often seen in the eyes of those around me: Can you trust this Glenn Turner?

When he interviewed me for *Playboy* in 1967, Nat Hentoff asked how I chose my clients. My answer, and it has not changed in the years since, was that ". . . a large part of the decision is a result of sitting down and talking with the fellow . . . much depends on whether I can become a little sympathetic to his situation."

In the first weeks and months of my representation, I had a number of opportunities to sit down and talk with Glenn Turner. My initial sense of his trustworthiness was reaffirmed, and I became decidedly sympathetic to his situation.

In all those miles, all those cities, all those days, I learned a great deal about Glenn Turner. Most of it came from people who worked for him or with him or against him. It was quite a story.

Turner was born in 1934, the year after I was, in Marion, South Carolina. He was the first child. In the next few years his sharecropper parents would have five more, four boys and finally a girl.

There was very little money—in a good year the father would earn slightly more than five hundred dollars—but the children grew strong because there was a lot of love. And there was usually food, the solid, basic diet of the Mid-South—ham hocks, greens, vegetables, and breads. Glenn was the oldest, the skinniest, and the one his parents worried about most—because he'd been born with a severe harelip and a cleft palate, two conditions that made his days at school increasingly difficult.

By the time he reached the ninth grade he found himself in the middle of a vicious circle: if he went to school and fought the kids who taunted him because he couldn't speak the way they did, he got a caning from the teacher; if he skipped school, he got one from his father (who knew a boy with a harelip needed all the education he could get).

Turner solved the dilemma by running away from home and school.

Over the next few years, waiting until he was old enough to join the Air Force, he worked at whatever he could find. He was almost seventeen, a little old for the ninth grade, even in Marion, but he'd missed the better part of two years because of operations on his lip. He looked better now, and people had less difficulty understanding him. But there was no mistaking the fact that he had several handicaps.

He thought the Air Force would be the beginning of a new life. His first and only assignment was latrine duty. Three months later it was learned that on top of everything else he had a perforated eardrum. He was given a medical discharge.

Back to the farm. Back behind the mule. But eventually back to a school where he earned a high school equivalency diploma, and by chance, another operation. As he put it, "I finally had an upper lip. Not much of a one, but at least I had one." According to Glenn, each change brought a bit more confidence, less fear of facing the world.

In 1955, just after he'd turned twenty-one, Glen found the way out of Marion, South Carolina. Sewing machines. He answered an ad for a salesman, and the manager, sensing the growing confidence of this awkward, unusual young man, hired him on straight commission.

It was not all uphill from there. Unusual successes were followed by the more usual failures. But over the next few years Turner learned he could sell. Belief in himself and in the product, and long hours of hard work, made him one of the most successful door-to-door salesmen in the history of both the Monarch Sewing Machine Company and later the Singer Sewing Machine Company.

The people he sold were people like himself—frequently poor, often black, and each one in his own way somehow handicapped. The sociologists would probably call it "identification"—and they would probably be right. But it was more than that. Apparently there was an unstated but clearly understood exchange of pride: "*You* can sell; *I* can buy. And we both know it."

By the time he was thirty Glenn Turner had made and lost several small fortunes. Once, when a finance company repossessed his car, he said, "Well, at least it's a Cadillac they're taking."

He also lost a wife. I've never heard him say much about it, but apparently the scars are still there. In 1957, then twenty-three, Turner lived and worked out of Knoxville, Tennessee, where he met a plain, friendly girl named Phyllis who worked in the drugstore of the Knoxville YMCA.

Her background was much the same as his. Neither of them wanted that back-country, sharecropper life. They were married by a justice of the peace and moved to Philadelphia, where Glenn was once again selling sewing machines. Their son Terry was born there.

Then, in 1957, shortly after their second child had been stillborn, Phyllis Turner came down with Hodgkin's disease. She lived less than a year. By the time he came out of the shock of his wife's death, Turner was more than eighteen thousand dollars in debt.

Two years later he met and married another girl, Alice Berkeley. She became the adoptive mother of his first child, and the mother-to-be of their own three children, a daughter and two sons. Together they fought back to financial health.

Various business ventures followed. Now, all of them were successful, the furniture stores in Knoxville and Charlotte, and the sewing machine sales he couldn't stop even though it meant moonlighting. But about this time he discovered franchising, and all but ignored his other ventures. After the IRS took over a furniture store for underpayment of taxes, Turner threw himself into what was for him a brand-new field. Cosmetics.

Investing five thousand dollars in Holiday Magic to become a distributor (which meant you had the right to bring in other people and get the lion's share of their purchase price) looked like the start of a bright new chapter in the life of Glenn Turner. But when the man who'd sold him the franchise failed to give him any instruction on how to sell cosmetics, and left town within a day with the five thousand, Turner began to wonder.

Typically, he made the next moves on his own. He spent his own money to travel to New York for the last day and a half of the five-day school in how to sell cosmetics. He learned enough to teach himself the rest. Soon it was the sewing machine story all over again. Glenn Turner became the hottest salesman in Holiday Magic.

At this point the stories begin to conflict. Whether Glenn left, as he claims, because Holiday Magic was not keeping its promises to the scores of people he'd brought into the program, or whether he simply wanted to start his own company along similar lines, is not clear. In any event, by 1967 Glenn Turner, former sewing machine salesman, had formed his own company—KOSCOT: "Kosmetics for the Communities of Tomorrow."

And the earlier successes were repeated, but not right away and not without a great deal of effort.

On August 22, 1967, Glenn Turner incorporated Koscot Interplanetary. The office was a single room in an apartment complex in Winter Park, Florida, a site chosen for its proximity to the almost finished Disney World in Orlando.

Turner had five thousand dollars in borrowed capital and a small group of devotees who had followed him from Holiday Magic. Each one had been convinced that Glenn Turner's company would live up to the promises it made and that their experience would be the opposite of what had happened to them in Holiday Magic.

Turner also had two other assets. He had Jerri Jacobus, once one of the most successful cosmetologists in the business; and he had a man named Bob Hansche, who owned a mink farm in Wisconsin. Typically, their association was a result of Glenn Turner's salesmanship. He had talked Jerri Jacobus out of retirement and he had talked Bob Hansche into supplying him with mink oil on credit.

The mink oil, which Hansche had been experimenting on for years and trying unsuccessfully to sell to the largest cosmetics companies as a base for a new product line, had been tested and approved by the government as a potentially valuable cosmetic ingredient.

With a few modifications, the original concept of the company was borrowed from Holiday Magic—that is, there was to be a national network of independent distributors and supervisors whose investment enabled them to sell cosmetics on a retail—door-to-door —basis, to sell the right to sell by recruiting others into the program, or to do both.

A distributorship cost $4500, $2500 more than the investment necessary for becoming a supervisor. There were several lower gradations, down to a coordinator for a hundred and twenty-five. But it was the higher positions that enabled the investor to earn the greatest returns: if a distributor brought another distributor into the company he or she received $2750, and a supervisor got $1000 when a new supervisor was recruited into the company.

There was trouble from the very beginning. While the first Koscot distributors were out in the field selling franchises and creating a staggering sum of initial capital, the established companies were giving Glenn Turner and his fledgling operation a hard time.

He wanted to rent a larger office, but the rental companies wanted more than the usual security deposit; he wanted capital to build his own combination office and warehouse, but no bank would lend it to him. And finally, he walked into the office of one of the largest cosmetics manufacturing plants in the country and gave them a large chunk of cash for an initial order that he needed within two weeks. The company argued, but finally agreed to his terms. It filled the order six months later.

In the meantime, early investors were complaining to the company. Every complaint received the same answer, based in part on the repeated promises of the manufacturer, "two weeks." By the time the orders were eventually filled, a handful of people had complained to their states that the new company looked like a massive con job.

The complaint was the same: "They're only interested in selling distributorships. There isn't any product at all."

In time there was product, such a great deal of it that the full line consisted of more than 120 items, and the related services had erupted into scores of new companies. There was a trucking company to transport the product, a credit card company so that any acceptable credit card could be used to buy products, a wig company, a fur company, and a clothing company. Turner once joked, "I think I've started a company company."

I had not seen the events of the first two years. But during the latter part of 1969, all of 1970, and part of 1971, I saw Glenn Turner at first hand. I saw him operate under enormous pressure from all sides. If he was, or is, a con man, he did not exhibit the telltale signs I'd observed in so many clients of dubious character over the past fifteen years.

He was generous to a fault. And by turns he was naïve and cunning. But he was never sneaky, never small, and he created trouble for himself by trusting his proven lieutenants to a degree that bordered on the ludicrous.

Certainly he was in it for the money. He was the first to admit it. But the money was not the sole attraction. What made Glenn Turner run, in my opinion based on hours of seeing him in action, was the satisfaction of helping other people like himself to make a living they never dreamed was even possible until they met him.

Until he started his own company, Turner's fortunes had gone up and down as if controlled by gravity. But in the first months and years of forming Koscot the success was more than even he had imagined before. In less than two years, an operation that had begun with five thousand dollars of borrowed money was producing two and three times that amount every hour of every day.

It was a staggering reality, one that Glenn Turner tried to take in stride, tried to pass off as something he'd expected all the time. But it was a hard act to play, much less to follow. Suddenly the harelipped country boy from Marion, South Carolina, was sought after by investors, bankers, politicians, religious leaders—by a class of people foreign to his background and often foreign to his liking.

When I met Turner in October of 1969, Koscot was one of the fastest-growing corporations in the United States. It probably stood alone as the most frequently sued. As far as Turner was concerned, the success and the litigation were no more than he could handle. In a sense I disagreed, for if it all wasn't too much, it was certainly too soon. No man could withstand all that was happening to Glenn Turner, yet he was withstanding it far better than anyone, myself included, could have predicted.

This is not to say that when the biggest of the bubbles finally burst Glenn Turner was blameless, that he had no part in the troubles. He was at fault. He was at fault on many counts. But his mistakes were those of inexperience, indecision, egotism, and blind faith in the honesty and the loyalty of those who served him. Despite many warnings to the contrary, Turner continued to give second, third, fourth, and fifth chances to people even the greenest corporate president would have dismissed long ago. He simply could not believe the obvious worst about one of "my people," as he described them.

Yes, I trusted Glenn Turner.

In Turner's case, my other criterion for accepting a client—being sympathetic to his situation—was met early on. He explained that he had been trying to alter some of his sales practices to meet the objections of several states, but that he couldn't get a clear answer as to just what it was he was doing wrong—or why certain practices that were allowed in one state were forbidden in the next. He said that he was beginning to feel they simply wanted to put him out of business.

After I'd met with the lawyers who had represented the company around the country (prior to the time he retained me, Turner never really had an in-house legal department staffed by lawyers) I got a better picture of what Turner had been talking about. The law in the area of multiple-level sales was vague at best, and in many states there were no laws at all.

Granted, Koscot had its share of what Turner called the "high rollers," the type of salesman who is interested only in the commission money he gets for bringing new people into the program and could not care less about seeing to it that the new investors attended the retail schools being held all over the country. Granted also that the company's difficulty in getting the product manufactured and transported gave the operation in certain states all the earmarks of a first-class fraud. But I agreed with Turner that these problems called for governmental regulation—not concerted action to destroy the company.

I had seen this kind of attack before. It isn't always a matter of bad faith on the government's part, and I was not convinced that it was bad faith in regard to Turner and Koscot. But the power of the government is so great that any action of this sort immediately creates a massive financial and public image problem for a company. By the time the issue is thrashed out in the courts there is no company left to run. Victories of this sort are called "pyrrhic," for although you may win the battles you also lose the war.

Turner needed experienced legal help. He needed lots of it and he needed it fast. As a client he fulfilled the basic criteria of my firm and its practice. And his situation represented a challenge, another of the elements that determines whether or not we accept a case.

The courtroom in Columbus, Ohio, was packed with more than two hundred Koscot distributors, supervisors, and retail sales people. The date was October 20, 1969. I had met Glenn Turner less than two weeks before, but my crash course in Boston and Orlando had paid off. I was ready for my first court appearance on behalf of Koscot.

Along with Turner and Malcolm Julian, Koscot's engaging young president, I was joined at the defense table by almost my entire legal staff. I'd brought them along to see at first hand what kind of legal problems this company faced, because they would soon be out in the various states trying to find solutions.

The state of Ohio, which had asked for a temporary restraining order to stop Koscot from selling any more franchises, or distributorships, was represented by Assistant Attorney General Scott Rawlings. An impressive young man with a soft, but articulate manner of speaking, Rawlings entreated the court to grant the injunction in order to protect the people of Ohio from the admittedly successful wholesale efforts of Koscot's advance men.

Suddenly there were reactions from the spectators' benches, and the judge looked up to see a couple hundred of Ohio's "good people" shaking their heads in vigorous disagreement with the notion that they needed to be protected from this company.

Rawlings continued his argument to the court. After a few minutes I realized that the plan he was describing was one that the company had not been using in Ohio for months. He was describing the old plan, under which a supervisor could not move up to the distributor level until he or she found a replacement on the lower level. (This plan, known as the double-level plan, was legal in numerous states, but as there was increasing opposition to it, the company had begun to phase it out.)

When Mr. Rawlings finished, he had mentioned other elements of the marketing program that were no longer used in Ohio. I put Malcolm Julian, the Koscot president, on the stand to clarify the situation. After he had testified I told the court that it appeared Mr. Rawlings did not have all the information he should have about the present workings of the company in his state. Citing my very recent agreement to represent the company and the fact that Mr. Rawlings and I hadn't had an opportunity to confer, I told the court that if it granted the relief sought by the attorney general it might issue an order that didn't accurately address itself to the relief sought.

I asked the judge to stay the injunction for ten days so that I could get together with Mr. Rawlings and bring him up to date on the new marketing plan. The court agreed, and denied the injunction sought by the state.

Turner was jubilant. He shook my hand, and the hands of all the attorneys on my staff. I'm sure that if he could have gotten to Scott Rawlings he would have pumped his hand, too.

My subsequent meetings with Rawlings cleared up many of his objections and the state of Ohio remained open to Koscot.

We had begun what would be a most interesting year.

Following hard on the success in Ohio, I took off on a whirlwind tour of the states where Koscot was having serious legal problems. My main interest was to hire some local lawyers for the company and to brief them on what the problems were, but also to meet with as many state officials as I could in order to find out their objections, suspicions, and even their fears. The point was to resolve these difficulties as quickly and peaceably as possible.

The flight log of my Lear Jet over the next thirty days reads like a script for an airborne version of *The Fugitive*.

| *1969* | Route | T.O. Landing |
|--------|-------|--------------|
| 10/19 | Boston–Columbus, O. | 1722–1905 |
| 10/20 | Columbus–Indianapolis, Ind. | 1451–1530 |
| 10/21 | Indianapolis–Baton Rouge, La. | 1015–1150 |
| 10/21 | Baton Rouge–Indianapolis | 1630–1800 |
| 10/21 | Indianapolis–DuPage (Chicago) | 1810–1858 |
| 10/22 | DuPage–Meigs (Chicago) | 1620–1635 |
| 10/22 | Meigs–Minneapolis | 1847–1955 |
| 10/23 | Minneapolis–Omaha, Neb. | 0733–0817 |
| 10/23 | Omaha–Scottsbluff, Neb. | 2015–2115 |
| 10/24 | Scottsbluff–Omaha | 2305–2405 |
| 10/24 | Omaha–Sidney, Neb. | 1246–1340 |
| 10/24 | Sidney–Omaha | 1703–1754 |
| 10/25 | Omaha–Des Moines, Iowa | 1042–1105 |
| 10/25 | Des Moines–Galesburg, Ill. | 1202–1236 |
| 10/25 | Galesburg–Houston, Tex. (Hobby) | 2238–2430 |
| 10/26 | Houston–Intercontinental (Houston) | 1824–1838 |
| 10/26 | Intercontinental–Orlando, Fla. | 2140–2324 |
| 10/27 | Orlando–Miami, Fla. | 2438–0110 |
| 10/28 | Miami–Orlando | 0121–0158 |
| 10/28 | Orlando–Miami | 1500–1600 |
| 10/28 | Miami–Orlando | 2327–2416 |
| 10/29 | Orlando–National (Washington, D.C.) | 0851–1041 |
| 10/30 | Washington–N. Philadelphia, Pa. | 1557–1640 |
| 10/31 | N. Philadelphia–Detroit, Mich. | 0910–1034 |
| 10/31 | Detroit–Lansing, Mich. | 1053–1138 |
| 10/31 | Lansing–Pittsburgh, Pa. | 1543–1640 |
| 10/31 | Pittsburgh–Boston | 2320–2440 |

| *1969* | *Route* | *T.O. Landing* |
|---|---|---|
| 11/2 | Boston–Orlando | 0855–1204 |
| 11/2 | Orlando–Miami | 1228–1317 |
| 11/2 | Miami–Orlando | 1320–1407 |
| 11/2 | Orlando–Miami | 1811–1900 |
| 11/2 | Miami–Orlando | 1922–2010 |
| 11/3 | Orlando–Baton Rouge, La. | 2002–2156 |
| 11/4 | Baton Rouge–Wichita, Kans. | 1300–1451 |
| 11/4 | Wichita–Kansas City | 1945–2034 |
| 11/5 | Kansas City–Jefferson, Mo. | 1515–1548 |
| 11/5 | Jefferson–Austin, Tex. | 1731–1914 |
| 11/6 | Austin–Little Rock, Ark. | 1345–1453 |
| 11/6 | Little Rock–Indianapolis | 1704–1821 |
| 11/7 | Indianapolis–Albuquerque, N.M. | 1703–2004 |
| 11/7 | Albuquerque–Phoenix, Ariz. | 2020–2130 |
| 11/8 | Phoenix–Albuquerque | 1142–1250 |
| 11/8 | Albuquerque–Salt Lake City, Utah | 1910–2023 |
| 11/9 | Salt Lake City–Van Nuys, Calif. | 0032–0215 |
| 11/10 | Van Nuys–Salem, Ore. | 0938–1144 |
| 11/10 | Salem–Sioux Falls, S.D. | 1444–1729 |
| 11/10 | Sioux Falls–Midway (Chicago) | 1800–1925 |
| 11/11 | Midway–Columbus | 1917–2015 |
| 11/12 | Columbus–Charlotte, N.C. | 1707–1817 |
| 11/12 | Charlotte–Columbus | 2311–2412 |
| 11/13 | Columbus–Wilkes-Barre, Pa. | 1728–1828 |
| 11/13 | Wilkes-Barre–Columbus | 2230–2340 |
| 11/14 | Columbus–Miami, Fla. | 1642–1934 |
| 11/16 | Miami–Orlando | 1640–1735 |
| 11/16 | Orlando–Columbus | 1750–2000 |
| 11/17 | Columbus–Dulles (Washington) | 1535–1645 |

Toward the end of this merry-go-round I started listing the complaints I'd been hearing around the country. Based on this information, I put together a new policy statement on November 16, 1969. Within days it had been sent to every attorney general with whom the company had had any dealings, and shortly after that a copy went out to the distributors.

It stated that the company was setting up a legal department, and that in the future every effort would be made to see that company policy was in line with the laws of the various states. It announced guidelines under which the company would operate and asked the recipients to notify the company of any infractions, misrepresentations, or misunderstandings in the field. In effect, it put the company on notice that things were going to be different.

The major complaint was that Koscot was using an "endless chain" marketing plan. This meant that, if true, every single citizen of a given neighborhood, city, state, and eventually the country could wind up with a Koscot franchise—and there would be no buyers because everyone was a seller.

Although the logic was theoretically faultless, I knew this was not the achievement of the company. But was it the company goal?

I asked Malcolm Julian if Koscot had set any quota, any limit to the number of distributorships that could be sold before saturation occurred. He told me they'd set a limit of one per four thousand people in a given state. However, his sources for that figure were not sufficiently impressive, so I decided that Koscot should commission an independent study.

The idea of employing outside experts began to make more and more sense to me the more I learned about the top management of the company. Almost everyone I met at the main offices in Orlando was imbued with Turner's self-help through self-confidence philosophy, and as admirable as their accomplishments were, these executives were nonetheless basically all salesmen. Few had any real training or experience in high-level corporate management, finance, or law.

I contacted Wayne Smith, a business associate in Washington, D.C., who was responsible for my meeting Glenn Turner in the first place, and asked him to find a consulting company with solid credentials. As a result of his efforts a contract was signed between Turner and the Checchi Company, a highly respected management consulting firm in the nation's capital.

Over the next months and years, Checci produced a series of reports on the various needs of Turner Enterprises. But it also provided, under employment contracts, several experienced financial and business advisers who held posts of responsibility within Turner's empire.

Later, with the help of these people, I convinced Turner to hire outside consultants in other fields, such as advertising, marketing, and public relations.

Bit by bit, and while the legal troubles were lessening because of the massive effort by my firm and some excellent lawyers on retainer in the field, Turner was building a competent corporate structure aimed toward the day when the national quota of distributorships had been reached (forty thousand) and the company could concentrate solely on retailing cosmetics.

At least, that was my goal, Turner's, and that of the people who then held the top company positions.

One of the initial problems when I agreed to represent Turner stemmed from the less-than-subtle sales techniques being used by people in the field to induce new people to come into the company. The basis for introduction into the company was almost always the "Golden Opportunity Meeting." Top salespeople, from the home office, or state or regional directors, would go into a community, rent a hall for one or several nights, and then publicize the event (usually by passing out handbills on the main streets and buttonholing people).

The format for these meetings, based on company manuals, rarely changed. After fiery introductory speeches where at least one local success story was touted, figures were written on a blackboard to represent how much money could be made with the company. Then there would be a guest spot, or speech by someone higher up in the organization, and finally the retail or "Alice" portion (named after Glenn Turner's wife, Alice) where the speaker would explain how much money could be made in selling cosmetics door to door.

After I had heard several complaints from attorneys general about the exaggerated figures allegedly being used at opportunity meetings, I attended a meeting myself. The authorities were right, to a degree. Speakers were putting up earnings figures that would have done justice to a team of salesmen.

We went back to the drawing board and drafted new guidelines for the field. Along with these we sent the latest distributorship quota, based on the report done by the Checci Company, one distributor per every seven thousand persons in the state.

By this time I had set up a proper legal department, small but staffed with people I knew and could trust completely. At my suggestion, and with Turner's concurrence, it hired a troubleshooter to roam the country unannounced, making sure the new policies emanating from headquarters were being followed.

Bit by bit we dug a fire line around the country. Occasionally one spot or another would flare up again—because of an unscrupulous employee or an intransigent public official—but the number of legal actions was lessening. By late 1970 most states in the nation were open to Koscot and its younger corporate sibling, Dare To Be Great (a motivational course offering both retail and wholesale positions).

Another important innovation that we introduced was the voting trust. Set up in April of 1970, the purpose of the trust was to check the legendary, free-wheeling spending of Glenn Turner, who never seemed able, up to that point, to distinguish between cash flow and actual profit.

The attorneys general I'd talked to on my twenty-thousand-mile trip in the fall of 1969 had expressed doubts that I could get Turner to follow my advice. This, plus the fact that conventional business-men and money-lending institutions were also worried that as sole stockholder Turner could do pretty well as he pleased, led us to set up the voting trust.

Actually there were three trusts, one for each company—Koscot, Dare To Be Great, and the House of Koscot, a subsidiary. Seven members made up each trust, four company officials and three out-side consultants, with Ben Bunting (Turner's number-two man) as a company member of all three trusts. That meant that Bunting, myself, and two outside consultants were on each trust.

Bunting was by then acceptable to all the outsiders because of his established conservatism—in opposition to the philosophy of such men as Hobart Wilder, who believed that "Mr. Turner should get everything he wants." With Bunting as a member, the vote could be predicted as 4–3 on the conservative side.

Although I was a member of all three trusts, I never had to cast a vote, chiefly because Glenn had the option of withdrawing any request for spending. We were working so closely by then that if I opposed him, he usually backed off the issue.

The voting trust was disbanded in December of 1970 for several reasons. One, the company was in much better financial shape, and Turner's proclivities toward extravagance didn't have the same ef-fect as they'd had six months earlier. Two, with a single exception, Turner was signing all the consent decrees that I was working out with the states, thus lessening the need for a "board of overseers."

All this while Glenn Turner had been an ideal client. I'd agreed to defer any large fees until after the company was back on its feet, but he was always current with payment for expenses. (And with the Lear Jet costing more than a dollar a mile, there were some good-sized expenses.) More importantly, he had dispelled the doubt put in my mind by several state attorneys general that he might refuse to take my legal advice when it conflicted with what he wanted to do.

I can't say we didn't have some classic verbal battles now and then. But for the most part Turner did what I advised, and without grumbling.

By early 1971 I was making progress toward what I considered the most important legal goal—a federal regulation that would outline the legal dos and don'ts for companies involved in multilevel sales programs.

I'd felt from the beginning that the best and most workable solution to Turner's legal problems would be a federal judgment or consent order. (By early 1971 he'd signed agreements with many states, but they represented a crazy-quilt pattern, and it was hard to educate company personnel on the state-to-state rules.)

The Federal Trade Commission had been requesting data from Koscot for some months, and the legal department had been furnishing the requested data. Still, no action that might result in a voluntary decree of some sort had been either initiated or proposed. I was told that things were moving slowly at the FTC because of numerous important personnel changes that were going on within the agency. We had no choice but to wait.

After the Post Office had requested and obtained interviews with key company personnel in February 1971, I began to be concerned that that agency had plans to lay back for a time, and then attempt to institute criminal proceedings against Turner and his companies. This suspicion was prompted by the fact that in cases I had defended during the past decade, such as the Great Plymouth Mail Robbery, this precise strategy had been used.

In addition, quite a number of the attorneys general with whom I had negotiated had expressed the view that the task of regulating the activities of an interstate company such as Koscot should more properly be borne by a federal agency, rather than leaving the matter in the hands of the states. In each such instance I agreed heartily.

In the light of all of these circumstances, I asked, through Deputy Attorney General Richard Kleindienst, that I be permitted to meet with representatives of every federal agency that might have an interest in Koscot, or some jurisdiction over its activities, in an effort to explain to them my problems as counsel and solicit their cooperation. Such a meeting was called, and was scheduled for April 14, 1971, at the Justice Department in Washington.

Just prior to that date, however, the FTC finally acted. On April 8, 1971, a letter was sent from Charles Tobin, secretary to the Federal Trade Commission, to Hobart Wilder, the new corporate president, enclosing a notice of a proposed complaint and an invitation to negotiate a consent order. I responded immediately that this invitation would be accepted; nonetheless, because of my concern over the Post Office investigation, I went forward with the meeting with federal agencies.

The large conference room was adequately, even expensively, furnished, but it had an unmistakable aroma of big government. The decor was Twentieth-Century Sub-Cabinet level, right down to the American flag in the corner and the half-smiling picture of President Nixon on the most conspicuous wall.

It was not a comfortable room, nor did the people who filled it appear at ease. Some of the expressions ran from mild displeasure to open hostility, all of it directed at me for causing them to be there.

The assembled group, which for the most part either looked at their watches or glared menacingly at me, included three high-ranking Justice Department lawyers (Donald Santarelli, a senior assistant attorney general; John Keeney, the head of the Frauds Division; and Bruce Wilson of the Criminal Division) two top lawyers from the Securities and Exchange Commission (Richard Nathan, the assistant general counsel; and Stanley Sporkin), and the Federal Trade Commission's representative, Richard Foster, the assistant director for general litigation.

William Lawrence, the assistant general counsel, and a lawyer by the name of John Tarpy were there on behalf of my old friend, the Postal Service. We had asked that the White House representative be Virginia Knauer, the head of the Consumer Affairs Office, but she couldn't make it, so she sent her assistant, Louis Engman.

Under different circumstances it might have been a congenial gathering of some of the government's best legal talent and consumer affairs specialists. But, with the exception of Santarelli, no one in the room was noticeably content to be there. For one thing, as someone pointed out, they were not accustomed "to being forced to meet for the convenience of one private practitioner."

On that unhappy note the meeting began. What I had hoped would be an exchange of ideas quickly degenerated into a series of complaints and then a twenty-minute speech by me, in which I tried to point out that Koscot had been attempting to comply with the multifarious state and federal regulations, to establish a hard-and-fast system of "dos and don'ts" for its people in the field, but that it really needed a uniform federal guideline.

In the months prior to the meeting there had been rumors that the postal inspectors were preparing a criminal case against Turner and his companies. I alluded to this when I told the group that I thought it singularly unfair for government bodies to refuse a request for guidelines so that another governmental arm could come in later and slap that same company with a criminal action. I directed these remarks to the representatives of the Postal Service.

I might as well have saved their time and my breath. The meeting lasted barely half an hour. The most vivid memory of the other side was a great deal of muttering and some heavy glowering.

I had been given a chance to say my piece, though, and that plus some good news on another front made me feel that the meeting had not been a total loss.

The good news mentioned earlier was that the Federal Trade Commission, the main governmental arm having jurisdiction over companies that operate in the manner of Turner's companies, appeared ready to sign a consent decree that would cover Koscot's operations nationwide.

During the spring and early summer of 1971, I conducted a series of lengthy meetings with attorneys for the Federal Trade Commission, Consumer Protection Bureau, in an effort to negotiate a consent order. Although Koscot was the only corporate party, we tried from the outset to write an agreement that would cover all Turner operations and companies.

Chief counsel for the FTC team was Charles W. O'Connell, assisted by Robert Galler and another young attorney. There were about a dozen negotiating sessions in all, and the range of topics covered by the negotiations was enormous, with the minutiae and possibilities discussed bordering on the infinite.

By late in July we had hammered out a document that counsel for both sides was prepared to recommend to their clients. Mr. Turner, his company officers, and I as counsel signed the proposed order on August 7, 1971, and submitted it to the commission.

During the negotiations, I had explained to Mr. O'Connell and his associates that any document drafted by lawyers would most likely be difficult for laymen to understand. So I proposed a handbook, which I would write, converting the meat of the regulatory provisions into laymen's language. I also suggested that this handbook be printed, bound, and distributed to all past and future franchisees of Mr. Turner's companies. I promised to submit a draft of the document to them for review, so that if any of them felt that I had not used proper language in interpreting the order, we could come to some agreeable version before publication.

They told me that this seemed an excellent idea. I agreed to begin work on the handbook just as soon as the consent order had been executed, and by the time the sixty-day period of publication had expired, to have an agreed and printed document ready for distribution on the very day the order became effective. This is the way we left the matter.

Next, I called a meeting in Orlando of all Turner executives, to explain to them the contents of the consent order, the meaning of its language, and the modifications in sales programs that would be required by it. This meeting took place early in August.

It was a long meeting. I had a lot to say, and certain things to get off my chest. After I had explained what the FTC order would mean to the companies, I told the group that once the order had been worked out and the handbook written, my original work agreement with Turner would be completed. In all probability my services would end.

Then I added that, in regard to the details of the federal order, its provisions had "damn well better be obeyed or there would be serious consequences."

There were no sounds of surprise or protest. Everyone at the meeting knew exactly what I was talking about. In the last few months there had been reports, at first just isolated incidents but then with some regularity, that several key people in the field were ignoring the orders of the legal department. According to the reports, opportunity meetings were being conducted in direct violation of the agreements we had signed, or the court orders that had gone out, in several states.

Finally, when the rumors became more frequent, I went to Turner and told him that he had to harness these people, that they had to live by the rules laid down by the legal department through negotiation and litigation. He promised to set "his people" straight, but continued to resist my suggestion that their actions were intentional, that they were knowingly breaking the law.

A cynic would have concluded easily that Glenn Turner would not fire these people because they were bringing in the big money. To me, his attitude was based on a refusal to face disloyalty. He simply wouldn't believe that any of his trusted lieutenants would knowingly jeopardize Turner Enterprises.

When the Orlando meeting broke up, two things were clear. One, an agreement with the Federal Trade Commission was all but a fact; and two, I was bowing out.

*          *          *

On October 8, 1971, the Federal Trade Commission informed me that the proposed consent order was not satisfactory. A few weeks later I met with Mr. Foster, the assistant director for general litigation, to discuss the areas of disagreement, but we came up at loggerheads.

When I told Glenn Turner what had happened, he was visibly upset. All the old prejudices against big government rose to the surface. It took me two months of pleading to get him to agree to another meeting with the FTC.

I remember one meeting in Orlando where I told him, "Glenn, I agree that the FTC is asking for more than it is entitled to. But, damn it, *some* federal order is better than none. If we can salvage an agreement with them, you'll have protection for the future. If we can't, then it's just a matter of time before they shut you down completely."

Turner's response was, "They don't really want to talk. They're out to get me and that's all there is to it."

Eventually I prevailed. On January 3, 1972, I met with Robert Petofsky, the director of the Bureau of Consumer Protection. This time Glenn Turner was there, too—he'd insisted on a chance to meet with the "head man," and make a personal attempt to persuade him.

Turner was impassioned if not eloquent, but Petofsky wouldn't budge. His staff had worked out a new agreement, and that was all he would discuss.

To Glenn's credit, he finally saw the handwriting on the wall. He agreed to sign the new order.

Three months later we had no word from the FTC. Then, in March, I got a call in my Boston office from FTC Secretary Charles Tobin: the commissioners had decided to reject the revised consent order. I called Charles O'Connell, who'd been so decent and professional in all my dealings with him, to see if there were really any possibility of further negotiations with the FTC.

It didn't take long to see that we'd come to a dead end. According to O'Connell, the commission would only be willing to talk about new demands, specifically that the company make full restitution to each and every franchise purchaser who requested it. This was an impossible demand, mathematically as well as financially.

When I told Turner what had happened, he was as close to bitterness as I'd ever seen him. "Isn't it funny, Bailey, that the government warned you, way back when you agreed to represent me, that

I might not be trustworthy, that I might not follow the legal advice you gave me?"

I knew just what he was talking about. Back in 1969, when I made my first tour of the country on Koscot's behalf, many of the state attorneys general warned me that Turner might not follow my advice, no matter how much good faith they attributed to me and my efforts. It had all come full circle.

I had another point to bring up with Turner. It was not a pleasant one. I told him that, based on a number of things I had heard —such as grand jury activity in Orlando—there might be a little collusion going on between government agencies. I mentioned Mr. O'Connell's surprise at his own Commission's action in refusing the second proposed consent decree. It was clear to me that a negotiated consent order by the FTC would fly in the face of a criminal indictment by the Post Office or the Securities and Exchange Commission. Therefore, I felt that the FTC had been dissuaded from making a fair compromise by some other agency that was trying to build a criminal case.

Turner's response was again tinged with irony, "It looks to me as if your idea of dealing fairly with all these people and giving them all the information they wanted about me and my companies wasn't so good after all. I think they were out to get me all along, and just used you to pick up a lot of free information."

As much as I would have liked to, I couldn't deny his charge with any real vigor.

Hindsight affords one a wonderfully simple but not always pleasant perspective. After the abortive liaison with the FTC, I no longer represented Glenn Turner or his companies on any regular basis. He had a number of able lawyers on retainer around the country who could better afford to spend vast amounts of time on his problems. I continued to monitor the criminal actions that were pending against him. I made sure that he had an experienced criminal lawyer on call in Orlando, and from time to time I communicated with that lawyer.

After March of 1972, I appeared on Turner's behalf only twice. Once I attended a meeting in New Jersey, and in January of 1973 I met with almost all of his state counsel in Orlando (they were on the verge of pulling out for nonpayment of fees, but we were able to work out a payment schedule).

I felt that I had given Glenn Turner and his companies good counsel. Until the time in mid-1971 when the FTC talks came up empty and the coloration of the board of directors changed from conservative businessmen to high rollers, we had succeeded in turning back the wave of litigation that threatened to swamp the company. By early 1973 the waters were darkening again, and this time it looked like a tidal wave.

It was of small consolation to me that I had not been paid any fees since mid-1971. What was most bothersome was that I may have added to Turner's difficulties by convincing him to enter good-faith negotiations with the government. Had I been too trusting? Perhaps Glenn was right, perhaps the government took advantage of our willingness to cooperate so that it could buttress its criminal case.

Eventually, Turner *was* right, at least to the extent that it would be a long time before he'd see the end of his troubles with the government. There are times when a client's hunch is more accurate than his lawyer's reasoning.

But neither Turner nor I even guessed at the bottom line—a line that read indictment for *both* of us. That, however, is another story. And it comes later in this book.

# The Happy Hooker's Best Friend

----

MAYOR Lindsay called him a "rogue cop," the Knapp Commission called him a "prime witness." Prosecutor John Keenan called him "a liar, a crook, a perjurer, . . . and a murderer." I called him Billy Phillips. He was my client.

When the Knapp Commission began its famous hearings into corruption within the ranks of New York's Finest, it already had the help of a very knowledgeable honest cop, Frank Serpico. But there was a problem with Serpico, just as there always is with honest cops; they know only so much. What the commission needed was a very knowledgeable *dishonest* cop. That's where Billy Phillips fit in.

The Knapp investigators tapped Billy Phillips on the shoulder at a time when he was riding high, higher in fact than ever before.

Shortly before he was caught, Billy had just added a very special client to his protection list—or, as the police themselves call it—"the pad." This special client was a high-priced call girl and madam by the soon-to-be-famous name of Xaviera Hollander. Within months, she would be known to the country and the world as "the Happy Hooker."

And Billy Phillips, television star of the Knapp Commission hearing, would be known to the country and world as a crooked cop, turned informer. Such is fate.

The attendant notoriety of the Knapp hearings made both Billy Phillips and Xaviera Hollander household words around New York City for quite some time. Both achieved fame, of sorts, but the lady was quite a bit more fortunate than the gentleman. True, she was forced to leave New York and give up her lucrative East Side business, but once resettled in Canada, she capitalized on her troubles.

*The Happy Hooker* was a great success. Soon there was a sequel to it, plus a magazine column, and although there have been periodic rumblings about deportation, there has also been the beginning of "a film career." All in all, not a bad shake.

Billy Phillips had to readjust and relocate, too. As a government witness of special value, he was allowed to remain on the payroll of the New York City Police Department and continue his time toward retirement. He had to move to another city and live under a false name, but that was a lot better than living in fear of his life in New York. When he came to town to testify or to provide information, the city paid his bills, and marshals protected him every step of the way.

Phillips thought he'd made the best of a bad deal. He knew he was a marked man, both in and out of the department, and there was street talk of a two-hundred-thousand-dollar contract on his life, but he believed that he was too important to the cases that grew out of the Knapp investigation for anyone to try and kill him —the fate of the honest cop, Frank Serpico, who had part of his face blown off in a rather suspicious drug raid.

Still, there are other ways of getting a man. Some of them are even legal, or at least they look that way.

Early in 1972, Billy Phillips got a phone call. He was wanted in New York. But this time he was not to go to the Office of the U.S. Attorney, which was the usual case, but to the District Attorney's Office in Manhattan. That bothered Phillips. Like the police department itself, the office of Frank Hogan, the venerable New York D.A. for more than three decades, was none too pleased about the Knapp Commission and its highly publicized hearings. The D.A.'s Office felt the hearings implied it was not doing its job. To put it mildly, there was bad blood between the two governmental bodies.

Phillips had been in the District Attorney's Office before, but it was not home ground. He felt apprehensive when he got on the airplane that morning. And well he should have. Before the day was out, he had been accused of murdering a pimp and a prostitute, and shooting a customer.

\*       \*       \*

When he joined the police force in 1957, Billy Phillips was twenty-eight years old. He'd knocked around more than a little. He had the street-quick glibness and charm of so many East Side New Yorkers who'd gone on the force before him, but his past was checkered with problems. Some were of his own making. Some weren't.

Billy was the second child and only son of an Irish-American couple who also grew up on the Lower East Side. His mother was plagued throughout her life with a series of illnesses, from rheumatic fever to goiter, that would have "tried the patience of Job," as the Irish Catholics are fond of saying. She died in 1947, when Billy was seventeen and his sister eighteen.

His father was an enigma. One moment he was the sternest of parents, beating his young son for disobedience, and the next he was showing off the boy to his crowd of friends at the Giants game, later propping him on the bar at the corner tavern and handing him pretzels and small glasses of beer.

Most importantly, Billy, Sr., was a cop. In fact, he was a detective. And his job and life style—he was always the best dressed and the first to buy a round—made an early, deep impression on his son.

Billy Phillips wasn't even twenty when he and his father had a serious fight, a fist fight. After he knocked his father down, Billy left the house. He didn't see his father for two years; he didn't talk to him for almost seven. During all that time, Billy Phillips, Jr., was on his own.

He had a variety of jobs, some good, some not, and he lost a number of them because he couldn't seem to get up on time. There was too much fun—football, baseball, and drinking beer. And women. He figured there would be time to settle down.

High school had been a laugh. He left before he was a senior. Years later he got his diploma by taking the New York State Equivalency Examination. It wasn't that Bill Phillips was dumb, it was that he never saw the point in studying too hard. And so he never did.

After a series of what he called "nothing" jobs, he joined the Air Force. Initially he did very well, and he was learning to fly. But that meant a six-year enlistment, rather than the four he agreed on, so he said no. Three days later he was shipped to Korea. But the war was waning, and Phillips spent a quiet time.

Back in the States, he was assigned to a base in Arizona. There he met a thin, quiet, and very attractive girl named Camille Bates. They got married. After his discharge, they moved to New York.

He spent thirty dollars on a cram course, enrolled in the Police

Academy, and became a policeman. He had had a number of jobs, most of them good, if not promising, but Billy Phillips wanted something more. In the back of his mind he knew that whatever troubles his parents had had, money was not one of them.

Billy Phillips, Sr., had always been able to take his family to the shore or the mountains each summer. And he had paid for all his wife's medical bills, as well as those of his mother. When it came down to crunch, he had the cash.

Somewhere along the line, when he was quite young, Billy Phillips, Jr., learned the truth—his father was a crooked cop. Nothing big, just the usual corruption.

Within months of his appointment, Billy Phillips, Jr., was following in his father's footsteps.

It all started so simply. Billy, Jr., did not start out with the idea of making all the illegal money he could. In fact, he started out with a very commendable goal—he wanted a gold shield, the detective's badge. (Years later, Billy would admit that as he got closer to thirty he realized he was patterning himself after his father in dress, style, and profession.)

Detectives did not wear uniforms. They had more influence. They were "somebody," in the close-knit world of the New York City policeman. So Billy Phillips went all out for the extra arrests that might bring him a commendation, which meant he would be that much closer to the gold badge.

He'd been a cop less than a year, and was taking a few college courses at night. (The degree, or progress toward it, didn't hurt either, when it came time to appoint detectives.) On the way to class one night he spotted two characters whose behavior bothered him. (From the very beginning, Billy Phillips had a keen eye for the out-of-order.)

When he began to follow them, rather clumsily, the two men ran. Phillips sprinted after them, caught them in a stairwell, and found a gun on one of them. The arrest for carrying an unlicensed weapon qualified Billy for a commendation.

But first there was the matter of the "hat." A hat, in police parlance, is the five bucks you have to give the officer who types up the report. And the report is necessary if you want a medal. In New York, and many other cities, the arresting officer has to *ask* for his medal. And the police clerk who types up your request is always, according to long-standing tradition, given his hat.

That was the first time. Billy got his commendation, after a good bit of finagling that should never have been necessary or tolerated, and he was officially part of the system of corruption.

He wanted that gold shield, and if that meant playing the game according to the rules of corruption, well, that was okay. Billy Phillips was never a very strict moralist. He knew about police corruption from his father's bragging, and he heard the others in his class at the academy talking about how much money they would be pulling down as soon as they got out of the academy grays and into the blue uniform—which they called "the money suit."

After the first time, it was easy.

There were a few other habits that made the pickings even more attractive. Billy Phillips was not a model husband. In fact, he was stepping out while the ink on his marriage certificate was still wet. When he and his wife got back to New York (and he settled her in a neighborhood across the river from Manhattan) he eagerly joined a group of roustabout rookies in their afterhours games.

Making the rounds of the bars, picking up women, it all took money, cash money. And the prime source of cash money for a New York City policeman was the street. It wasn't long before Billy Phillips was collecting his share, and then some.

In fairness to Phillips, it should be noted that during the time he began his police career, the corruption was so endemic, so widespread, that it was actually hard to be an honest cop. (Anyone who doubts that simple fact should read a book called *Serpico*.) Graft was such a plain fact of precinct life that a man who wanted no part of it had to promise not to blow the whistle on his mates. And then he was considered, according to Billy, "some kind of queer."

The other side of the coin is that Billy always knew what was going on; and when it turned to his advantage, he played the game with skill and zest.

At the height of his troubles, Billy Phillips told the late Leonard Shecter (who co-authored *On the Pad*, Billy's life story) about the process of corruption: "It's a slow deterioration of yourself, your morals and your aspects as to what is right and what is wrong. This deterioration happens from the time you come into the job and take your first five-dollar bill. After you do that, you are more or less on the hook and you just become progressively worse."

Such moralizing does not come naturally to Billy Phillips, and he might never have summed it up that way if he hadn't been caught. Nonetheless, it is a very accurate appraisal.

From his first assignment in East Harlem, where the awful variety of crimes and criminals makes bribery and protection the way of life, to his appointment as a detective assigned to a posh East Side Manhattan precinct, he learned the ropes.

There were a few things that even Bill Phillips wouldn't do, such as scavenging a DOA, or "dead on arrival," for all his worldly goods. And when he made a score, when he accepted money to let someone off, he never cleaned his victim out. "Always leave them with something. That way they're happy," was his motto. But even these twinges of conscience or common sense hardly dented his take.

After he'd been a cop for ten years, Billy was making at least four hundred dollars a week in unreported, tax-free income. Cash money. Good weeks brought a thousand.

Given those figures, it might be assumed that Billy Phillips was one of the richest crooked cops in New York. That would not be a wise assumption. Phillips's take was far less than that of certain officials, the lieutenants and the captains, who had more experience and opportunity. Billy was playing the game, and he was very good at it. He wasn't greedy, but then he wasn't exactly shy either.

Until 1965, when he went too far and lost his gold badge—the department's term for being busted from detective to uniform patrolman is "flopped"—Billy Phillips also worked hard at being an effective cop. He spent days of his own time on cases that promised no reward other than satisfaction.

In a clean department he might have become an outstanding cop. But he didn't work in a clean department, and his personal code of morality did not include high standards.

When Billy was flopped—for telling a bar owner in Queens that the two men in the back were cops; ironically, he was doing the owner a favor, gratis—he owned a snappy red Triumph sportscar, part of three airplanes and a flying school, and more expensive clothes than most mid-level advertising executives. His taste in women ran to knockouts, most of whom were stewardesses or nurses, or any other younger girl whose irregular hours matched his.

After eight years on the force his reputation as a "money man," one who could pull down an excessive amount of illegal cash, was well known among his peers on the force.

More than half of those eight years had been spent as a detective, which gave him a wide circle of friends within the department who could be useful when someone wanted Billy to arrange something, like buying out of an arrest. (That's not at all hard to do: the arresting officer who suddenly can't identify the defendant when he gets into court can scuttle the most airtight of cases. Once, when Billy was about to testify falsely, he realized the judge was in on the deal; he got so mad he testified truthfully, and the man was convicted. As Billy got off the stand, the judge said, "That's one you owe me.")

What this means is that when Billy got flopped back to a beat in Harlem, it hardly even slowed him down.

Usually, when a crooked cop is transferred from one New York precinct to another, he goes on collecting his share of the pad in his old precinct for two months. This is done under the theory that it takes about that long to "get established" on the pad in his new location. Billy Phillips followed this rule, but it didn't take him any two months to get started. He knew all the signs on the street that spell money.

What Billy did miss was the added clout of being called "Detective Phillips." And when he was off duty, and drinking in the backroom at P. J. Clarke's, the famous New York saloon where *Lost Weekend* was filmed, and where Billy ran with a fast crowd, he liked being known as the detective. And as he said several times, "It didn't hurt with the broads either."

It was almost poetic justice that the deal that turned into Billy's downfall was struck in Clarke's back room.

One April afternoon in 1971, Billy Phillips stopped at P. J. Clarke's for a drink after work. The first person he ran into was hardly one of his favorites. The man was Sammy Meyers, who made his money, it was said, by tipping off investors to inside information so they could make a stock killing. Like Phillips, Meyers's deals were not always strictly kosher.

Sammy told him about a madam who wanted to get on a pad. Even though he didn't particularly like Meyers, Billy's ears perked up when he heard the word "pad."

"What's the problem? Doesn't she know anybody?" Phillips asked.

"Not yet. I took a buddy of mine over there last night, and he tried to con her that he was a cop. But I think she smelled it. Would you be interested?"

Is the Pope Catholic? When Meyers's friend from the night before showed up, and confirmed the story of the high-class madam who needed to pay for antipolice protection, the trio decided to pay her a visit.

As they went out the door, Billy Phillips said, "Hey, what's this broad's name?"

"It's kind of weird," said Meyers. "She's Dutch or something. Her name's Xaviera Hollander."

One might have thought that Billy Phillips and Xaviera Hollander would have hit it off. Both were good-looking people, skilled in their respective professions. Phillips was forty, just six feet, and muscular. He had dark hair, moderately trendy sideburns, and deep blue eyes. Though his face could look very tough, his easy-going, backroom charm usually softened it. He told stories very well, usually on-the-job oddities that only a policeman would run across. And his raucous, free-flowing language added to every story. As Leonard Shecter put it, his vocabulary was "pure New York City cop."

Billy Phillips did not hit it off with Miss Hollander. For one thing, he wasn't too keen on scoring a prostitute. A lot of things could go wrong. For another, and this was probably a more important reason, she was "slow pay." According to Billy, "She was tight as a crab's ass."

Still, in a little over a month's time, he did three jobs for Hollander and her circle of friends. He made less than a thousand dollars. One job was supposed to cost her thirty-five hundred dollars; she paid fifteen hundred down, and then it turned out that the fix money wasn't needed. She refused to pay the rest. Billy was very angry, but there was little he could do about it. He wasn't going to beat up a madam.

The job that tripped Billy up was one he'd have turned down if he had known all the details.

Xaviera Hollander had a boy friend who helped her out around the apartment. Most people thought that was all he did, but he had other work. And it made prostitution look like peanuts, even the kind of high-class East Side prostitution à la Hollander.

He worked for an insurance firm. That was a legitimate job. But he had a deal on the side where he cashed stolen checks, through his firm and without his employer's knowledge. What made it significant was that the checks were stolen by the Mafia. The boy friend was a small cog in a large Mafia-run stolen check ring.

When he was caught, he was holding a check for a quarter of a million dollars. The other part of the indictment charged him with possession of a forged instrument. It was very serious.

After learning the case was too hot for Phillips's police connections to fix, Hollander asked, through a go-between, if Phillips knew a lawyer who could get to the judge. By chance, Phillips ran into Sammy Meyers, again at P. J. Clarke's, and put the question to him. Of course.

A meeting was set up, then another, and finally the payoff was arranged at the lawyer's office. Phillips was to be there with Hollander's go-between, an unusual little man known as Teddy Ratnoff.

Ratnoff, another character from Clarke's back room, ran a one-man business—Microsync Research and Development Corporation. Translated, it meant that Teddy Ratnoff was an electronic eavesdropper—or, if you prefer, a bugger.

As Leonard Shecter wrote, "Much more is known about Teddy Ratnoff's eavesdropping equipment than is known about Teddy Ratnoff. It was good eavesdropping equipment. No one is that sure about Teddy Ratnoff."

Not only did Ratnoff deal in secret listening devices, he was himself a plant. No one knew it, not Hollander or any of her crowd, and certainly not William Phillips, but Ratnoff had been trying for some months, prior to meeting either Xaviera or Billy, to get on the payroll of the Knapp Commission. In his zeal to prove himself an asset to the corruption-hunting commission, which was in a fallow period after its initial success with Frank Serpico, Ratnoff volunteered to help the Knapp investigators find a madam who would pay off the police. Had the commission more money, it would never have had to rely on the likes of Teddy Ratnoff; and ironically it would never have found Billy Phillips, who turned out unquestionably to be its star witness.

(There was a further irony. Ratnoff did not know Hollander when he first learned that the commission was looking for a prostitute/madam who was on the pad. He learned her name from Robin Moore, author of *The Green Berets* and *The French Connection*. Moore was interested in doing a book on electronic surveillance, and someone suggested that he might find the life and not-so-hard times of Teddy Ratnoff intriguing. The two met for lunch at Toots Shor's, and although Moore didn't get what he wanted, Ratnoff got the name of Xaviera Hollander from Moore, who was then busily ghostwriting *The Happy Hooker*. Moore thought it would be a good idea for Teddy to bug Hollander's phone and bedroom, so he could get some spicy verbatim quotes. Ratnoff came out way ahead.)

For days prior to meeting in the lawyer's office, Ratnoff had been wearing one of his own sophisticated listening devices during his talks with Phillips. Worn around the waist, the battery-operated device picked up conversation through a mike hidden under the tie, and broadcast it several blocks away to two Knapp Commission investigators sitting in a parked car.

The lawyer's name was Irwin Germaise. The less said about him the bettter, except for two points: one, the judge he swore he could bribe was later driven from the bench, a fairly rare occurrence in New York; and two, he affected a pearl-handled cane he said—and Ratnoff definitely believed—contained a gun. The point is that Teddy Ratnoff, for all his seediness, was taking quite a chance. He thought that Germaise was armed, and he *knew* that Phillips was.

The Knapp agents had assured Ratnoff that if his bug was discovered they could be in the lawyer's eighth-floor office in two minutes. He doubted it. But he was determined to prove his worth to the commission.

Shortly before Ratnoff arrived, ostensibly to make the payoff for Hollander, Germaise told Phillips that he was worried Ratnoff might be "wired," the term for a person who is carrying a concealed recording or transmitting device.

Phillips was incredulous. In his usual blunt terms, he said, "He's not wired. He's a shithead, a shmuck. He's nothing."

Germaise insisted. "No, I think he's wired."

"He can't be wired. He's not that smart. He's like a flunky in the whorehouse. That's all."

When Ratnoff walked into Germaise's inner office the next day at four o'clock, the agents were parked across the street. They listened as Ratnoff got the okay from the secretary to enter.

What they couldn't hear was Billy Phillips get up and walk over to Teddy, and throw his arm around his shoulder, as if in friendship. When Billy slipped his hand down the man's back, he felt the wire. His blood went cold. So did Ratnoff's.

Phillips's first words, unwittingly broadcast loud and clear to the agents, were oddly formal, "Irwin, the man is loaded."

Then everyone held his breath. Did Phillips or Germaise know Ratnoff was transmitting? Would they shoot him, either way? The agents had ten seconds or so to make up their minds. Should they wait it out and see if Ratnoff could convince Phillips it was a harmless device, such as a page? Or should they race up there immediately and save his life?

When Ratnoff said nothing for the moment or two, the agents were out of the car and into the building. One of them stopped to grab the nearest policeman, and explain that his presence was needed to protect a man's life. At first the cop didn't want to go. He was busy ticketing a pretzel vendor.

Brian Bruh, a big young investigator on loan to the Knapp Commission from the Intelligence Division of the Internal Revenue Service, was the first one to burst into the office. There was something almost Keystonic about the scene: neither Phillips nor Germaise knew it, but the Knapp people had no arrest powers. All they were doing was saving a life that may have been in danger.

Seeing the door to the inner office, Bruh knocked on it. Nothing. He pounded, and it was opened slightly. That was all he needed; he slammed it open.

Ratnoff's face was the color of bad pork. Germaise looked scared. As for Phillips, Bruh said later, "It was like sticking a pin into a balloon. You could see it on his face. He was a beaten man. There's no doubt in my mind that he thought he was under arrest at that time. Of course, we had no more arrest ability than the average citizen."

All Bruh had done was to identify himself and the other agent as being from the Knapp Commission. Then he looked at Ratnoff and said, "We want him out of here."

Ratnoff was only too happy to leave. Billy Phillips, no slouch when it came to thinking fast, started to leave with him. Bruh barked, "Hey, stop there. Get back inside."

Phillips returned. It was not the beginning of the end. It was the end.

The Knapp agents "turned" Billy a few days later, on the street in front of P. J. Clarke's. It was only fitting.

"Turning" means that a crooked police officer has agreed to help uncover evidence of police corruption. Phillips really had no choice. For one thing, he knew what would happen to him if he went to prison (which was the obvious ax the commission held over him); and for another, his father was no longer living. He didn't have to worry about the effect of this news on the father he had, curiously, come to love all over again. As for Billy's wife, she was never really a factor in his decision. She didn't know he had lost his detective rank until three years later. That was the kind of man he was.

For the next four months Billy Phillips was an undercover agent for the Knapp Commission. He made most of the agents' fondest dreams come true.

During the televised portion of the hearings, Phillips took the stand without a mask or a blindfold or a voice-altering device, and told the history of his own years as a corrupt cop.

Beginning with that first five-dollar hat so the clerk would type up his commendation papers, he ran through the litany of all the types of graft and bribery that he had taken part in—the stopped motorists who couldn't afford another ticket but could afford a few dollars (from tens to hundreds, whatever the traffic would bear) for the arresting officer; the far more lucrative arrangement after a ticket had already been written, an arrest made, and courtroom testimony had to be bought (the price was always higher for lying under oath); and the fortuitous discovery of the safecrackers Billy caught before they'd opened the safe. He got five hundred dollars from them, left them alone while he circled the block a few times, and went back in and took the eighty dollars they'd found in the cracked safe.

And there were the names he named. All those sergeants, captains, lieutenants, and various other officers, high and low, Billy had worked with over the years. If the investigators had a good lead, Billy Phillips named the right names.

From the smallest transgressions (the "flute," or free coke bottle full of whiskey, that the neighborhood bar gave up without question, not knowing or really caring if it was for the patrolman who picked it up or his superior back at the precinct house) to the purchase of perjured testimony and the buying of judges. If the Knapp investigators asked the right questions, Billy gave the right answers.

It was quite a show. For days on end New Yorkers sat transfixed in front of the television screen. The viewers had heard all about the twin Mr. Cleans, Frank Serpico and David Durk, the good cops who blew the whistle on their own; now they were seeing and hearing the real article, the corrupt cop. So many pious disclaimers from the department went up in the smoke of the klieg lights as Phillips testified. You couldn't listen to him and deny it all.

But the public hearings were only a part of Billy's usefulness to the Knapp investigators. For months prior to the televised hearings he had been invaluable as the one weapon the commission most needed—a crooked cop on the inside.

Just like Teddy Ratnoff, Billy Phillips was wired—battery pack—transmitter around the waist under the sport coat, and microphone hidden under the tie. He set up meeting after meeting, passed money, made deals, and finally trapped some officers in a deal with the Mafia. It was dirty, dangerous work, and he hated it. But he had no choice.

Little wonder then that the word on the street was the mob had put a two-hundred-thousand-dollar contract on his head. And that the police themselves were unofficially furious, or that he truly needed the complement of federal marshals (and the immunity from federal prosecution) that accompanied him wherever he went. It wasn't overcaution or theatrics that decided his wife's move to Arizona or his own relocation to another city; it was simple necessity.

Little wonder also that someone got to Phillips in the only non-violent, apparently legal way possible: indictment.

Certainly there must have been a crooked cop or two somewhere in the city who would have chanced the odds and tried to do Billy in. But the memory of Frank Serpico, and the headlines following his unfortunate shooting by a "crazed junkie," were still too fresh. (When Serpico was in the hospital, a day after being shot in the face, he got a card that had been altered to read "Die quickly." Under the message was written "You scumbag." According to Serpico, that was known as the worst thing one cop could call another.)

Indictment was the way, indictment for murder. Then who would believe him?

My associate Gerry Alch took the first call from Billy Phillips. It came some weeks prior to the indictment. Would we take the case? We would see.

There are certain kinds of cases I've usually stayed away from. One is the gang rape. I would have no stomach if someone came to me, and admitting his guilt, asked me to defend him against that charge. Let some other criminal lawyer take that one. Another type is the defense of an admittedly crooked cop.

I've defended accused policemen before. Once, in Ohio, I defended eight of them and the gambler they'd been supposedly working the numbers racket with, but I took that one because I felt the prosecution was playing too rough.

When Gerry Alch told me that Billy Phillips wanted me to defend him on a double murder charge, my first question was, "Did he do it?"

Gerry said that Phillips swore he didn't, that it was a frame because he'd turned—and there was no other way, short of outright murder, that they could shut him up. (Phillips was slated to be the chief witness against a number of New York City policemen when the Knapp Commission work was done and its recommendations for indictment were handed down. A crooked cop can still be an effective witness, but a crooked cop accused of murder suffers an immediate credibility loss.)

Gerry also said that Phillips had agreed to take a polygraph test just as soon as we could set it up. I liked that. I told Gerry I'd agree to take the case if he passed, but I wanted to meet Phillips first.

"Oh, Lee, there's something else. We'll probably have to scale down the fee. He's got some money, but not much."

Well, that wasn't exactly good news, for a major murder trial can really run up expenses during the investigative phase. Still, it sounded like an intriguing case. From what I knew of the work of the

Knapp Commission, and what little I had read or heard of Phillips's role, the idea of a framed murder indictment had a certain, sickening plausibility.

On that gray April day in 1972 when John Keenan, the assistant district attorney in charge of homicide, read Billy his rights and told him he had a right to remain silent, the right to contact an attorney, and that anything he said could be used against him (in other words, the Miranda warning), Phillips knew he was in big, big trouble.

Even pimps and prostitutes have to do something on Christmas Eve. In 1968, in a beautifully furnished apartment on Manhattan's fashionable East Side, a pimp known as Jimmy Goldberg watched television. One of his girls, a nineteen-year-old named Sharon Stango, was entertaining Charles Gonsalez, a regular, in one of the back bedrooms.

Goldberg was a rather odd man. For one thing, his real name was Jimmy Smith. Goldberg was his alias. For another, although he had a good stable of girls, he was almost always in debt. He was not much of a businessman.

While Gonsalez had been waiting in the lobby for Sharon to arrive, he noticed a chunky man in a tan raincoat. The man asked for 11-F, Goldberg's apartment. After the doorman had cleared him by phone, the man had gone upstairs.

Sharon used her own key to the apartment, and after she had provided a little Christmas cheer, Gonsalez paid her. He then washed up, and went into the living room where Goldberg and the man in the tan raincoat were arguing about money.

At this point there were four people in the room: the pimp, the prostitute, the john, and the man in the tan raincoat.

According to Gonsalez, the argument turned hot. The man in the coat wanted a thousand dollars that he claimed Goldberg owed him, and when Goldberg continued to stall, the man became furious. He pulled out a large gun (a .38 special) and shot Goldberg/Smith to death from six inches away. Then he did the same to Sharon Stango, who had screamed. Then he shot Gonsalez, and, thinking he'd killed him, he walked out.

And what did all this have to do with Billy Phillips? Two things. One, he had testified before the Knapp hearings that in 1965 he had scored Jimmy Smith (alias Goldberg) for fifteen hundred dollars, a few months after he had made some money betting on football games with tips from Smith. According to Billy Phillips, that was the last time in his life he had seen one Jimmy Smith/Goldberg. Two, in October of 1971, a detective named John Justy watched Phillips testify before the Knapp Commission on television (and, one must assume, he was not too pleased at what he heard) and suddenly a light went on; this witness Phillips looked, Justy would later claim, very much like the police artist's composite sketch of the man who had killed Jimmy Smith/Goldberg. When Assistant D.A. John Keenan read Phillips his rights, five months later, it was because Phillips had become the prime suspect in that killing.

I met Billy Phillips for the first time on a Monday morning in March of 1972. He'd come up to my Boston office to take a polygraph test. I can't say that I found him a warm and wonderful human being. After all, here was a man who had admitted to everything from petty bribery to perjury, and he'd admitted it on television. Still, he gave the distinct impression of truthfulness when I asked him the preliminary questions about the facts of the case against him. I don't claim infallibility when it comes to detecting mendacity, but one way or another I have had a great deal of experience with liars.

I found Phillips to be a good-looking, rather hard type, with a streak of Irish charm a yard wide and still visible beneath his nervousness. He reminded me of so many of the Boston cops I used to know when I was just starting out, despite that special New York veneer.

Nonetheless, I wasn't about to believe a word he said unless it was backed up by the polygraph.

To run the test, I had decided against my usual stalwart, Charles Zimmerman of Boston, in favor of a man named Bill La Parl, who worked for him. My reason was that La Parl had been a policeman before going into private industry as a polygraph examiner. La Parl would have a better line on what kind of man Phillips was.

La Parl and Phillips got on well from the beginning. Billy remembers that La Parl warned him that if he thought he could beat the test, he should just forget about it. Phillips, who knew at least something about the machine and had seen it used in some of his own investigations as a detective, said, "I'm here for the sole purpose of taking this test, passing it, and having Mr. Bailey represent me."

He passed it, and I agreed to represent him. Billy Phillips was no Ernie Medina, but the test showed that he, too, was not guilty of the crime with which he was about to be charged. That was enough for me.

S. Edward Orenstein, Phillips's civil lawyer, was in on the case from the beginning, and his New York office on lower Broadway became our pretrial headquarters. When Billy was called before the grand jury in late March, we had to face our first conflict. Should he testify or should he take the Fifth?

Ed Orenstein felt that Billy was going to get indicted no matter what he said, and thus there was no point in letting him go before the grand jury where he would have to waive his immunity (which he had as a result of being a Knapp Commission witness).

I disagreed. When dealing with a "tarnished" client—and Billy Phillips was never going to strike anyone as a choir boy—you don't want to add to that tarnish. I thought Billy should testify. For one thing, I could later argue to a jury (if it came to that) that Phillips had never refused to answer qustions, as had so many other indicted or suspect New York City cops.

Phillips was convinced that if he passed the polygraph test, the Knapp Commission people would rally to his defense and help to get him off. To an extent, he was justified in thinking that; he had been their salvation. But high-level criminal proceedings in the largest city in the nation are layered with machinations. One should not predict lightly.

Part of the problem was the District Attorney's Office. Without going into all the history, it is enough to say that the Knapp Commission had embarrassed the D.A.'s Office, which is charged with overseeing much of the work of the Police Department. Add to that the near-hatred that many cops and police officials felt for Phillips, the turncoat, and you had two rather formidable foes.

In the end, the other side had more clout. On March 20, 1972, Billy Phillips was indicted by the grand jury for the murders of Jimmy Smith/Goldberg and Sharon Stango, and "the felonious assault on the life of one Charles Gonsalez."

Later, Phillips told Leonard Shecter how he felt the day he got indicted:

> Bailey comes out and he says, Bill, you've been indicted. I says, fucking son of a bitch. Oh, did I feel like shit. Now I don't want to let them know I feel like shit. I put on my little act, smiling, fucking around, I wouldn't let them know it bothered me, but it fucking tore me up. I says, those rotten bunch of bastards.
>
> I then had to go down to be fingerprinted and photographed. That's a real fucking winner. Go down to the photograph bureau, right? And sit there with the numbers on my chest and all that spinning me around in the chair. That really fucking pissed

me off, but I wouldn't bend at all. We go back upstairs and they're going to drive me over to the Fifth Precinct. First they got to put handcuffs on me. What for? Where am I going? Handcuffs. A million fucking reporters, photographers all around taking pictures of me in handcuffs. I didn't lower my head; I didn't bend a bit for them bastards. I walked out there with my head stuck as high as I could get the goddamn thing.

Get to the Fifth Precinct, and I hear a lot of shit from a lot of cops when I walk in to get booked. Now I got to get arraigned. This is the worst day of my life. I've had some bad days, but this, this is the worst, and it gets worse as it goes on.

Were it not for the presence of John Keenan, a good and decent man, it would be easy to say that Billy Phillips was indicted solely because he "turned." That he got it because he was a marked man who had dared to expose the corruption among New York's finest. But Keenan would not have stood for that. Keenan believed Phillips was guilty. What, then, was the case against Billy Phillips?

He was charged with murder on the basis of eyewitness identification—three years after the alleged crime.

I accepted the Phillips case because a combination of facts bothered me: here was a turncoat cop who had blown the whistle on his former mates, but now he was being charged, three years later, with a set of murders on the basis of eyewitness testimony. If I had learned one thing in all the years I had been practicing criminal law, it was to doubt the testimony of late-blooming murder witnesses.

Even before I got the results of Bill La Parl's polygraph test, I had a strong hunch that Billy Phillips was being framed. An important factor that influenced me was that Billy had a very strong alibi.

Fortunately, from Phillips's standpoint, the murders had taken place on Christmas Eve, one night out of the year when a person has a fairly good chance of remembering where he or she was and what they did. And what the Phillipses did that Christmas Eve was to visit two different sets of relatives and friends. Everyone present at both parties remembered the visits, as did Camille Phillips, Billy's wife. And a co-worker and friend of Camille's who had driven her home from the office party remembered that he had stopped in for a few drinks with Camille and Billy.

Phillips himself was the opposite of a solid citizen. No one disputed that. But the people he had spent Christmas Eve with were all very solid. It was the kind of alibi that is usually called airtight.

In almost any other situation, the alibi, once checked out by the

D.A.'s Office, would have been enough to quash the indictment. This was not, however, just any old indictment. It was a murder indictment against the "rogue cop." Because of that, the case went to trial.

From the standpoint of the defense, we had two problems: one was the presence of John Keenan as the prosecutor; and the other was the presence of John Martin Murtaugh as the judge.

Keenan is probably one of the best prosecutors in the country. In his early forties, he slips quietly into court in modest dress, sometimes looking for all the world like a political accident who will surely be voted out in the next election. To the contrary, he is more than able—a sharp legal mind combined with an excellent sense of barely contained moral outrage. Smooth-looking jurors may discount him at the beginning of a case, but by the end they listen to everything he says. He comes on like Diogenes. It is not easy to go against John Keenan.

By a similar token, it is not easy to go *before* Judge Murtaugh. There are judges whose idea of civil defense is to draw all the wagons into a circle. Judge Murtaugh is not one of them, but on occasion he can give that impression. On balance, he is a tough judge who cannot always be second-guessed; in other words, just when you think you have him figured out, he surprises you. This was part of the difficulty, but the greater part was that Judge Murtaugh and District Attorney Hogan were friends from the old days. That kind of background makes life difficult for a defense attorney and hell for a defendant like Bill Phillips.

Another part of the problem was timing. Judge Murtaugh had just come off the Black Panther case, in which he had all but voted for conviction, only to hear the foreman repeat "Not guilty" 156 times, thereby freeing the defendants on each and every count. It was a hard act to follow.

Once he was indicted, Billy Phillips regained some of his famous self-confidence. But I knew he was very worried—and I can't say I blamed him. The case against him was based on the identification and eventual testimony of some very strange people. The government witnesses included prostitutes and their customers. Given his background, Phillips knew that people with so little to lose might well say anything on the stand.

I don't imply that the prosecution knowingly put on witnesses it knew would say the convenient thing. The government often has to make use of people it would not deal with otherwise. A witness is a witness is a witness. That's a fact of courtroom life. And when a pimp gets killed, the people in the room are not likely to be ministers and bank presidents (but notice I don't say that *never* happens). Nonetheless, my client had reason to worry. I could tell him to relax, that he was in the middle of a gigantic frame, and he would nod his agreement. But that didn't stop him from worrying.

We had not even picked the jury when I learned that Judge Murtaugh was going to be very tough with us. I had argued, during pretrial, that we should have the names and addresses of all the witnesses that the government planned to call, and I got a bit vocal about it. I said it was allowed in all the "better" jurisdictions. Judge Murtaugh listened to me for a while, and then he let me have it:

"Counsel, we have graciously permitted you to represent the defendant in our jurisdiction. . . . It ill befits you to make aspersions as to the manner in which justice is being conducted in New York State."

All I could possibly reply was, "Yes, Your Honor."

We lost all the big battles during the pretrial phase. When I argued that I should be able to bring out the fact of the Knapp Commission and Billy Phillips's special relationship, Judge Murtaugh stepped on me again. I said, "I am not permitted to argue to the jury that the police have a motive for framing this man?"

The judge said, "I don't think you are."

On a beautiful day in late June, we began the task of picking Billy Phillips's jury. It strains the meaning of words to say that it was a jury of his peers. This jury, all solid, taxpaying citizens, would be allowed to hear that the defendant was a corrupt cop; but it would not be allowed to hear that he had cooperated with the Knapp Commission in a unique admission, from the inside, of the depth and breadth of police corruption. It was neither fair nor just.

We ended up, after all the hassling, with a jury of ten men and two women. (Billy didn't want *any* women; he felt they'd hang him for being an unfaithful husband.) It was a fairly well-educated group, and I was for the most part satisfied. I had to worry about two extremes: those potential jurors who would be certain Phillips was being persecuted by the government, and those who felt a guy who admitted to so many misdeeds should be hung with something. I wanted a mix of people. I think that's what we got.

The prosecution, of course, wanted people who had never even heard of the Knapp Commission, and there were moments when I thought John Keenan wanted nothing but the barely literate. That's when a trial most often resembles a game, rather than a search for the truth. It would have greatly eased the prosecutor's already-lightened burden if he could find a dozen people who by some quirk of fate had never heard of the Knapp investigation.

Ultimately neither side was particularly pleased with the jury—which meant it was a fairly typical jury for a case of this sort.

John Keenan dropped a bomb in his opening statement. He told the jury that the admittedly sketchy eyewitness testimony of the Christmas Eve group would be buttressed by four witnesses who would swear they had seen Phillips in the Smith/Goldberg apartment on the evening of the twenty-third! Of course, two of these witnesses happened to be prostitutes—if the killing had taken place in a shoe store, some of the witnesses would be shoe salesmen, right? —but, according to Keenan, they were still excellent witnesses with the full blessing of the District Attorney's Office. (Immediately, the press dubbed them "Hogan's Hookers.")

What hurt was that under the rules of evidence the government had no obligation to tell us of the existence of these new witnesses. Billy Phillips may have been on trial for his life, but procedure is procedure and must be followed.

When John Keenan mentioned the news of the twenty-third, I looked at my client, and he mouthed the words, "No way." Again, I couldn't blame Keenan. He was simply using what his police investigators had given him as evidence. Still, it hurt. And what hurt the most was that, as he told the jury, these witnesses would testify that Phillips had come in, angry, demanded his money, and when he didn't get it threatened to kill Jimmy Smith if he didn't have it by the next day.

It was almost too neat, but juries are not necessarily made up of skeptics. And when more than several people take the stand, it is hard for most jurors to believe that all of them are lying. I had my work cut out for me.

Keenan's opening was, from a professional standpoint, an admirable piece of work. He projected the image of a calm, thorough, and obviously decent public servant. And the image was accurate. He played his appearance and his style for all they were worth. At one point he told the jury that on the twenty-third Phillips had taken Smith/Goldberg into the kitchen and said, in a very loud voice, "If you don't have that money by tomorrow night. I'll blow your f . . . ing head off." And then he added, "But the defendant didn't say 'f . . . ing.' He said the whole word."

In my opening statement I admitted that Billy Phillips had known Jimmy Goldberg, the pimp who used the name of Jimmy Smith, that he had placed some football bets with him in 1965, and that he had scored him for some shakedown money the same fall. I denied the killing. Under different circumstances I would have asked the jury to ponder why a man who had supposedly murdered another man would volunteer his association with the deceased while testifying, on television, to his own criminal activities. But the judge's ruling kept me from asking that question.

Instead I told the jury that we would show Phillips's innocence by pointing to the identity of the real killer.

Anyone who watches television knows that such statements are the stuff of which Perry Mason was made. But I was dead serious. My own investigators had turned up the name of a man who had a solid motive for killing Jimmy Smith. The man was also a pimp, and he had just lost a very valuable asset—a beautiful, hard-working prostitute—to Jimmy Smith. Our information was that the girl had been making a thousand dollars a week for the jilted pimp when she joined Jimmy Smith's family.

That made Billy Phillips's thousand-dollar-total debt rather pale in comparison. On balance, I think things were about even in the surprise department.

The case against Phillips had begun, according to the government's theory, during the unmentionable Knapp hearings when Detective John Justy saw Phillips on television. Suddenly, Justy saw what he thought was a resemblance between Phillips and the police artist's sketch of Smith's killer, back in 1968.

That was step one. After that, Justy went out and reinterviewed all the important witnesses. Lo and behold, several of the prostitutes agreed that the man on the other side of the one-way glass at the station house (Phillips) looked just like the man in the tan raincoat who had killed Jimmy Smith.

And so did Charles Gonsalez. And so did Richie Stevens, a building employee who claimed that he was in the apartment on the night of the twenty-third because Jimmy Smith was letting him take his Christmas "tip" out in trade. More than three years later, all of these witnesses agreed with Detective Justy that Bill Phillips looked like the killer; in fact, they thought he was the killer.

That was the bulk of the case against my client. I waited, not so patiently, as Keenan put his string of witnesses on the stand.

First it was a quartet of prostitutes—Terry Rogers, Vicki ("Lolita") Lewis, Doris Lee (a.k.a. Cora Tyrone), and Donna Charmello.

The testimony of the first three was generally in agreement: each had seen Phillips several times during the months preceding the killings. That placed him.

The next witness, Donna Charmello, was the one who really put the blocks to Billy. She said that she had been in the apartment on the twenty-third, taking part in the freebie holiday celebration, when there was a knock on the door. She testified that she ran to answer it because "the early bird gets the worm." There was Phillips. He came in and went off to the kitchen with Jimmy Smith, and through the open door she could hear the loud cursing and the demand for money. And the death threat.

I had not spent too much time in cross-examining the first three prostitutes, just enough to let the jury see that they were hardly the most positive and convincing of witnesses. Miss Charmello was more damaging, so I spent almost half an hour with her. (She was also the most striking looking of the quartet. Juries shouldn't take such things into consideration, but they do. And the lawyer who forgets it might well be jeopardizing his client's welfare.)

It wasn't the most revealing cross-examination, but I think it planted a few doubts. For one thing, she said that she could hear everything that went on in the kitchen between Smith and the man in the tan raincoat (but later witnesses who were also in the room that same night testified that they could not hear anywhere near that well). For another, she said that Detective Justy had interviewed her for the first time in May of 1969, five months after the killing, and though she did not tell him of the party on Christmas Eve, she did get her dander up sufficiently to hint that a policeman might be involved. She said, "I told him maybe he didn't really want to find out who did it, and that he ought to try digging up bones in his own back yard."

Detective Justy, however, did not take the hint, nor did he include her statement in his report. Apparently it wasn't until three years later, when he saw Phillips blowing his whistle on television, that he got Donna's message. That's the kind of doubt that troubles a fair-minded juror.

The trial was half over when Keenan put his "star" witness on the stand. Charles Gonsalez, at the time of the murders, was forty years old. He was short, fat, and unattractive. For sometime he had been a regular at Jimmy Smith's, where his particular favorite was nineteen-year-old Sharon Stango. This little daytime bookkeeper's assistant from New Jersey must have looked like the moon and stars to poor Charles Gonsalez. On Christmas Eve he waited just for her. He met her in the lobby and they entered the apartment with her key, went straight to the bedroom, and after he'd played and paid, he cleaned up and went into the living room.

There he witnessed the cold-blooded murder of Jimmy Smith and Sharon Stango, and took a bullet in his side that was meant to kill him.

The jury watched him intently as he shuffled up to the stand. It's hard not to feel sympathy for a man who was almost killed. And in case anyone missed that point, the prosecutor had Gonsalez open his shirt and display his scars.

There were no surprises in his testimony. The *way* he testified was more than a little unusual. His voice was high-pitched, nervous, and startlingly loud. He seemed to be speaking in capital letters. And he used "Mr. Keenan" almost every other time he opened his mouth, occasionally at both the beginning and end of his sentences.

If ever a witness appeared eager to please the prosecutor, it was Charles Gonsalez. Of course, some of this zeal was perfectly understandable, as Mr. Gonsalez had almost lost his life, but his testimonial fervor seemed a bit odd when it came out that he had originally described the killer as being shorter and slimmer than Billy Phillips.

On direct examination by Keenan, Gonsalez shouted that after he "had sex" with Sharon Stango he washed up and went into the living room, where he saw a stranger like Phillips, who was "five feet eleven, a hundred ninety pounds."

He then described the killings and his own narrow escape, using simple, effective language. When the prosecutor asked him if the man who had done the killings was in the room, Gonsalez said yes, and when asked to point him out, he left the witness stand and advanced on Phillips, finger shaking as he pointed. He looked like a possessed man.

When the bailiff restrained him, Billy Phillips looked at me and smiled. It would have taken an awfully cool murderer to do that.

On cross-examination I went into the matter of the earlier description that Gonsalez had given Detective Justy:

"Did you ever give a policeman a description of the man who shot you?"

"No, I did not."

"Never in your whole life?"

"No."

"Were you asked to give one by a policeman?"

"No."

"Nobody ever asked you how big he was?"

"They asked me how tall he was, yes."

"Did you tell them?"

"Yes, I said five foot eleven, a hundred ninety pounds."

"Didn't you, in fact, say between five eight and five nine to Detective Justy?"

"I said five nine."

"You said five nine?"

"Right."

"Do you wish to correct your earlier testimony that the killer was five eleven?"

"Yes, I do. I say he's five eleven."

"Now wait a minute. You say that the first height you gave of the killer was five feet nine inches, right?"

"Right."

"Now, when did you change that to five feet eleven inches?"

"Because he appears taller to me."

"You mean Phillips does?"

"Yes."

For an important prosecution witness, Charles Gonsalez displayed several other weak points.

I asked if he had seen Phillips before on television or in the newspapers. He said he'd seen Phillips's picture in the paper after he was indicted for murder. I then asked him if he had ever seen him prior to that time, and he said, "I never seen him before in my life."

Several of the jurors registered visible shock. After all, Phillips was the man who had allegedly shot Gonsalez.

There were a number of small holes in the overall testimony of the government's witnesses. Some said the door between the kitchen and the murder room was open; some said it was closed. Some said Phillips was a regular at Jimmy Smith's (one of the girls even called him "Philly," and said that's what she always called him, even though no one else did) and some said they'd never seen him there before. Both Gonsalez and Detective Justy said the killer had been five nine and weighed 170 pounds; apparently, in three years' time Phillips had grown two inches and put on fifteen pounds. Justy said the killer's face was "pockmarked," as did several other witnesses; Phillips has a clear complexion.

Still, none of these holes was clearly large enough for my client to walk through. And I was taking such a beating from Judge Murtaugh on evidentiary rulings that the jury had no real idea of just how inconsistent some of the testimony had been. (For one thing, based on information Billy gave me, I could have shown a relationship of long-lasting antagonism between Phillips and Detective Justy, but without being able to argue that the police had a motive for framing Billy it would do little good.) I can't say that at the end of the government's case Phillips was in grave danger of conviction, but he had clearly been hurt more than he should have been by the witnesses.

It was mid-July, and the case was in its fourth week when we began the defense of Billy Phillips. It would all rest on the strength of his alibi—and the credibility of his alibi witnesses. Every one of them was a nice person, but unfortunately most nice people have never been subjected to harsh cross-examination in a major murder case. And you could bet your last dollar that John Keenan was not going to go easy on them just because they were nice people. He had the burden of proof.

The defense was not the only one with a problem. Keenan had a monkey on his back—the honor and integrity of the New York City Police Department. If he won a conviction against the department's chief accuser, both Phillips and the Knapp Commission would be greatly discredited. Nonetheless, in this as in all murder trials, there was no question as to which side had more to lose.

As the first witnesses for the defense, I called the people who had actually spent Christmas Eve of 1968 with Billy Phillips. They provided the jury with a fascinating contrast of human beings from those called (and relied on) by the government. The prosecution witnesses had been, for the most part, prostitutes and their customers; the Phillipses' family and friends were the type of people who wouldn't even use the *word* "whorehouse."

The story that they told, pieced together, was this:

On the afternoon of December 24, Camille Phillips went to an office Christmas party. She and Leo Slack, a co-worker who often drove her to and from work, left the restaurant where the party was held at four-thirty. He drove her home and stopped in for a drink. The first thing that Leo and Camille saw was Billy's unusual Christmas present for his wife—fifty one-dollar bills attached to the Christmas tree. (The present was a big hit; Camille even had her picture taken in front of the tree.)

Camille, Billy, and Leo Slack drank Tom Collinses until seven or seven-thirty, when the three left the house together. Slack left in his car for Pennsylvania, where he was to spend Christmas in his old home town. Billy and Camille drove to the home of Billy's aunt and uncle, Frank and Martha McKee, for a small Christmas Eve gathering. Billy's great favorite, his maternal grandmother, was also there.

The Phillipses left the McKees' at ten o'clock, and went on to another party. And there was no forgetting this one, for it was a very special occasion. Billy's cousin, Margie, was going to get married, and her mother and father, Tom and Rita Leavey, wanted all the relatives in to celebrate. Engagements, of course, happen all the time, but this one was different, for Margie Leavy had recently left the convent to return to the secular life, and had just gotten engaged to a young Irish-American by the name of Peter Callaghan. It was not the kind of occasion a Catholic family would soon forget.

John Keenan, himself a Catholic and the product of a string of Catholic schools right up through law school, did the best he could to discredit or confuse these good people. And he scored a few points along the way. But he made one crack that brought me right out of my seat.

He asked Camille Phillips, who looked to be in shock all the time she was on the stand, why she and Billy had not bought an engagement present for the Callaghans-to-be. His tone was very sarcastic, because he wanted to imply that the party had never happened.

"I object," I shouted, "that's rude!"

I was dead serious. He could imply all he wanted to, but he had to do so within the proper bounds.

Even though Judge Murtaugh overruled my objection, Keenan took it personally and shouted back, "I object to Mr. Bailey's comments. I have never been rude in this courtroom, and I ask for an apology, sir."

He was angry, but so was I. "You won't get it. I don't think you have any right to challenge anyone for not giving someone a gift."

After I'd called all the family and relatives who were at the two parties on Christmas Eve—and all of them testified that both Camille and Billy were there all night—I called Mike Armstrong of the Knapp Commission. He testified that, yes, Officer Phillips had once killed a man in the line of duty, but that was the only such occurrence, and the department had not seen fit to question the incident. (This testimony was necessary because the prosecution had introduced evidence of a boast that Phillips had made to Ratnoff that he had once killed three men. With his usual delicacy of language, Phillips had said, "Yeah, once I blew away three fucks up in Harlem." As Bill explained to me, and I had no reason to doubt, he was trying to scare Ratnoff into thinking he was dealing with a very tough cus-

tomer. Cops, and especially crooked ones, do this kind of thing all
the time.)

And then it was time to call the defendant himself. It was now
August, and we were close to the sixth week of trial. However, no
sooner had I announced my intention to call Phillips when we ran
into a few roadblocks.

All that summer, prior to the trial, Billy Phillips had been having
taping sessions with Leonard Shecter, a New York writer who'd
been a columnist for more than twenty years with the *New York
Post* before he turned to the writing of books. Shecter and Phillips
had a contract to do a book on Billy's life.

There was nothing illegal about their project, but it cost the
defense dearly. When the government found out about the projected
book, it subpoenaed the rough draft that had been sent to the pub-
lisher. Shecter put up a valiant fight, but it was a lost cause from
the beginning. And once Keenan had the material, he used it very
effectively.

Judge Murtaugh ruled that he would decide if the material should
be turned over to the prosecution. He would do so by reading the
manuscript to see what parts, if any, would be relevant to the government's cross-examination of Phillips. Long before Billy took the
stand, Judge Murtaugh turned the material over to Keenan. He had
decided the whole thing was relevant, which hardly surprised me.

I did not keep Billy on the stand for very long. It was absolutely
necessary that he testify in his own defense, but to drag out his testimony might have made the jurors think we were worried about the
substance of the government's case. I wanted him to hit the highlights, and then do the best he could under Keenan's cross-examination.

I had Billy detail, quickly, his life as a crooked cop, his work for
the Knapp Commission (he could describe it, but I couldn't argue
to the jury that he was being tried because of it), and then we got
into the events of December 24, 1968.

He explained where he was and when. He simply could not have
committed the murder and been home in time to have a drink or
two with Leo Slack and then show up at the McKees' at eight o'clock.
I asked him if he knew Jimmy Smith/Goldberg and he explained
their relationship, stating that he had never seen him again after
the fall of 1965. He stated firmly that he had never seen or talked
to any of the other witnesses, the prostitutes or their customers who
had sworn he was the killer.

And then it was John Keenan's turn. He all but jumped out of his chair to confront the witness. But after all the smoke had cleared, I think Billy had stood up extremely well. He gave at least as good as he got.

Keenan tried to score a strong point by suggesting that Billy had a motive, that he would have killed for a sum as small as one thousand dollars because he was heavily in debt. It wasn't entirely true, but it sounded that way after Keenan led Billy through a recitation of his outstanding debts. When the figure reached forty thousand, it sounded very damaging. Still, I felt the jury was not buying the suggestion that a man with those liabilities would kill for one-fortieth of what he owed. Also, Billy had substantial assets in his home and his flying business, and the jury knew it.

Keenan proved just how very good he is by reading to Phillips, as background for some of his questions, from the first chapter of the Phillips-Shecter manuscript, rather than from the transcript of the Knapp Commission hearings (which covered the same ground). By doing this, he planted the idea that here was a crooked cop about to make even more money by telling his life story. It was an excellent tactic.

All in all, though, Billy Phillips stood up well. He was just too seasoned a witness, having appeared in so many courtrooms in his years as a policeman. Also, he was on trial for murder. I could tell that John Keenan was not entirely pleased when he sat down.

I had two more witnesses I wanted to call. The second was far more important than the first. Judge Murtaugh allowed me to call one of them.

Billy Peterson, the doorman in the late Jimmy Smith/Goldberg's building, had been a government witness against Phillips. I put him on for one simple reason: although Donna Charmello and Richie Stevens (the handyman who had been at the party on the twenty-third with Charmello, Sharon Stango, and Peterson) had testified that they heard the loud argument between Smith and the man in the tan raincoat, Peterson testified that he had heard nothing. All of them had been sitting in the same room. It was an interesting discrepancy, the kind that creates a reasonable doubt.

My final witness was to be a man named John Benner. Benner was the night doorman. He would have testified, as I explained to Judge Murtaugh at the bench prior to calling the witness, that at three o'clock in the morning of the killing, three men drove up in front of the building. One of them came to the door and said he wanted to see "James Goldberg." Benner rang apartment 11-F, but there was no answer. The man left, but not before Benner noticed that he had a heavily pockmarked face.

John Keenan objected to my calling Benner. He said the evidence was "too remote." In sustaining his objection, Judge Murtaugh stated that in his opinion the evidence didn't have "probative force."

And so we were ready for final argument.

Most of my summation was spent in dissecting the testimony of each one of the seven main witnesses against Phillips. There was room for reasonable doubt with each one. If they weren't lying, then they were rather sadly mistaken about the events of Christmastime, 1968. The one point that I really hammered home was before even one of the so-called eyewitnesses ever identified Bill Phillips, they had all spent hours being interviewed by the same man—Detective John Justy. And then several of them had considerable trouble picking out Phillips when they watched him through the one-way glass at the police station. The ring of truth just wasn't there.

I told the jury that the case against Billy Phillips was maliciously assembled, that I was sorry but I could not produce the real killer (we had subsequently learned that he was a loan shark, not a rival pimp, but we couldn't get supportive witnesses to come forward, and the government quite naturally showed no great interest in helping us to smoke them out or even to investigate the suspect), and I closed by saying to the jury, "Walk out with the knowledge, please, Mr. Foreman and gentlemen of the jury, that justice is walking with you, because if you do, walking behind you will be William Phillips."

John Keenan, faced with a tough job, delivered a classic final argument. He made the most of what he had. He stressed that each of the government's witnesses, in his opinion, was more than candid, some even to the point of admitting crimes (he didn't mention that most of the crimes were too old to prosecute.) As for the question of motive, he sidled neatly around it by saying that even though Phillips owed money it made no difference, because the government didn't have to prove motive. He painted Billy Phillips in colors so dark that he suggested to the jury that Phillips would have no compunction to go on television (as he had) and mention his dealings with a man he had killed.

It was a good job, but I think he lost some jurors with that last point.

All that was left when Keenan finished was for the judge to instruct the jury on the law, and for the jury to deliberate.

I had had trouble with Judge Murtaugh throughout the entire

case, from the standpoint of his rulings, which I felt were far too favorable to the government. But when it came time to charge the jury, he outdid himself.

In the twenty years that I have been associated with the law, I have never heard a charge so blatantly unfair to the defendant. I had more than a dozen objections, for the record, to the individual charges. I promptly asked for a mistrial based on the instructions. It was promptly denied.

The judge charged the jury that "in the administration of the law and in protecting the interests of society, it is very often necessary to resort to the testimony of those who live or have lived outside the law. It is necessary sometimes to descend into the gutter or sewer in the prosecution of crime. Very often it is necessary to bring creatures from the depths of depravity and put them on the witness stand and let the jury determine whether such witnesses are testifying truthfully. A witness of that kind does not stand on the same footing as a person of good character, but it isn't for the prosecution, whose business it is to prosecute crime, or for the court, whose business it is to uphold the law, to choose and select witnesses." (That was tantamount to saying, Don't be too worried about the unsavory character of some of the government's witnesses. It was almost a stamp of approval for their testimony.)

If that charge was biased, Judge Murtaugh's instruction that dealt with the defense witnesses was even worse. "You may also consider the testimony of the relatives and friends of the defendant. Was this testimony inconsistent with the defendant's having been at the scene of the crime at the time the shootings occurred? If so, did witnesses accurately recall the times of the events of December 24, 1968? Did they have an interest in testifying as they did; was their testimony influenced by love and affection for the defendant?" (In other words, don't discount the testimony of the hookers and their less-than-solid citizen customers, but be very careful about the testimony of Billy Phillips's aunt and uncle, and his wife!)

And Judge Murtaugh told the jury, "You may consider any criminal acts or immoral acts admittedly committed by the defendant. You may consider his general background in determining his credibility as a witness. You may consider his testimony that he has committed perjury on numerous occasions. Would you rely on his statement if they were statements made to you in our everyday affairs?" (It's hard to paraphrase that as meaning anything other than: "Can you believe *anything* this man has said?")

Finally, he gave an instruction that I was not even sure I was hearing. I have referred to it ever since as the "guilt-by-dirty-word instruction." Judge Murtaugh said, "You may consider the evidence as to the use by the defendant of a four-letter word beginning with the letter *f* or, in any event, the use of the plural or of the present participle of that word. In determining the credibility of the witnesses who testified that the defendant was in the house of ill repute operated by James Smith . . . on December 23rd and December 24, 1968, and who also testified to the use by the defendant of that four-letter word or its present participle in addressing James Smith . . . you may consider the evidence which is not disputed by the defendant that in the conversation recorded by the Knapp Commission . . . the defendant made use of this very four-letter word or the plural thereof or its present participle. I repeat, the admitted use of this objectionable four-letter word in the recorded conversation may be considered by you in determining the credibility of witnesses who testified that a man was in the house of ill repute on December 23 or December 24, 1968, and that the man made statements that included this four-letter word and who identified the man as the defendant Phillips." (Leonard Shecter, Billy's co-author, was stunned by this instruction, and later wrote, "My God, if we are going to identify and convict on that kind of language then we are all guilty.")

The jury left to begin its deliberations, and we went down the street to Ed Orenstein's office to have a drink and try to act civil while passing what had to be the most difficult, nonviolent moments in all of human existence.

Billy Phillips was not in a good mood. He couldn't stand the thought of food and passed up the tray of sandwiches that had been brought in. He drank his Scotch. And he waited.

We had left the courtroom at one o'clock. By the time the sun set, there was no word. Then, at ten minutes to ten that same night, we received word that the jury had asked for the testimony of Charles Gonsalez.

Many people think it is a bad sign when the jury asks to have testimony read back to it. I have never subscribed to that theory. I think it can mean that the jury is doubtful, and wants to be sure before it votes to acquit.

My theory was not the prevalent one. Almost everyone in the room was wearing a long face.

We heard nothing more from the jury until eleven the next morning. And still it wasn't a verdict. This time it wanted to hear my cross-examination of Gonzalez, plus all the testimony of Richie Stevens.

Shortly after lunch, one of the jurors had a heart attack. At least, that's what we were told at first. It turned out that she was suffering from indigestion. Nonetheless, she was off the panel for the moment.

According to New York court rules, the defense can ask for an automatic mistrial any time the number of jurors dips below twelve. Spirits rose. The worse thing we could get, it looked like, was a mistrial. And that's not bad when you're on trial for murder.

But it didn't make Billy Phillips happy. I could understand his feelings. He didn't want to have to go through another trial.

Because of my client's worry, and my own strong feeling that the jury was on our side, I asked that the sick juror be replaced by the second alternate juror (a student from Columbia). Not long after, the jury reported to Judge Murtaugh that it was deadlocked. (You never know which way, but we had little doubt that the great majority was for acquittal, and that one or two jurors were holding out for conviction.)

Murtaugh didn't want that kind of result. He sent the jury back for further deliberation. At half past three in the afternoon, the jury sent still another note. It said it was hopelessly deadlocked.

Now a curious shift took place. We, the defense, began to resist the idea of a mistrial. We were convinced that things were going in our favor, and that given enough time the jury would convince the holdouts (or holdout) and acquit. But the prosecution, in the reverse of the normal procedure, was urging the court to accept a mistrial. Judge Murtaugh sent the jury back for one more try.

More than seven hours later, at 10:30 P.M., the jury (that had been out more than a day) sent word it was unalterably hung. The jury wanted out. Finally, a few minutes later, the judge granted the jury's wish. He accepted the fact that it was deadlocked, thanked the jury, and discharged it.

Then Judge Murtaugh did something very strange—and in my opinion improper. He said to the jury that the case of the people v. William Phillips, Jr., would "be tried again." A judge should never say that, for there is no guarantee that a case that ends in a hung jury will ever be retried. There's a whole laundry list of reasons why it may never go to trial again. And it just isn't fair for the judge in the original trial to announce in open court that the defendant can expect a second tour through hell.

*　　*　　*

Either Judge Murtaugh was a fortune teller, or he knew something no one else knew. But he was right. In late fall of 1974—almost six years after the murders, and more than two years after the jury had almost acquitted Billy Phillips (We later learned that the vote for acquittal was either 10–2 or 11–1) the District Attorney's Office tried Phillips a second time.

From the summer of 1972 to the fall of 1974, Billy Phillips lived in a world of suspended animation. Still under government protection, and still being paid his salary by the New York City Police Department (at the request of the federal government), he continued to live, and sometimes work, under an assumed name in a city several hundred miles from New York. If he remembered his early religious training, he would have called it Limbo, the Catholic term for the place between Heaven and Hell.

I had promised Billy that if the government ever tried him again, which I had strong doubts about, I would defend him. But when the time came I had trials and troubles of my own (which will be explained later), and had to break that promise. I was very sorry not to be able to keep that commitment, for I believed that Phillips had been framed in the first place, and that he should never have been tried—not even once.

At my urging, Henry Rothblatt of New York, a justly famous criminal trial lawyer (and my co-author on a series of law books devoted to the practice of criminal law), agreed to defend Billy.

There were other changes in the cast. The D.A.'s Office was represented by one of John Keenan's assistants, Jack Litman, and the case was heard by Judge Harold Birns.

This time the trial ran for eight weeks, slightly longer than the first. Although the government called more witnesses, the case was essentially a rerun. Based on the reports I was getting from time to time from both Henry and Billy himself, it looked as if Phillips was finally going to get his "not guilty" verdict.

There was even a touch of the bizarre: toward the end of the case, and after he had again testified as the government's star witness, Charles Gonsalez was himself arrested. For impersonating a police officer. He had been picked up with a badge and a gun in a New York subway station. Unfortunately, the jury was of course not allowed to learn of this incident. It seemed to me almost symbolic of the government's case against Phillips.

On Thursday, November 21, 1974, Lynda and I were in Detroit, trying a long-delayed case that had predated Billy's. When we got back to the hotel, there was an urgent message to call Henry Roth-blatt. I got a sudden knotting feeling in my stomach.

When Henry answered the phone, I could tell by his voice that it was bad news. After deliberating for eleven hours—and once again calling for the testimony of Charles Gonsalez—the all-male jury had found Billy Phillips guilty of two counts of murder in the first degree.

I was stunned. Lynda immediately burst into tears.

What went wrong? What had happened? I had no clear idea, but I learned several interesting facts.

The jury returned its verdict of "guilty" at 3:57 P.M. At 4:00, officer William Phillips, Jr., was removed from the payroll of the New York City Police Department. As the defendant left the court-room, a cordon of twenty-five police officers arrived to escort him to jail. The "rogue cop" was getting the royal treatment—or the royal shaft.

I also learned from Henry Rothblatt that something most unusual had occurred on the day before the jury went out to decide Billy's fate. A juror who had been sitting for the entire eight weeks of the trial was removed. The reason: he had taken a plea in a marijuana case and was slated to be a prosecution witness against his former co-defendants.

A juror who has had prior contact with the government is supposed to reveal that fact before he is sworn in. This juror had not done so. The judge's remedy was to replace him at the eleventh hour. But what had his continued presence, and then his sudden unexplained absence, done to the rest of the jury? There was no way of knowing.

The worst part of it was that Henry Rothblatt learned that the prosecutor had known about the juror since late October—and had not seen fit to notify either the court or the defense.

It sounded to me as if Billy Phillips had been convicted by a jury that was at the least tainted—and at the worst poisoned.

The conviction will be appealed. Rothblatt announced that within seconds of the verdict. In the meantime Billy Phillips, the "turned" cop, is in jail, still hoping to be granted bail. If there is any other more dangerous situation for that man, I cannot imagine it. As Billy once said to me, "If I ever go to jail, every con in the place will want a piece of me."

Fortunately, no reporter bothered to seek out Xaviera Hollander in Canada, where she had set up her new shop, and ask her what she thought of the conviction. It was probably just as well. She and Billy had never gotten on, and she might have said something about "justice."

Billy Phillips was not a good man. No one ever suggested otherwise. The point was—did he commit murder? On that point, and that point alone, justice was never a factor.

On Friday, November 22, 1974, the *New York Daily News* ran a banner headline. In type easily two inches high, it screamed: PHIL-LIPS GUILTY IN 2 MURDERS. On page 8 a columnist devoted a paragraph to the atmosphere of the day before, the day Billy sweated out his fate. He ended his account with a comment that may have been far more accurate than even the writer realized. He wrote, "The Knapp Commission and its revelations were long ago. There were few spectators in court. Nobody seemed to care much whether Phillips would continue his waiting inside jail or out."

Callous? Certainly, but nonetheless pretty close to the truth. Nobody really wanted to hear about the corruption of the police department anyway. But the story had been told, and now Frank Serpico was far away and Billy Phillips was locked up. The only real losers were the people of New York, and Serpico, and Phillips.

Some people would say that because Billy had been a crooked cop, the murder conviction was actually a form of "rough justice," therefore what difference did it all make? To my way of thinking it made a hell of a lot of difference, for that just isn't the way our system works.

On Sunday night, November 24, I got a phone call from Billy. He was calling me from the jail. He said, "Lee, I just wondered if you're going to be able to help me get out of here."

I answered immediately, "Billy, you are one guy who does not belong in jail for murder. It may take a long time, but I'll do everything I can to get you out of there."

"Thanks, that's what I wanted to hear. Now I can go back to my cell and get a good night's rest."

No one ever said that Billy Phillips didn't have guts.

# Midwestern
# Gothic

L Y N D A looked up from the case file she was reading. She screwed up her face in revulsion, and said, "Lee, is there something unusual about the Midwest?"

"What do you mean?"

She put down the investigators' file on the murder case I was trying in Chicago. "This thing is so . . . sordid. In a way you'd expect it would have happened in some horrible part of a huge city, not out here in the middle of all this beautiful, clean country."

"What's that got to do with the rest of the Midwest?" I was waiting for someone to come on the line, and hadn't really given her question much thought.

"It seems to me that there have been so many brutal killings in this part of the country. There was the case that Truman Capote wrote about in Kansas, the . . ."

"Clutter," I said.

". . . family. And the man in Chicago who killed all those student nurses a few years ago. And your own cases, like the murder of Sam Sheppard's wife. And the one you just tried in Kansas City. Oh, cor, I could go on and on."

She was right. I hadn't really thought about it before, but the heartland had its own brand of grisly violence. In her present mood I didn't want to tell Lynda, but I remembered reading about a Wisconsin murder case in the early fifties. A number of women had disappeared in a quiet, rural area upstate, and the trail finally led to a lonely farmer by the name of Ed Gein. When they searched his farm they found the makeshift graves of eighteen women. And when they searched his farmhouse, they were horrified. Ed Gein had chair seats and lampshades made of his victim's skin. Among the more bizarre facts that were actually printed was the account of the wash-line of human breasts he had strung across the living room.

We didn't pursue the subject, but as usual Lynda had made a very cogent observation. Sometimes it takes someone from the outside to show us facts we'd rather not see.

Certainly the two cases I'd been working on in the Midwest were far from ordinary.


For years I have been lecturing about the power of an indictment to harm, and to harm not just once but repeatedly. For some incredible reason, many otherwise intelligent citizens believe that if the indictment does not end in trial and conviction, then the defendant has not been harmed. Perhaps that is what they learned in their sixth-grade civics class; if so, it wasn't true then and certainly isn't true now. I have scores of cases in my files to prove that the simple fact of being indicted guarantees at least some harm and damage—and in most cases a great deal.

There are hundreds of people in this country right now who learned the hard way what happens when you are named in an indictment and charged with a crime you did not commit. Too many of these people have been called into the boss's office and told, in oily tones of mock sympathy, that "under the circumstances" and "for the good of the company" there is no longer a job for them.

That's one part of it. Another part is the wife or husband or friend or relative who breaks under the pressure of the inevitable publicity—and such "breaks" are rarely repaired. The damage of a wrongful indictment is like a fire in a closed room; eventually it touches everything. To some degree, everything (and everyone) gets burned.

Finally, of course, there is the part played by the skeptic, the person who invariably says, "Well, he got off. But you can't tell me there wasn't *something* to it. The government [or the state or the district attorney] doesn't indict a person unless they've got something on him." The less said about such people the better, except to note the unfortunate fact that they greatly outnumber those who feel the end of the case is the end of the matter.

All of this leads to a point about the two cases that make up this chapter. The first case is that of Tom Cochran, a Missouri business-man who heads an interstate company that provides a variety of industrial products and services. Along with a business associate, Tom Cochran and his company were charged with hiring two thugs to blow up a truck owned by a competitor.

The second case is that of Silas Jayne, a seemingly larger-than-life figure who was tried for conspiring to murder his own brother.

Each case contains more than enough odd and unusual elements to justify the use of the word "gothic," which means, among other things, "emphasizing the grotesque." But there is a central difference in the treatment of the two cases. In the Jayne case, the second case, everything is told as it actually happened; in the Cochran case, the names of the two individual defendants and the name and nature of the corporate defendant have been changed.

"Tom Cochran" is not my client's name. People who followed, or were part of, the case, will identify him readily enough, but there is no need to publicize further the real name of the man who lived through the gross indignities of this trial.

The story, however, needs to be told because it illustrates most dramatically the problem of overzealous prosecution. What happened to "Tom Cochran" shouldn't happen to any American citizen. But it did. And that's the point.

As for Silas Jayne, his story needed to be told, too. It would have been wrong to change his name, as the reader will find out.

According to all the accepted values, Thomas Cochran had it made. By the age of forty he had accomplished a great deal. The Cochran Company, which he had built from nothing, was one of the largest in the Midwest.

A pleasant, outgoing man who knew what he wanted, Cochran had married an attractive woman who had given him several equally attractive children. The years of back-breaking work that had gone into the founding and growth of the Cochran Company had returned dividends. There was not much in the way of material goods that Cochran did not have, or could not buy if he felt like it. All in all, Thomas Cochran was a satisfied man, and although he continued to work as if there weren't enough hours in the day, he was a happy man.

There had been some rumbling about the possibility of an antitrust investigation because of the swiftness of his company's rise, but Cochran wasn't particularly worried about that. Most self-made businessmen have their detractors.

Then, in February of 1969, it all turned sour. What must have looked like a perfect life to so many people in the small town of

Lebanon, Missouri, suddenly and without warning turned into a perfect nightmare.

It wasn't even light when State Trooper Thomas Davis began to patrol the outskirts of Ava, Missouri, one snowy morning in late February 1969. The trooper had received a call about two men who had been seen walking on private property, and when he noticed two strange men in a late-model sedan, he pulled them over.

Seeing that the occupants were two very tough-looking customers, he wished he had a search warrant, for their behavior bothered him —and after a few questions he was even more bothered. Then he noticed a familiar object protruding from under the driver's seat. It was the handle of a pistol.

That was all the "probable cause" he needed. He ordered the men out of the car and searched it. In the trunk he found two more guns, plus ten sticks of dynamite made up into a bomb.

The men, placed under arrest, denied any knowledge of the bomb. Their story was most unusual. They had been hired, they said, to blow up a large truck that belonged to a man named Hamilton, a man who had recently left Cochran to form his own supply company. According to the informant, who had a long arrest and prison record, a man named Jones had hired them over the telephone to discourage the competition by eliminating the costly new truck.

The more colorful of the two men was a gangly forty-two-year-old named Alfred Earl Harflinger. He had an extensive criminal record. His companion was a younger man named James Nash.

Both men were tried for possession of the bomb, convicted, and sentenced to ten years in jail. (Nash died in prison a short time later, of natural causes.)

Some months later the grand jury handed down another indictment. Apparently based at least in part on the testimony of Harflinger, it charged Harold Jones, Thomas R. Cochran, and The Cochran Company with various crimes, ranging from antitrust law violations to a conspiracy to violate the federal firearms act by scheming to blow up the truck.

Harold Jones ran an industrial security business that did work for Cochran. According to the indictment, Jones hired the two thugs to blow up the truck, but the man who really pulled the strings was Tom Cochran.

In most of the infamous midwestern cases, the crime was brutal and horrifying, the kind of crime that struck fear in the hearts of

all those who heard about it. But in the Cochran case there had been
no actual crime of violence committed. The bumbling ex-convicts
who were allegedly hired to bomb the truck, and who had in truth
been scouting the area for weeks, could not find the vehicle when it
came time to perform. Then, to top it off, they were caught with the
bomb in their car for nothing more overt than "looking suspicious—"
or, simply, for being from out of town.

Nonetheless, the Cochran case turned out to have its own brand
of gothic weirdness for one reason: it turned on the testimony of
Alfred Earl Harflinger, a man who was a walking argument for his
parents' sterilization.

Immediately after the indictment, Cochran contacted O. J. Taylor,
a corporate lawyer from Springfield, Missouri, who had handled a
number of his legal matters in the past. Ironically, everyone's first
concern was the antitrust charge, so Cochran added another corporate lawyer. His name was Earl Jinkinson, and he was a distinguished
older lawyer who was a partner in a large corporate law firm in
Chicago. Earl Jinkinson looked as if he had been sent over by Central Casting to play the judge. He was tall, trim, silver-haired, and
had a voice to match his impressive demeanor. For years he had been
a high-ranking government trial lawyer with the antitrust section of
the Justice Department, and he was more than well experienced in
that branch of the law.

I never learned whether it was O. J. Taylor, Earl Jinkinson, or
even Tom Cochran himself who finally realized that the bomb charge
was more of a problem than everyone had thought when the indictment came down. Whoever it was, someone finally suggested that
they needed the services of an experienced criminal lawyer.

I got a call from Mr. Taylor, who asked if they could come to my
Boston office and discuss the possibility of my representing Mr.
Cochran. When I learned that Cochran had a company plane at his
disposal, I suggested that they come to my home in Marshfield instead, as it would be a lot simpler than flying into Logan Interna-
tional Airport.

On a bitter cold day in late January 1973, Thomas Cochran, O. J.
Taylor, and I sat in the office in my home and they told me about
the case. I had to nod my agreement when Mr. Taylor said, "Perhaps the conspiracy-to-bomb charge should be given at least as much
weight as the antitrust charge." We talked for several hours, and they
left to fly back to Missouri.

After they left, I called the office in Boston and talked to both my partners, Colin Gillis and Gerry Alch, about a number of pending cases. Then I asked Gerry to put John Truman on the line.

Ever since I had hired John Truman and Mark Kadish, the exceptional young lawyers who had been Ernie Medina's Army defense lawyers, they had both been working all but nonstop. Kadish had been to court with me on several cases, but thus far Truman had been stuck in the library, researching and writing briefs.

"John, how would you like to go home?"

Truman had no way of knowing what I was talking about, so all he could say was, "Huh?"

"Don't worry. You aren't getting canned. I've just been asked to defend a criminal case in federal court in Kansas City, Missouri. I thought maybe you'd like to come along and carry the briefcase."

I knew exactly what was going through his mind. Neither John nor his wife Laura had been home much since he'd come to work for me, and the Missouri natives have a strong affection for their part of the country.

Finally, Truman found his voice, "You know, don't you, that my father was . . ."

"Yes. I know."

". . . the clerk of that same court. Oh shit, I'd love to go. And Laura could see her folks, and . . . well, damn, yes. Of course."

Never having had a huge law firm—the number of lawyers in mine has never exceeded a dozen—I can't say from personal experience why they do it, but too many of the big firms have the horrible policy of hiring bright, promising young lawyers and then forgetting about them. They wait for them to claw their way up the ladder. I asked John Truman to come on the Cochran case because he needed the courtroom experience, and because I knew I would get an excellent performance from him. And to be candid, I knew it wouldn't hurt to go into Missouri with the grandnephew of Harry S Truman.

Nonetheless, I would not have assigned him to the case unless I was convinced he could handle it. Even if he had been the trial judge's son. There was no doubt in my mind that John Truman could handle it. I had seen what he had done in defense of Captain Ernest L. Medina.

I accepted the case in early February. Truman and I made several trips to Kansas City (Missouri, not Kansas) and found to our great delight that the case had been assigned to Judge John W. Oliver. Still in his early fifties, Judge Oliver had a reputation for across-the-board fairness. In addition, he was one of the most scholarly judges I'd ever run across.

The pretrial phase took a long time, almost a month, but I soon learned that it was worth every minute. Judge Oliver had an obvious concern over the legal rights of the defendant. You didn't have to try and "educate" this judge, which is a term that defense lawyers often use. If there was a legitimate problem, be it on evidence or the protection of witnesses or whatever, he grasped the meaning right away.

The minute I met Judge Oliver I knew it was going to be an enjoyable experience to defend Tom Cochran. Oliver was as different from Judge Murtaugh (Billy Phillips's judge) as a man could be.

Toward the end of the pretrial period, there had probably been hundreds of hours of lawyers' meetings. As it was originally laid out, I had the responsibility of the bomb charge, and the other lawyers would concern themselves with everything else. (Defendant Harold Jones was represented by Harry Claiborne, a well-known criminal lawyer from Las Vegas.) But we soon came to see that the antitrust charge was like an albatross (rather than the other way around, as had been the original point of view). I suggested that we go to the judge with our theory of the case, and try to make it official.

We asked Judge Oliver to split the indictment, try the bomb charge first, and then (depending on the outcome) take care of the antitrust element of the charge later.

He agreed to do so, commenting that it would be the most "judicious" way to proceed.

What this meant was that, if the government could prove that Cochran was behind the bomb plot, then, obviously, he was the kind of man who might well violate the antitrust laws. If not, why blow your competition away?

The government fought us tooth and nail to keep the original charges together. And well it should have, for the prosecutors had a real problem—they only had one important witness.

Originally, there were two mad bombers, Alfred Harflinger and James Nash. But Nash, after being convicted and sentenced to a ten-year term for possession of a bomb, went to jail and died. There was nothing sinister about it. He was only forty years old, but he simply died.

That left the government with only one of the hired bombers, and on his shoulders rested the government's case. If the jury believed Earl Harflinger, Cochran and Jones would go to jail. If it didn't, they would be free men—to the extent that they had been found not guilty of the bomb plot. There would still be the antitrust element, unless the judge felt that the two were intertwined, which was our fond hope.

The government's problem was that Earl Harflinger would come to the witness chair direct from the state prison. His entire history would be brought into issue on the simple question of whether or not he was a credible witness.

That was hardly a new problem for the prosecutors. The government often uses, has to use, known criminals as witnesses for the simple reason that they were *there*. And so the prosecution had to go ahead, had to reply on the witness Harflinger.

The chief prosecutor was a government lawyer by the name of Thomas Howard. As luck would have it, he had been hired into the government, years ago, by one of the men who sat across from him, one of the defense team—Earl Jinkinson. It wasn't a good break for Howard.

I almost felt sorry for Tom Howard. He wasn't a local government man, from the U.S. Attorney's Office, given a chance to shine by prosecuting a notorious case; he was a Justice Department specialist from Washington, one of the main trial lawyers in the antitrust section. He was experienced in that distinct and special field of law. But here he was, stuck with prosecuting a grisly bomb-for-hire case. And if that wasn't bad enough, his whole case rested on one of the least credible witnesses ever to take the stand in a federal court.

The trial began in March of 1973. Harflinger was not the first witness. He was the "biggie," so they were saving him for later.

The first witness of any consequence was the man who owned the new truck that had escaped an explosive end. His name was Arthur Hamilton. Mr. Hamilton had worked, for a number of years, for a company that had been bought out by Cochran. He testified that he had been hired by Cochran, even given a raise, but that eventually there was a falling out. He said that on January 3, 1973, he "threw my keys on the desk and quit."

He then started his own company, in direct—though on a very small scale—competition with the Cochran Company. I had information to indicate that Mr. Hamilton had walked off with a customer list, but his contention was that he had merely contacted the customers he used to deal with when he worked for the company that Cochran took over. I couldn't shake his story on cross-examination.

I didn't spend too much time with Hamilton. I wanted the jury to cogitate about the likelihood of Thomas Cochran, who owned a fleet of trucks that serviced twenty states, hiring two thugs to dynamite a one-truck competitor. Admittedly, Hamilton had taken some local Missouri customers away from Cochran. But would an elephant put out a contract on a flea?

And then the government called Alfred Earl Harflinger. He took the stand on Monday, March 19, and under direct examination by Howard, told this story:

One day during the week prior to February 22, 1969, Harflinger and Nash went to Harold Jones's office in Saint Louis, where they discussed the "job." Harflinger said that Jones told them he wanted to have Hamilton's new truck blown up, but that he was actually acting for someone else. Jones wanted the job done on the weekend of the twenty-second, and how much would it cost? A thousand dollars apiece, said Harflinger—one for him, and one for his friend Nash.

Jones quibbled, according to Harflinger, and it was finally agreed that the two men would do the dynamiting for five hundred dollars each—five hundred "up front," and five hundred on completion.

Harflinger testified that a couple of days later he and Nash drove down to Ava to look for the truck. They checked out Hamilton's farm, but the truck wasn't there. So they drove into town, where, as luck would have it, they saw the truck. (Harflinger said he knew it was the right truck because it had the name "Hamilton" painted on its side!)

Then they went back to St. Louis and told Jones they had seen the truck. Everything was ready.

Howard was properly polite with the lanky Harflinger. He asked him to "please describe what happened next." Harflinger testified that on Friday night, February 21, he drove to a crossroads near Rolla, Missouri, and met Nash. There they made the ten sticks of dynamite into a bomb, and though it was snowing terribly hard, they drove on to Ava in search of Arthur Hamilton's doomed truck.

Again, he said, they couldn't find it. They even got out and tramped around Hamilton's farm. Remembering where they had found the truck the last time, they drove into Ava.

They cruised the roads around Ava for quite some time, but they never spotted the truck. So, Harflinger said, he called Jones and asked him if perhaps there was something else he wanted them to blow up. According to Harflinger, Jones told him to call back later.

That he did, but by then the picture had changed considerably. By 7:30 A.M. Harflinger and Nash were in jail and under arrest, having had their meeting with Trooper Davis. Harflinger testified that he called Jones from the jail, and that Jones told him to "sit tight," that he would see everything was taken care of. Neither Harflinger nor Nash ever heard from Mr. Jones again.

I asked Judge Oliver if I could begin my cross-examination the next morning, and he agreed. I wanted a full night to mull over, with John Truman and investigator Andy Tuney, the best way to use the wealth of information we had uncovered on Mr. Harflinger.

It was a long night, and the glasses were filled and emptied quite a few times, for there was a lot of ground to cover. Andy Tuney, the former Massachusetts state detective lieutenant who has been working with me since we bumped into each other—on opposite sides of the fence—in the Boston Strangler case, had been out beating the bushes. He'd learned that investigating Alfred Earl Harflinger was like touring the Aegean stables—the "dirt" was everywhere.

One of the most startling bits of information that Andy picked up was that Harflinger was facing the strong possibility of being indicted for murder. Not just one murder, either. It looked as if he could be charged with three killings. (Two stemmed from a housebreaking in Mount Vernon, Illinois, and the third was the result of an argument in a bar.)

What made all this so important was not merely the effect it might have on his credibility, but it indicated that Harflinger had been dealing with the prosecution, literally stringing them along so he could get immunity for these crimes in exchange for his testimony against Cochran and Jones. The government was willing to grant him immunity—that's done all the time and is perfectly legal—but Harflinger had "immunity" mixed up with "amnesty." And the latter was what he wanted. He wanted to get off scot free.

Tom Howard may have been frustrated, but he wasn't dishonest. In all of his discussions with his witness, he always stressed that he could promise no deals, other than the standard immunity (which meant that nothing Harflinger said on the stand in this case could be used against him in any case or prosecution). But Harflinger wasn't satisfied. He was still holding the government off when the trial began. He even refused to testify, but when Judge Oliver carefully spelled out the protection that the grant of immunity carried, and put on a little judicial pressure, Harflinger agreed to testify.

We knew about his unreasonable attempts to all-but-blackmail the government into granting him freedom in exchange for his testimony. And I could hardly wait to bring it out in front of the jury. We also knew, from uncontestable records and transcripts, that Harflinger had committed perjury both in court and before a grand jury. When you looked at his record hard and long enough, there was hardly a crime that the government's star witness had not committed.

Harflinger had, in fact, conned the U.S. Attorney something beautiful. Tom Howard had very little experience with "red hots," Judge Oliver's term for experienced criminal witnesses like Harflinger. The witness had no real interest in getting Tom Cochran; he was interested in getting a new trial for himself, plus immunity for a string of violent crimes all the way up to murder, that he had committed. He was trying to get the U.S. Attorney to give him immunity—which the witness thought was amnesty, and which would give him full and complete coverage for all of his past sins, known or unknown. Harflinger was very much afraid that one or more of these crimes would catch up with him, that he would be prosecuted, and that this time it would be the Big House for sure. And once back in, his terrible record would ensure that it was for keeps.

Unfortunately for Harflinger, the point of use immunity is that you are only protected for that which you disclose. And if you don't disclose, you don't have any protection. He wanted amnesty, but no matter what he thought, that wasn't what he got from the prosecutor.

The government had still another problem with Harflinger. The witness got the chief prosecutor to draw up a waiver of the attorney-client privilege (between Harflinger and a man who had represented him prior to his trial) that stated Harflinger could withdraw it at any time he (Harflinger) wanted to. Unfortunately, Mr. Howard, with his extensive background in antitrust legislation did not see what the pen-smart convict was doing to him.

When I pointed out to the judge that the government had been thoroughly sucked in, that we were talking about all kinds of murders and other heinous crimes that completely overshadowed the crime with which Cochran was charged—conspiracy to possess a bomb—and the problem of the conditional waiver, it touched off a tremendous argument. There were three or four days of discussion.

Harflinger, meanwhile, whom the judge had ruled would have to be reimmunized before he could be forced to testify in front of the jury, was balking. He said, "I'm not going to testify, no matter if the judge gives me immunity or not." And what could the judge do to him? He was already serving a ten-year sentence. The worst the judge could do was hold him in contempt and order him to jail. Not much of a penalty.

Poor Tom Howard just didn't have enough experience with red-hots. He couldn't communicate with Harflinger. Finally, Judge Oliver ruled that a conditional waiver of the attorney-client privilege was a nonentity in the law, and a waiver is a waiver, and once given it couldn't be retracted. Therefore, Tom Howard's document wasn't worth the powder to blow it to hell.

I protested when it was suggested that the Justice Department grant new immunity, which could only be done at the request of somebody as high as Henry Petersen, because I felt that this would degrade the American system of justice by putting a murderer on the streets, absolutely protected, now that the government knew about the murders.

I said, "If you immunize him now, I'm going to make him admit the murders on the stand, and that will protect him from ever being prosecuted. So you're putting a killer on the streets to try and get a businessman for a conspiracy to possess a bomb." Henry Petersen's answer was, "Well, I didn't know those facts when I signed the original immunity thing, but I'm committed to it now. There's no turning back. Harflinger gets immunity."

Harflinger decided to take the immunity.

After the trial began, but before Harflinger took the stand, I received a confidential document that verified what I had felt about Thomas Cochran from the very beginning. The document was entitled, "Report of Polygraph Examination." It read:

At the request of Mr. F. Lee Bailey, Esq., attorney for Mr. Thomas R. Cochran, a truth verification examination (polygraph test) was extended to Thomas R. Cochran (42) on March 9, 1973, at the Hilton Inn Hotel, Kansas City, Missouri.

The purpose of the examination was to determine whether or not the detection of deception technique could support, corroborate and/or substantiate Mr. Cochran's statements when he denied having willfully caused anyone, in February 1969, to possess and/or transport dynamite anywhere.

Transcript (Marlin, Beck, etc.) and other sundry pertinent

facts and features were made available to the undersigned examiner.

No restrictions in the scope of questioning were imposed either by Mr. Bailey or Mr. Cochran.

CONCLUSIONS:

It is the considered opinion of the undersigned examiner that, based on the reactionary patterns exhibited, Mr. Cochran's statements, asserting that he did not, in February 1969, willfully cause anyone to possess and/or transport dynamite anywhere, can be supported, corroborated and substantiated as having been made in candor.

P.S.   A total of five (5) examinations were the basis of this:
Two (2) Reid Technique
Two (2) Backster Technique
One (1) Controll-Examination
A Keeler Polygraph Model 6388M2 was used during the examination.

> [signed]
> Charles H. Zimmerman
> Chief Examiner
> Scientific Security
> 80 Boylston Street
> Boston, Mass. 02116

As I have said so many times before, innocence never *guarantees* that a defendant will be acquitted, but it always helps to have a successful polygraph test in the back pocket. I had no hope of its being allowed into evidence, but it made me all that much more eager to go after the government's chief witness.

Alfred Earl Harflinger took the stand at nine-thirty in the morning. It was Tuesday, March 20, 1973. Thirty-seven months had elapsed since the time of the alleged bomb plot.

Harflinger had the usual prison pallor, but he has nonetheless a prepossessing sight. He was large, aggressive, and shrewd, like a nasty Ichabod Crane. No one in his right mind would have wanted to meet him in an alley, dark or light.

I wanted the jury to get the message right away that they were listening to a witness who was used to lying under oath. We knew that he had lied at his own trial, so I began with a line of questions to draw out that admission.

Q. Mr. Harflinger, you have told us that when you came on for trial in the bomb possession case, that you attempted to win it by telling the jury that you weren't guilty, right?

A. Yes, sir.

Q. But prior to that time you tried to win it completely legitimately, did you not, on a search and seizure question? [He lost on that issue and later, in prison, wrote an appeal brief on the same issue.]

A. Yes, sir. . . .

Q. . . . when you took the oath [in his own trial], you took it knowing that you were going to lie, right?

A. I did.

Q. And you were looking at an American jury empaneled with the power to find guilt or innocence in the hope that you would deceive them so that you could go free, right?

A. Yes, sir.

Q. And then when you wrote this rather elaborate brief for the United States Court of Appeals of the Eighth Circuit, in an effort to have your conviction overturned, you repeated the same false statements, did you not?

A. I did.

Q. Okay, and the reason that you lied before the jury and the reason you lied to the Eighth Circuit was to get out of jail, correct?

A. That is true.

What I was bringing out was no great shock to the jury. Yesterday, it had heard Harflinger being cross-examined by Harold Jones's lawyer, Mr. Claiborne. But I wasn't just covering the same ground. Harry Claiborne had, as agreed, peeled back the first few layers. I was going after the rest of the onion.

Q. As Mr. Claiborne said yesterday, there is hardly a con in the pen that doesn't want to hit the street, true?

A. There are very few.

Q. And if there are any that don't want to hit the street, you are not one of them?

A. I am not.

Q. You would like to get out tomorrow, right?

A. Yes, sir.

Q. And if you can accomplish it, you would get out very shortly, won't you, if you can accomplish it?

A. If it is possible, I will do everything within my power.

Q. I am sure that you will. Now, Mr. Harflinger, is it fair to say that when you lied to the jury in your own case, that you didn't really lose much sleep about the whole business, it didn't keep you awake at night, the fact that you had committed perjury, did it?

A. No, sir.

Q. Have you not in the course of your adult lifetime lied whenever necessary to protect yourself from any kind of harm, including imprisonment?

A. No, sir.

Q. Do you mean that you are an honest thief?

A. I don't know any honest thieves.

Q. And you certainly don't know of yourself as an honest thief, do you, Mr. Harflinger?

A. I wouldn't classify myself as such.

Q. No. Well, in order to be in the business of living beyond the law, it is frequently necessary to lie, in order to stay on the street, isn't it?

A. Probably, yes, sir.

Q. Well, of course, when you use the name Jim Burnett, that is a lie, isn't it?

A. Yes.

Q. When you sign up for a Gulf Credit Card, you don't say, "I've got a string of felony convictions that would croak that," you don't tell them that, do you?

A. No, sir.

Q. Because if you did, you would never get the credit card.

A. Right.

Q. And so you practice fraud and deceit whenever you have to, right?

A. That is true.

Q. Now, Mr. Harflinger, you understand that the agonizing question that may be dumped in your jury's lap is whether or not to believe you, right?

A. Right.

Q. It can be and will be, in all probability, extremely important to them to decide whether or not today in this courtroom you have spoken the truth. You understand that?

A. Yes, sir.

Q. Now, I think we have established that at the time of your own trial you lied as necessary for your own well-being, true?

A. Yes, sir.

I was hammering home the point of his earlier perjury because I was sure that Harflinger would say, as he finally did, that all those other times were different—*this* time he was telling the truth. And it was certainly within the realm of possibility that he was being truthful. The way the law works, when two sides are in total conflict, and there is no outside party or mechanism to verify one over the other, the jury has to decide which one to believe.

I had no doubt that Harflinger was lying, but I wanted the jury to get such a full picture of this career criminal that it couldn't even *imagine* believing him.

As I'd expected, Harflinger testified that "yes," he had lied at his own trial, but now he was going to tell the truth, and "let the chips fall where they may." (I thought that a rather specious answer, since Harflinger had nothing to lose.)

And as he later admitted, he had something to gain when it came time for the parole board to hear his petition for early release. I looked at the jury, and I could swear that two of the jurors winked at me.

The day before, the jury had finally heard about Harflinger's famous immunity (or "amnesty") for other crimes he'd committed, but it didn't know what those crimes were. I set out to fill that gap in the jury's knowledge.

I wanted to show that contrary to his testimony Alfred Earl Harflinger was trying to cut a very special deal for himself, and that he needed desperately to do so because he had a lot to hide.

I asked the witness if the crimes for which he was seeking immunity were more serious than the one he was presently imprisoned for, that of possessing a bomb. He fenced with me a bit, so I put it to him directly. "Now, Mr. Harflinger, do you know whether or not you are accused of murder?"

Again he fenced. He said that he knew his "name was on a warrant," but he didn't know if that meant he was accused. Quickly he realized that wouldn't wash, so he said, "It's an accusation, but it's not—doesn't mean that I did do or I didn't do it."

Considering the leeway that Judge Oliver had been giving me, I decided to put it as plainly as I could. "Let's solve that. You tell this jury—" and I pointed to the jury box—"did you do that murder?"

Howard was out of his seat instantly with an objection. Within seconds the judge had us at the bench, where he decided that the best course was to hash things out in the absence of the jury.

We spent the better part of two hours in chambers. But it turned out to be quite productive for the defense. At that point in the trial, I knew that Harflinger was accused of one murder and under investigation in relation to another.

As we walked into the judge's chambers, one of the prosecutors handed one of the defense lawyers several pieces of paper. He kept one and passed a single page to each of the rest of us, thinking they were copies of the murder indictment. Suddenly, after we had been arguing the law for quite a while, it dawned on all of us that what we had been given was not four copies of one indictment, but four separate indictments. Each one was a formal charge by the state of Illinois against Alfred Earl Harflinger.

One was for murder. Another was for attempted murder. The third was for burglary, and the last was for robbery. It was quite a little surprise package.

But if we were surprised, the judge was shocked. Under his ruling, the prosecution had been ordered—once trial began—to share numerous documents with the defense. Lawyers call such documents "Brady material," after the name of the Supreme Court case that ordered the sharing. (Prior to that decision, defense lawyers often had to wait until a government witness took the stand before they were given any information from the government's files. This meant there was not time to really study the documents or to conduct a meaningful investigation based on their contents. For decades this practice had worked a hardship on criminal defendants.) It really bothered Judge Oliver that we had been kept in the dark so long.

That set the judge's temper on edge, and the one who felt the cutting most was Thomas Howard, the chief prosecutor. Howard and Oliver had not gotten on well from the outset, but the session on the twenty-ninth was most difficult for Mr. Howard. To make matters worse, kindly "Judge" Earl Jinkinson, to whom Howard deferred simply because of the former's age had developed the habit of snorting at the prosecutor, "Damn it, Tom, if I'd known you were so stupid, I'd never have hired you in the first place."

Howard took a real pasting from the judge, and when we reconvened, at 11:36 A.M., I was allowed to ask Harflinger almost the exact question I had framed. Judge Oliver had overruled Howard's objection, but I was limited by the fact that at the time I had asked the witness about, the state charges had not been drawn up. Still, it was a sweet victory for the defense. I was at the heart of the onion.

The courtroom was absolutely packed when we got back in. Word had spread that the witness was being questioned about a *murder,*

and that he might actually confess to it on the stand. Courtroom
buffs know the meaning of such legal terms as "immunity," but the
general run of spectator does not. I would imagine the word passed
rather swiftly that a very unusual scene was about to unfold.

Q. All right, Mr. Harflinger, what I am trying to learn is
whether or not as you stood before Chief Judge Becker and
heard immunity granted, which you interpreted to be amnesty,
you had in mind some specific crimes for which you thought
you might be prosecuted. Were you thinking then of some specfic
crimes that you thought might be charged against you when you
heard the immunity granted?

A. Not any specific charge, Mr. Bailey.

Q. I don't mean charges. I mean were you thinking of some
things that you had done before going to prison and after your
trial that worried you?

A. Yes, sir.

Q. And were you hopeful that the action of Judge Becker on
the motion of Mr. Howard would protect you from prosecution
for those crimes?

A. I was.

Q. All right. Now I will ask you whether or not one of the
things that was in your mind when you got the immunity that
you thought was amnesty was an incident that took place on
October 10, 1971, in Jefferson County, Illinois.

A. I imagine. I don't know the date, but that is probably
right.

Q. Was it an incident that involved a man named Allen?

A. I don't know any names.

Q. Was it an incident that involved the breaking into a house?

A. Yes, sir.

Q. At 766 Fairfield Road?

A. I don't know the address, sir.

Q. All right. But were you remembering, when you were
thinking about the amnesty, that in October of 1971 you had
broken into a man's house?

A. Yes, sir.

Q. That while in the house you had taken a .38 caliber
weapon and attempted to rob some of the people in it?

A. Yes, sir.

Q. That you had shot and killed one of the occupants of that
house.

A. Not an occupant of that house, sir.

Q. Well, who was it that you shot and killed? Tell the jury.

There was absolute and total silence in the courtroom. But Harflinger didn't even pause.

A. It was a person that wasn't in the house. When I was leaving, when I was crawling the fence, a man jumped at me and I turned around and shot him.

Q. And you killed him?

A. I don't know that I killed him. He was running when I was crawling away.

Q. But I am talking about what you knew on March 10. You read in the newspaper that he died, didn't you?

A. I did.

Q. And you believed that, didn't you?

A. I did.

Q. So you knew that you could be prosecuted for a murder you had committed, correct?

A. Yes, sir.

Q. All right, and while in the house, with that same pistol you shot another man, didn't you?

A. I did.

Q. Why did you shoot him?

A. He was running toward the door and screaming, yelling.

Q. Was he an occupant of that house?

A. He was.

Q. Now, Mr. Harflinger, as you got the immunity that you thought was amnesty, you also were mindful of an incident that occurred in the Sportsman's Lounge in Alton, Illinois, were you not?

MR. HOWARD: I object, Your Honor.

THE COURT: The objection will be overruled for the grounds stated in chambers.

We had learned of the incident at the Sportsman's Lounge through Andy Tuney's digging and certain courtroom gossip. The story we were told was that Harflinger faced the possibility of still another murder charge.

The Sportsman's Lounge in Alton, Illinois, is probably just like tens of thousands of other bar-restaurants in the Midwest, or anywhere else in the country for that matter. Unlike the great majority of gin mills, however, it was the scene of a murder.

One night in January of 1971, while Alfred Harflinger was still out on bond (his conviction in the bomb case was being appealed), he and a group of friends showed up at the Sportsman's Lounge. The lady who ran the bar was about to close, and had just told the patrons that she would serve no more drinks. Then Harflinger and his party arrived.

Apparently she knew them, for she promptly served them the drinks they ordered. Seeing this, one of the more thirsty patrons walked up to the bar and complained. He, too, wanted a drink, and who did these latecomers think they were, and all of that.

Soon it was a hot argument. It began with some name calling, and it ended when one of the men at the bar pulled out a gun and shot the complaining customer.

According to our information, the man who did the shooting was Alfred Earl Harflinger. However, the investigation was still open because the police in Alton wanted to arrange a lineup to see if one of the witnesses could identify Harflinger, and they had to wait until we had concluded the Jones-Cochran trial.

That was not the way Harflinger told the story on the stand. He said that "the other guy did it." According to Harflinger, the angry patron had walked behind the bar, started to argue, and then grabbed a beer bottle. He hit Harflinger with the bottle, and "one of the two other people that was with me shot the man."

"Five times?" I asked him.

"No, sir."

"How many times?"

"Shot him once there and then went over and shot him again in the leg. Shot him twice."

"I see. Well now, Mr. Harflinger, did you feel that the gentlemen with you was shooting Mr. Lafferty because he was defending you from an attack?"

"I don't really know why he shot him. I just know that he did shoot him."

"Did you report the matter to the police?"

"I did not."

By this point in the testimony, the jury appeared to be slipping into a state of dazed fascination. Some of them looked openly incredulous, but you couldn't have dragged them from their seats if the room had been on fire.

I left the details of the shooting for possible later questioning, and I asked Harflinger if the Sportsman's Lounge incident had been in his mind when he refused to testify unless he received immunity. He agreed that it was, and then he admitted that he had not even told his court-appointed lawyer, much less the prosecutors, about the matter.

"Because you kind of thought, 'Well, gee, if I tell him the price of my testimony is a couple of shootings, of murders, they might not give me immunity.' Didn't that thought pass through your mind?"

"It did."

I wanted the jury to understand exactly the quality of the man they were listening to, a man whose credibility was essential to their deliberations. I made the point that Harflinger had been very selective in what he told his own lawyer, and finally I put it to him bluntly: "Did you tell him that what you wanted was to get away with murder?"

"No, sir."

"All right, and that is precisely what you want today, isn't it, to get away with the murder of Mr. Allen?"

"Yes, sir."

"Yes, and your testimony here today, you hope, will help you get away with murder, correct?"

"That is true."

The reporters in the press section were scribbling madly, spectators were murmuring, and most jurors looked at the witness as if the terrible meaning of his words was momentarily incomprehensible. It is one thing to read such testimony in the newspaper, but it is quite another for decent human beings to hear a flesh-and-blood admission of murder described so offhandedly as the motive for concealing information.

Still, I didn't want even a single juror to miss the import of what Harflinger was saying. So I asked him, "In other words, what you hope, Mr. Harflinger, is that you will be able to leave prison, walk out on the street, never to be tried for the murder you committed, and go back into civilization, correct?"

"Yes, sir."

"Do you have any line of work in mind?"

"No, sir."

"Does your reformation to the point where you are now a teller of truth include the fact that you no longer think there is any possibility that you might live a life of crime?"

"I will not live a life of crime again, sir."

With the next few questions, I was able to bring out that as late as the previous Friday Harflinger was trying to get at least some assurance that he could trade his willingness to testify in this case for a bar to any further prosecution, at best, and a reduction of sentence, at worst.

"Okay. Now then, right up until last Friday your desire to tell what you described as the truth was not enough to cause you to come into this court until you had these other things, was it?"

"Yes, sir."

"You were wheeling and dealing for your own future, is that a fair statement?"

"That's a fair statement."

"And you fully admit, that as you give your testimony this day to these jurors, that all you hope to get out of it is the right to walk free, despite killing a human being in cold blood, and the right to walk free on the streets of America. That's all you want, isn't it?"

"That's true."


As so often happens in an intensely emotional trial, moments of deep seriousness are suddenly followed by lighter, almost humorous episodes. Perhaps the human psyche needs such forms of comic relief. Certainly they restore a sense of balance.

We had one such episode before Alfred Earl Harflinger left the stand.

I had just concluded a series of questions that was aimed at showing Harflinger's fondness for the "I can't remember" answer if there was any chance of being disproven.

I hadn't been able to pin him on that one, and I was a bit disgruntled as I shifted to a new line of questioning. On direct examination, he had claimed that in September of 1971, he had gone to the Cochran Company and asked to see Thomas Cochran. The president was not in, but Harflinger did see "a woman in the office," where he waited for a short period of time, according to his story.

I felt sure that Harflinger had never set foot in the offices of the Cochran Company, so I began by questioning him as to the woman he allegedly saw.

Q. . . . Mr. Harflinger, I want to know a complete description of the lady that you say you encountered in the offices of the Cochran Company, on which you say is now September 3, 1971, and I mean top to bottom.
A. I can't give it to you.
Q. You can't give it to me?
A. No, sir.
Q. Do you have any description at all to give me?

A. No, sir.

Q. Now, do you remember whether or not she was Chinese?

A. She wasn't Chinese.

Q. Was she black?

A. She wasn't black.

Q. Was she Indian?

A. She wasn't Indian.

Q. Does that lead you to the inescapable conclusion that you saw a white lady?

A. It does.

Q. Then why didn't you answer and give me a description by at least saying she was white? I know you are chuckling. Tell us, please. Do you want some time out for humor or are you ready to answer my question?

A. I will answer it as best I can.

Q. All right, when you were asked for a description, you didn't say she was a white lady, did you?

A. I did not.

Q. You now tell us that she was white.

A. She was a white lady.

Q. Because you realize that if you give a wrong description and Cochran can prove that no such woman was anywhere near that place, it can punch a hole in your testimony, you know that, don't you?

A. I do.

Q. And therefore you choose to give no description so that we have nothing to disprove.

MR. HOWARD: I object to this type of examination. It is improper. He should ask the witness for his knowledge and not to speculate.

THE COURT: You have made your objection. Your objection will be overruled. . . .

At this point, the judge informed the lawyers that he had a meeting to attend and he wondered if we would agree to breaking just a bit earlier than usual. I welcomed the break, for I wanted the jury to go out to lunch and chew over Harflinger's suddenly diminished powers of observation.

After the lunch break, however, we got right back to it. Whatever the witness had eaten, it hadn't done a thing for his memory.

Q. Mr. Harflinger, in view of what occurred almost two hours ago, you will recall I asked you to describe a particular young lady.

A. Yes, sir.

Q. And you said that you were able to offer nothing by way of description, right?

A. That is true.

Q. And then after we ran through the available races, you agreed that she was white.

A. I did.

Q. And I pointed out at that time that you seemed to be smiling.

A. Yes, sir.

Q. And the reason you were smiling is because you were thinking to yourself, "My God, he's got me trapped on that, hasn't he?"

MR. HOWARD: Just a moment. I object to that.

THE COURT: The objection will be overruled.

Q. (By Mr. Bailey) Isn't that true, Mr. Harflinger?

A. No, it was just the way—you can't describe anybody by their—she wasn't bald, she had hair.

Q. And you had some more help for that. Let's go through this by detail. After saying that you had nothing to tell us, you tell us that she was white and had hair.

A. That is true.

Q. That would be a fairly safe bet about any woman, wouldn't it?

A. Two arms and two legs.

Q. Okay, and did she have features in her face, nose, eyes, mouth, and so forth?

A. She had those.

Q. Do you remember those, as you sit here today on the witness stand helping the jury to find the truth?

A. To describe her nose or her eyes or her lips or her face, her features, as opposed to someone else's, no, I couldn't. She was just a normal human being.

Q. Are you telling us that if she were to walk in here now, this lady that you saw, you just wouldn't know her?

A. I would not.

Q. Well, Mr. Harflinger, let's see if we can scratch up a little more here. Was she over 7 feet tall?

A. No.

Q. Was she over 6 feet tall?

A. No.

Q. Was she between 5 and 6 feet tall?

A. I believe that is a fair description.

Q. On what do you base that estimate?

A. There was nothing outstanding, as far as I was concerned about the lady; in other words, she just wasn't a midget, she wasn't a giant, she wasn't obese, she wasn't so skinny you could see through her.

Q. Okay. Do you remember what she was wearing? Did she have clothes on? You would remember that.

A. She was dressed.

Q. Do you remember what she was wearing?

A. No, I don't. . . .

Q. . . . Now, Mr. Harflinger, do you as a man experienced with legal matters, to the extent that you have described to this jury, do you presently feel that if you were to give a precise description of a human being that it might not fit people that we can prove were there, is that your feeling at the moment?

A. No, sir.

Q. It is not. Have you ordinarily had this much difficulty in describing a person that you met in broad daylight for a matter of minutes, or is this unusual in your experience?

A. It is not unusual.

By this time, there were so many holes in Harflinger's credibility that it was like a used target. And I still had a few more shots. I asked him about the telephone call he claimed to have had with Harold Jones in late 1971. He said that it was "not very long."

I asked him, "Less than a minute? Quick like that?" and I snapped my fingers.

"Just long enough that he said, 'You've got your point across.'"

I then produced telephone company records that indicated a call had been made from a certain filling station—the same phone Harflinger claimed to have used, but again the government had only Harflinger's word for the fact that it was he who had placed the call. According to the phone company record, the call had lasted over *four* minutes.

"Are you willing to change your testimony now so that it will fit the documentary evidence and tell this jury that you spoke with Harold Jones for four minutes, are you willing to do that?"

"No, because I don't know."

"Didn't you just say it was probably less than a minute, Mr. Harflinger?"

"I said it was a brief conversation, that was probably about right."

"And it was probably less than a minute, right?"

"I didn't say how long it was."

By insisting, even after it was warned, on putting Harflinger on the stand as its witness, the government had severely damaged its case. The admission of the murders and the robberies had the jury recoiling in horror. But there was one more problem in regard to Mr. Harflinger; because of a motion that we had made on Cochran's behalf, a motion to suppress Harflinger's testimony because his initial arrest in the bomb possession case was based on an illegal search of the car by the state trooper, we had created a situation where Harflinger was a potential witness for the defense.

(Harflinger had always maintained, without wavering an iota, that there had not been a pistol in the car, and the trooper had made it up so that he had "probable cause," the legal necessity, to search the trunk. Actually, Andy Tuney had found support for this view, but I couldn't use it in court because the source refused to get involved, and it would be futile for us to try and force him. He had given Andy the information off the record.) Judge Oliver had put off ruling on the motion, but it was still pending when Harflinger took the stand, which meant the government had a distinct problem: it vouched for his truthfulness in regard to the case against Cochran, but it could not at the same time vouch for his veracity in regard to the story of his arrest.

I had Harflinger in a very difficult position before the jury—he was swearing to the truth of both stories.

In answer to one of my final questions, Alfred Earl Harflinger looked me directly in the eye and said, "I told you the truth all the way through on every question." His next response was, "I want the jury to believe that I am telling the truth."

And when I asked if he wanted the judge to believe him, too, because that would help him get out of jail, he said, "I do."

"And," I said, "if he believed you, you know there wouldn't be a question for the jury, don't you?"

"Yes, sir." It was as if Lewis Carroll had been writing courtroom drama.

I was through with Mr. Harflinger. I looked at the judge and said, "That's all."

(I later learned that Judge Oliver had been very impressed with my cross-examination of the government's star witness. A courthouse source told me that, while Judge Oliver was lunching with several other judges, one of them said to him, "What's this Bailey like? Is he really any good?" Judge Oliver, I was told, replied, "I've seen lawyers *kill* a witness before, but this guy's an embalmer." I have treasured that compliment ever since.)

Now it was Earl Jinkinson's turn to cross-examine, on behalf of the corporation. The tall, distinguished gentleman stood up, and in his marvelous, stentorian voice said, "Your Honor, due to the testimony I have heard from this witness, I adopt the cross-examination of counsel for co-defendants and do not wish to examine this witness."

I then put Whit Moody, the assistant prosecutor, on the stand and asked him if the government vouched for the testimony of Mr. Harflinger. He said, "Yes, we do."

Then I asked, "Does the government take the position that he is telling the truth about the illegality of the search?" And he replied, "No, we take the position that he's telling the truth about the bomb episode, but as to the illegality of the search he's honestly mistaken."

And that's the way it was left before the jury.

That night I had another long meeting with John Truman and Andy Tuney, and I listened hard to what John had to say about the probable effect of Harflinger's testimony on the good people of Missouri who made up the jury. We talked long into the night before I made a crucial decision.

The next morning, at nine-thirty, we told Judge Oliver that the defense was not going to put on a case. We felt that the testimony of the government's star witness had been so damaging to the government's case that there was little or nothing we could do to improve on the situation. With that, the defense rested.

Final arguments were short and to the point.

Chief prosecutor Tom Howard had an unenviable job. He had to try to reconstruct his main witness. All things considered, he made a creditable closing argument. But there wasn't much anyone could do to make Earl Harflinger believable. Howard met the issue of his star witness's less-than-sterling-character head on: "When you want someone to do a job like this [the bombing] you don't go to the local Sunday school teacher. You go to the hardened criminal." Indeed.

The government had taken an hour for its final argument, which was given by Howard and his assistant, Mr. Moody. We decided to take the same amount of time.

Earl Jinkinson went first, for a very few minutes, and lashed the government pretty heavily for not giving the jury better evidence.

I took less time, perhaps only fifteen minutes. A witness like Alfred Earl Harflinger did not deserve a lengthy argument.

I wasted no time in going after Mr. Harflinger. The government had tried to explain why it was that the witness had told them one story and the judge another. Fortunately, I wasn't faced with the alchemist's dilemma of trying to turn a base metal into gold; all I had to do was prove it was base. I described Harflinger as ". . . one of the most ridiculous pieces of human trash that ever walked into a courtroom, deceiving everyone as he went, including the gullible lawyers for the government. That is how this case arose."

I cautioned the jury about the need to keep the evidence separate, because we had three defendants—the company, Cochran, and Jones—and then I gave our view of the case.

"We start and did start, and I suggest to you we have never left this position by reason of the utter failure of the government to prove any case at all against Tom Cochran, whose name hasn't come up enough in this trial to even keep up his own interest. He started, presumed innocent. [The government] assumed the burden of proving him guilty to a point where no juror, no single juror, could conscientiously attain or retain a reasonable doubt, the kind of doubt that would make you hesitate in a serious matter.

"Now, that definition will be more elaborately explained by the very capable trial judge. I simply put to you that my brevity is in that context, that there is nothing before you that could even begin to lead you down the path to the point where you would say, 'In my own heart I am satisfied that this gentleman, who is an honorable citizen—' from all you know, just like you all—'had in mind and somehow aided and encouraged a guy like Harflinger, that he had never even met or talked to, admittedly, to have a bomb in his car down in Ava, Missouri.' "

The next point that had to be dealt with was the prosecutor's incredible suggestion, in his closing argument, that Cochran was a bad man because he used bad language. There had been testimony that when Cochran learned Hamilton (the man who owned the new truck) was soliciting some of his customers, he allegedly said to a subordinate, "I think this guy has got some of our property. I think he is stealing from us. I think he has got the customer list and I want you to go down there and nail the son of a bitch, and if he has done what I think he has done, I want you to sue him."

(I found it intriguing that a year after a New York judge had told the jury in a murder case that it could consider the defendant's use of "a certain four-letter word beginning with *f* or the plural or its present participle," in judging his character and perhaps even in determining his guilt, we now had a prosecutor in Missouri who took the same line of reasoning in regard to a certain three-word expression beginning with *s*. Good old New York, always setting the trend.)

When Tom Howard made his comment about Cochran using "s.o.b.," John Truman nudged me and whispered, "Remember Uncle Harry and John Kennedy."

I remembered them all right. I told the jury, "Now, people that indulge in what we call 'legal self-help' shoot the guys they don't like or bring them out or buy them out. They don't resort to the courts. Mr. Cochran has done exactly the reverse, by Mr. Howard's own admission, of what you would expect of a person with a violent disposition, and there is no evidence that he has anything of the sort, and I must say that I agree with brother Jinkinson, that I don't believe that a man is to be condemned and indeed convicted in a court of the United States by good and honest men and women because he has used the same language that our late President once used in describing big business, 's.o.b.s.'"

I was warming to my subject:

"But if you are to condemn him for the use of that language, it should have nothing to do with your verdict, and I want you to know that I, too, am guilty. Before I came out here to cross-examine Harflinger, I said to my brother Claiborne, or he said to me, I can't remember, 'Let's go out there and nail that son-of-a-bitch.' Now, ladies and gentlemen, take a look at Alfred Earl Harflinger. My life is dealing with felons. I would have to assume from listening to Mr. Howard, and from watching him try and handle a couple of low-life witnesses, that he hasn't got much experience with them. Harflinger might once have been a human being. Thanks to the misery and cruelty that is our present system, he progressively became worse and worse. You heard a history studded with assault with intent to kill, armed robbery, using pistols, but you heard that he wanted immunity and he knew how to get it, become a witness in a criminal case and get some naïve lawyer to think, 'Oh boy, I'm going to make a big one out of this. Here is my witness. All he wants is immunity. Rush him right in and get the immunity without even bothering to find out what the effect of that might be.'

"Ladies and gentlemen, immunity is a machinery. Once the United States brings it to a trial judge, he has no choice, and it can immunize from prosecution every crime and conception, including the cold-blooded murder of an innocent citizen who happened to be outside a house where Mr. Harflinger had just in a flash completed burglary, armed robbery, and assault with an intent to kill on the occupant.

"Well, the United States discovered belatedly that all Al had won was the chance to avoid conviction in the State of Illinois, for a whole pack of crimes, including murder in the first degree, and that all he really wants is to void his own conviction, and he may not get much opposition on that, so that he can walk the streets of America that you and I own and he does not.

"Now, ladies and gentlemen, I am not going to make Mr. Claiborne's argument. He will do it for you. I say to you on behalf of Mr. Cochran, for an American jury to dignify the statement of a man whose life has become nothing more than a walking lie, who lied to you on the witness stand even after a jury, a judge, and the distinguished Eighth Circuit Court of Appeals, to whom he wrote this brief, found him to be a liar, he sticks by it because he wants out.

"I hope that your rejection of any consideration of this witness in this case against any person, in summary and in reflection of the outrage that people ought to feel when you find that the United States government, even though unwittingly at first, is so bloodthirsty that the awful price it will pay to try to put in testimony on a crummy little bomb case is to trade a man a capital conviction as his pay, and Harflinger said, 'That's right, that's what I am getting paid, and I love it,' and you bet he does.

"Mr. Howard did not mention to you, and it is because it wasn't an important factor, the alleged trip which I very severely doubt that Mr. Harflinger claims he made to see the Cochran Company. It is very funny that he admits, 'I never saw Mr. Cochran there, never heard him, can't remember a single person who might remember him there,' in a busy company. Well, he knows better. He is an experienced lawyer. You give too much detail in a false story and one can disprove it. You give no detail and it stands alone. Anything that Harflinger says that stands alone is automatically unworthy of belief as a matter of simple experience."

After quickly running through the testimony of another government witness, one who sounded like he was in the wrong courtroom, I finished by saying, "I know that my client would like to hear me cover the case very thoroughly. I have to take the chance, as I have for years, that when an American jury hears no evidence against a man, that it doesn't take them long to find that the presumption of innocence with which he began a trial remains in place . . ."

* * *

It took the jury exactly five hours.

Harry Claiborne, who should be even more famous than he is, gave a marvelous final argument on behalf of Harold Jones. He was very emotional, almost righteously indignant, and when he finished there was very little meat left on the bones of Harflinger's testimony.

Judge Oliver's charge to the jury was a model of judicial fairness and clarity. I remember particularly that he admonished the jury not to view the trial as a contest, with one side inevitably winning and the other losing. "When justice is done," he said, "the government never loses."

Late in the afternoon Harold Jones and Thomas Cochran heard the foreman read the words, "We find all defendants not guilty on all of the charges listed in the indictment."

The next day the *Kansas City Times* quoted Cochran and Jones as saying they were "elated with the verdict. It certainly restores my faith in the jury system" (Cochran), and, "I'm grateful that you can still find justice in our courts. I never, never was in doubt about the verdict" (Jones). And then the reporter went on to make the same kind of error that Judge Murtaugh had made when he said, in discharging the Phillips jury, "There will be another trial." The reporter wrote, "Both men and the Cochran Corporation still face federal charges of attempting to monopolize the industrial supply and service business in Missouri and other areas. This count of the indictment will be tried later in the federal court here."

The mistake is that no one should ever say, publicly or through any media, that there *will be* a subsequent trial. Too many things can happen; witnesses can die, prosecutors can change their minds, or judges can dispose of the matter short of actually going to trial.

Judge Murtaugh, as it happened, was right. Billy Phillips was tried again. Thus his statement was accurate, but highly prejudicial. Unfortunately, no one will ever know if the judge's statement had anything to do with the decision to retry Phillips.

As for the reporter's statement, it was dead wrong. Several weeks after the acquittal in the bomb conspiracy case, Judge Oliver reviewed the indictment and dismissed the remaining charges. I didn't see it, but I would bet in the blind that the account of the dismissal was buried in the back pages of the paper, along with the other obituaries.

There is one happy postscript. In the early fall of 1974 I received a copy of the Cochran Company's latest annual report. It stated that fiscal 1974 had been its best year ever. It was a very good year for the company, and, by its end, a very good year for Tom Cochran.

But as I glanced at the pictures of Cochran that accompanied the "President's Report to the Shareholders," I thought he looked as if he'd aged quite a bit in one year.

Being indicted can do that to a man.

I had barely caught my breath after the Cochran case when I found myself back in the Midwest. This time my client was on trial for murder and conspiracy to murder. In Cochran, the violence was muted by the failure of the alleged bomb plot, but in the case of Silas Jayne there were no failures and the violence was very real. Without exaggeration, the Jayne case was the most bizarre murder case I've ever had.

Silas Jayne. When I first heard the name, it made me think of the farmer in Grant Wood's famous painting, "American Gothic," a tall, spare man who scratched the land for a hard living. When I met my client for the first time, I saw that, outside of his being tall, there was no resemblance whatsoever.

In his early sixties, Silas Jayne was a big, strong-lookng man who resembled a heavy Joseph Cotten, with his wavy hair and straight back. Jayne trained and dealt in horses, but he was not the sort that comes to mind when someone says "horse show." Yet he was a fixture around the Chicago horse world, as was his younger brother, George.

For ten years, at least, the rough-edged, outgoing Jayne brothers had provided area horse show people with a stream of tackroom gossip. Big, loud, and apparently violent, Silas had been threatening to kill George for almost a decade. According to the stories, he didn't care where he said it or who heard him. The two brothers had a blood feud, and scores of witnesses had heard Silas roar that he would kill his brother some day.

Over a period of time that stretched from 1961 to 1965, witnesses at five different horse shows had heard Silas threaten to kill his younger brother. No one knows just how serious Silas actually was—he had a reputation for being a "terrific card" among the horsey set—but there was little doubt that *someone* was after George Jayne.

In 1965 he and his stable hands were shot at by a sniper. Later his office in the stable was riddled with twenty-eight shots, two of his horses were poisoned, and his car was vandalized.

In the summer of that same year Cheri Rude, a professional rider whom George had hired away from Silas, was about to run an errand for George. She got into his Cadillac, turned on the ignition, and was blown to bits. George said, quite rightly, "It was meant for me." A coroner's grand jury studied the matter, but all it could conclude was that the murder was committed by "a person or persons unknown."

Apparently, George was convinced that his brother was behind the bombing. He initiated an investigation by the Cook County sheriff's office. A grand jury eventually indicted Silas, based on the information of two men who claimed that they had been hired by Silas to kill George. But the stories had changed by the time of trial, and the indictment was dismissed.

Early in 1967, at the urging of relatives, George and Silas got together to see if they could patch things up. Apparently, it was a successful meeting. Then, a few months later, someone threw several sticks of dynamite at George's house, so he hired a private detective as a bodyguard.

Not long after, Silas was sitting in his living room in Elgin, watching television. At his side were two loaded pistols. Suddenly, according to Silas's account, two shots struck the wall above his head. He grabbed his pistols and fired once through the door and again through the window. Then he took off after his assailant.

When Silas got to the front yard, he saw a young man limping down the walkway, obviously wounded. He hurried back, picked up a rifle, and went out again. This time he fired a fatal shot.

The dead man turned out to be the son of George Jayne's bodyguard.

There was another investigation, but no charges were brought against Silas. According to people who had become self-styled experts on the "feud," Silas was convinced that George had tried to have him killed. Yet there were no more incidents all through 1967, 1968, and 1969.

On October 28, 1970, George Jayne and his family had just enjoyed a nice dinner in celebration of George, Jr.'s, sixteenth birthday, which fell on the next day. After dinner, George, his wife, and their daughter and her husband went down to the recreation room to play some bridge.

As George was shuffling the cards, a man poked a 30.06 rifle through the open basement window and shot George Jayne to death.

Despite the open secret of the feud between George and Silas, the immediate investigation brought no charges. Then, seven months later, the state police (who had received an anonymous phone tip) began a whirlwind search for the killers. Moving swiftly through an incredible chain of human events, they brought their findings to a prosecutor.

On May 22, 1971, the grand jury indicted three men for the murder of George Jayne. One of the men was Silas Jayne.

According to the indictment, Silas had hired two men to kill his brother. One was Joseph LaPlaca, a carpet installer in his late forties; the other was Julius Barnes, thirty-seven, who worked at the stockyards in Chicago.

Silas's request for bail was denied, and he took up involuntary residence in the Cook County Jail. About four months later he called my office to see if I would take his case. He stated that he already had a lawyer, but it didn't seem that they were compatible, and after reading an excerpt of *The Defense Never Rests* in *Ladies Home Journal*, he had decided that I was the man for him.

As I was booked up solid, the original negotiations involved his being represented by Gerry Alch, and his co-defendant LaPlaca's hiring Mark Kadish. Part of the deal was that, if I suddenly found myself with a hole in my schedule, I would defend Silas and Gerry would defend Joe LaPlaca. But all of this was strictly in the talking stage. First we had to learn more about Mr. Jayne.

I sent Mark Kadish out to interview Silas at the Cook County Jail. He spent several hours with him, and also talked with Jayne's original lawyer, who turned out to be an extremely decent man who gave us all his files on the case. When Mark got back to Boston, he told me that his meeting had gone very well, that he found Silas Jayne to be open and direct—and he had heard the most fantastic story he had ever heard from a defendant.

Mark said that Silas appeared to be entirely candid (though Mark said he couldn't even hazard a guess as to whether or not the man was telling the truth.) If there were any gory details to the long-running blood feud between Silas and George, they were forgotten rather than withheld, for Silas went on at great length about the threats and the counterthreats, shootings, bombings, and beatings.

Silas Jayne was equally candid about his own history, regaling Mark with the story of how he had shot the man who fired into his living room, and he described an episode in which he had discovered three men in the process of robbing his safe. Instead of calling the police, which apparently was definitely not his way of doing things, he got a *machine gun* and "blew them all away." (Later we learned that this was apparently true, and that after investigation no charges were filed against Silas, just as none were filed after the shooting that followed the living room incident.)

As to the killing of his brother George, Silas was adamant that he had not done it, that in fact it was a frame-up. But as Mark noted in his report, the problem was twofold: one, Silas Jayne appeared, by his own admission, to be the type of man who could have done it; and two, Mark got no real feeling, one way or the other, as to whether or not Silas was telling the truth.

I hired Steve Delaney, one of the best private investigators in the business, and sent him to Chicago to begin the arduous task of building a defense file.

Mark Kadish handled the great bulk of the pretrial work, from brief writing to oral argument. When the Supreme Court of the United States abolished the death penalty, Mark thought the decision contained sufficient latitude that its theory might be applied to the problem of bail for Silas Jayne. By this time Silas had been in jail for almost a year, and he was anxious to be out and helping with his own defense. Eventually, Mark argued the bail question all the way up to the Supreme Court of the State of Illinois. But before the highest court could rule, the trial began and the point was considered moot.

As the months prior to trial wore on, Mark, Gerry Alch, and Steve Delaney began to assemble their facts. The picture that emerged was every bit as bizarre as Mark had said it was after his first visit with Silas.

When George Jayne was killed, in 1970, no one in the area was surprised that his brother Si was a prime suspect. In fact, George's widow, Marion, was pushing the police to check out the possibility of Si's involvement. The police did check, but nothing came of it for more than half a year. Then, the police got a break, so to speak.

In early May of 1971 an anonymous caller phoned the police and told them to check out one Mel Adams, a thirty-nine-year-old ex-convict who lived in Posen, Illinois. The police did, and eventually Adams cracked—or so the story goes—naming three other men as co-plotters in the murder of George Jayne; one of the men was Silas.

According to the police and Adams, this is what had happened: Adams had a friend by the name of Ed Nefeld, the chief of detectives in Markham, Illinois, a town not famous for the simon purity of its police force. After they had become particularly good friends, Nefeld let Adams in on a little business venture—the for-hire killing of George Jayne. Nefeld asked Adams if he knew anyone who wanted the job, and Adams said he would like to check it out further.

So Nefeld introduced Mel Adams to Joe LaPlaca, a good friend of Silas Jayne's, and Joe, according to the story, offered Adams ten thousand dollars to do the job. LaPlaca even took Adams up to the area, fifty miles away, where George lived, to show him the lay of the land. Next there was a meeting with Si, held in Si's car, where Silas allegedly struck the deal with Mel Adams to have his brother murdered. Adams told the police that Si at first wanted him to machine-gun George, but later backed off on that idea and several others that were even more bizarre, and gave him two pistols.

By June of 1970 Adams was becoming disenchanted with the whole thing, but—as he told the police—LaPlaca said Si was willing to raise the ante to twenty thousand dollars. This rekindled the interest of Mel Adams, who then asked if Silas would bump the take another ten grand if he (Adams) brought in a third man to make sure the plan worked.

Si agreed, said Adams, and Mel enlisted the services of one Julius Barnes, a man who worked with Adams in Chicago's stockyards. Apparently, Barnes was the first to suggest that the only right way to do the job was with a high-powered rifle. Then Adams and Barnes took the rifle, which had been provided by Adams's girlfriend, and they went out to *Silas Jayne*'s farm to do some target shooting as practice!

A few months later, on October 28, Mel and Julius drove up to Palatine, where George Jayne lived. They did the job.

After the Illinois Bureau of Investigation (the IBI) had Adams's confession, he was made a witness for the state and given immunity. He was to be the government's star in the trial of three men who were arrested and charged, on May 22, 1971, with the plot to murder George Jayne—Joe LaPlaca, Julius Barnes, and Silas Jayne.

According to the IBI, what clinched the case against Silas Jayne was that the ballistics test of the murder showed that the fatal bullets matched those dug out of a tree on Si's farm. That, plus the discovery of one of Silas Jayne's handguns in the possession of Julius Barnes, convinced the IBI that Adams was telling the truth when he claimed that Silas had hired him and the others to murder George.

There was one other problem: Julius Barnes, the alleged trigger man, had confessed. Yes, he told the police, he had been hired by Adams and LaPlaca; and yes, the money man who hired all three of them was Silas Jayne.

That was the government's theory of the case, and as the defense investigation began in earnest, it would have been hard to find anyone in Chicagoland who didn't believe that the prosecution had an airtight case.

In answer to the charges, our clients said, "No. We are innocent. Totally and completely." As Silas told Mark Kadish in their very first interview, "Sure, someone paid to have my brother George killed —but it wasn't me, and it sure wasn't my friend Joe LaPlaca." He said one other thing that was very intriguing. He said that he had never met Melvin Adams in his entire life.

Steve Delaney, who had been hired by my office to work on the case, was immediately recognized by Frank Jayne and other pro-Silas family members as a crackerjack investigator. In order to guarantee that the case would have his undivided attention, Frank Jayne asked if they could hire Steve and pay him directly. That was fine with us, because we knew that, with Steve on the case full time, it would make our job just that much easier. There is no substitute for a top-flight criminal investigator in a tough case, and Steve (like Andy Tuney and John McNally) is one of the best.

After he had finished his preliminary investigation, Steve reported that he "had never seen the odds piled up so high against a guy." Unfortunately, that seemed to be the consensus of opinion among the lawyers, too.

One thing pleased us greatly. In late 1972 the case was assigned to Judge Richard Fitzgerald, a Chicago jurist with a well-deserved reputation for fairness and intelligence. That had to help our side. From the first day of pretrial hearings, Gerry Alch raved about the judge.

As Alch and Kadish got deeper into the case, aided by Steve Delaney's digging, they began to learn more about the world of George and Silas Jayne.

Too often when one hears the words "horse show," one tends to think in trite images: Caroline Kennedy on her pony; men and women in jodhpurs and riding caps; and the spectators lining the show ring, sipping from silver flasks, their hundred-dollar cashmere sweaters tied casually around their waists.

As with any stereotype, there is some truth to it, but the world of horse people is much more complex—and less glamorous—than that. The horse show world does have its share of the so-called beautiful people, but it also has its share of the rest of society, from top to bottom. Organized crime, for example, has always been interested in horses, and not just those that you bet on at a little window or over the phone.

As for the Jayne brothers, they fit somewhere in the middle between the social poles of the North Shore and the South Side. They were a huge family; Silas was the oldest, George the youngest, of fourteen children born to a farming couple who lived in Barrington, Illinois. Sometime in the 1940s both George and Silas became involved in the horse business. Originally they had worked as a team, but George struck out on his own toward the end of the fifties, which, apparently, caused a good deal of friction. Nonetheless, both did fairly well (especially the younger brother). George eventually became a judge of the prestigious American Horse Shows Association, and not long after there were frequent arguments between the brothers over rules and decisions.

One other point, unearthed by Delaney, was that both Si and George were money lenders in the horse business. As in so many other businesses, it is not uncommon that those who do the bankrolling are not total strangers to violence. Indeed, there was the fact that George's house had once burned down—at the very time that Silas was trying to sell his own house to George. The uncharitable suggested that Si really knew how to close a deal.

As with so many of the other feud stories, including the reputed threats on George's life by his brother Silas, this rumor was uncorroborated. Still, it added to the whole aura of suspicion that had all but convicted Silas Jayne before we ever went to trial.

Then Delaney came up with something that had to be checked out. He learned that shortly after the killing Marion Jayne had let it be known that she would pay a handsome sum to anyone who could prove that Silas was behind the death of her husband. Not long after, she was seen riding around town in the company of two policemen from nearby Markham, Illinois.

In December Gerry Alch filed a motion to suppress certain evidence that the government planned to use, and the hearing turned out to be a perfect opportunity to learn more about the possible influence of George's widow on the police investigation. The defense called four witnesses: Marion Jayne, Melvin Adams, and the two policemen—Nefeld, the Markham chief of detectives, and Lawrence, a lieutenant.

From all accounts, particularly those of Kadish and the clients, Alch did an excellent job. During the day-and-a-half hearing, Gerry (and also Mark) asked probing question after probing question, and even though he could not establish a direct link between Marion's reward money and the subsequent indictment, he accomplished far more than was evident to the casual spectator. He created a record of pretrial testimony regarding several important points that would serve to "contain" these same witnesses when the time came for them to testify at the trial itself.

As Gerry knew so well, the defense lawyer's best protection in cross-examining government witnesses is what the law refers to as "prior inconsistent statements." Now we had a record to back us up. That is, we had a record in so far as three of the four witnesses were concerned—Lieutenant Lawrence took the Fifth Amendment.

Shortly before the trial was slated to begin we learned two things: one, neither Markham detective would testify; and two, I would be available after all. Gerry informed the clients that we could shift to the contingent arrangement—whereby I would represent Jayne and Alch would represent LaPlaca—if they still wanted to. They did. I told Lynda to start packing. We were going to Chicago.

On trial eve, so to speak, we faced the fact that it was going to be very hard to win this one. There was a mountain of evidence. There was Mel Adams's "confession," which had earned him immunity, and there were the matching bullets—some in the tree on Si's farm, and one in his brother's body. There were the weapons, the 30.06 and the "Enforcer," a small .30-caliber pistol once owned by Si that had been turned over to the police when they arrested Julius Barnes. Finally, we had just learned that if the circumstantial evidence of the long-standing feud was not enough, there was now the matter of Silas Jayne's fingerprint, which appeared on one of the bills that Adams claimed was the payoff money.

Against all that evidence we had Silas Jayne's entire defense: "Someone else did it."

On that less-than-happy note, we went to trial.

The rest of the trial cast should be mentioned. The prosecutor was a man in his early thirties by the name of Nicholas Motherway. Mark and Gerry had warned me that Motherway was "up" for this trial. The conviction of Silas Jayne, and all the beneficial publicity that would flow from it, was to be the climax of his career as a public prosecutor. If anyone doubted Motherway's zeal, all such doubts were erased when we learned that above the prosecutor's desk was a huge photograph of Silas Jayne—that he used as a dartboard.

Motherway, a rather good-looking man of medium height with reddish-blond hair, was known to be a little bit short on the handle.

The word was that he could be provoked in court. When I met him I found him to be friendly, but somewhat cautious.

The trial judge deserves the most comment because I had never been before a better one. Richard Fitzgerald was a silver-haired, quite handsome judge, in his middle fifties, who kept himself in fine physical shape. As I soon found out, he was very highly respected by the lawyers in the community, and the reasons for that respect were not hard to discern.

His rulings were good, he was always extremely pleasant, and you wouldn't know he was running his own courtroom unless you attempted to test him on the point—in which case you quickly found out. He was very informal in chambers, in trying to work out problems, and would always reach out for a solution that was agreeable to both sides if that was possible without ruling summarily, as some judges are prone to do.

The Jayne trial fell during a very busy and complicated time for me, and Judge Fitzgerald was more than understanding. He let me use his outer office for making and receiving telephone calls in order to try and keep a handle on things. His kindliness and patience meant a lot to me.

One other interesting aspect of the case is that it was the very first one Gerry Alch and I had tried together. Gerry had been a member of my firm since 1968, and a senior associate for more than four years, but outside of hearings and pretrial motions we had never actually tried a case together. Having Gerry around was a professional and personal tonic.

In addition to being an excellent trial lawyer, Alch is the legal profession's answer to David Frye. On many occasions I've seen him meet someone only momentarily, then turn right around and do an almost perfect imitation of his speech. (I was not at all surprised when this talent surfaced in the Jayne case.)

Having a heavy hitter of Gerry's caliber made things a great deal easier for me, especially since there was no conflict between Silas Jayne (my client) and Joe LaPlaca (Gerry's). If the need arose, one of us could cover for the other's client.

The trial of the case really boiled down to two important factors: the testimony of Melvin Adams, the self-confessed "hit arranger," who had been granted immunity from prosecution and therefore had nothing to risk in telling his story; and the confession of Julius Barnes.

Julius was represented by a black lawyer, about my own age, named George Howard, who was sometimes described to me as the "black mayor of Chicago." He certainly knew his way around, was well respected and active in the criminal bar, and a pure delight to work with. I seldom saw George Howard without a smile. About five feet six inches tall, he had a great string of admirers, both because of his ability and because he was an unusually handsome man. His excellent understanding of the local legal community, in particular the judge and the prosecutors, was most helpful.

He had a marvelous speaking voice, deep and impressive, and sometimes, when the substance got weak, the rhetoric was so overwhelming that you were persuaded by what you thought you'd heard. He was also a most cooperative lawyer. His client, Julius Barnes, was in a far different position than either Jayne or LaPlaca because he had made a detailed confession to the crime of murder (for reasons that he would later testify were extremely bizarre).

George agreed to let both Gerry and me cross-examine witnesses before he did, because he recognized that we had been able to prepare far more fully than he—due in chief to Steve Delaney's longtime presence on the scene.

When Mel Adams took the stand, we all went to work. Adams, who worked in the same glue factory with Julius Barnes, had had some sort of criminal conviction while in the Air Force, but had kept a decidedly low profile since he got out. A good-looking, blond-haired man of average height, but with a solid build, Adams was reasonably articulate for a man of limited education.

In answer to Motherway's questions, Melvin Adams told his story to the jury: Si Jayne and Joe LaPlaca invited him into Jayne's car, parked in the parking lot of the Blue Moon Café, and there they offered him the job. He said that Silas told him he wanted his brother dead, that Silas gave him two guns, and told him he could come out to his farm any time he wanted for target practice. Adams said that although he did go up to the area of George Jayne's home with Joe LaPlaca on many occasions to "case it," he really didn't have the stomach for the job.

So, according to Adams, he went to his good friend and co-worker, Julius Barnes, and said, "Julius, I've got a little hit job to do. Do you want in on it?"

And Julius Barnes immediately responded, "Sure. Why don't you give me the details?"

Just the way that came out struck me as completely unlikely. Barnes was a simple, poorly educated black man who supported the woman he lived with; from all indications, his was a very regular, if unremarkable, life, with no criminal difficulties whatsoever. Physically he was large and cumbersome, and he looked tough, but there was no history to back up the image of Barnes as a hired gun. Nonetheless, that was Adams's story.

Adams went on to say that he and Barnes "cased" George Jayne's neighborhood on numerous occasions, "to get the lay of the land." There was a problem, here, in my opinion. For Adams to travel around George's expensive, all-but-lily-white neighborhood with a black man of Julius Barnes's size and shape would hardly have gone unnoticed.

Again, it struck me as highly unlikely, but that was Adams's story.

He testified further that he had borrowed a hunting rifle, a 30.06, from a police officer, by getting his girl friend Pat to do the actual borrowing. The cover story was that the rifle was to be used on a hunting trip—which wasn't far from the truth, after all. Adams said that he and Joe LaPlaca once went out to the Silas Jayne farm to "home in" the weapon by taking some practice shots. They stood, he said, in a cornfield and fired some 100 to 150 yards into a large tree. Both the field and the tree, he said, were on the property of Silas Jayne.

(Indeed, bullets were found in the tree he described and they matched the murder bullet taken from the body of George Jayne. And the tree was in fact on Silas's farm.)

The time that elapsed between the making of the contract and the ultimate execution of George Jayne was better than a year, and during that time it seemed like the hostility between the two brothers had cooled. If Silas had made the contract, he had very little reason to suspect that it was still "alive" and operating.

Nonetheless, according to Adams, he and Barnes went out there on the night in question, drove around a while, stopped—and put up the car hood. This was Adams's idea of how to be innocuous, so that passsers-by wouldn't wonder about a strange car in the neighborhood. I thought it was more like asking for someone to stop and offer help, and getting a good look at the culprits in the process.

In any event, Adams said that Julius went to the cellar window, knelt down in front of it, and then a large blast was heard. According to Adams, Julius Barnes came back and reported that the deed was done.

Adams went on to testify that sometime after he had "switched," gone over to the government, he had a private conversation with Marion Jayne, George's widow, who had been offering twenty-five thousand dollars (in cash) for information leading to the arrest of the culprit. At about the same time Adams had begun to cooperate with the government, Marion Jayne had shown him a suitcase filled with reward money. So, with immunity, and the possibility of having received twenty-five thousand dollars, Melvin was probably doing all right for himself.

Whatever his motive, Melvin got wired up with a hidden recorder and went to see Julius Barnes, with whom he had deposited the murder weapon, after offering Julius a good sum of money simply to hide the guns. Adams had set things up so that Barnes was to return the guns to him while Mel's recorder was in the "on" position, and while they both were under police surveillance.

The recording was not a "hit," but it got close enough to the top of the charts for the police to buy it. Not long after, Barnes was arrested, and after him Joe LaPlaca and Silas Jayne.

At trial, Barnes pleaded "not guilty" and told a quite different story. In his opening statement George Howard said that Barnes knew nothing about the shooting, but he did know that one day, at work, his buddy Mel had come to him and said, "Julius, I've got a good bit of money to give you if you will just store a few things for me, no questions asked." In exchange for five thousand dollars, Adams gave Barnes two guns: one was a .30-caliber pistol, known as an "Enforcer," which had been purchased by Silas Jayne, and the other was the murder weapon itself. Barnes simply stuck the weapons in a closet, and when Adams asked to have them back, he returned them—but the return was duly recorded by the police.

When Barnes was picked up and taken down to headquarters, he said he didn't know anything about any shooting. But then Mel Adams entered the room. Adams said, "Julius, it's okay. Just tell them we did it." According to Barnes, this was a signal. Adams, said Barnes, had called him before the pickup and said, "If you get arrested, don't worry. I have immunity and you will get it, too. Just tell them whatever they want to hear."

So, with a little bit of leading, Barnes confessed to all the things that Adams had told the police were true. The confession was then signed.

When Adams finished his direct examination, I had the first crack at him. There were a number of details that I wanted to establish before attacking his credibility.

The first thing I wanted him to do was to say, without any doubt, that the photo I showed him of the Blue Moon Café was an accurate photo of the place where he had his first and only meeting with Si Jayne. After he had stated, on two or three occasions, that the current photo was accurate, I felt I had him sufficiently locked in on that point.

Next I asked him to describe his "sighting in" of the murder weapon on Silas Jayne's farm. Using aerial photographs that we had taken earlier in the year, I asked him to point out exactly where he had been standing when he fired the practice shots, and he did so with great certainty and no hesitation. He stated that the practice session had taken place in October, the same month as the killing.

Once that was established, I left it and switched back to the issue of the Blue Moon Café. The witness looked decidedly uncomfortable as I introduced evidence to prove that the photo he had so positively identified was a current photo of the Blue Moon, which had been extensively redecorated since the time of the alleged meeting in Si Jayne's car—so much so that one could hardly call it the same place.

Then I introduced evidence to show that in October of 1970, on the day when Adams supposedly sighted in the gun, the spot he swore he'd stood in was covered with corn stalks over twelve feet high. Since the bullets dug out of the tree were at a point five to six above the ground, and the tree was 100 to 150 yards away, this would have been a difficult feat to accomplish. This kicked off a great ruckus, with both sides eventually calling experts to establish whether or not 1970 had been a good year for corn. All of the expert testimony was really not necessary, and in fact was rather foolish, because the tenant farmer who rented the land from Silas kept meticulous records showing height and also exactly when the corn was cut.

The prosecution's mistake was in thinking Adams was talking about corn that was raised for human consumption, when actually it was feed grain—which is not cut until November.

There were many other minor inconsistencies in Adams's testimony, and the more he talked the more he tripped himself up, especially on details. But he never did budge on the principal claims of his testimony: that Silas Jayne hired him; that he in turn hired Barnes; that the two of them did the killing; and that Joe LaPlaca then brought him the thirty thousand dollars in payoff money, from which he then paid Barnes.

We could not very well dispute the fact that Silas Jayne's thumbprint was on one of the bills that the police took from Melvin Adams when they first arrested him shortly after the shooting (but couldn't hold him because they didn't have enough information). The print was as clear as it could be, but the fact that Adams had a bill with

Si Jayne's print on it did not in and of itself prove anything criminal.

When I concluded my cross-examination, which went a full day, Gerry Alch took over and banged away at him for the better part of another day.

One of the few humorous moments of the trial occurred when Gerry had Adams get down from the stand and take the rifle, the actual murder weapon, to demonstrate how he had fired the practice shots. Adams immediately pointed this lethal weapon right at the jury—and all twelve jurors hit the deck. Chastised, he turned in the other direction, whereupon the judge hit the deck. Finally Gerry got him straightened out, and with the rifle pointed at the window wall, the examination continued.

After establishing the distance from the spot of firing to the tree, and the height at which the bullets had been retrieved from the tree, Gerry demanded to know how it was possible—when the corn was twelve feet high.

Furious, Adams turned to Alch and shouted, "I told you, it was *cut!*"

Gerry's purpose, and accomplishment, was to work incessantly on the details, and reviewing his testimony, to see which would change and which would remain constant. By this time, Adams had been tripped up with sufficient frequency so that his standard answer was highly qualified—to the extent that everything "would be," or "might be," or "may be" the truth—but he was not going to stand behind it unequivocally, because he couldnt remember what else he might have said that would contradict it.

By the time that George Howard rose to undertake the cross-examiantion of Melvin Adams, George had heard enough equivocation to realize that a firm hand would have to be exercised or Melvin Adams would run without control. At about the third question, when he got a "maybe" instead of the affirmative response he was looking for, George Howard decided to take matters into his own hands. In a most authoritarian manner, Howard said to the witness —in the presence of the jury, and very loudly—"Mr. Adams, I don't want no more 'maybes' from you, and I don't want no more 'could bes,' from you I want some 'yeses,' and some 'nos!' "

Although this broke up the entire courtroom, plus the judge and the jury, it did not get George Howard the "yeses" and "nos" that he wanted. Adams was just too slippery.

(Later that afternoon, during a conference in the judge's chambers, we were arguing a very fine point of law when Judge Fitzgerald turned to Gerry and said, "Mr. Alch, can you tell the court just what you want?" With a perfectly straight face, Alch said, "Your Honor, I don't want me no 'maybes.' I wants me some 'yeses' and some 'nos.'" The judge laughed so hard that he had to get hold of himself before he could resume the bench. Gerry had mimicked George Howard's voice perfectly, and George was laughing as hard as the judge. Still later, Alch would occasionally do the same thing during side bar conferences, out of the jury's hearing. The spectators who were too far away to hear anything could see the judge laughing and struggling to regain his composure. Finally, one of the reporters stopped Gerry and asked what he was saying that seemed to make the judge laugh. Gerry said, "I don't know. It might be my Boston accent.")

When Adams left the stand, I think the general impression was that he had been dented, but not destroyed. It was still an open ball game. By the time that Julius Barnes's confession had been put in evidence, the betting was roughly one thousand to one against the defense.

Nonetheless, all three defendants took the stand in their own defense, and by and large they did a pretty creditable job.

Barnes' explanation of his confession was that he had trusted Mel Adams—who had promised him he would get the same deal that he, Adams, got—and that is why he told the police what he did. His story was that Adams had tricked him. He didn't make a terribly impressive witness, but they didn't crack him, either.

Joe LaPlaca explained that a good deal of his association with Adams was for "other reasons." In particular, he painfully had to admit to the jury that things hadn't been all that good at home for some years, and Melvin Adams was a guy who could "fix him up." Joe LaPlaca, a wispy little underfed Italian of about forty-five, would not be mistaken for Don Juan.

By contrast, Silas Jayne on the stand looked big, hearty, and robust. He was an irascible witness, but try as he might, Motherway barely touched him on cross-examination. Silas did explain one other possible reason for George's demise. That was that he had taken George to task for having associated with some bad people who were allegedly involved in the narcotics business; and George had failed to deny his involvement.

There was also evidence presented that Silas and George had had a run-in over the rumor that George was mixed up in doping horses. In judging horse shows, the animal's demeanor, as well as its beauty, is an important factor, and points are won and lost in respect to the horse's conduct. Rumor had it that George and his friends were tranquilizing the animals in order to make them appear especially well trained. Silas was apparently worried that George's actions might be mistakenly attributed to him, since they shared the same last name, and he and George had several long conversations. According to some sources, George had agreed to leave the area, in exchange for Silas's pledge of silence, and had told several people that he would soon be leaving Chicago for the West Coast.

And that was about the best we could do in our effort to explain why someone other than brother Silas might have wanted to get rid of George.

There was also the question of the reconciliation between Silas and George, which had taken place in the presence of several of their sisters. At the trial, one of the sisters testified for Silas—and one testified against him. The difference in their testimony about the reconciliation was not great, but the flavor was different. As a result of the sister who testified for the prosecution, you could infer that it wasn't a very solid reconciliation. The other sister contradicted that, saying she felt very relaxed about it, and it looked to her like the boys were going to get along.

That was back in 1967, or so, some three years before the shooting. There had been an absence of any recent provocation that might have triggered Silas's desire to make the contract, but there had been enough violence between the two men so that the prosecution was able to argue that it was a continuing dream on Silas's part that his brother would become one of the dear departed.

The final arguments were in many ways a draw. But there was evidence that you simply couldn't talk your way out of—including the thumbprint on the payoff money. (Silas said he had given money to LaPlaca any number of times for any number of reasons, and LaPlaca said he'd given money to Adams, from time to time, mostly for girls, and that was probably how Silas Jayne's hundred-dollar bill got in Adams's pocket); the fact that Adams actually had several of Jayne's weapons (Silas said that they were stolen); and the fact that the bullets were in the tree, despite the cornstalk problem. (We theorized for the defense that Adams had in fact killed George Jayne himself—Steve Delaney, for one, was absolutely convinced of this—and then for some reason decided to implicate Silas and went out in November, after the killing, and fired into Silas's tree—at which time the corn *had* been cut, which was why he recalled that the corn was down.)

What we were left with, then, was a good bare-bones story, accounting for the murder of George Jayne, with a lot of holes in it that couldn't be reconciled. Had it not been for the confession of Barnes, I'm satisfied that we would have had no real problem.

The jury was out for the entire afternoon, and most of the next day. When they returned, they gave one of the most anomalous (irregular, exceptional, abnormal, take your pick) verdicts yet to be recorded in Chicago.

All men had been charged with murder, and anyone who hires or acts as a middleman for a hit is guilty of murder; and all men had been charged with conspiracy, for the agreement among themselves to commit the murder. Barnes was alleged to have conspired with LaPlaca and Jayne, although admittedly he had never met them, because of his dealing with Adams, the middleman. The rule is that when one engages in a conspiracy, one becomes a co-conspirator with all the others also engaged, whether he knows their identities or not. So it seemed very unlikely that there would be any split verdicts in this case.

The jury found Julius Barnes guilty of murder, but not conspiracy; and they found Silas Jayne and Joe LaPlaca guilty of conspiracy, but not murder!

The odd result was based on a very, very unlikely view of what had happened. For Jayne and LaPlaca to be guilty of conspiracy they would have had to have made an agreement with Barnes, Adams being the middleman, to have the murder done—and then done nothing to help! No furnishing of the weapons, the target area, the money, or anything else—simply making an agreement and then walking away.

But that's how the verdict came in. When he heard the verdict, Gerry Alch, who was feeling pretty pessimistic about the outcome of the case by the second day of the jury's deliberations, turned to me and said quietly, "We can live with that."

What he meant was that Silas Jayne and Joe LaPlaca had already served a full two years in jail awaiting trial, and had willingly postponed the onset of the trial until I could be available to try it. Because they received a sentence of a minimum of six years and a maximum of twenty, they would be eligible for parole after serving another two of the six years, or a total of four.

The community apparently considered the case a draw. In a sense Motherway had gotten a conviction; in a sense he very sorely lacked the conviction he had been seeking. Indeed, at the time of sentencing he attempted to persuade the judge to give Silas Jayne the maximum sentence on the ground that he was really guilty of murder, even though the jury had acquitted him of that charge. And therefore the judge should view him as a murderer when sentencing him for conspiracy.

Fortunately, Judge Fitzgerald took a dim view of this concept, realizing its "novelty." I had pointed out, heatedly, that Motherway had lost the ball game and was now seeking to reap the spoils despite the loss—which was hardly a fair way of determining the sentence of a man convicted of something considerably less than murder one.

As of this writing, late fall of 1974, the appeal for all three defendants is being handled by George Howard. Investigator Steve Delaney is still working on the case, hoping to uncover that elusive bit of evidence that will exonerate Silas Jayne. Despite the vagaries of his most unusual case, with Howard and Delaney in the picture Si has a far better chance than most men *ever* would.

I have not had a major criminal trial in the Midwest since 1973. It is probably just as well. The trial of Silas Jayne would be a very hard act to follow.

# Twisting Slowly, Slowly

No one ever promised *any* of us a rose garden, but in the spring of 1973 I began to feel as if I'd walked into one.

In less than a year, Lynda had turned our domestic life into an almost orderly, full-speed-ahead tranquility. That might not make much sense to people who sleep under the same roof night after night, but that small army of people who travel constantly know what it means to be able to relax while on the road. Lynda went everywhere I did, which made my life both easier and happy.

She was making her mark on the house in Marshfield, too. Bit by bit, there were small touches. A different picture here, a different arrangement of furniture there—our own pattern was coming to the fore, and it was good.

The office in Boston was booming. Gerry Alch had a full calendar of cases to try, as I did, and Colin Gillis could hardly clear his desk of the matters that piled up whenever he left to teach one of his law classes. Everyone was busy. Truman was working with me on the Cochran case, and Mark Kadish was helping Gerry Alch with Silas Jayne and LaPlaca. Al Johnson, Jimmy Merberg, and Mario Misci were all busy with a variety of matters, and investigators Andy Tuney, Steve DeLaney, and John McNally had all been hired for cross-country cases. It was a hectic, exciting time.

And then, in May, it all fell apart. Not immediately, and neither entirely nor inevitably, but that's when it began.

For years people had been telling me that all criminal lawyers who have gained some degree of national attention get their lumps sooner or later. This society does not always take kindly to mavericks (and that's what a good criminal lawyer really is), to those who make a living by rocking boats. I knew all the case histories, from Clarence Darrow through Willie Fallon and beyond, but I thought I'd paid my dues already. (I'd been censured in Massachusetts and suspended from practice in New Jersey for one year, for what amounted to "overzealously" representing my client.) And I did not disagree when an English barrister told me, in London, "Our two countries treat their criminal lawyers quite differently. In my country they are apt to be knighted, while in yours they are more likely to be indicted." That kind of trouble just wasn't in the cards for me.

I also knew that most defense lawyers get in trouble because of their clients. Looking back over the list of the last few years, I couldn't see that any of them was likely to involve me in any personal difficulties. Ernie Medina? His case was a closed book, and he was fitting in beautifully at the helicopter factory in Menominee; Billy Phillips was still tied up trying to pay his own dues; Tom Cochran and Silas Jayne were nothing more than the next cases on the calendar. As a matter of fact, as criminal clients go, I'd had a string of princes.

If I were to get involved in personal trouble, personal legal trouble, because of someone I had represented in the recent past, my only guess would have been Glenn Wesley Turner.

As early as the summer of 1972 I had begun to hear talk that Turner was going to be indicted by some branch of the federal government—and perhaps even more than one. But I filed these rumors away in the back of my mind. I had always told Glenn that if he ever got into a heavy criminal case I would defend him. So I knew I was obligated. But I never thought I would be caught in the same web. It just never seemed possible.

Once the Federal Trade Commission had backed off the second of the consent decrees that Turner had signed, it was clear that Glenn either had to collar his overenthusiastic people in the field or face renewed legal action. For a time it looked as if he was doing just that, but then there was an emotional rupture, and some of his top people left to form companies of their own.

The group that took over control of Turner Enterprises was not as cautious as their predecessors had learned to be, and soon the money and the complaints were flowing in at almost the same rate. I tried to warn Glenn that he was heading for trouble, but he was euphoric over the financial rebound. Time passed, I got caught up in the problems of other clients, and we did not communicate as often as we had during the days when I was actively the general counsel.

Early in 1972 the word got out that a federal grand jury was looking into Turner's entire operation, and I began to suspect that the
broken agreements with the Federal Trade Commission had resulted
from pressure by the Justice Department. (Had the consent agreements I had worked out ever been signed, a criminal prosecution
would have been all but impossible.) In the summer of 1972 I learned
of an ugly remark made by an assistant federal prosecutor in Miami
that *I* was to be one of the targets of the grand jury investigation. I
immediately checked this rumor with a friend high in the Justice
Department, and was told that the matter had no substance; and
further, that the "spokesman" in Miami was resigning the following
week because of his big mouth.

Because I was loaded with a heavy trial schedule, Turner hired
one of my friends and former associates, Jim Russ, of Orlando, to
represent him in connection with the grand jury proceedings. Ben
Bunting, the second-in-command of the Turner companies during
most of the time that I actively represented them, and Raleigh P.
"Rip" Mann, the number-three man, sought my advice as to how they
might protect themselves against unwarranted criminal charges. I told
them that I could not ethically represent them individually and the
Turner complex at the same time, and suggested that they seek their
own lawyer. Not long after, I got a call from an attorney named Dave
Fleming in Los Angeles. He identified himself as the lawyer who had
represented Dita Beard (the ITT lobbyist who touched off a scandal
over the question of whether ITT had "bought" its way out of a
federal antitrust suit by promising to put up four hundred thousand
dollars to fund the Republican National Convention in 1972 in San
Diego). Mrs. Beard avoided testifying before the Senate inquiry because of an illness that kept her hospitalized in Denver. One could
infer that the Nixon people were more than happy about her absence.
Fleming thought so, and allowed as how the Justice Department owed
him a favor, which could help Bunting and Mann.

I am always suspicious of lawyers who claim enough influence, for
any reason, to be able to "take care of" cases in the federal system.
Although I imagine that such things can be done, the collusion of a
great many people, some of them young and idealistic, would be required to stop an impending indictment. Nonetheless, I advised
Fleming to use whatever credibility he had to persuade those in
charge that Bunting and Mann were honest men who had tried their
best to operate the companies in a truthful way. That much I had
witnessed personally.

Barely two weeks later I got a call from Ben, who was in Washington with Fleming, another lawyer, and Mann. His story was chilling.

The lawyers, he said, had just met with "the top man" in the Justice Department. Immediately after the meeting they returned and began to grill Ben as to what he could say about me. He told them that he could say a good deal, all of which would show that I had done my damnedest to give the companies good representation when they badly needed it, and to install safeguards in the operating practices that would prevent misrepresentations by the sales force. Bunting was told, "Well, you're not cooperating, we can't represent you." The message was plain. A "cooperative" Bunting could take immunity in exchange for a promise to say something damaging about me, even if he had to dream it up. To his ever-lasting credit and my good fortune, Ben Bunting simply wasn't built that way. He fired the lawyers.

I asked what Rip Mann had responded when the same offer was put to him. "I think he's going to play the game," said Ben. "He explained to me that he's got a family to think of . . ." I wasn't particularly worried about Rip, because our contact had been very limited. But I was livid to find myself the target of such cheap tactics. It was just one more example of lawyers for the prosecution trying to "buy" incriminating testimony without much concern for its truth. If the Bar Associations would somehow find the courage to disbar prosecutors for such tricks, our profession might stand a chance of winning the respect and public confidence it so sorely lacks. (I hold little hope for such a development in my lifetime.)

I very quickly asked for and got a meeting with Henry Petersen, chief of the Criminal Division of the Justice Department. I had known Henry for some time, and had deep respect for his integrity, a respect he had always said was mutual. When we first sat down— Henry, myself, Wayne Smith, and John Keeney, Henry's top assistant —Henry said: "Lee, the last name I ever want to see crossing my desk for a recommendation of indictment is yours. Were you an officer or director or stockholder of these companies?"

I said "No," and explained what my role had and had not been, and suggested that I had done enough work with federal agencies on Turner's behalf so that these facts could be quickly checked out. I also related the "deal" offered Bunting by his lawyers, and suggested that moves of this sort did not seem to comport with Henry's way of doing business. John Keeney spoke up.

"Fleming met with me," he said. "He asked me what Lee Bailey had to do with this whole affair, and I gave him no answer. That was all there was to it."

I had no way to dispute Keeney's account. I did know that *some-one* in the Justice Department had indicated to Fleming that my head on a platter would make for a tempting trade. Henry assured me that his office would not tolerate perjured testimony in order to get an indictment against me, and the meeting ended.

Rumors persisted to the effect that Turner would soon be indicted, but nothing happened. In March 1973, on the day I was preparing a final argument in Tom Cochran's case, I got a call from Wayne Smith.

"I just talked to Justice," he said. "Six people—prosecutors and postal inspectors from Florida—have recommended that you be indicted. But don't worry. I am assured that you will be given a chance to tell your side of the story." That was gloomy news, but I felt confident that given a chance I could quickly and emphatically show the absence of any wrongdoing on my part.

I heard nothing more until the day, six weeks later, when I was —ironically—preparing a summation in Silas Jayne's case. Wayne called again and said: "John Keeney just called and said, 'The time is now.' You're to call John Briggs, the U.S. Attorney in Jacksonville, and make the arrangements to testify."

I called Briggs, who seemed very courtly. He arranged for one of his assistants to inform me of the topics I would be questioned about, and set a time and date—2:00 P.M. on May 3, 1973—for me to appear.

Lynda, Al Johnson, and I arrived in Orlando the day before. On the morning of May 3 Al went down to Briggs's office to discuss what promised to be a serious problem.

In order to give a full account of my relationship with Turner and his companies, it would be necessary to discuss many conversations that fell within the attorney-client privilege. Although I had an ethical right to invade that privilege to the extent necessary for my own protection, in doing so I might well taint the entire grand jury proceedings against any suspect I had represented. I had expected Briggs to say, "That's okay, the government is taking the position that these defendants destroyed their attorney-client privilege by making fraudulent use of the advice they got." This is a well-settled rule of law, and very common where fraud is claimed. But Briggs's response was a surprise—and taken at face value, an encouraging surprise. He told Al quite angrily that under no circumstances was I to testify to any privileged communications. Al suggested that the matter be brought to the attention of a United States District Judge for a ruling. Briggs exploded. "I will be the

judge of this matter," he said. "If you guys try to hold up these proceedings by going to a judge, Bailey won't testify at all. And another thing. I don't want him on the stand all day. He's not going
to take over my grand jury. I didn't want him down here in the first
place."

When Al reported his conversation with Briggs, I was puzzled,
but heartened. If Briggs disallowed the use of the fraud exception
to wipe away the attorney-client privilege, he could hardly be considering charging me with fraud. Still, his apparent fear at the
thought of having a judge rule on the matter smelled a little. My
testimony was postponed until the following day. In an effort to
clear the air, I arranged a conference with Briggs and his staff that
evening.

At 7:30 P.M. we gathered in Briggs's small conference room. Al
was with me. Sitting with Briggs were Kendall Wherry, his assistant,
Jay Johnson, a young Justice Department lawyer, and Postal Inspector Billie Wayne Baron. Briggs suggested that I run through the
testimony I proposed to give without any attorney-client conversations, to see where we stood. I did so for about ninety minutes.
When I had finished, he asked me a few questions for clarification,
then smiled and said, "Mr. Bailey, if you give to the grand jury tomorrow the facts you have related to us here tonight, you will have
accomplished your purpose in coming down here." Al and I, much
relieved over this assurance, picked up Lynda in the reception room
and went back to the hotel to relax.

The following day I testified for more than two hours. Feeling that
there was no further need for a judicial ruling on the privilege
question, I stayed far away from any attorney-client conversations.
As I gave a lengthy narrative of my representation of the Turner
companies, the grand jurors smiled. When I was through Jay Johnson asked me questions about a few documents I had never seen
before, and I left Orlando with a promise to send by letter any information I might be able to dig up about the documents.

As I left the U.S. Courthouse, Bob Johnson, a reporter from the
*Tampa Tribune*, accosted me. "Mr. Bailey," he said, "I have some
highly reliable information that you are going to be indicted. I'd
like a comment." This was the same Bob Johnson who had related
the same "hot tip" to an Orlando attorney a few days before. I decided to draw him out a bit.

"Tell me your source, and I might comment."

"Oh, I can't do that, because I absolutely promised I wouldn't
give out his name. But I can tell you that it's a former Assistant U.S.

Attorney, now practicing in Tampa, who is going to be a special prosecutor, mainly to get you."

"Sorry," I said. "No name, no comment." I walked away.

The exchange was discomforting, but I still felt that I could rely on John Briggs's honesty in his remarks the night before. He knew that I had every right to disregard his wishes and tell the grand jury *all* that had transpired, and that I had waived the opportunity to do so because of his statement that my testimony, even without touching on confidential matters, would "accomplish my purpose in coming to Orlando"—which was obviously to avoid indictment.

I tracked down the history of the documents, including the name of a man who had forged my name to a certain letter that was sent to the field, and forwarded the information to Briggs. I thought everything was fine, when I got another hot tip: Indictment imminent, and you, Lee, are part of the package. I called Henry Petersen at once to find out what kind of double cross was in progress. For the first time in our acquaintance Henry did not return the call—to this day.

Gerry Alch happened to be in a nearby city, and I asked him to drive down to Orlando to speak to Briggs, and to suggest that he call as witnesses the many other lawyers who had represented Turner. They would surely testify that I had gone to great lengths to keep the Turner companies honest. Briggs refused, saying, "We have no question that Mr. Bailey's conduct as a lawyer was proper."

Gerry reported back that Briggs was going to give the grand jury everything I wanted—except the testimony of the other lawyers.

That same morning, May 18, 1973, Lynda and I climbed into the Duke and headed for the Enstrom factory in Menominee, Michigan. The company, which I own, manufactures helicopters. We had with us Verne Lawyer (who happens to be a great one) and Howard Gregory, a very successful aviation businessman from Des Moines who was considering becoming an Enstrom dealer. As we were climbing, I got a call from the Des Moines Flying Service—Mr. Gregory's company—on the radio. A Mr. Garland had called, I was told. (Ed Garland, a crackerjack young attorney from Atlanta, had gone with Alch that morning to see Briggs.) He had left no message.

That was bad. If there had been good news, a message would have been left and the caller would have been Gerry Alch.

When I got within range of the factory, I called on the company frequency and got Ernie Medina. It was immediately apparent that he had some bad news, and was reluctant to break it while talking over a radio that all the employees in the room could hear.

"It's okay, Ernie," I said softly, "it'll be all over the news soon enough. What's the word?"

Medina choked a bit. "Sir, they've got an indictment." He didn't have to say more.

I switched off the radio and leaned back. We were flying over beautiful country, the picturesque farmland of northern Wisconsin, and the brilliant morning sun was spilling into the cabin. But I didn't notice anything at all.

At first the news seemed totally unreal, like something straight out of Kafka. But as I ruminated, I began to remember certain things, certain signs along the way that perhaps I should have heeded long ago.

One scene flashed into my mind with unusual vividness. It was several years ago, a party atmosphere, and I was sitting at a table with the late Jake Ehrlich, a magnificent criminal lawyer with whom I'd had a particularly fond relationship. (Melvin Belli calls me his "illegitimate son," but Jake used to call me his "legitimate son.") Jake was a guest at the opening of the San Francisco Envoy Club, and a group of us were sitting at a table drinking Scotch and soda.

After a while Jake looked at me and said, "Lee, there isn't much more you can do as far as handling heavy cases is concerned. You've handled the most prolific murderer of all time, the most famous murder case of the century, the biggest robbery in the history of the country, and about the only thing that remains for you to round out your career is to get indicted and tried by some son of a bitch."

Rest in peace, Jake, and the knowledge that you were right.

Stripped of all its legal language, the indictment in *U.S.* v. *Koscot et al.* meant that Turner, three of his corporations, eight of his past and present employees, and I were charged with defrauding people by getting them to buy into his various programs. It was classified as a mail fraud case because the companies had used the mails in conducting their business.

What the government was saying was that they never intended to run a legitimate business, that our only real purpose was—as the prosecution's first witness later put it—"to get the check." According to the indictment, "the scheme to defraud" began at the very moment the first company (Koscot) was started, way back in 1967, and that when the various defendants entered the picture, each one eagerly joined the conspiracy. As for me, my role was not spelled out in the indictment, but I could see that the government would allege I had aided the scheme by making it look as if the company was sincere in its efforts to operate legitimately. It was a neat little package.

The only problem was that it simply wasn't true. First of all, a couple of the people named in the indictment wouldn't have been capable of conspiring to cut grass, much less bilk people out of money. Secondly, there was just too much evidence of the company's legitimacy to be consistent with an elaborate, long-standing fraudulent scheme. And finally, there were literally hundreds of lawyers, governmental and in private practice, around the country who knew my role was to keep the company and its personnel from breaking any laws.

Why then did they go after us? For one thing, and there is no denying the fact, Turner and some of his people exhibited all the mannerisms of the classic con man. The flashy clothes, the block-long Cadillacs and Lincoln Continentals, and the wads of money that were always flashed at the meetings. It *looked* like a con, and therefore, after investigating him for more than five years, the government finally concluded that Turner had to *be* a con.

Now of course it wasn't all that simple. There had been people out in the field who clearly defrauded the public by promising them astronomical earnings for little or no work. But Turner, even more after I entered the picture, had been weeding them out. But the point of the indictment was conspiracy. And that just didn't wash.

I think the government went after Turner because he symbolized (in their minds) all that was wrong with multilevel selling. And that when he didn't just roll over and play dead the first time they hit him, and when he in fact protested his innocence and fought back repeatedly, he became a marked man. There were other reasons, less obvious ones. In my opinion the government—at least certain of its small, faceless little bureaucrats—was scared of Glenn Turner because of his ability to rouse the have-nots. There was a potential there that scared hell out of them. So they balled up all their complaints, justified and unjustified, into one package labeled "criminal conspiracy."

The next question was, Why include me? Unfortunately, the answer was all too apparent to me. And it was spelled p-o-s-t-a-l-s. It was an open secret that the postal inspectors were livid over the way I described them in my first book, *The Defense Never Rests*. I'd detailed the way they completely bungled their job in the Plymouth Mail Robbery case, where their singular inability to solve a crime was exceeded only by their hamhandedness at criminal investigative work. I knew they disliked me with a fierce passion, but until May 18 of 1973 I never knew just how deep it went—and how much power they had. I don't think that I would have been indicted if any other federal investigative force had been involved.

Just knowing that I would have to deal with the postals was enough to further blacken my mood.

On the Monday after my indictment, I called my entire staff together in the Boston office. Outside the spring weather was beautiful, but inside we were a tense and anxious crew. I told them bluntly that we might as well begin to think and plan in military terms, because there was no mistaking the fact that we were at war.

I wasn't exaggerating. The office would have to go on what was tantamount to a full alert. There would be no more nine to five, and leisurely lunch hours. It was going to be an all-out effort, nine to nine, plus weekends, and I had to know who I could count on and who wanted out. Again, the reaction was heartening. I began to assign tasks. I had already decided to move for a speedy trial and also for a separate trial, so there was an incredible amount of work that had to be done before June 15th, the first date for filing motions.

Later that same evening, Lynda and I were talking over coffee. I'd explained to her how well everyone in the office had responded to the "alert."

She toyed with her spoon for a moment, drawing lines in the cloth napkin. "What do you expect will happen, hon?"

"I think our motion for a speedy trial will be granted. I think we'll be severed out, get a separate trial, and we'll be able to show that the government has no case against me. It'll rule our lives and foul up the office for the next month or six weeks. But then we can get back to work."

"Well, that's not really so bad then, is it?"

"No," I replied, "it could be a lot worse."

My first moves were all taken with one thought in mind: speed. A criminal lawyer makes his money by being available, and if the word got out that I was going to be stuck in a complicated trial along with eight other human and three corporate defendants, clients would begin to look elsewhere. When you run an office with a monthly overhead of fifty-five thousand dollars, it doesn't take long to get behind the eight ball. A separate and speedy trial was an absolute must.

My first move, which I made at the staff meeting in the Boston office on the Monday after the indictment, had been to put Mark Kadish in full and complete charge of the preparation of the defense of my case.

Mark had two main tasks. One was to set up the machinery of the investigation to support my defense, which meant uncovering a wealth of documentary evidence before he could even begin to interview witnesses, and the other was to manage the legal research that had to be done immediately for the briefs to be filed in support of my motions for a speedy trial and for severance.

The date for filing motions was June 5—just ten days away—so Mark and John Truman rolled up their sleeves, and those of the law clerks, and plunged in. It was to be Medina all over again, flat-out work with no stones unturned. The team produced seventeen motions and memoranda of law in ten days, averaging twenty hours of work per day. The motions were excellent. (Mark said they were "very good, considering the time frame.")

The early hostility on the part of the prosecution should have warned me that I was in for a long, unpleasant battle. But during what I thought were moments of objectivity, I had analyzed the government's case. I felt that our own investigation would turn up sufficient evidence to produce one of two results: either a dismissal of the charges against me before we ever got to trial, or a separate and therefore short trial.

One of the reasons for my feeling of confidence was that our legal brief in support of severance had been written by an acknowledged expert in the criminal law field, Prof. Alan Dershowitz of Harvard. We retained Professor Dershowitz (and one of his senior students) to research and write the brief because of his reputation—and because we simply hadn't the time to do it ourselves with seventeen other legal documents to prepare.

All the motions, those my office had produced and the motion written by Professor Dershowitz, were filed by June 5. Chief Judge George C. Young, to whom the case had been assigned, immediately set June 15—not even two weeks away—as the day on which he would hear oral argument on all the motions.

I was pleased by the judge's willingness to hear the motions so soon. It seemed to me an indication that he was inclined in favor of severance. But then the government got in the act. It opposed my motion's being heard separately from those of the other defendants, arguing that since the magistrate had given them an additional two weeks to make their motions, hearing mine first would be a duplication of effort. I think the government's phrase was "judicial economy would not be favored by such a procedure."

The judge's response lifted our spirits. Judge Young ruled that he would hear just my motions (for severance and for a speedy trial) on June 15th, and hold the others in abeyance until he had ruled on mine. I took this as a very good sign, a strong indication that he would grant me a separate trial.

I was dead wrong. The June 15 hearing before Judge Young swiftly deteriorated into what Kadish called a "bad scene." First the government objected to some general, and I felt innocuous, comments I had made on the Mike Douglas television show shortly after the indictment came out (I was keeping a commitment made months before) and to certain public statements made by Glenn Turner and one of his company lawyers. We were completely surprised by this and wasted more than an hour in argument.

Then an unfortunate exchange took place between Judge Young and a lawyer I'd recommended to Koscot, and who had come to court under the mistaken impression that he had been asked to defend me. When his name came up on a minor matter, he stood up and began to argue with the judge from the spectator seats in the courtroom. Finally, the judge said, "Don't let that young man leave the courtroom. I have some things I want to ask him." And the lawyer stood up and shouted, "I've got some things I want to tell you, Judge."

The whole thing must have left a very unpleasant taste in the judge's mouth. When we got around, at last, to argue my motions we could see that a good deal of his patience had already been spent.

He gave Gerry Alch forty minutes to argue the motion for a speedy trial and Alan Dershowitz thirty to argue the severance motion. Alch did an excellent job in his argument. So did Dershowitz, on the legal basis for severance, but Judge Young tripped him up by asking for specific examples of matters between Turner, myself, and others that he could cite as examples of the attorney-client privilege.

Something was very wrong. How could a sitting judge, in open court, ask for disclosure of privileged information that John Briggs had conceded could not be used against Turner or his associates? That "I've been had" feeling flooded through me like a hot flash.

Dershowitz, of course, had no response, since I had not briefed him on any of the conversations between Turner (and the others) and myself. And yet here was a U.S. District Judge inviting him to tell all the world that which had been treated as confidential through centuries of practice.

Bernie Dempsey, the special prosecutor hired by Briggs and the

Justice Department to try the case—and the same man who had seen fit to "leak" the news of my impending indictment to Bob Johnson of the *Tampa Tribune* before I testified in the grand jury—explained things very quickly. "There *is* no attorney-client privilege in this case, Your Honor, because the fraud exception applies. I have three hundred witnesses to call and the government's case will take fourteen weeks. We don't want two trials."

John Briggs, who was telling all the world through his indictment that Turner and Co. were "con" men of the first water, had in fact "conned" me beautifully. Belatedly, it was plain. He couldn't afford the risk that his grand jury, having heard my complete testimony, might refuse to indict, so he talked me out of pressing the matter by giving a false assurance that if I went along with him I would be all right. It had been a scheme from the start, and his great concern over my taking the question to a federal judge for a ruling, when his grand jury was about to run out of time, was apparent.

(I suppose he felt pleased at what he had accomplished. Nonetheless, it dismays me that federal prosecutors think they must stoop to conquer. Had I pulled a stunt like that, the Massachusetts Bar Association would have been after my license in a minute. But then, who is to prosecute the prosecutors when they commit fraud? Must we have an Archibald Cox to be checked on by a Leon Jaworski, to be checked on by a . . . ? It's like the timeless question of who guards the guards.)

Based upon Dempsey's representation, Judge Young denied my motions and delayed the trial for as long as he legally could, under the rules of his court, 120 days. He warned the government, however, that if it attempted a joint trial of great length and I had to be severed out along the way, that could be the ball game so far as I was concerned.

As I learned much later, the prosecutors had considered this risk, and took it deliberately, not because they wanted to, but because in their minds there was no choice.

The windows of the rental car were tightly closed, and the air-conditioning unit battled valiantly against the midsummer Florida sun. It was July 18, and we'd been summoned to Orlando for additional pretrial hearings.

I heard Lynda sigh, and looked in the direction of her glance. There, off to the left of the highway, some two hundred yards ahead, a huge billboard totally dominated the view.

On one side was the American flag, and on the other a man dressed in the same color scheme struck a defiant pose. Across the top of the billboard were the words "Welcome to Orlando. Home of the UNSTOPPABLE Glenn W. Turner."

We were on our way back to court because there had been a major change in the dramatis personae. Two weeks before, all counsel and defendants had been notified that Judge Young had removed himself from the case. He'd turned the case over to the Fifth Circuit's youngest judge, Gerald B. Tjoflat, who had agreed to rehear the original pretrial motions.

Hope springs eternal, as they say, and to me this meant another shot at a severance. As soon as I heard the news I put Kadish and Truman back to work beefing up our original briefs.

Two of the other defendants had recently hired lawyers from Florida, so I checked with their counsel to see what they thought of the new judge. I was pleased by what I heard. Judge Tjoflat (pronounced SHO-flat) was forty-three years old, a former trial lawyer who specialized in defending insurance companies. That didn't exactly make him a defense lawyer's dream, but at least he'd had trial experience.

Florida Governor Kirk had appointed Tjoflat to the state bench in 1968. He'd run successfully for the same position two years later, and in 1970, President Nixon appointed him a Federal District Judge, on the recommendation of Sen. Edward Gurney.

Almost immediately he started to earn a reputation as a no-nonsense, work-horse judge who knew the law. I asked other Florida lawyers about him, and as the reports began to filter in, it appeared that if he had a known flaw it was that he was almost too tough. But I liked that. There is nothing better in a complicated case than a judge who takes charge, firmly but fairly. From all accounts it looked like a plus.

Another thing I liked was that Judge Tjoflat had a solid academic background. Born in Pittsburgh, he'd been schooled in the South, with an undergraduate degree from the University of Virginia and a law degree from prestigious Duke, where he'd been editor of the *Law Review*.

I got my first look at Gerald Bard Tjoflat on July 19 in Federal Court in Orlando. He lived up to all his advance billing: tall, apparently in excellent physical shape, and obviously intelligent, he took charge the moment he entered the courtroom.

Given the circumstances, it took some doing. In addition to the ten defendants, there were at least fifteen out-of-state lawyers plus several local counsel. As the *Orlando Times* pointed out the next day, it resembled a bar association meeting. Ironically, the front page headline in that day's *Orlando Sentinel* read: ORLANDO TOPS NATION IN JOB GAINS.

If a lawyer rambled on, Tjoflat cut him off or brought him back to the point at hand; if counsel forgot the specifics of a case he was citing, the judge sent his clerk out for the record of the case; and if an attorney made an unfortunate reference to circumstances other than the case at hand, he received a sharp rebuke and a testy lecture.

As I learned from one of the local lawyers, this tough exterior was no act. Not long ago he'd given a waitress thirty days in jail for contempt of court. Her crime: a tableful of jurors she'd been serving left a scanty tip, so she remarked, "Have an innocent day!"

In 1972 Judge Tjoflat had the unpleasant judicial duty of ruling on the city of Jacksonville's school busing case. His decision put 60 percent of the city's youngsters on the bus each morning. One of them was his own daughter.

I thought Judge Tjoflat's presence increased my chances for an early out, especially when he agreed to rehear the motions for severance.

Our renewed pretrial hopes were centered on a 357-page brief, the product of still another all-out effort by John Truman. Again, we stressed two reasons for a separate trial: first of all, I felt that my chances for a swift acquittal (or even a dismissal of the charges) would be greater if the jury did not have to sift out my defense from that of nine others, some of whom might have trouble mounting a credible defense; and secondly, my motion for a speedy trial was still pending. We were ready for trial, whereas many of the other defendants had only recently found counsel who could devote the necessary time to preparing their defenses.

By late August, with the trial only days away, Judge Tjoflat was not the only change in the cast of characters. Nor would he be the last.

One of the new additions was my lawyer. When Judge Young ruled, back in June, that all defendants would go to trial together, I figured the time had come to hire good counsel.

I chose Theodore I. Koskoff of Bridgeport, Connecticut. I had met Teddy Koskoff quite by accident a few years ago when I was speaking at a convention of the American Trial Lawyers Association. Much of the discussion that day had centered around the less than impressive job done by several of the defense lawyers in the trial of the Chicago Seven.

The comments had nothing to do with politics or philosophy, but simply with the manner in which the defendants had been represented. I made a remark about the difference between the defense effort in that case and reports of the sterling defense of the New Haven Panthers by a man named Theodore Koskoff. Suddenly a large, rotund man seated to my right on the dais got up and said, "Thank you very much, Mr. Bailey. I'm Teddy Koskoff."

We became friends. Shortly after that, when Turner was looking for legal help in the Northeast, I recommended Koskoff.

The combination of his legal skills, honed over thirty-five years of practice as a trial lawyer, plus his familiarity with Turner Enterprises and my work for them, made Teddy Koskoff an ideal choice as my defense counsel.

The government's team appeared to be the finalists in a game of musical prosecutors. John Briggs was nowhere to be seen, having turned the case over to Bernie Dempsey. But Dempsey didn't last too long. When it was learned that Judge Tjoflat would hear the case, Dempsey faded from view. According to courthouse scuttlebutt, he was hardly a favorite of the judge's.

In the middle of July the case was turned over to still another special prosecutor and former Assistant U.S. Attorney by the name of Hugh Smith. Blond, seemingly pleasant, the thirtyish Smith was a member of a Tampa law firm also represented at the prosecution table by a senior member, Michael Kinney, who was to handle the cross-examination.

The government's second string consisted of two young men, Robert Leventhal, an Assistant U.S. Attorney, and Jay Johnson, a lawyer with the Justice Department in Washington who had been working on the case for several years. Finally, there was Billie Wayne Baron, the postal inspector.

The prosecution was something less than a seasoned, cohesive unit —Hugh Smith, who would present a case the government had worked on for over five years, running up a bill of who knows how many millions of dollars, was appointed in mid-July of 1973. But the defense was worse off.

With the exception of myself, no defendant had a lawyer who'd been retained before the middle of the summer. Turner and Ed Garland (who'd been recommended, to my great delight, by Jerris Leonard) were newly wed, as were most of the other defendants and their counsel.

At first glance it might seem that things were even: the chief prosecutor was new and so were most of the defense attorneys. But this kind of logic ignores the reality of the situation. The government, no matter who was in charge at the time, had been preparing its case since 1968. The files of the postal inspectors were thick with documentation. Hundreds of potential government witnesses had already been interviewed, their statements taken and typed, and their strategic value to the government's case duly recorded.

The defense knew nothing of all this. No files had been turned over, though boxes of them were available. Except for me, not one defendant had interviewed a "count" witness or any other witness. And the government was talking about calling three hundred witnesses. We were up against the power and weight of the system. In a multidefendant conspiracy trial the inequities all but cry out for reform. But that's the way it is. And that's what we were facing.

Our hope lay in the new judge. Orally and in writing we had pleaded with him to recognize the basic unfairness of the situation. As federal judges go he was brand new; no barnacles marked his bench. Just a few years ago he was down in the trial pit, and we thought his memory was clear, that he knew the immense difficulty of coming into a hard case cold. We held our breath for over a month. On August 30, eleven days before the trial was slated to begin, Judge Tjoflat denied my motion for a separate trial, ruled that all defendants would be tried together, and moved the site of the trial from Orlando to Jacksonville, which happened to be his home town.

The judge knew it would be a long trial. To a Miami reporter he made a guess of eight weeks. Initially, the estimates of the lawyers in the case ranged from three to six months. Later they would double.

On the last day of the pretrial hearings in Orlando, Ed Garland argued eloquently for a continuance of six months. He pleaded that he would need that much time just to prepare an *adequate* defense for Glenn Turner, citing that the government that very day had turned over four huge cardboard boxes of documents for his "perusal."

Judge Tjoflat was not totally insensitive. He postponed the trial for one week.

With the guesses at the trial's length running from a minimum of two months to a maximum of six, it appeared that Lynda and I would probably be in Jacksonville, Florida, long enough to qualify for residency. Jacksonville was, as the saying goes, a nice place to visit, but we had no great desire to live there.

One thing was certain, a motel was going to become both expensive and confining, so the defense team began to scout around for a convenient place where we could rent apartments on a short-term basis.

Teddy Koskoff and his able young assistant Tom Nadeau had been looking at apartments for several days when they found a fairly new, not-to-expensive complex in Arlington, a South Side suburb just ten minutes from the courthouse—and five minutes from a private airport.

In keeping with the poetic bravado of northern Florida, the apartments were called Villa Granada.

If you drive too fast down Crane Avenue, you can easily miss Villa Granada, as most of it is hidden behind a tiny shopping center that houses a Seven-Eleven store, an unfinished drugstore, a dry cleaners, and, oddly, two laundromats. Yet, once inside, there is a surprisingly pleasant layout of at least a dozen three-story buildings, two swimming pools, and several grassy courtyards. Here and there a lone pine tree stands in splendid defiance of the traffic flow, a stubborn symbol of the architect's integrity, the builder's foresight, or a lucky mistake.

The apartments themselves were conveniently laid out with the kitchen at the small end of the L and the living room at the other. The number of bedrooms, which varied from one to three, determined the width of the main room. Despite many examples of corner-cutting and sloppy workmanship (the obvious tilt of the eaves, as seen from the balconies, the light switches installed upside down, and the water taps that give the opposite of their labels) there was, at least at the beginning, a curious charm to the wood and stucco buildings of the Villa Granada.

Within days, the Koskot et al. retinue had become the prime tenant. Someone joked that the name should be changed to Villacot. With the exception of the local attorney, every defendant and every lawyer took rooms. Single additional apartments were rented for investigators, secretaries, aides, office equipment, and the burgeoning file system. To make life more palatable, Glenn Turner provided a color television set for every apartment.

Daily maid service was available for anyone who wanted it. (After the first few days Lynda, an inveterate picker-upper, complained, "Damn it, Lee, I don't see why we should pay a maid ten dollars a day just to make our bed." I laughed. "Honey, we're not paying it.

Glenn is. And if you say you don't want it you'll hurt his feelings.")

We had a two-bedroom apartment, as did Teddy Koskoff, Glenn Turner, Ed Garland, and Mark Kadish. The other two-bedrooms were shared by various combinations: two lawyers, two defendants, a lawyer and his client.

When the investigative arm became fully operative, a three-bedroom apartment—No. 106—was turned into command central. Regular and WATS (Wide Area Telephone Service) lines were installed alongside IBM Selectric typewriters, and the furniture had to make room for filing cabinets, desks, and steel shelving.

Our apartment soon reflected our temporary position as the only married couple in residence. Small touches began to appear: a framed painting from the house in Marshfield, slightly better dishes and silverware. But there was a limit to what Lynda could do in the moments stolen for homemaking. Toast still had to be made in the oven, and the ashtrays had little stickers on the bottom that read "29 cents."

The few compulsive members of the team, like Mark Kadish, kept their apartments neat. The rest, despite valiant initial efforts, soon lapsed into the habits of a lifetime. Closets became clothes hampers, the same quickly rinsed dish and cup served for every meal, and most refrigerators held only fruit juice and beer.

Originally the lawyers' meetings were held in our apartment, but when the crowds got too big I had to switch them to 106. It was less pleasant but more functional. Within weeks it would become just another routine, another pattern, an accommodation. But the stakes would remain the same.

In the first week of September, with the trial all but begun, I had to make a hard choice that would cause still another change in the cast of characters. I had to decide if it would be better, under the circumstances, for me to defend myself.

I had absolutely no disagreement, dissatisfaction or disappointment with the work of Teddy Koskoff. The question, which we had discussed early on, centered on whether or not I was granted a separate trial.

In my view, the attorney-client privilege prevailed—no matter what the government said. I had the right to invade it as much as was necessary for my own protection, and that called for a moment-to-moment judgment throughout the trial, with the other defendants present, as to what I was willing to sacrifice for their protection. No one could do that for me.

On Friday, September 7, Judge Tjoflat granted my motion to go "pro se."

I know the immediate reaction of many people to the news that a lawyer is going to defend himself. I know the old saw, and in fact had used it analogously in *The Defense Never Rests* in explaining why I use a literary agent: ". . . any author who tries to represent himself in the publishing field is in the same league as that lawyer who represents himself in court—he has a fool for a client."

Why did I decide to defend myself? The reasons were based on tactics and personality. First of all, I had been directing my own defense from the very beginning. Only in court, during the hours of pretrial, did I have to sit back, to force myself to wait and see if any of the other lawyers made the point I thought should be made. Many times I had to tug sleeves, to whisper, to pass notes. This is not my style. And for me to do so during the trial while the other defendants sit in silence would look very odd to a jury.

Another reason was the need for immediate reaction during cross-examination. There is no way under the sun that a criminal lawyer—defendant can function effectively by tugging on someone else's sleeve or whispering in his ear. For one thing, there is not enough time. When a witness falters or makes a damaging admission inadvertently, the cross-examiner must move in immediately. Once lost, such opportunities rarely present themselves a second time.

I am by nature an aggressive lawyer. I cannot sit back, as Teddy Koskoff can, waiting for just the right moment to make a move, waiting for the opponent to slip. I have to force the issue. That's the way I am.

There were two other reasons.

One, I knew more about this case than anyone else because of the time I had put in representing the various companies and individuals. There is only one co-defendant whom I did not represent in some manner in the past four years.

Two, when Judge Tjoflat denied my motion for a separate trial, a motion predicated heavily on the importance of the attorney-client privilege, he relied in so doing on the government's allegations of proof. According to the government's proffer, their representation of what they can prove, the attorney-client privilege would be eliminated.

I disagreed with that ruling because I didn't believe the government could prove that. I thought the government had made a false proffer. Therefore, the principal reason I decided to defend myself was that I refused the government's "invitation" to damage the other defendants in order to help myself. I planned to conduct my defense as if the attorney-client privilege were still in effect. And nobody else should bear that responsibility.

I don't say that to blow my own horn. What I mean is that, because I had spent so much more time than anyone else on the defense team with Glenn Turner and his companies, I was in the best position to decide what should fall under the attorney-client privilege and what should not.

Another serious aspect of the case affecting my decision was that so few of the defense lawyers had adequate time to prepare. By early September many of the lawyers were relatively new and some were brand new. One of them, a man named Hernandez, had been in the case but a week when he made his first appearance in court on September 7. He moved for a continuance for his client, but Judge Tjoflat denied it.

Later that same day Ed Garland was arguing that he needed more time to prepare Turner's defense. Employing figurative language, Garland said, "Your Honor, I've been in this case for two months now, and I've just reached the trunk. I need time to get to the branches." At that, Mr. Hernandez leaped up and said, "Judge, Mr. Garland worked for two months before he got to the trunk. I haven't even found the tree yet." The judge joined in the spontaneous laughter, but did not grant a continuance.

When Judge Tjoflat ruled that I could defend myself, he said that I would have to do it alone. There would be no splitting of the defense role between myself and Teddy Koskoff. What's more, he ruled that Mark Kadish could assist only in the role of investigator.

The judge wanted it clean and neat. No fuzzing of the lines. There were already too many lawyers (nine) and defendants (thirteen—ten human and three corporate) in the courtroom. So, if the lone attorney-defendant wanted to defend himself, fine. But he had to go it alone.

Teddy Koskoff was upset. He had not expected Judge Tjoflat to cut him out of the case entirely. In a characteristic gesture, he offered to stay on and help plan the defense for nothing. I was sorely tempted to accept. But I knew all too well what happens to a medium-sized law firm when one of its senior partners is tied up with one case for a long time. I couldn't accept Teddy's generous offer, nor could I express just how much I appreciated it, so I thanked him and hoped he understood my feelings.

I would miss Teddy's counsel, and we would all miss the work of Tom Nadeau, Teddy's younger associate, who had impressed everyone on the defense team with his quiet ways and his thorough, professional manner.

I was sure of only two things: one, with defense lawyers' fees ranging from five hundred to a thousand dollars a day, plus expenses, it was sure to be a very costly trial; and two, my client would be paying the biggest per diem of all.

At precisely nine-fifteen on the morning of Monday, September 17, 1974, the heavy oak door behind the judge's bench opened and the clerk gaveled the courtroom into silence. The marshall intoned, "Everyone please rise. This honorable court is in session, Judge Gerald Bard Tjoflat presiding."

Settling his swirling robe, the judge took the middle chair of the three behind his bench, and instructed the clerk to call the case.

"This case," the clerk read carefully in a firm voice, "is The *United States of America* versus *Koscot Interplanetary, Incorporated, et al.*, number 7371 Orlando Circuit . . ." and the last, the distinguishing word, "criminal."

I looked over at Glenn Turner, resplendent in a white suit, blue shirt, and red tie. As usual, he grinned at me. His attitude from the beginning had been, "If you look scared, they're going to think you're guilty. I'm not scared, and I'm not guilty, and I'm not even worried. So I'm not going to go around with my head hanging down." And he didn't. He smiled his way through the next three days—especially as he watched the way the jury was shaping up.

By Wednesday afternoon we had our jury. The panel contained eighteen people, twelve regular jurors and six alternates. By sex it broke down into eleven women and seven men. There were six blacks and twelve whites.

It was a good jury for Glenn Turner. I wasn't terribly happy with its educational level, and the government probably felt the way I did. As I looked at the jury all I could think of was one of Glenn's Golden Opportunity meetings. This didn't necessarily mean it would be a tough jury for me, but I had wanted more people who could understand certain legal concepts that were part and parcel of my own defense case. As I learned the jurors' occupations, I was concerned about the ability of some of them to grasp such fine points as, for example, being a principal and being the lawyer for a principal.

Captain Hall, the second to last alternate juror empaneled, probably had the most education; he was a retired Navy man who ran his own string of businesses. Several other jurors had some college experience, and most had at least a high school diploma. Their occupations included one canteen worker; a mechanic; a widow with six children; a man who worked on the loading dock of a Jacksonville newspaper; a retired longshoreman; two telephone operators; a business machine operator; a man who ran an addressograph machine; and a woman who worked in the bad check department of a bank.

I'm sure the government's worry was that a panel of "salt-of-the-earth" types might be influenced by Turner's self-help philosophy and his rags-to-riches story. (If the whole matter hadn't been so deadly serious, it might have been funny.) Nonetheless, that was the jury of our peers.

And then there was the judge. Ever since he had refused to grant me a separate trial I had been studying him, trying to find out his attitude about the defense. I was beginning to suspect a progovernment tilt, to borrow a word from Henry Kissinger.

The more recent information about the judge was less encouraging. A Nixon appointee, he reputedly prided himself on the number of defendants he could get to plead to lesser charges, thus avoiding unnecessary trials and reducing the backlog. There was nothing wrong with this trait, nor even unusual, but I worried a bit about his "law-and-order" reputation, and his personal background, which was certainly antithetical to that of a Glenn Turner.

Judge Tjoflat was a high Episcopalian, in fact a power in the local church. He was exactly the sort of man who would be appalled by some of the charges against Turner and his companies.

I kept thinking of something that Clarence Darrow had written years ago:

> Beware of the Lutherans, especially the Scandinavians; they are almost sure to convict. Either a Lutheran or a Scandinavian is unsafe, but if both-in-one, plead your client guilty and go down the docket. He learns about sinning and punishing from the preacher, and dares not doubt. A person who disobeys must be sent to Hell; he has God's word for that.

Granted, Darrow was having a bit of fun. And he was referring to jurors not judges, and Lutherans and Episcopalians are not identical. Still, the similarities were too close for comfort.

We got underway, officially, at nine-fifteen on Tuesday morning, September 20, 1973. Judge Tjoflat became the first contestant in the boredom sweepstakes by reading the entire first count of the indictment to the jury. When he finished, Hugh Smith would make the government's opening statement, for which he'd asked and received three hours. Ed Garland and I, in that order, would split an equal amount of time.

The judge's reading of the first count took almost an hour. It was tedious, boring to those who had already read it; the jury, which was hearing it for the first time, paid valiant attention for the first five minutes and then began to flag.

I turned back to the spectator section and smiled at Lynda. I could tell from her expression that she sensed my anxiety. All I wanted to do was get on with it.

The judge closed in standard fashion and it was time for the chief prosecutor to make the government's opening statement.

Hugh Smith carried a thick pile of yellow legal-sized sheets up to the lectern. He smiled perfunctorily at the jury, most of whom smiled back. With his blond hair layered with several long, sun-bleached whitish strands, Smith looked like Florida's version of the boy-next-door grown up.

For three hours he tolled off the charges, describing what he called "a scheme from front to back." He alleged the knowing participation of everyone, those who left early as well as those like me who'd come later, and everyone like Turner who was still active in the company. At one point near the end he called the whole operation a "gigantic and successful fraud," a phrase that all the papers used the next day, along with his characterization of Turner Enterprises as a "Franken-stein monster."

Smith had done a pretty good job. He'd outlined the structure and the practices of the companies, from the beginning to the time of the indictment, making sure to tie in all of the defendants. He'd gone over the promotional practices, spending most of his time on those of the last few years, which were the most questionable, as I well knew because they were the kinds of actions that turned me away from the company. When touching on the legitimate efforts of many to build and increase the companies, he gave them quick lip service. As the papers would point out the next day, it was a damning in-dictment of all the companies and anyone who'd ever had anything to do with them.

At lunch, when Smith was two-thirds of the way through his open-ing, Teddy Koskoff (who had stayed to hear the opening statements) wolfed down his Bloody Mary, shook his head, and observed, "It's go-ing to be a typical vicious conspiracy case where the prosecutor throws so much garbage that what hits one or two will foul up all of them. And he knows that if he throws enough he's bound to hit somebody, sometime."

The courtroom was very quiet when Ed Garland began his opening statement.

The right side of the spectator section of the courtroom had been appropriated by friends of the defense, much like the split in a congregation at a wedding, and in the first row sat Ed's father, seventy-year-old Reuben Garland. For half a century Reuben Garland had practiced criminal law in Atlanta. He was a living legend.

Ever since the senior Garland had turned up at the trial for the first time, defense people remarked on the obvious and touching closeness between father and son. If his father's tie was slightly askew, Ed would straighten it, unself-consciously, or he'd brush off his father's coat, making the gesture seem affectionate rather than functional. Now, as his son prepared to make the first opening statement for the defense, Reuben Garland's proud red face flushed even redder.

I glanced back at Lynda, sitting in the same row. She gave me one of her magnificent smiles. I could see that she was nervous. She liked Ed Garland, and wanted very much for him to be good today.

And he was good. Among other things, he said:

"We will show you that the United States, through its attorneys' office, investigated for three years in Orlando the process of bringing these charges after the postal inspectors had done so for six years, and we shall show you throughout this time that Glenn Turner and the others who at different times were involved with him throughout this period constantly went and said, 'Show us how you want us to do it and we'll do it your way.'

"The evidence is going to present to you one of the most tragic stories of an individual citizen and those people who joined with him who are average citizens, being hunted and hounded by the forces of government.

". . . The evidence, ladies and gentlemen, . . . will show no criminal intention in this case, and you will get the facts and there are many of them, the fact that distribution systems were set up by these people in an effort to supply the people with the product, the fact that trucking systems were set up with an attempt to supply the people with the product, the fact that in 1969 after having counsel, Glenn Turner went to F. Lee Bailey and said, 'Will you represent me?'

"And the evidence will show that thereafter Mr. Bailey hired and set up a staff of some of the finest attorneys in America to go to the attorneys general, some fifty or more attorneys, many of whom will come here and tell you how they tried to work out whatever problems might exist, and we will show that this was done, and we will show it was done in good faith with an attempt to comply with the laws that were rapidly changing, because the age of the consumer and the consumer politician, we'll show, has come and it's begun to change, and even to this day there are only twenty-three states that have passed any laws that either regulate or control a multilevel marketing program in this country.

"But we will show that the government destroyed, by going one step further, this man's ability to have his attorney, by indicting his attorney, the man who should be standing here where I am standing, to attempt to destroy his right to defend this case.

". . . I want to say to you in conclusion that I believe at the end of this case you will realize that the issues are not the issues stated by the government in its opening, and that this is not the case of the United States government versus Glenn Turner and these other people, but this is the case of the United States government against the American people."

When Ed finished it was 3:10 P.M. We all went back to the defense room for a break. The general consensus was that Garland had done a good job. Teddy Koskoff rated it "a B, maybe even a B plus." Mark Kadish was pleased, though he thought Ed had said too much about the obstructionist role of the government (which we had agreed I would stress). I thought Ed had done a fine job, and I told him so. But I had a hard time getting through the wall of praise that Reuben Garland had set up around his son. The senior Garland was telling everyone within earshot, "My boy is the best trial lawyer in the country." Then he saw me, winked, and pulled me aside. "Of course that doesn't include you and me."

I told Reuben that I agreed, and then I walked down to the end of the corridor. There were various groups in the hallway, but I wanted to be by myself for a while. There were a few things I still had to think about, a few adjustments to make in my opening statement that was now only minutes away.

Back in the courtroom, Judge Tjoflat was instructing the jury on the function of the grand jury (Smith had objected because Garland mentioned that Turner had not been called before the grand jury—it was a small point and we didn't think it warranted an instruction, but the judge did). I shifted around in my chair, mentally urging him to hurry.

Finally he said, "We begin the trial with a clean slate, no evidence whatsoever presented, and at this point in this case, there is no evidence presented. . . . You may proceed, Mr. Bailey."

There were so many things I wanted to say that I felt I could talk through the night. But it was late and the jurors were beginning to sag. Instead I hit the highlights, yet managed to cover the main story. When I finished, I was surprised to see that I had talked for only an hour.

I began by giving a little personal history and then shifted into my relationship with Glenn Turner. I described my legal work for Glenn, ending with the collapse of our negotiations with the FTC, and I made sure the jury knew how I felt about him personally.

". . . I liked the cut of the man, I liked the things he said, I liked the humility he showed, the honesty he showed admitting some mistakes he made. I liked the way he told me he didn't know much in many areas of running a business, but would be willing to bring in experts who could do that for him. . . . I didn't turn Mr. Turner down."

I thought I could detect a slight glimmer, a slight difference in the way several of the jurors were looking at Glenn. Perhaps I was just imagining it. But they *were* looking at him steadily now.

The government I saved for last.

". . . The evidence will show, ladies and gentlemen, that during 1971 and 1972, while we were being led down the primrose path by one agency, another agency was sneaking around trying to put together a criminal case. They already had a plan. If the Federal Trade Commission had ever signed that order this case wouldn't be here today, and the evidence will prove to you beyond any doubt that, in one of the dirtiest moves in politics, one agency called the other one and said, 'Don't sign it! Don't sign it,' and persuaded them not to do it. So when you hear all this talk of criminal conduct, when you hear all this talk of evil intent, bear in mind that you are going to hear some evidence of conduct not very admirable on the part of not the government, but the people who were then running it.

". . . There are a number of overt acts here. I had originally intended to go through them all. I will not. I will hope that as evidence appears in this case that you will do this, because it is cruel and inhuman treatment to keep you here any more today, and the Eighth Amendment prohibits it.

"As evidence comes in this case from the prosecution's side, be alert for something to explain it in cross-examination or countervailing evidence from the defense side, and vice versa.

"I ask no favor of you, but be fair to both sides. If something seems confusing because I didn't take the time to go into it in argument in a case that involves some three years, indeed, the opening statement can go on for days to cover all the details.

"Keep that same open mind until the close of the case. Everybody has made you a lot of promises about what they are going to show, and I am making a promise, this statement to you is a promisssory note, and if it turns out to be no good at the end of the trial, I would expect to be in some trouble. But that is where the promises are paid off, when we stand back up here again the next time to sum up for you what has been proven in this case as against what was claimed with all the grandiosity of rhetoric at the outset, that will be the day of reckoning. If you will keep an open mind until that is concluded, and then until the judge explains to you, as only he has the right to do, what the law must be as you take it from him and apply it to the facts and deliberate your verdict. I ask no more.

"Indeed, ladies and gentlemen, I thank you for your extreme patience. I am sorry I was last, but it works out that way. I have asked for no more than it says right up there [I pointed to the Latin words, *Fiat Justicia,* carved in the oak paneling above the judge's bench]: 'Do justice.' "

The crowd in our apartment was so large on Monday evening that Lynda spent most of her time standing in the kitchen. Normally she would be on the couch, but tonight, with all the defendants and their lawyers crowded into the living room, she said she had to make room for those with, as she put it, "most at stake."

By necessity, we'd formed a large circle. Ben Bunting said it looked like an Indian war council. He was right.

The purpose of the meeting was to discuss whatever anyone knew about the three witnesses the government had finally told us they would use in the first week. In most cases the sides exchange witness lists as soon as they know who they will call. In our case, we'd been having a great deal of trouble getting Hugh Smith and his boys to tell us who they would call, much less in what order. As we got closer and closer to the first day of witness testimony, getting a list from the government was about as easy as getting tapes from the White House. Finally, on Friday they gave us three names—Jimmie Earl James, Lynn Garrett, and Bill Sant. But the order was, as they put it, "tentative."

In any criminal case, the more time you have to prepare for a specific witness the better job you can do on him, provided you have the money to hire an experienced investigator to dig up material. At the opening of our case we had three investigators, and one of them, Andy Tuney, was on my payroll and had been concentrating on my defense. So I had called a meeting to see what the defendants knew about the three names on the government's list, names of people who all had worked for or with the company at one time. If the lay defendants could give us enough background on the witnesses, I could send my investigators out to substantiate it, and maybe to find out other helpful facts we could use on cross-examination.

All three witnesses on the list, James, Garrett, and Sant, had come into the company as Koscot distributors, but Jimmie James and Bill Sant had later gone to work for the company at headquarters in Orlando, where they eventually held middle-management positions. Apparently the government would present them as honest men who became disgruntled with company policies and got out rather than be parties to anything fraudulent.

There were, as I well knew, a number of people who fit that description, especially farther down the line of power, whose complaints never reached the top. I wanted to find out from the other defendants if these witnesses belonged in that category.

There was one thing I'd learned about my co-defendants: when it got down to scratch, you could usually count on them for a straight answer. They told me what the three witnesses would probably say against them, and then they told me why. By the end of the evening I had all three witnesses in much better perspective—and I thought I'd found a few skeletons in each closet.

The old juices were flowing, and I launched into a demonstration of what I would do to Jimmie James, Bill Sant, and Lynn Garrett when they took the stand. It was eight parts braggadocio, and impassioned, if nothing else. I had to smile to myself, because I was so obviously using Glenn Turner's standard trick—"jack 'em up!"

When I finished, Jess Hickman, the jolly giant who used to be a major-league pitcher until his arm went bad, jumped out of his chair and hollered, "Gol dang! I just cain't wait to get to that cotton-pickin' courthouse tomorrow and watch Mr. Bailey rip those jay birds apart! It's going to be outasight!"

At the door, Roger Zuckerman, Jess Hickman's courtly young lawyer, shook his head and smiled. "Lee, that's the first time I've ever seen a criminal defendant who's anxious to be in court."

Jimmie Earl James was the government's first witness. At thirty-six years of age, he appeared pleasant though not distinctive. Of medium height and build, he was dressed neatly. Yet there were hints of flashier days, the carefully combed hair, the patent leather slip-on shoes, and the dark red blazer. The lone assertive touch was his pair of modish rose-tinted glasses.

James had owned his own filling station in Greenville, South Carolina, on the day in 1966 when one of his regular customers, a logger, told him about the fabulous money he was making as a distributor with Holiday Magic, a cosmetics company. Jimmie James went to a few meetings, liked what he heard, and invested five thousand dollars to become a distributor.

Soon he came in contact with the hottest salesman in all of Holiday Magic, Glenn W. Turner, and when Turner left the company to form his own, Jimmie Earl James went with him, as one of the first Koscot distributors. He weathered the tough early months, and by late in 1968 he was making more money than he'd expected.

As he rose in the organization he was asked to tell his success story at opportunity meetings. The story began to assume mythic proportions because Jimmie loved to tell how he'd become so motivated by Glenn Turner that he gave away his filling station for one dollar to devote all his time to Koscot.

By 1970 Jimmie Jones had his eye on the presidency of Koscot. It wasn't an unreasonable hope, for he'd been a state director and then a vice-president in charge of customer relations. But there had been a few problems, so Turner gave him a trial demotion to "get his attitude right."

Apparently it didn't help. The relationship went from bad to worse, and Jimmie James left Koscot in 1971. He attempted to start his own company along the exact lines of Turner's. When that failed to get off the ground, James drifted through a few other franchise operations, and then returned home to Greenville, South Carolina. When the government found him, he was, once again, the owner-operator of a filling station.

In an important case, and especially one the government had spent over five years preparing, the lead-off witness was expected to provide some very damaging testimony. Jimmie James didn't disappoint.

In response to Hugh Smith's careful, almost boring interrogation, James gave his version of why he left Koscot. He testified that as director of customer relations he began to hear repeated complaints about unfair and even outright dishonest practices. He said that he went to Orlando and asked for a meeting with Ben Bunting and, later, Malcolm Julian. (Julian, who had been trained by Jimmie James, had risen faster than his mentor and eventually got the job

James wanted, president of Koscot.) He testified that his protests fell on deaf ears, so he asked Malcolm Julian about the policy statement I had written, which had been sent out over Malcolm Julian's signature to all distributors calling for a strict adherence to ethical business practices. James said he asked Julian if it really meant there would be changes made.

Hugh Smith said, "And what was Mr. Julian's response?"

"Mr. Julian told me, 'Proceed as usual. Get the check.' "

Soon it became a litany. Whenever he could squeeze it in to his answer of one of the prosecutor's questions, Jimmie James would repeat, "He told me, 'Proceed as usual. Get the check.' "

Malcolm Julian sat shaking his head in disbelief and bewilderment, trying to contain his anger.

Malcolm was not James's only target. The witness implicated everyone but Jess Hickman, who had come into the company after Jimmie James had left. As for me, James testified that he'd heard me address a rally in Portland, Oregon, and say that I had "joined forces with Turner" to get him out of legal trouble. At the defense table I whispered to Bunting, "It was about as likely for me to say I'd 'joined forces' as it was for Malcolm to say, 'Proceed as usual. Get the check.' "

As soon as the lunch recess was called, I grabbed Mark Kadish and told him to get a private investigator up the Greenville, South Carolina, as soon as it was humanly possible. When I returned to the defense room where the defendants and their lawyers had lunch every day, Turner was ribbing Malcolm Julian.

"Malcolm," he kidded gleefully, "people have been telling me I had a few bad apples in the barrel, but I never figured you for one of them. Just imagine, you were going around telling people to 'Get the check.' Hey, Jess, Uncle Harry, did you hear that? You just can't tell about some people, can you?"

Several others joined in, and by the end of the lunch break Turner's strategy had paid off: Malcolm Julian was laughing and kidding along with the others. He had just learned the hard way that a conspiracy trial is seldom fair.

On the stand Jimmie James had sounded decidedly holier-than-thou, but the other defendants had a different story. They described James as a disgruntled former employee who had attempted to raid Turner's shop before being asked to leave. There were also hints that he might have been a target for the original indictment, but there wasn't enough hard information, so the defense team decided to see what was brought out on the stand before making any final plans.

We also agreed that only two lawyers would cross-examine Jimmie James. Ed Garland would go first, on Turner's behalf, and I would follow on my own (even though no one expected James to hurt me in any way), and if possible I would also repair whatever damage he might have done any of the other defendants.

Hugh Smith took the better part of three hours to examine Jimmie James on direct. Except for a rare hardness of tone, everything about the chief prosecutor was soft. He wore a light tan suit, he spoke in a voice almost totally free of inflection, and only the occasional prissy set of his mouth betrayed his pleasure in the damaging information he was eliciting from the witness.

It appeared that Smith wanted the jury, and the judge, to notice the sharp difference between his manner and mine—which was known to be less than quiet when dealing with hostile or unfriendly witnesses.

That was another reason why the defense team agreed that Garland would take on the witness first. The jury's exposure to Ed Garland was limited mainly to his quiet but effective opening statement.

By this time the jury had to have noticed two things: one, although Garland looked the part of the successful, young, big-city practitioner (with his tailored suits, British shoes, and plain, expensive-looking dark ties with tiny figures), in reality he spoke their easy blend of country-city talk far more naturally than Mr. Smith (who in his opening statement couldn't bring himself to echo the Turnerites' well-known "Go, go, go" shout, substituting a weak "Yeah, yeah, yeah"); and two, for some unknown reason Judge Tjoflat did not like Ed Garland at all.

Almost without exception, the judge's response to an objection by Garland was met with an impatient, "Overruled." Most of the time he didn't even bother to look at the young lawyer as he said it, and when he did look his treatment was even worse. Once Judge Tjoflat cut him off before he had finished, and Garland protested that he'd like to state the grounds of his objection for the record. The Judge barked, "Sit down, Counsel, you're through."

After Garland had been slapped down half a dozen times, I kidded him. "Ed, you've really got that judge wrapped around your little finger." Garland laughed, but it was apparent that he could not understand why Judge Tjoflat was singling him out for such harsh treatment.

Garland's cross-examination of Jimmie James was a careful, effective piece of work. He smiled at the jury, he smiled at the witness, and he even smiled at the judge. And when he was through, Jimmie

James had repudiated a number of damaging things he had said about Glenn Turner, and a few other defendants as well.

The witness's admissions about how much "Mr. Turner" had helped him overcome personal problems and set his life on the right course sounded so much like a testimonial that the prosecutors squirmed in their chairs. At this point, a spectator seated behind Lynda turned to a man next to him and said, "Excuse me, but I just got here a few minutes ago. Isn't this supposed to be a prosecution witness?"

Garland had not been able to get James to recant on his testimony regarding Malcolm Julian, so I agreed to let Julian's lawyer, Charles Pillans of Jacksonville, take the next turn. Pillans, a thorough practitioner, took the witness back over his testimony with care, and when he finished his client was in a better position. It was late in the day, and although Pillans wanted to nail James for his "Proceed as usual. Get the check" ritual, everyone was tired. He noted the time, informed the judge that he would have a few more questions of the witness first thing in the morning, and suggested a recess. The judge agreed and court was recessed for the day.

Later that evening, after one meeting and just before another, Mark Kadish came into our apartment with a big grin on his face.

"I think I've got something for you on Jimmie James. And I think you'll like it if you can only figure out how to use it."

"Well? Don't just stand there grinning."

Kadish turned one of the dining chairs around, sat down, and hung his arms over the back. "Our investigator just called from Greenville. He got there late this afternoon and nosed around for people who knew Jimmie James, but he couldnt find any right off. So he drove out to Jimmie's filling station, and had a most interesting conversation. It turns out that Mr. James has a real thing about blacks . . ."

"I'd heard that, but I thought he now had a black man working for him?"

"He does, but do you know what he calls him, in front of his white customers and the man himself? He calls him 'the nigger.' "

I was damn interested, but I had to make sure. "How reliable is this information?"

"The guy who told the investigator is Jimmie James's son."

That night, after the final meeting, I sat up for quite a long time. Short of physical violence, bigotry angers me more than anything else, and I wanted to make the most of what we had just learned. I relished the possibility that the man who had been flat out lying about Malcolm Julian might be exposed before the judge and the jury as a racist.

It would have to be done just right, though. If I confronted James with this charge and he lied his way out, it could be a dangerously inflammatory step, one that Judge Tjoflat would not appreciate.

I also had to think about the other lawyers. It's one thing to take a chance on your own behalf, but when you have the rights of a number of co-defendants to keep in mind, it can be an entirely different matter. And I had no experience in that field.

The next morning Charlie Pillans questioned Jimmie James for another forty-five minutes. He scored a number of small points, and cast further doubt on the man's veracity, memory, and character. Then he turned him over to me.

There had been some discussion among the defense lawyers as to just how hard I should go after the witness, just what the proper "tone" should be. The question arose because I had made several loud and angry objections to Hugh Smith's opening statement and his direct examination of the first witness.

Roger Zuckerman of Washington was one of the lawyers who cautioned me to "cool it," so I wouldn't contrast too sharply with Smith. I told Roger I would keep it in mind.

I began easily with Jimmie James, almost on a friendly basis. The witness was not fighting me, and I got him to admit that he couldn't really remember exactly what I had said at the meetings he'd attended. Then he admitted that he'd only seen me in passing a few times in the halls of the Koscot building in Orlando, and that our two or three meetings had been nothing but hand-shaking, followed by the usual innocuous comments on the weather.

At the end of an hour I had cleared myself of the few damaging statements the witness had made about me in his direct testimony. Then I went into other areas, and at one point Jimmie James made the statement that he always treated everyone "fair and equal."

Within minutes, he'd said it again. That was what I had been waiting for. I picked it up as part of my next question, and again he stated his dedication to fairness and equality.

I could see Frank Martin, LeRoy Beale's Georgia lawyer, look over at his friend Ed Garland and smile ever so slightly. He knew I had found the key I had been probing for. The point now was—how well would the witness resist my efforts to use it?

Under the rules of federal court, a lawyer may not pursue a potentially volatile line of questioning unless he has the information to back it up—the usual phrase is "to tie it in." Armed with the investi-

272      F. LEE BAILEY  /  *For the Defense*

gator's report, plus other facts, I was determined to bring out the
fact that Jimmie James was fired from Koscot largely because of his
racist beliefs and attitude.

I moved into a collateral matter, hoping to confuse the witness.
Previously, my questions had been asked in an even tone, and the
only emotion I displayed was mild exasperation when the witness displayed a conveniently hazy memory as to any date or number that
might be helpful to the defense.

As I shifted into the area of why James left Koscot, I used a harder
tone.

Q. Now, you told us, I believe, that the reason that you were
discharged, according to what you were told at this time, was
that you weren't pumping up Mr. Turner's image enough?

A. This is part of it, yes.

Q. There were some other reasons, too, weren't there, Mr.
James?

A. I'm sure.

Q. You have been openly criticized by Mr. Turner for reasons
having nothing to do with not pumping him up, had you not?

At this point the witness began to show signs of nervousness. He
had not expected the line of questioning to come when it did.

A. Openly criticized by Mr. Turner?

Q. That is right.

A. Not to my knowledge.

Without glancing at my notes, I moved to the side of the lectern. I
lowered my voice.

Q. I call your attention to a meeting of Senior State Directors
at the Langford Hotel on May 6, 7, 8 and 11 of 1969 and ask if
you were there?

A. Yes, sir. I believe I was.

Q. Were you sitting in a room with the other Senior State Di-
tors, including, specifically, Delane Frazier, when Mr. Turner
ran down the list of the shortcomings of each of those directors
and ways they ought to improve themselves?

A. Yes, sir.

Q. All right, and when he got to you, did he say "Now, as to
you, Jimmie James, the reason you are not being promoted is
because, number one, you can't get along with Preston Harris,
whom you are supposed to work with, and number two, because
you don't treat black people fairly and this company won't put

up with that?" Do you remember him saying that to you in front of all those men?

Hugh Smith was on his feet. The witness looked toward him and then answered.

A. He didn't say that.

Mr. Smith: Your Honor, may we approach the Bench?

The court reporter moved to the sidebar, carrying the portable recorder, and the lawyers gathered at the far end of Judge Tjoflat's bench, in view of the jury but out of its hearing.

Mr. Smith: The objection is fairly obvious, at this point, Your Honor, that the question—the witness answered that that was not the statement made. That Mr. Bailey has asked an extremely improper question—

The Court: Well—

Mr. Smith: —intending to prejudice—

Mr. Bailey: I would never have asked that question without substantial evidence to back it up. It is part of the reason of the firing.

The Court: Well, I think that because of the Jury that I would like to tell the Jury the question is not evidence in the case, that he has adopted it—

Mr. Garland: Your Honor, I object to that—

The Court: Be quiet.

Mr. Bailey: Judge, I think that is fair. At the same time, I want to put on my opportunity to present evidence of that. It won't come until the evidence is through. I don't want it to look like a slap. I researched this very carefully before I ever put the question.

Mr. Smith: Such a statement—that could be an error if Mr. Bailey does not put on any evidence.

Mr. Bailey: You will have to leave that on my shoulders, Mr. Smith.

The relationship between myself and Smith, originally polite but cautious, began to change at precisely this point. Minus any evidence to support his view, Smith had just suggested I had no foundation for my line of questioning.

We went around and around for several more minutes, with the judge implying that I was using a "tactic," and me arguing that I had everything I needed to tie in my line of questioning. I told the judge I didn't like the implication that I was engaging in what he had called "tactics and strategy," and he said, "I am not talking about anything unethical. I'm simply saying, though, that when you get to a matter of race it is more volatile than some other kind of argumentative question."

Mr. Bailey: That is true, Judge, but I expect the same number of white Jurors would be offended by a bigot.

The Court: What I'm saying—I'm not saying who may or may not be offended. Sometimes an old southern darkie can look through things better than a white person can, you know. I mean, you know, a lot of them get home, they know they have been had by a song and dance man before the white man does.

Mr. Bailey: That is right. It would be a foolish tactic if I couldn't back it up.

The Court: It could be in the first place.

Mr. Bailey: Well, maybe.

I found the judge's comments quite a bit more revealing than I think he wanted them to be. When the jury was brought in, I felt a different, a more tense, mood in the courtroom. And it included everyone, from the bench to the benches.

My use of the term "black people," just before the conference at the side bar, had been the first time any emotional trigger words had been heard in the trial. No juror seemed alarmed, but there was an alertness in the air that hadn't been present earlier.

I continued my cross-examination of Jimmie James:

Q. Mr. James, you told us that you remembered the remark about not getting along with Preston Harris and what had been said in front of the other state directors. Do you remember any other remark Mr. Turner directed at you as a criticism on that day?

A. Mr. Turner was continuously criticizing me, Mr. Bailey. I could name several remarks he made, not only me, but several people in the company.

Q. Do you remember anything specific that you were criticized for as he ran down the list on that day as to the Langford Hotel in May of 1969 beyond Preston Harris?

A. Specifically, no.

Q. Do you remember any criticism from Mr. Turner for your attitude toward racial problems?

A. He may have. He may have.

Q. Did he tell you he did not like your attitude, Mr. James?

A. Yes, I'm sure he did, if that would be the case.

Q. Do you remember, I want you to search your recollection, do you remember Mr. Turner at any time telling you that you have got to treat these black people fairly to advance in this company; do you remember that?

A. He didn't have to tell me that, sir.

Q. Did he tell you, just did he tell you?

A. He didn't have to tell me that.

Q. Did he tell you or didn't he?

A. Not only him, but Mr. Bunting and several others as well. I knew that. Why would anybody have to tell—as a matter of fact, right now—

THE COURT: Wait a minute.

Q. Excuse me, Mr. Witness—

THE COURT: Mr. James, he just wants to know whether or not you were told that. That is all. . . .

Q. Did he or did he not tell you that?

A. Yes, sir.

Q. When did he tell it to you?

A. In the—at the meeting.

Q. At the meeting, right?

A. That's what I said.

Q. So, when I asked you a few moments ago didn't he tell you, Jimmie James, you got two shortcomings: one, you don't get along with Preston Harris, and, two, you don't treat the black people fairly and you have got to, that was correct, wasn't it?

A. No.

Q. Then you tell us what he did say at the meeting.

A. I couldn't tell you word for word, but he certainly didn't phrase it like that.

Q. Did he or didn't he? I believe you answered this question. Did he or didn't he criticize you for your attitude towards black people at this meeting at the hotel?

A. He did.

Q. All right. He told you he did not like your attitude, right?

A. I have answered the question, yes.

Q. Now, you say you have discussed the same problem with Mr. Bunting?

A. I have.

Q. Did he tell you the same thing?

A. Did he tell me the same thing?

Q. Yes. . . .

Q. I take it from the responses you have given, that even

though Mr. Turner may have in fact criticized you, you say that criticism wasn't justified; is that right?

A. It was not justified.

Q. Because, as you told us today, all men are equal in your eyes?

A. Yes, sir.

Q. You stand on that statement, do you not?

A. I stand on it.

Q. Do you remember where you were that night, sir, after the meeting broke up?

A. I don't.

Q. Were you with some other state directors having a drink or two in the evening?

A. No, sir, not a drink or two, because I've probably drunk about a drink or two or three in my life. [At this answer, several defendants almost laughed out loud.]

Q. You were sitting around having cocktails on a social basis?

A. I wasn't drunk. I knew what I was saying.

Q. Mr. George Stokes suggested you were drunk. You would not get drunk on a drink or two?

A. I wouldn't get drunk, period. . . .

Q. Did you discuss what Mr. Turner had said that day about you with any of the other state directors in the evening?

A. Again, sir, I may have.

Q. Was one of them a gentleman named Delane Frazier?

A. Again, it could have been.

Q. Did you indicate that you found it a little bit embarrassing that he should criticize you openly the way he had done that day at the meeting?

A. I didn't really appreciate it, if that's what you mean?

Q. You expressed that thought, didn't you?

A. Yes, sir, I did.

Q. Did you also say to Delane and to the others, "He's right about one thing, I hate niggers"?

A. No, sir.

Q. Did you make that statement or didn't you?

A. Absolutely not, and you heard me correctly, sir. I absolutely did not say that.

Jimmie James made the answer sound as emphatic as he could, but he was clearly nervous. And the atmosphere in the courtroom was equally tense, for it had changed noticeably when I used the word

"niggers." I had barked out the word, trying to give it as much mean-
ness and venom as I could. It hung in the air, an all but palpable
accusation. Within seconds the witness was showing signs of strain.
He sat motionless, but he was biting his lip frequently now, and the
jury was staring at him.

My pace had been very fast, so I slowed it a bit by pausing, and
then picked up the speed again. My voice was firm and loud.

Q. You say that you did not. You do not use that word at all,
do you?

I knew that if James denied using the word, I could put the investigator on the stand to refute him, thereby impeaching that statement and casting doubt on the rest of his testimony as well. The
witness must have had similar thoughts.

A. I'm sure I've used it, yes, sir, because I'm from the South.

Several jurors who had been watching me returned their gaze to
the witness. As soon as James said he used the word, I had what I
needed to asked the next two questions without objection from the
prosecutor. I almost shouted them.

Q. As recently as last week, perhaps, in Greenville?

James went literally pale. His hand gripped the top of the witness
box.

A. I may have.
Q. Describing your own employee, LEE GRIMES, whom you
call a *nigger* on a daily basis?

Jimmie James must have known we had checked him out, but he
never expected it had been that thorough a job. His answer startled
the entire courtroom. Even I was not prepared for it.

A. He enjoys it.

I waited a moment for the impact of his answer to sink in, and then
I said, as I picked up my notes and returned to the defense table,
" 'He enjoys it.' And you believe all men are equal in your eyes?
Thank you. No further questions."

Hugh Smith was on his feet like a shot, objecting to my final remark. But the jury hardly noticed him. All eyes were on Jimmie
James, the "fair and equal" man.

One black juror, a woman who had betrayed absolutely no emotion up to that point, appeared stunned. She stared at the witness.

The lawyers went to the sidebar, where Smith prevailed in his argument that my last remark should be disregarded. The woman paid no attention as the Judge said, "Ladies and Gentlemen of the Jury, I want you to disregard the comment Mr. Bailey made when he sat down. It was not addressed to the witness or anyone else. You may proceed, Mr. Smith."

The judge could have saved his breath for all the apparent effect it had on the jury. The black woman in the front row continued to stare at Jimmie James all through Smith's less-than-enthusiastic redirect examination. The juror next to her, another woman, kept patting her on the knee the whole time, saying what even an amateur lip reader could recognize as "Calm down now, calm down."

If the impact of the government's first witness had turned out to be something less than the prosecution had anticipated, the effect of their second witness must have come as a total surprise—and another disappointment.

We had been told that the second witness would be one Lynn Garrett, a former Koscot and Dare To Be Great distributor on the West Coast. The defense team had been preparing for his appearance for several days. But instead of Garrett the government called William Sant.

Smith told the court, in explaining the shift, that both Sant and Garrett were in town, but that Sant was under pressure from his new employer, and if he didn't get back to Denver by Monday, he might lose his job. I didn't buy it, even though I had no hard evidence to the contrary. It sounded to me as if the government was so distressed by what the defense—and our investigative team—had done to Jimmie James, that it wanted to throw us off stride and bring on someone we'd had no time to investigate.

I felt that the prosecution did not want to end the day with the memory of Jimmie James lingering on in the mind of the jury. So, at three o'clock on Thursday afternoon, William Sant took the stand.

Almost immediately, it was clear that Sant would be a more credible witness than James, the government's closet bigot.

William Sant had a pleasant way about him. Within a few minutes of his direct testimony he had several jurors smiling along with him. In his early thirties, with an oval face going to flesh, Sant had a manner of speaking that combined a mature directness with more than a little boyish charm. With regard to names, dates, and places, Sant was clear and fairly confident. His memory was markedly better than that of the first witness (who answered one question by saying he was so confused that he couldn't remember his own name). Sant had a habit of pausing before he would answer certain questions, as if he were trying—out of concern for accuracy rather than slowness—to get the facts just right.

I watched Sant very carefully as Hugh Smith, again using a low-key approach, took Sant over the ground of his positions with Koscot and Dare To Be Great. Some of the prosecutor's questions were asked so quietly that the witness had to ask that they be repeated.

Sant's rapport with the jury increased with each answer. At times he seemed almost to enjoy his role, for most jurors were smiling at his mock self-deprecation and his manner of using facial expressions to complement his answers.

Sant only testified for a quarter of an hour on his first day. The government asked to close the jury's day early and the judge agreed. The witness's testimony had been damaging, but hardly devastating.

Sant took the stand again the next morning, Friday, September 28, 1973. Hugh Smith led him through an explanation of a document that Sant had helped to write. It was a training manual for instructors in Dare To Be Great, Turner's motivational program.

Instead of just using the witness to identify the document, and then reading selections from it to the jury himself, Smith had Sant do the actual reading. Initially, it appeared to be a smart move. Sant turned his back slightly to the judge so that he now faced the jury, and he began to read.

It was clear that the jury, for the most part, was favorably impressed with Sant. His mild, almost self-deprecating manner brought mirror reactions from several jurors—smile for smile, frown for frown. As he tripped over the pronunciation of certain words, the jury nodded as if in understanding. There was clear rapport. I didn't like it.

I had nothing personal against Bill Sant. As with so many scores of Koscot and Dare To Be Great employees, I had met him only once or twice at company functions. He came across, on the stand, as a pleasant, affable person, which was pretty much the way I remembered him.

But there was a difference. Now, all of Sant's affability was directed to the jury, and he was a government witness. I won't say that butter wouldn't have melted in his mouth, but the coloration of everything he was saying seemed intended to convince the jury that he, Bill Sant, was a nice guy who had gotten hooked up with a gang of thieves. And that just wasn't the case.

Sant had been reading to the jury for over thirty minutes when

I noticed something that bothered me. When it continued, it made me downright angry.

If he read a passage in the manual that made the company policy look suspect, Sant read the words with a perfectly straight face. But when he read a passage that made the company sound good, he did a little dance with his face. The eyebrows would go up or the eyes would roll slightly. To me, the clear import of the facial gestures was as if he'd said, "Don't pay any attention to this stuff. It's premium-grade fertilizer."

I began to watch him more closely.

Soon he was padding his part to include facial comments that stressed questionable passages. I almost objected, but decided to wait. I wanted to be sure that it was intentional. A few lines later he did it again. I was mad, and the tone of my voice reflected it, but I didn't shout.

"Excuse me, Your Honor. Excuse me, Mr. Sant. Judge, I'm going to ask you to direct this witness not to improvise his testimony with facial expressions every now and then."

My objection apparently startled the judge. He looked down at me and said sternly, "That is enough. That is enough. Go ahead, Mr. Sant."

I persisted. "Your Honor, you deny my motion to give the order?"

"Yes, I just want him to testify."

Now I was really getting mad. "I seriously ask for a hearing. I can testify about what he is doing."

The judge's response did nothing to soften my mood: "That is enough. I'm not going to have any argument before the jury."

That hurt. I'm in complete agreement with the rule that lawyers should not be allowed to sneak in clearly inadmissible evidence by including the gist of it in their objection made in the jury's presence. And that wasn't what I was doing, but the judge's comment implied that I was. I asked for permission to approach the bench.

MR. BAILEY: May the record reflect the following: this witness has been testifying in the narrative. He is facing the jury. The Judge is sitting about ten feet from him and his back is to the Judge. He has repeatedly, during his testimony, and I have observed this with my own eyes, when he comes to certain portions of the testimony and [is] describing what a prospect should be told, looked to the jury, raised his eyebrows and rolled his eyes, as if to say, "Isn't this a fraudulent attitude to take."

I have asked the Court to restrain him from doing that. I want the Jury withdrawn. I want to take the stand and testify what I have seen under oath and have this Court admonish the witness in the presence of the Jury.

Then the judge said something that, on reflection, turned out to be an amazing comment. He admitted I was right.

THE COURT: I will take that as a proffer. You don't need to get on the stand under oath.
MR. BAILEY: All right.
THE COURT: Okay. I'm going to permit the witness to testify.
MR. BAILEY: Will you admonish the witness?
THE COURT: No. I am not going to admonish him. I haven't seen it.
MR. BAILEY: You can't see it.
THE COURT: It is a matter that you can bring out on argument and cross-examination.
*(End of Sidebar Conference)*

Clearly buoyed by the judge's ruling, Bill Sant smiled slightly at the prosecutor and resumed his reading.

Anyone who has the task of reading a business training manual knows they are not the highest form of literary achievement, and Koscot's was certainly no exception. Within a few minutes we were all on the threshold of boredom, but suddenly, as I looked at Sant, I realized to my great surprise that he was at it again. The eyebrows were arching and the eyes were starting to roll.

He was reading a passage about how to attend a rally with a prospective customer, how to give him what the manual referred to as "the bird-dog treatment."

As he finished reading this passage, Sant could not resist another little eyebrow-arching. That did it.

I shot out of my chair. "I renew my objection as previously stated."

Judge Tjoflat overruled me immediately, which only increased my anger.

What was getting me so mad was that the transcript of Sant's testimony would not indicate what was actually going on. Court reporters have a hard enough time just getting the words down. They rarely attempt to record nonverbal expressions, which means that when a case is appealed, all the Appellate Court sees is the bald transcript of the words that were spoken.

I tried to remedy that situation by saying, "Let the record show that the court does not observe the witness."

The judge repeated his ruling and instructed the witness to continue. I could feel the skin on the back of my neck going red. The frustration of the past months was welling up, and I was very close to an eruption.

Sant read but one line before he fell back into his habit of raising his eyebrows.

Again I objected, this time in an even louder voice.

Again the court overruled me.

In a strong tone I repeated my objection, for the record, that the court wasn't able to see the witness.

Then Judge Tjoflat, who could see that I was extremely agitated, took what I thought was a very unfair step. He sent the jury out of the room for a five-minute recess, and before the marshal had left the courtroom to accompany the panel back to the jury room, he told the marshal to make it fifteen minutes.

He must have sensed that we were on the edge of a real donnybrook. He was right.

When I finally got to the bench, the judge said, curtly, "Go ahead and put whatever you want on the record."

MR. BAILEY: Yes, I will, sir. I move that the Court—I move that the Court, in light of the Court's refusal to even observe what this witness is doing after my report which I understood you to accept, interrupt the testimony of this witness and take him off the stand.

I have never in a United States District Court seen a practice tolerated as low as this. This Court knows this stenographer isn't even looking at the witness anymore than you are. He is sitting there using his eyebrows and everything else he can to convey his opinion to the Jury. It's not going in this record. The Fifth Circuit will never see it and he does it over and over again and you tolerate it.

THE COURT: Mr. Bailey, I'm watching the witness except for his eyes.

MR. BAILEY: And his face.

THE COURT: No, I can see his face.

MR. BAILEY: Well, I disagree with the Court. You can't see it, Judge.

THE COURT: You can disagree with it. I know you want his testimony interrupted.

MR. BAILEY: I resent that remark.

THE COURT: That's all right, and I'm not going to climb down from the Bench and sit in front of the witness and watch him and tell him he can't do this or he can't do that.

MR. BAILEY: I asked you for a simple instruction. You wouldn't give it.

THE COURT: No.

MR. BAILEY: The record will so reflect.

THE COURT: The record will reflect it. I am observing the witness and you will have the opportunity to cross-examine the witness.

We began a little waltz where the judge claimed he could see almost all of the witness's face and I claimed he could see hardly any of it. Then he made a comment that brought all of the other lawyers very much into the picture. He said, "I am going to permit the witness to testify, and when it comes to facial expressions, I'm sitting here and watching the defendants and several lawyers [It had become apparent very early on in the proceedings, that when Judge Tjoflat said "the lawyers," he meant the defense; when he was talking about the lawyers for the prosecution, he called them "the government"] make expressions throughout the entire trial and haven't said a word about it."

That brought several murmurs, and I asked the judge if he was talking about me. He said he wasn't, that he was talking about "other defendants and other lawyers," but his point was that he had tolerated a lot of "face making" from our side of the room and perhaps he had to do something about it.

In effect, he was turning the tables on us. I tried to bring the discussion back to my original point, and asked that the witness be made to face the prosecutor ". . . instead of making a Go-Tour for the jury, and then you can observe him."

But the judge again turned it around, by saying, "He can look at the jury in the same fashion, for example, as Mr. Garland while he questions a witness spends his entire time looking at the jury."

A moment later, he added, "And I have seen you looking at the jury while you questioned them." That was too much for me. There was nothing in the federal rules that said a lawyer couldn't look at the jury any time he felt like it.

I snapped back, "I'd be a damn fool if I didn't, Judge."

We danced around a few more times, and then Judge Tjoflat indicated he had heard enough.

THE COURT: I think that from what I have seen, I am going to permit the witness to testify.

Judge Tjoflat was visibly upset. Our loud exchange, in the absence of the jury, was the first open threat to his total control of the courtroom. He'd said a few things he probably hadn't meant to say, such as his comment on the conduct and demeanor of the defense lawyers, one of whom, Frank Martin, looked almost as upset as the judge.

I had one more point that I wanted to make in support of the record in case we had to appeal. I could see that Judge Tjoflat was about to declare a recess, but I got in one more statement: "Let the record show, and I'd like all counsel to take a position that the court does not require the stenographer to watch the witness and note what he is doing and says that it's fair tactics for him to sit there and roll his eyes as he testifies. May I have the remarks of counsel?"

Before I'd finished my last word, Frank Martin was on his way to the center of the group huddled around the bench. Martin has an articulate drawl, and the southerner's disarming slowness usually masks the hardness of his questions. This time there was no mistaking his fervor. He was mad.

Now it was obvious that the judge wanted to get off the bench for a few minutes, but Martin cut right in. "Your Honor, before you leave, may I say something, because I would like some direction from you."

Settling back in his chair, Judge Tjoflat was confronted with something I am sure he had never seen in his four years on the federal bench—Martin was pointing a finger at him, actually waving it in a clearly accusatory manner. "You have intimidated me as I stand here right now by your remarks that you are watching certain defendants and certain lawyers making movements and expressions, and unless you exclude me, I want you to know that I am intimidated by you and Mr. Beale [Martin's client] does not have effective assistance of counsel . . ."

And then Martin paused ever so slightly . . . "because I think I have received a veiled threat from you."

The courtroom was dead quiet. No one had expected Frank to wade in so soon. The judge shook his head, as if he had suddenly found himself in the middle of a very bad dream.

THE COURT: I haven't said anything about any specific person. I said there's a lot of commotion from time to time at the defense table. I simply make that remark. I haven't called anyone to task for it. I don't think it's gotten to the point where any comment is necessary.

Martin had no intention of letting it go that easily. "Would you tell me if you are including me?"

THE COURT: I haven't seen you do anything specifically inappropriate. I'm talking about whenever you get as many people in the courtroom as there are here, there's a lot of moving around, a lot of talking while witnesses are testifying, and while questioning is going on, and at times there's facial expressions.

With what would only be read as sarcasm, Martin said, "Well, I thank you for excluding me. Thank you."

As he rose to leave the bench, Judge Tjoflat responded in kind. He turned back to Frank Martin and said, "I'm sorry if you feel intimidated. We are in recess for fifteen minutes."

Back in the defense room, the scene was one of unrestrained glee. As Lynda and I walked into the room, Glenn Turner pounded his fist on the table and stood up. "Hot damn, Bailey. You really know how to put it to him. That judge has been pushing us around since the day he got this case, and now we've started to fight back. The tide is turning." I didn't agree, but I said nothing rather than spoil the fun. People under indictment need all the hope they can get.

It was a moment of general release, and everyone was smiling. Everyone but Ed Garland. He moved over to where I stood in a far corner of the room. "Lee, I'm afraid the time is going to come when I'll be forced to do what you just did."

"You may have to," I said quietly. "If you don't stand up for your client's rights soon, he's just going to run roughshod over you for the rest of the trial." Ed said nothing, but he gave me a long, steady look.

I noticed that Lynda, who had been enjoying the fun heartily—adding her own funny cracks—had stopped smiling. I turned to follow her gaze and saw that John Truman had just walked into the defense room.

"That son of a bitch Hugh Smith!" Truman was boiling. He lowered his lanky frame into a chair, lit a cigarette, and muttered, "Now I know why Lee calls him 'Cheap Shot Smith.' "

"What's the matter, John?"

He looked at me, and he was angry as hell. "As soon as you left the courtroom, Smith went up to the bench and told the judge that he had been observing the witness—and that he had seen none of the facial expressions you objected to!"

I turned immediately and left the room.

In the time it took me to walk the fifty yards or so from the defense room to courtroom number one, I tried to check my growing anger. This Smith was developing into something more than just a thorn in my side.

I learned years ago that in the heat of trial lawyers are not always gentlemen, in fact are seldom gentlemen. But in bitter, intense trials, the change for the worse usually doesn't occur until late in the proceedings. Hugh Smith, however, was revealing his true character at the very beginning.

I had calmed down a bit by the time I reached the courtroom. Judge Tjoflat was telling the marshal to see if the jury was ready, but I interrupted him.

"I have . . . a very important point for the record. I understand that after I stepped out, having inquired of the court whether we were in recess, Mr. Hugh Smith went to the bench and told you as an officer of the court he observed the witness and said that what I had complained of hadn't happened."

I was really mad, and I made a suggestion for a very unusual procedure: "Now I want him [Hugh Smith] on the witness stand and I want it under oath, and I want to call my own witnesses."

I finished with a strong statement, but I meant every word of it: "Judge, this trial can't run if the lawyers lie to you."

Judge Tjoflat was shocked. Apparently he felt I was on the verge of losing control over my emotions. He said, "Mr. Bailey, just calm down."

I apologized to the court for being "upset," and explained that I was upset because I had watched what happened. I could tell Judge Tjoflat didn't think I was gaining any control over my emotions. For one thing, I was shouting again.

The judge said, his own voice rising, "Will you just calm down?" He explained that Smith had made his statement to the court reporter, not to the judge.

I asked that Smith repeat what he had said in the form of a representation to the court.

Smith stepped up, eagerly. "I will make a proffer at this time. I have been observing the witness during the course of the direct examination, but I have not observed the conduct mentioned by Mr. Bailey and I have been paying close attention to his facial expressions.

"I think the sole purpose in my observation for the objection to the conduct of the witness is to break the witness's testimony."

If my temperature had gone down at all, Smith's statement sent it right back up again. I asked the court for permission to put Mr. Smith on the stand, under oath, in front of the jury. I knew the jurors had seen Sant's facial gymnastics, and I wanted them to hear Hugh Smith say it had never happened. I wanted to put Hugh Smith's credibility on the line.

The judge would not let me examine Smith in front of the jury, but did agree to let me put him on the stand.

Hugh Smith was not pleased about this turn of events. He took the stand looking both angry and worried. After a few preliminary questions, I asked him: "You have seen the witness looking at the jury and reading from the document as he gives a narrative of the document, have you not?"

Smith replied that he had, and I asked him the central question: "Have you seen him at any time today while reading from this document make facial expressions?"

A. I have not.
Q. Not once? You never saw him lift his eyebrows, sir?
A. No.
Q. You never saw him roll his eyes?
A. No.

Smith's denial infuriated me. He had to have seen the witness doing his act in front of the jury, yet there he was on the stand, under oath, saying that he had seen nothing of the sort. I've had hundreds of heated exchanges with prosecutors during trial, but I rarely felt that we were engaging in anything other than an honest difference of opinion. In Hugh Smith's case there was total disagreement, but I didn't believe it was honest.

Frustrated by Smith's denial, I decided then and there to call the entire panel of prosecutors. In an angry voice I said, "Mr. Johnson, take the stand."

Unfortunately, I accompanied my words with an abrupt gesture. I pointed from Johnson to the stand, much as one might order an obstreperous student to the front of the classroom.

Smith, who had been excused, was on his feet with an objection, but he was careful to keep his tone of voice more pleasant than mine: "Could the court afford counsel the basic courtesies counsel is—"

At this point the judge could see I was about to erupt, and he leaned over the bench. "Just calm down, Mr. Bailey."

Of course that kind of comment had the opposite of its intended effect. The exchange that followed was fast, loud, and on my part angry.

MR. BAILEY: I am calmed down.

THE COURT: You are not calmed down.

MR. BAILEY: I want to elicit testimony from an incipient witness.

THE COURT: Just calm down, count to ten, would you please.

MR. BAILEY: I counted to twenty, Judge, and I am still mad.

THE COURT: Then count to 50.

MR. BAILEY: Is that going to evaporate an injustice my counting to 50?

Now the judge seemed to be losing his control:

THE COURT: I don't want you to scream at me.

MR. BAILEY: If I screamed at you, I apologize.

THE COURT: I don't want you rolling your hand over there and telling Mr. Johnson to get on the stand. I don't want you any more since after developing the collateral issue of "nigger" yesterday and sit down with a big flurry.

Suddenly we had another can of worms in front of us. It seemed to me that Judge Tjoflat had just outdone me in the area of "collateral issues."

MR. BAILEY: Judge, it is not my fault. It is not my fault that the prosecution's witness turned out to be a bigot.

THE COURT: Mr. Bailey—

MR. SMITH: Your Honor, I object to such statements.

MR. BAILEY: He raised it. Why do you criticize me for bringing in the fact that a man calls a black man a nigger?

THE COURT: I am talking about the way in which you ended the examination and sat down.

MR. BAILEY: I would assume—

THE COURT: Just a minute.

MR. BAILEY: It was a natural reaction. I don't think it right for people to use the word "nigger" and I presume you don't either.

We went around and around on this point for a few more minutes. The judge told me to calm down again, which didn't help things, but finally we all began to regain our composure.

Judge Tjoflat made the point that my last question to Jimmie James was not really a question, but rather a statement that he felt was intended only to influence the jury. As often happens after sharp exchanges, this one ended with a touch of humor.

The judge said to me, "You didn't put a question to the witness." I replied that I had, he said that I hadn't, and then, after thinking for a moment, I said, "It was a bifurcated question which was intended to give him no possibility of an answer."

There were surprised laughs from both sides, and even Judge Tjoflat joined in. "Good enough," he said, "swear in Mr. Johnson. Let us see if we can go on with some kind of demeanor."

We couldn't, though. Jay Johnson denied all (flippantly); Robert Leventhal admitted seeing some movement but basically disagreed (densely); and to the shock of the defense team, Mike Kinney refused to be questioned (adamantly).

And Judge Tjoflat refused to compel him.

And that was the straw that broke Ed Garland's back. He rose, made an objection, and Judge Tjoflat, in turn, blew up. He blew up because the basis of Ed's objection was the judge's "attitude of laughing and levity" during a Garland cross-examination.

When Ed finished the courtroom was absolutely silent. Even the marshals, normally the most passive figures in the courtroom, looked apprehensive. As for the judge, he was clearly angry now. He rose from his chair, almost fully out of it, looking for all the world as if he were about to vault the bench and go after Garland with his bare hands.

THE COURT: Do you have anything to say to the Court? Stand up on your feet. Do you have anything further to say to the Court?

The judge's admonition to Garland to "stand up on your feet" was barked out, like a military command. If it had been meant to scare Garland, it hadn't worked. Ed looked steadily at the judge and replied that he had nothing further to say.

Judge Tjoflat was hopping mad. He is a man whose temper is always just below the surface, and it often erupts with suddenness. Clearly, he didn't like Garland's comments, especially not with several local newspaper reporters seated in the front row. Nor had he been at all pleased with my objections, but with Garland's refusal to say anything else, it looked as if the judge's anger was lessening.

Then Frank Martin, who had complained earlier of having been "intimidated," stood up and objected to the way the judge had dealt with Mr. Sant the previous day. (Instead of having the clerk hand a document to the witness, which is the standard procedure, the judge got up, out of his chair, and went to the end of the bench to hand the paper to the witness himself.) Martin claimed that this created the impression in the jury's mind that the judge was more considerate of a government witness than he would be of one called by the defense.

This got Tjoflat even madder. After a few more words with Martin, he turned to the defense side of the courtroom and snapped, "Does anybody else want to make criticism of the court?"

The ensuing scene was so heated—and so unusual—that I never expect to see the likes of it again. Judge Tjoflat made every defense lawyer stand up and put on the record any objection or criticism he had of the judge's conduct of the case.

To their everlasting credit, the defense lawyers did not cave in under this most unusual display of judicial wrath. Two declined to speak (one because he was scared and the other because he felt it best for his client that he keep still). The rest laid it on the line, all of their complaints, and with each answer the judge got more and more angry.

When he got to me he was all but fuming. Ironically, we now had the reverse of the earlier situation.

I spoke on the record for about ten minutes, and although I praised the judge for what I truly believed was his honest attempt to be impartial, I told him—since he'd asked—just what I thought of the way he had been treating Ed Garland.

"I do not think the court has been halfway fair to Mr. Garland. I am watching a young man of considerable talent whom you didn't let prepare a case, and I know it, who has worked every day since he took it, defending a case I should be defending, the most difficult mail fraud case I have ever seen, and you bark at him in open court like he was a little boy not entitled to your respect, and you let the jury get that impression. You might not mean to. You speak off the hip a lot, and you are usually right, in my opinion, but I don't think there is any occasion for the way that Mr. Garland is treated . . ."

After I'd sat down, I caught Ed Garland's eye. He'd been staring at the judge, but he turned to me and smiled a thin smile of gratitude. It made me feel good—the smile, not the exchange with Judge Tjoflat. I was pretty sure I had made my point.

The quiz of the prosecutors was soon finished, and although it hadn't turned out exactly the way I'd hoped, I was pleased that we had finally cleared the air. It had been a knock-down, drag-out affair, with no one pulling any punches. But it was a very necessary, and ultimately healthy, emotional release.

The tone of the courtroom was almost back to normal, and when the judge made some comments about demeanor, pointing out that I had a different demeanor from Mr. Leventhal, I couldn't resist answering, "I hope so."

The judge was about to send out for the jury when Hugh Smith interrupted, in what struck me as an unusually civil, almost friendly tone of voice. I should have known he had bad news.

Smith said, "Could we hold up the jury for a minute . . . I noticed that Mr. Bailey's wife, during the exchange with the bench, has become extremely upset."

The judge's response surprised me even more: "Yes, she's been crying out there."

I didn't know what they were talking about.

All I could say was, "I'm sorry. I didn't notice that."

Then the judge said, "She's been having a day out there."

At this point I hardly knew what to say. Lynda is a real trouper, and has been with me during every trial since our marriage, but she has always been able to contain her emotions until we get out of the courthouse.

I asked the judge for permission to take her out of the courtroom before the jury came in, in case any of them knew who she was and began to speculate on what had taken place while they were gone. But it turned out that Lynda had already left.

I told the judge I hadn't even know that she had left; his response bothered me. He said, "There are a lot of things you fellows aren't aware of that I can see, you know."

It struck me as a particularly ill-timed remark, so I said, "And there are some things we can see that you can't. That's the reason for this whole colloquy, Judge."

Fifteen minutes later I found Lynda in the defense room. Her eyes were red and swollen, but she appeared to have gotten control of herself. I asked her how she felt, and she put her head on my arm and almost started to cry again.

"Oh, Lee, I was doing just fine. I mean I was mad as hell at that judge for letting Sant get away with all those faces he was making, but I was okay. Then, when you started to defend Ed Garland, to stick up for him, and tell that judge how wrong he was for the way he was treating him—well, I just started to cry. And I couldn't stop.

God, I must look a perfect fright."

Not to me she didn't. She looked especially beautiful.

It would be nice to report that our first flap with the judge was also our last, that one good blowup cleared the air and assured an impartial judicial mien that lasted for the rest of the trial. Unfortunately, that wasn't what happened.

One week after the first fight with the judge there was another. In some ways it was worse, because it was more intense, more personal, and private. Because it occurred in chambers, and because Judge Tjoflat sealed the transcript, I can not describe it here. I will say that it was the most emotional session I have ever had with a judge—and I am sure I speak for every other lawyer who was in the room. It made my disagreement with Col. Ken Howard, the judge in the Medina case, look like a high school debate. And as things worked out, it was the key to a calmness that eventually settled over the trial, a calmness that lasted for quite some time.

Trouble began on another front. This time the renewal of hostilities involved the prosecution; the judge was on the sidelines.

Hugh Smith, the chief prosecutor, was about finished with Bill Sant—who had been languishing on the stand for more than a week —when one of the defense lawyers came to him with a problem. The lawyer was Bert Salem, of Tampa, who represented Clyde Cobb, past president of Dare To Be Great, and one of the most fundamentally decent human beings in the entire case.

During lunch on Wednesday, Bert called his office in Tampa and learned that he was needed on an important matter if there was any way he could get back. He went to Hugh Smith and asked if anything affecting his client was likely to come up that afternoon. He explained his problem, but said he wouldn't go to Tampa if he was going to be critically needed in Jacksonville that afternoon.

Smith replied, "Well, as a matter of fact, the next witness is absolutely going to bury Cobb." Bert was startled, until he realized that Smith was joking. They discussed the problem, and Smith promised that he wouldn't bring up anything involving his client in Salem's absence. Bert caught the next plane.

Late that afternoon Bill Sant was still on the stand, and Hugh Smith was conducting the government's redirect examination. Smith handed the witness a document and asked him to read it to the jury. The document, an interoffice company memo of several pages, had already been introduced into evidence, but it had never been read to the jury. (In trial terminology, such a reading is referred to as "publishing" the document.)

Several of us got up to object on several different grounds, which was ironic, because although we knew that the document was signed by Clyde Cobb as president of Dare To Be Great, none of us knew about Smith's promise to Salem. For the moment, only Clyde Cobb knew that Smith was pulling another one of his cheap shots.

Frank Martin had asked for a bench conference because he wanted permission to stand near the jury box in order to watch Sant's eyes. The judge denied this, telling him, "I don't want lawyers sitting in the jurors' laps." Before we had disposed of the other objections, there was a brief exchange between the prosecutor and the judge that got under my skin.

The defense had insisted that Smith read the document to the jury, rather than having Sant read it. (We didn't want any more problems with Sant's visual underlining.) I made the point that it was better to have a lawyer read the document because he was an officer of the court and therefore the judge would have a swift remedy if the lawyer used improper inflections.

Then Smith cut in and said, "Can I roll my eyes?" The judge smiled, and said, "No, but you can use my bifocals."

I didn't learn until later that Cobb was getting very upset. (Unfortunately he hadn't told me about the promise Smith had made to his counsel.) I could see Clyde's problem, because at one point in the bench conference I had objected to the fact that Smith was using a 1970 document—the Cobb memo—to relate to what the witness had been saying about tactics used in 1971, and said, more pointedly than I realized at the time, "If I were Mr. Cobb's lawyer, I'd make heavy objection about that."

Well, Mr. Cobb's lawyer wasn't there to make his objection, as Smith well knew. In case there was any doubt in the mind of the chief prosecutor that at least someone considered it a low trick, it was erased as soon as the jury had left the courtroom for the afternoon break. Clyde Cobb stood up, muttered something at Smith, and threw his heavy trial notebook across the courtroom. Then he stormed out, banging the large doors as he plowed through them.

Clyde Cobb is a small man, but he is strong and his temper is stronger. Several of the lawyers went out and calmed Clyde down. Then they brought him back for one of the most unusual bench conferences of the trial.

The defense lawyers, by this time, had learned of the so-called agreement between Smith and Salem, and they were arguing on Cobb's behalf, when the judge stated that the record should indicate that Mr. Cobb was standing near the bench, and was involved in the conversation.

Suddenly, Clyde said (and it was the first time in the trial that any defendant had spoken directly to the judge, on or off the record), "Your Honor, I would like to be heard from if that is possible." Judge Tjoflat looked a bit surprised, but he let Clyde give his version of the Smith-Salem pact.

As Clyde put it, speaking quite nervously but with obvious strong feeling, "I conversed with him [Salem] over that issue. And he said, 'Clyde, there is no need to worry about it. You are low profile for the rest of the day. Mr. Smith has assured me that your name won't even come up.' And I said, 'Really?' He said, 'Yes,' and I asked him [Smith], I said, 'You are not going to turn that around on me, are you, Smith?' And Smith said, 'No.' "

At this, the judge was looking mildly uncomfortable, and he turned toward Hugh Smith for a response. To his discredit, Smith replied, "I have to point out one other thing. I had no discussion with Mr. Salem whatsoever as it related to the witness presently on the stand."

It was a sleazy evasion. Smith was saying, "Sure, I promised your lawyer I wouldn't mention your name to Garrett. But he never asked me not to mention it to Sant." Such tactics are not only unprofessional, they are the kind that can send innocent men and women to prison.

After the Smith-Cobb blowup and the second fight with the judge, the trial began to run at a much more even keel. Unfortunately, it ran with little or no speed. In contrast to the belligerency of the first month, we now faced the problem of boredom.

In the middle of the fourth week of trial we spent an entire day without the jury ever being called. First there was the possibility of prejudicial publicity (the losing decision in another Turner Enterprises case was widely broadcast throughout Jacksonville), and then the problem of possible jury-tampering (a juror's son received a phone call that he thought was an offer of money).

We spent the whole day on these two matters and nothing ever came of either one. We'd had two tempests in the same teapot.

(There was one light touch: the juror who had to report the so-called bribe offer was extremely nervous in the presence of the stern

Judge Tjoflat. She told him, "Your Honor, you're a very nice man, but you just plain scare me!")

After that, things went into a steady decline. By the sixteenth of October, one month into a trial that the judge had guessed would last six to eight weeks, only five witnesses had testified. Of that five, we had shown one to be a bigot and at least two to be liars. In addition, the defense had managed to introduce several Turner films, plus numerous documents, into evidence during the beginning of the government's case.

All of the witnesses had offered damaging testimony, but none of it was so devastating that we couldn't turn it around either on cross-examination or during our own portion of the case. As might be expected, the prosecutors were not happy about the way the trial was going.

Then, in a swift about-face, the government stepped on the gas. Instead of using several days for a single witness, they began to put on several witnesses in a single day. In the next two and a half weeks they put on seventeen witnesses.

One of the defense lawyers cornered an assistant prosecutor in the hallway and asked, "What's going on?" The government lawyer replied, "Well, after the first few witnesses, it was apparent that you had a better investigative force than we had anticipated. And, quite frankly, the postal inspectors' files on the witnesses leave something to be desired. It was obvious that we weren't beating you with quality, so we've decided to do it with quantity."

Whether or not they were actually "beating" us was open to debate, but there was no doubt that they were putting witnesses on in quantity. By the two-month mark the government had brought almost forty-five witnesses to the stand. Their top score was seven in one day.

At first, it was a drain on the energy and funds of the defense. Each witness had to be checked out, and unless he or she refused, interviewed by at least one defense lawyer or several, if the witness's testimony would mention more than one defendant (as almost all of the witnesses did). After the first few weeks, however, we got into the rhythm of it all. The government, of course, had only to check over the testimony briefly, compare it to their massive files, and be ready for the next day. But the defense was meeting a lot of new faces.

There were people of all ages, colors, and shapes, from all over the country. They all told essentially the same story: they invested and they lost their money and the company didn't give a damn about them. Carefully and slowly, one by one, we had to pick their stories apart, to show that in many cases they thought they were buying a free ride and never bothered to work. Or they were passed up for promotion by the home office and left in a huff. Or they were simply hustlers who had no intention of doing anything more strenuous than picking a money tree.

It was slow, grinding work, and at times I wondered if it was worth it. The jury was looking more tired and numb each day, as it sat and listened to tales of homes lost, savings accounts depleted, and spirits (allegedly) broken. It may not have been quality, but it certainly was quantity. And what did the government care how long it took? Their salary checks would come in, twice a month, no matter how long it dragged on.

Occasionally, Judge Tjoflat would flare up, rail at the prosecution for the way the trial was limping along, but soon he, too, was resigned to the snail-like pace.

One day in late November, well into the third month of the trial, I ran into Ed Garland at dinner. He looked, to borrow one of Turner's favorite expressions, "glazed over." I asked him how he felt, and he shook his head sadly. "You know, Lee, these witnesses are like the Chinese. The just keep coming and coming."

One of the few light moments in the entire parade of the wooden witnesses had to do with a witness who never got on the stand. The government had brought down to Jacksonville, from Washington, D.C., a very articulate young black man who was a computer operator. He was said to have lost forty-five hundred dollars in one of Turner's companies, and the prosecutors felt he would make an impressive witness for a variety of reasons, not the least of which was that he was still, years later, very bitter about his loss.

Unfortunately, other witnesses ran longer than the government had expected, so the prosecutors told the man he could have a free weekend in Florida, on Uncle Sam, and that they would put him on the stand come Monday morning.

On Saturday night he decided to kill some time by going to the dog track. There he bet two dollars on the Quinella, an event in which the bettor has to pick the winners of five races. By the time four out of five had come in, he was close to hysteria, and when his fifth choice won he was leaping and shouting like a madman. And for good reason—he had just won ninety-six hundred dollars.

On Monday morning he was still so "up" that the government decided he could no longer communicate his bitterness over the money he had lost with Turner. They sent him home on the next plane. When Glenn heard about it, he said, "See? All you have to do is stick with me long enough."

By late October the first signs of strain could be seen. It wasn't just the length and pace of the trial, which appeared to have no end in sight, or the travel, or the separation of families, or even the financial drain. Beneath the surface of all these problems was the special nature of a conspiracy charge.

All defendants were charged with *conspiring* to defraud, yet the government was putting on evidence to show only that (in its view) people had been defrauded. According to the law, and based on the common sense realization that a conspiracy is by nature a secret agreement, the government is not required to show by direct evidence that the defendants got together in a smoke-filled back room and agreed on the details of an illegal scheme. It's enough, generally speaking, for the government to show that because certain acts were done (which could be illegal acts or legal acts done for an illegal purpose), and because the defendants conducted themselves in a certain way, the whole thing added up to a conspiracy.

It might sound terribly complicated, but it comes down to simply this: if the government could prove that enough people had been defrauded and that all the defendants knew what was happening and went along, willingly, with what amounted to a scheme to defraud, then we were all conspirators.

Boiled down even more, the jury would eventually decide if Koscot and the later companies were set up for the purpose of defrauding people. The government said yes, and we said no. But when it came time for the jury to decide our fate, it would be allowed to *infer* that there was such an agreement, based on the acts and conduct of the defendants.

That's what made the case so murky. At best, if the trial stretched on too long, all the jurors would be able to remember would be certain impressions. It would be harder and harder for them to distinguish between isolated incidents of fraud and a grand, overall scheme to bilk the public on the part of all the defendants. It was not a pleasant prospect.

What I had to hope for was that when the jury finally got the case it had the presence of mind to say, "Okay, some people got burned. But where is the proof, of any sort, that these defendants got together for the purpose of burning them?" It was a lot to hope for.

I was growing increasingly angry at the length of the trial—it was cutting substantially into my firm's business—but the one who was

really suffering was Lynda. She has colitis, has had it for years, a mal-
ady that thrives on tension. When the pressure becomes too much,
the colon erupts in painful spasms, and it takes increasingly larger
doses of medication to calm it down. By the end of the second
month she had suffered several attacks, each one longer and more
painful than the one before.

We were faced with a Hobson's choice: she could leave Jacksonville and go home to rest; but if she did that she would worry so
much about the day's events in Jacksonville that it would trigger
another attack. If she came to court she might get so upset that the
result would be the same. Eventually I convinced her that she didn't
have to attend every session, and that way we were able to keep one
small step ahead of the problem.

At the beginning of November, spirits had been very low, as
everyone seemed to realize that we were in for a long trial. With the
government apparently willing to put on an endless chain of witnesses, the defense team's mood worsened by the day.

We all tried to adjust as best we could. I was about to go out of
my mind sitting in court listening to witness after witness who had
nothing to say about me. Finally, I decided that it would be better
for me to stay in the defense room, rather than sit in court as if I
expected to hear something damaging.

For the next few weeks I probably read every news magazine that
came out, and with more thoroughness than I had in years. It was
an incredibly boring time. Roger Zuckerman and Mark Kadish
called it my "current events period." To make matters worse, both
Lynda and I caught colds, and one morning I was so bushed that
after court convened I went back to the defense room, put my head
on my folded arms, and went to sleep sitting at a table.

I learned later that Kenny Robinson, the young Washington,
D.C., lawyer who represented the corporations, came into the room,
took one look at me, and burst out laughing. What struck him so
funny was that right next to my sleeping form was a copy of my
book—*The Defense Never Rests.*

He said later that he thought if he only had a camera he might
have taken his first prize-winning photograph.

Fortunately for all of us, by the last week of November the depression lifted. It seemed as if the government had lost its edge.
For one thing, we were scoring heavily on cross-examination of
many of their witnesses, and for another, the jury was beginning to
look mightily bored. (The jurors had to know the defense wasn't responsible for the agonizingly slow pace of the trial.) All the defense

lawyers and their clients seemed to be getting on well, and a few of the defendants took advantage of the judge's rule and left town for several days at a time, trying to make some money to feed their families—and their lawyer's family.

The last trial week in November opened slowly, like the others before it, but it turned out to be quite a week. Once the action began, it continued throughout the weekend, and culminated in our first Sunday session of court.

On Monday, November 26, during the morning recess, the judge's law clerk came up to the defense table and said, "Did you hear the news? Albert DeSalvo was murdered in prison in Massachusetts."

Suddenly, Mark Kadish shot out of his chair. "What!"

I was a bit puzzled. The DeSalvo case was years before Mark had come to work for me. I couldn't understand his sudden rush of compassion.

The law clerk said, "Yeah, Albert DeSalvo, the Boston Strangler."

"Jesus!" The expression on Mark's face changed completely. "I thought you said 'Bert Salem.' Boy, this trial must be getting to me."

During the lunch break, I was interviewed by several local and wire service reporters. They wanted to know my reaction to the news of the death of one of my most famous clients. There really wasn't a whole lot I could say. Once the state had blocked Albert's being tried as the Strangler, I felt it was only a matter of time before he met a violent end. DeSalvo should have been made the object of the most intensive medical and psychological testing known to modern science. Instead, he was locked up and forgotten. Now we would never know just what combination of mistakes produced such a horrendously warped mind—and so many terrible killings. And although I didn't mention it to the press, there was something else in the back of my mind; for all the time I had spent with Albert, I had never been able to empathize with him. In death, as in life, I couldn't help but think of him as a mutant, a human misfire of gross proportions.

By Wednesday afternoon I was a bit tired, and was looking forward to a relatively quiet night, especially because Lynda had not been feeling well. In fact, she had stayed back at the apartment all day, so I called to see if she felt like going out to dinner. I didn't like the sound of her voice over the phone at all, so I hurried back to the Villa Granada.

Riding back to the apartment with me was John Greenya, a Washington, D.C., free-lance writer who was collaborating with me on a new book. John had been in Jacksonville for all of September and October, but had stayed in Washington throughout most of November, working on the manuscript.

I had thought he and Lynda and I could grab a quick dinner at one of the steak houses near the apartment, but it now looked as if Lynda was in for the night. After stopping in briefly to see Lynda, John made other plans and went upstairs to Mark's apartment, where he was staying.

Lynda said she was feeling better, but she didn't look it. I asked how many Demerol she had taken, and she made a face. "One before noon, but three since then." I didn't like the sound of it. She hated taking pain-killers, and resorted to them only when the attack was particularly severe. Four was much more than her dosage on a rough day. I got her to take some soup and she went back to bed.

Shortly before ten o'clock, while I was on the phone, Lynda came into the room. Almost all of the color was drained from her face, and she was clutching her side. "I'm sorry," she said, "but this time it's really bad."

Twenty minutes later we were on our way to Saint Vincent's Hospital. I'd called John Greenya and asked him to drive us, as I wanted to hold on to Lynda. Charlie Pillans, the lone Jacksonville attorney on the defense team, had been good enough to call his senior partner, Chester Biddel, who called a doctor friend, a specialist who was going to meet us there.

At ten-thirty we screeched into the hospital parking lot and I took Lynda into the emergency waiting room. The doctor wasn't there yet, so we had to wait. But first I was required to go through that timeless ordeal of giving a receptionist the vital details. As Lynda sat with John, moaning as quietly as she could, I provided her name, address, religion, and social security number.

The girl taking the information was a hardened veteran of the emergency room wars, and she took it all down like a living computer. I was almost finished when a large man came up, recognized me, and said hello. He turned to the nurse and said, "This is F. Lee Bailey. Don't you know who he is?"

The receptionist, who could have cared less who anyone was, looked up at him and said in a tired voice, "I'm sorry. I don't watch much television."

The doctor arrived and Lynda was taken off for X-rays and treatment. Forty-five minutes later she reappeared, looking wan but better. Unfortunately the spasms had stopped before the machine could get a picture of them. She had obviously been given a good-sized dose of some tranquilizer.

Dr. Buelow, a very pleasant, fairly young internist, was shaking his head. "Mr. Bailey, your wife has accused me of mistaking her for a horse."

"Pardon me?"

"Yes, she thinks I gave her a dosage of medicine that was meant for a large animal."

As usual, Lynda had not lost her sense of humor.

An hour later, with Lynda back in bed at our apartment, I mixed a drink for John and myself and sat down to talk about the progress of the case. I told him that things appeared to be falling into a fairly steady pattern, and that I didn't expect any fireworks for a while.

I couldn't have been more wrong.

Q. Would you state your name please, sir?
A. Howard J. Zoufaly. That's Z as in Zebra, o-u-f-a-l-y.

The tall dark young man on the witness stand spoke carefully, like a person who prides himself on his good diction. His voice was firm, a shade too loud, and there was an annoying air of self-importance about him.

It was Friday, November 30. We had been prepared for Mr. Zoufaly for over two weeks.

We knew that he worked for a soft-drink company in Massachusetts, that he'd had a short, unproductive career as a Koscot distributor—and that he was about to give false testimony.

By the second month of trial we had finally worked out a system with the prosecutors, whereby they gave us, seven days in advance of when they would be called, a list of witnesses broken down by state. In late October we received a list of Massachusetts witnesses. I looked over the list, saw no names that I recognized, and made a mental note that we could forget about my home state, as far as any impending problems were concerned.

Nonetheless, as was our practice, we had all the people on the list checked out. Andy Tuney was more than busy in Florida, so we hired John McNally, the top-notch private investigator from New York who had worked with me on several previous cases. McNally interviewed all the listed witnesses, and there was nothing special about the results of any of the interviews, except that one witness, a Howard Zoufaly from Lowell, Massachusetts, refused to be interviewed. McNally then served him with a subpoena, and we forgot about him, in a sense, expecting that we would have a chance to talk with him sometime before he took the stand.

That was the last I heard of the matter for several weeks, until, on a day when all the defense lawyers were out of town, Zoufaly showed up in Jacksonville and announced his availability. As a courtesy, Charlie Pillans (who lived in Jacksonville) went downtown to interview him, accompanied by Harold Horne, a young assistant from Ed Garland's office who was still waiting to learn if he had passed the Georgia bar examination. (He had.)

The interview had barely concluded when I got a distress call from Mark Kadish; Mark said that Zoufaly told Pillans and Horne that on (or about) November 1, 1969, he had attended a Koscot Golden Opportunity Meeting in Millis, Massachusetts. According to Zoufaly's story, not only was I present at the meeting with Turner, but I spoke—advising people to invest their money in Koscot distributorships because Turner had a "great company"—and later, I autographed a book for Zoufaly.

He said he couldn't remember the name of the book, only that it was "about the law." (I knew it couldn't have been *The Defense Never Rests*, because that came out in late 1971.) Zoufaly also told Pillans and Horne that after the meeting he came up to me, as I was standing alongside Glenn Turner, and said, "Mr. Bailey, if I invest in this company, will I end up in jail?" and that I responded, "You stick with me and Glenn Turner and you'll be all right."

There were two problems: one, my alleged statement hardly sounded like the kind of thing I would have said under any circumstances; and two, I was not at the meeting.

I didn't even have to check a calendar to learn where I had been on that particular night. I remembered that meeting in Millis for one reason—that meeting was held on the same night my son Brian was in Children's Hospital in Boston, the same night I had visited him there. Brian had undergone minor surgery, and I went to see him, along with Wayne Smith, who brought Brian a gift from Glenn Turner.

Obviously, there was something very wrong with Mr. Zoufaly's story.

The government scheduled Zoufaly for testimony in mid-November, but had to postpone his appearance because it was taking too long to get through the witnesses ahead of him. On Friday, November 23, the prosecution was almost ready for Mr. Zoufaly, but I threw a snag into their plans by asking the judge if I could leave court early (there were hurricane warnings along the coast, and we had filed a flight plan for Boston that was safe up to mid-afternoon). The government agreed that it would call no witnesses against me for the rest of the day, and Judge Tjoflat allowed me to leave right after lunch.

Having scheduled Zoufaly twice in a row for Friday testimony, the government was tipping its hand. There is a practice, used by both sides in trial, known as "maximizing the impact" of a witness. This means that he or she is called as the last witness of the day, or better yet as the last witness for the week, so that jury has time to react to the testimony, to let it sink in. I was quite clear to me that this was the government's plan in regard to Mr. Zoufaly.

The importance of his testimony can not be understated: Zoufaly was the government's best hope for keeping me in the case, for blocking a directed verdict in my favor by introducing evidence that had to go to the jury because it involved a question of fact. Lawyers call this the kind of evidence that "drives a case over the rail," by which they mean the judge cannot rule as a matter of law that insufficient evidence has been offered against a particular defendant.

Whether or not Zoufaly was telling the truth had nothing to do with it—except ethically and morally. If the government could get his testimony that I was at a meeting urging people to invest in Turner's company, it could tie me into the alleged scheme to defraud. It would be up to the jury to decide if he was telling the truth.

The prosecution had had no success with its early theory that I was an officer of the company, and was now pinning its hopes on being able to show that I acted like one—thereby defrauding people who relied on my public statements. It was thin ice, and the government knew it, but it went ahead anyway.

I had been gone for less than half an hour, on Friday the twenty-third, when Prosecutor Leventhal attempted to call Mr. Zoufaly to the stand and to extract his testimony in my absence. The judge, however, was well aware that our earlier discussion was on the record, and he refused to allow the government to call the witness in my absence.

This action solidified my suspicion that the government was relying heavily on Zoufaly. I told Mark Kadish to redouble our investigative efforts, and by the middle of the next week—Zoufaly had again been listed a Friday witness—we had a comprehensive file with which to counter his story.

Included in the file were affidavits from my son Brian, his mother,

Wayne Smith, Gary Wilson (a consultant to Turner who had actually attended the meeting in question as an observer), and Andy Crane, then my chief pilot—all of whom could testify as to my exact whereabouts on the night of the meeting—and twelve people from Massachusetts who *were* at the meeting and could testify that I was not. It was quite a thick file.

The file also contained hospital records, copies of insurance forms, investigative reports, and my own affidavit. I never thought it would even be necessary to bring the file to court, much less use it, but I had not fully understood the government's passion to keep me in the case.

So, on Friday, November 30 (two days after Lynda's attack, which up to that point was the highlight of a week I expected to be uneventful), the government called Howard Zoufaly to the stand.

As he took the oath I sat quietly, my fingers wrapped around a thick brown file containing all the affidavits and documents we had so carefully and expensively gathered. The weight of all the documents and affidavits was not just that Howard Zoufaly was wrong—for this would have been a proper subject for rebuttal evidence—but that he could not possibly have believed that he was right.

After he had taught the prosecutor how to spell his name, Zoufaly began to settle in. Each answer took a bit more time than the one before, and when the prosecutor asked him why he was interested in Koscot in the first place, he gave a brief lecture on the importance and saleability of cosmetics, ending with the arch pronouncement, "I would suppose that ladies like to change cosmetics as often as they change clothes" (not one woman on the jury so much as grinned).

Within minutes, Leventhal had brought the witness to the meeting in Millis, Massachusetts. I waited as Zoufaly began to tell who was there, and when he said "Bailey," I made my move. My fingers closed around the thick file as I said, *"Objection!"* and headed for the bench.

Handing the file to the judge, I said, "Your Honor, a felony is now in progress. Mr. Zoufaly is perjuring himself, and I think it a legitimate question to ask if he has had any help."

The judge was not pleased. He did send the jury out of the room, but his first reaction was to castigate me for not bringing the matter to *his* attention before this point. I explained to him that I had reason to wonder about the government's role in this obviously false testimony, and therefore had no intention of putting my cards on the table until it was both necessary and tactically wise.

Finally, Judge Tjoflat looked toward the government lawyers and said something to the effect of, "What do you have to say about this?" I then handed the file of affidavits and documents to Hugh Smith. As I did so, I glanced at my watch and noted the time.

Smith began to flip through the pages, and less than one minute later, he looked to the bench and said, "I'm not impressed with this evidence." That rocked me. Smith had seen none of the evidence in the file prior to the moment I handed it to him, yet after looking at it for all of forty-five seconds, he was convinced that it did not impugn his witness. In fact, he stated that he was ready to put the man on the stand in front of the jury.

I thought this was a very strange attitude for a man who had taken an oath to support the truth. Here he was—without an examination of the contents of the file and all that it represented—ready to thrust the weight of the government behind a man who, for all he knew, might be a nut, a liar, or a teller of the Gospel.

In the absence of the jury, we conducted a voir dire examination of Mr. Howard Zoufaly. Roughly translated, a "voir dire" means that a witness is questioned about his story before he tells it to the jury. There are many reasons for conducting a voir dire, such as determining if the witness is credible, or to see if there are circumstances that warrant his testimony not be heard (coercion by the government, etc.).

During the examination, Zoufaly stuck to his guns. He was adamant that I had been at the meeting, and had spoken to him briefly after the meeting. He also said that I had autographed a book for him. However, he could not remember the name of the book, which he had sold, he claimed, along with a number of other books shortly after his daughter was born. He said he sold a carton of books to a used bookstore in Bedford, Massachusetts, and gave the location and a description of the store.

The longer he testified, the more apparent it became that the government was determined to put him on the stand in front of the jury. I asked the judge to require the prosecution to make a representation that its witness was telling the truth—and Robert Leventhal refused to do so. He cited the Canons of Ethics as the reason why he need not be required to make such a statement. It was a shabby performance.

What bothered me even more, though, was the growing realization that Judge Tjoflat was going to let the witness testify. He stated that he had observed the witness's "demeanor," and did not find it consistent with that of a mentally disturbed witness.

The situation was most unusual. The witness was ready to testify that I had appeared at the meeting and urged people to "invest" in Turner's company; but I had a thick file containing sworn statements from seventeen different people, statements that showed: one, that I did not appear on the night in question, before during or after the meeting; and two, I was somewhere else the entire night in question. Yet both the government and the judge seemed willing to let the man take the stand.

At one point in the proceedings, John Truman pointed to the words *Fiat Justicia,* above the judge's bench. "No one," he said to me in an aside, "seems to be paying much attention to that phrase." It means, "Let justice be done."

It was painfully apparent to me that the government had taken great joy in the discovery of Mr. Zoufaly, with his critically needed testimony. As far as they were concerned, he was their protection against the judge's granting me a directed verdict. Whether or not Zoufaly was relating historical truth was at that point secondary; he was just too damned good to lose under any circumstances. And testify he would!

I had no proof that the prosecutors had put Zoufaly up to his crazy story, but I felt that their refusal to check out my version of the facts was tantamount to what the law calls "a reckless disregard of the truth." I made this point to the court, but go nowhere with it. In fact, it looked to me as if Judge Tjoflat was about to allow Zoufaly to retake the stand.

Just then, I learned by telephone that Lynda had gone to the hospital again. It was an "ill wind" situation, for it forced the judge to recess for the weekend—which gave me the time I needed to prepare an immediate petition to the Fifth Circuit U.S. Court of Appeals in New Orleans.

We then began the most grueling weekend of the entire trial.

I had asked the judge to require the government to give, in simple terms, its side of the story. Not only did the judge refuse to do so, but no government lawyer stepped forward to vouch for the credibility of their witness. We were in a real hard box. My position was simple: either I could wait for the man to testify (and chance my conviction on the basis of his testimony) or I could try to stop him from taking the stand again. I chose the latter.

The chances of getting an appellate court to make a ruling that affects the conduct of a trial still in progress are not great. But the power does exist, and I decided to try and use it. As soon as I got back to Villa Granada, I put Mark Kadish and John Truman on full-time duty. John was to prepare a petition for the Fifth Circuit U.S. Court of Appeals, and Mark was to keep all the lines open for a flat-out investigative effort.

Mark was not terribly happy. He was engaged to marry a girl in Atlanta, and the wedding was not too far away, so he looked forward to his weekends with a bit more emotion than some of the other lawyers. But, as usual, he pitched right in. And Truman cranked up for a sleepless weekend. It was a red alert.

I notified the office in Boston that we might need to bring *all* the Massachusetts witnesses down to Jacksonville, and the machinery was put in motion. I dispatched Jimmy Merberg, one of the most bright and able young lawyers in the office, to interview Mrs. Zoufaly. As it turned out, that was the smartest thing I did.

Another smart thing was to put Lynda to bed. The day's activities had all but erased the good effects of the new prescription she'd been on since her attack two days ago. The only thing that would help her was rest and sleep. She resisted for a while, but finally gave in, though not without extracting a promise from me that I would wake her if anything "super" happened.

By late Friday I had dictated a lengthy appellate petition to Paula Days, an excellent secretary from my office in Boston, who was the latest resident addition to the Villa Granada troops. As soon as I had finished, Paula in turn dictated the petition to Western Union and instructed that it be sent to the Fifth Circuit U.S. Court of Appeals in New Orleans. I was asking the court to grant a writ of mandamus that would prevent Zoufaly from taking the stand on Monday morning, as it was now clear that Judge Tjoflat saw no reason to keep him off. I knew our chances were slim, but we had to try.

On Saturday night I heard from Jimmy Merberg. He'd had a most interesting interview with Mrs. Zoufaly at five-thirty that evening. According to the witness's wife, the book in question did not exist: she had never seen a book with my signature in their house or apartment, and she was sure that if one had existed Howard would certainly have told her about it—in fact, she said, it would have been proudly displayed. She did remember that when they moved into their present house there was a box of books, but that was still in the attic, and she had gone through it trying to find one with my signature. She did not recall Howard's ever selling any books at the time of their daughter's birth in 1969.

Mrs. Zoufaly also said that she had never heard her husband mention my presence at any Koscot meeting, and again, she felt that it was the kind of event he would have mentioned, as he was apparently one of my "fans." (I found that to be, under the circumstances, a rather ironic note.)

The sum total of Mrs. Zoufaly's conversation was to put the lie to her husband's story.

Jimmy Merberg had served Mrs. Zoufaly with a defense subpoena, and although she was less than thrilled with the notion of going to Jacksonville, she agreed to do so if it became necessary. She admitted the seriousness of the matter and promised to tell the truth. She asked only that she be allowed to bring her three-year-old daughter with her, as it would be all but impossible to get an overnight babysitter on such short notice. Merberg quickly agreed.

On Saturday we also learned that Western Union had lost our petition to the Fifth Circuit. It apparently had disappeared in the bowels of one of the company's computers. Fortunately, as a backup, I had already dispatched John Truman to New Orleans by plane with a typed copy. He hand delivered it that same afternoon.

Bit by bit, the stage was being set for a dramatic confrontation.

Meanwhile, Andy Tuney reported in. He had found the bookstore, interviewed the proprietor, and learned that this part of Zoufaly's tale was also false. The bookseller said he would have remembered any book bearing my signature, as he knew of me, and always put signed books on a special shelf. He also said that he had never heard of anyone named Zoufaly, but was sure he would have remembered the name—if he had indeed bought a whole carton of books from him—simply because the name was so unusual. He showed Andy his record book, where he listed larger purchases, and there was no entry for Mr. Zoufaly during the time in question.

Even if Zoufaly did stick to his story, we were beginning to get the kind of ammunition necessary to shoot him down. Nonetheless, I wanted to avoid any chance of his going on before the jury, something which the judge and the prosecutors seemed determined to bring about, and I asked for a further hearing on Sunday afternoon.

The next step was very expensive, but I felt that money was the least of my concerns at that point. I subpoenaed and had brought down to Jacksonville six of the twelve witnesses who had been at the meeting in Massachusetts that Zoufaly had attended. I wanted them ready for the sole purpose of marching them into the courtroom and seeing if he could identify them. I was pretty sure that the judge, and perhaps the jury, would get the point.

In addition, I had Mrs. Zoufaly brought down, simply for the purpose of putting her testimony in the record before she had any chance to confer with her husband.

When we got the court that afternoon, I learned that Smith had still another cheap shot up his sleeve. He stated that he wanted some sort of action taken against Jim Merberg for "upsetting" Mrs. Zoufaly, and making her cry. In support of this he put Howard Zoufaly on the stand, who testified that his wife had called him over the weekend while he was visiting friends in Tampa, and that she was quite upset. I readily agreed with this, but I suggested she was upset because she was in a position where in order to tell the truth she had to make a liar out of her own husband, and that that was enough to unnerve any woman. I also stated that Mr. Merberg could be on the next plane to Jacksonville and appear in person to relate that his conversation with Mrs. Zoufaly had been courteous and cordial, and not in the least bit threatening.

Next, I went to the bench with a typed summary of what Mrs. Zoufaly had told Mr. Merberg, and asked the judge to read it in camera (alone and off the record). He was reluctant to do so, but finally agreed. When he had read it, I suggested that Mrs. Zoufaly be met at the airport by a U.S. marshal, so that she could be brought directly to the court and in the presence of the judge, so that her statement might be taken before she could be persuaded to modify it in any way by anyone.

Hugh Smith then made a horrendous tactical and strategic mistake. He mentioned, almost in passing, that perhaps the judge had no right to talk to her, because he might be thereby violating her right to counsel. And that she was entitled to know what the ramifications of the privilege between husband and wife amounted to. It was a foolish point for him to raise, because, as he well knew, I didn't intend to learn from her any communications she had with her husband—but only communications which she had *not* had, which are not privileged in any sense.

However, when Smith mentioned Mrs. Zoufaly's right to counsel, I leapt immediately to the idea. I said to the judge, "Your Honor, I think you would be doing yourself and all the parties concerned a tremendous favor if you would see to it that *both* Mr. and Mrs. Zoufaly have counsel at the earliest possible moment."

After mulling the matter over for a minute, he agreed and soon two of Jacksonville's best criminal defense lawyers were called away from their Sunday golf game. Two hours later Edward Booth had been named as court-appointed counsel for Mr. Zoufaly, and James Harrison for Mrs. Zoufaly.

I waited until the lawyers showed up, to tell them that there were numerous witnesses already in the courthouse (the Boston plane had landed, bearing Mrs. Zoufaly and the small army of defense witnesses) whom they might want to talk to. Talk they did, for about two hours, and when they were finished it was very plain that: one, Mrs. Zoufaly was sticking by her story and completely contradicting her husband; and two, Mr. Zoufaly and the prosecutors were beginning to look a little green around the gills.

By now it was well past eight o'clock in the evening, and the defense room was beginning to look like convention headquarters. All the defense lawyers were back in town by this time, as was John Greenya (who had flown down on the same plane with the Boston group and Mrs. Zoufaly, without knowing who anyone was); and the defense witnesses we had subpoenaed were milling around, trying not to look excited. John Truman, who had not slept in forty-eight hours, was reinterviewing each one. Occasionally he would step into the room, from the smaller adjacent room where he was conducting the interviews, and say, "Next!" It was turning into a happy little group, which I took to be a good sign.

Shortly after 8:00 P.M. Ed Garland and Mark Kadish went off to interview Mrs. Zoufaly, with the permission of her court-appointed lawyer. At first they reported that according to Hugh Smith Mrs. Zoufaly now said she had been harassed by *me*, but Mrs. Zoufaly promptly denied it (Smith was not having a good day). In fact, after the interview Mark bumped into Smith in the hall and said, bluntly, "Do you have any corroboration of Zoufaly's testimony?" Smith was equally blunt. He said, "I'll tell you after you've committed yourself with the witness on the stand." As for Mr. Leventhal, no one knew exactly how he felt because he refused to talk to the defense.

At approximately 9:30 P.M. Ed Booth, Howard Zoufaly's counsel, was called to the judge's chambers for a conference. I went back to the defense room to have a cigarette, and was pleased at the rising mood of expectancy.

At 10:03 P.M. we were called to the judge's chambers and informed that Zoufaly had indeed "made a terrible mistake about describing my presence at a meeting I had not attended," and would like to throw himself on the mercy of the court. Zoufaly's appointed lawyer was of course properly concerned about the possibility of his short-notice client being charged with perjury.

There was actual whooping and hollering in the defense room when we got back. When Truman heard the news, he looked at the woman he was interviewing and said, "That's it! I'm not going to ask you any more questions." They both laughed. In the next room Mark Kadish was smoking a cigarette, something he does two or three times a year in his rare moments of near elation. Ed Garland, his broad face beaming, walked around the room repeating, "How sweet it is!"

I told Mark to tell the Boston-area witnesses that we would not have to put them on the stand after all, but I appreciated their presence, and I'd be giving each one of them a signed copy of *The Defense Never Rests*.

Garland said, "How about one for Howard?"

Back at Villa Granada, five of us crowded into the bedroom to tell Lynda what had happened that day. She was still under the weather, but a moment later she was sitting up and joking with the group, her face lit up with pleasure. Finally, Mark had her laughing so hard with his imitations of the prosecutors that I thought we'd better let her rest. We went out to the living room and discovered that no one had any booze. Garland disappeared, and was back shortly with several small bottles from the airline, and we did the best we could with what little we had. It was a fine time.

Just before we broke up, Kadish turned serious. He said, "Lee, I'll never forgive those prosecutors for what they did this weekend. I realize that you do certain things in the heat of battle, but I just can't believe it." He shook his head, "They want you *so* bad."

I wished I could disagree, but I couldn't. I had just seen how far they were willing to go. In order to stop them, I had to spend hundreds of man-hours—and more than four thousand dollars.

At 8:45 A.M. on Monday, December 3, 1973, Howard J. Zoufaly was back in the courtroom. This time all the bravado was gone. He stood quietly as his lawyer addressed the court:

MR. BOOTH: Your Honor, may it please the Court, following the Court's appointment yesterday of myself to advise and consult with Mr. Zoufaly, I did so. I conferred with him last evening for approximately two hours, at which time I had an opportunity to review with Mr. Zoufaly the matters and events that transpired on Friday of last week.

Mr. Zoufaly has authorized me this morning to advise the

Court that following the giving of his testimony before the Court here on Friday, the proffer that was taken up at the time, that he left Jacksonville and went to Tampa, and that during the time that he was gone, and the time he returned here yesterday, that he had an opportunity to consider and reconsider the matters that he had testified to before the Court, particularly as to those matters that relate to the testimony that he had given regarding the presence of Mr. Bailey at a meeting on November 1, 1969.

The more he considered these matters, the more misgivings he had and grave misgivings, the way he put it, about his ability to recall the events that transpired at that time, and about the validity of the testimony he had given. . . . And he came to the conclusion in his own mind that his recollection of events was such that he could not state with any accuracy before the Court, or support the matters that he had testified to under oath, and that he wanted an opportunity to come back before the Court and correct the testimony and recant and retract the statements that he made on Friday.

I would further advise the Court that from my conversations with Mr. Zoufaly, I do not believe and I certainly don't want to represent to the Court that the statements were made with any malicious intent nor with any sinister desires.

And then the judge said, which surprised me, "Or induced by anybody?"

MR. BOOTH: Nor do I feel in talking to him that these statements were induced by pressure from any source, but it is a matter that he has no confidence in the accuracy of his recollection of these events, and he has advised me and asked me to advise the Court that he cannot testify under oath and does not want to represent to this Court Mr. Bailey was in any attendance in this meeting in any way, shape, or form, and he has asked me to advise the Court of this this morning, and his desire to recant and retract his testimony.

So Howard Zoufaly, who up until the last minute, when he was pinned to the wall by the truthfulness of his own wife had been more than willing to testify falsely, was now being described as a nice, confused man who would like to change his story in the interest of truth. There was no point, however, in pursuing the matter. My hard feelings were reserved entirely for the prosecution.

Just to be on the safe side, Booth asked the judge if it was true that by recanting Zoufaly had eliminated the possibility of his being charged with perjury, and the judge said yes. Everyone joined in the motion to strike the testimony, and it was wiped from the record, a highly dramatic episode that no one would ever read in those pages.

When Booth had finished his explanation of his client's intention to recant, the judge said to the witness, "Is that a correct statement, Mr. Zoufaly?"

A newly meek Howard Zoufaly replied, quietly, "Yes, Your Honor, it is." Zoufaly had had his moment in the sun; and he came away badly burned.

There was a fitting end to the whole bizarre incident. Later in the morning, Mark Kadish was distributing checks to the six people who had come down from Boston for their expenses and witness fees, even though it wasn't necessary for them to testify. When he learned that Zoufaly had paid for his wife's trip, Mark called him at the hotel across the street and told him the money was a legitimate defense expenditure, and that if he would come over, we would reimburse him for the cost of the round-trip flight.

He arrived in short order, and as he pocketed the check, he said to Mark, "You know, I really shouldn't take this."

"Why not?" Mark said.

"Because I'm the guy that tried to shaft you people."

Then, as if things weren't sufficiently weird, Zoufaly noticed the pile of my books that had been autographed for the Boston witnesses. Apparently it was too much for him, and he said, "Boy, I sure would like to have one of those." Without batting an eye, Mark walked into the next room and asked me if I would autograph a free copy of *The Defense Never Rests* for Howard Zoufaly.

I realized he wasn't kidding, and after a moment's thought I said, "Oh, what the hell." I scrawled something as an inscription, signed the book, and slammed it shut. There was general laughter around the room when Ed Garland cautioned me by saying, "I hope you remembered to write down the date."

The Zoufaly affair marked the beginning of December. In the next weeks the government again stepped up its pace, averaging five to six witnesses a day. The testimony was repetitious and boring, but its cumulative effect was probably being felt by the jury —if the jury was still capable of feeling. Someone suggested that we take out the witness stand and replace it with a revolving door.

Late in the afternoon of December 4, the day after Zoufaly had recanted his testimony, Mark Kadish had a chance encounter with Hugh Smith in the hallway outside the courtroom. Mark was still bothered by the weekend debacle, and the extreme pace of the last few days. Smith remarked that Kadish looked tired, and Mark said, "Yes, I am. It's getting very difficult for me to participate in this trial because I can't see where you have any evidence to come that will satisfy me that Lee Bailey was properly indicted."

Smith reacted with his usual aplomb. (For one thing, as a special prosecutor named to the spot late in the summer, he had nothing to do with the indictment itself.) He told Mark that, the way it now looked, it might have been a strategic error on his part "to try Bailey along with the other defendants, but there really was no choice, because it was my opinion that Bailey could never have been convicted on the evidence if he had been tried alone."

Mark hardly knew what to say, but he repeated that he was surprised at how thin the government's case against me was, up to this point. Smith said that I "would be surprised" when the insider witnesses began to take the stand, and then told Mark that his trial strategy was to rely heavily on victim witnesses because of "the low mentality of the jury." Just then someone called Smith away, and the conversation ended.

When I learned what Smith had said, I had Mark dictate a statement covering his recollection of the conversation, and I later brought the matter to the attention of the judge. I felt that this was additional evidence that the government was out to get me, whether it had a case or not. The judge accepted the statement without comment, and that was the last I ever heard of it.

Shortly before Christmas, when the defense team felt that the case was progressing more than satisfactorily from our point of view, the lawyers were dealt a rude shock. Glenn Turner ran out of money.

It was Turner, and Turner alone, who was bankrolling the major portion of the defense costs, including the hefty per diem of several of the many lawyers. For the first three months of trial, Glenn had paid the tab for everything from lawyers to the maid service, and paid it for the most part with no complaints. I was paying my own expenses, plus the cost of the keeping my staff people in Jacksonville, but I, too, had benefited from the money spent for investigators and other backup help. By the end of the third month of the trial, Turner had laid out over five hundred thousand dollars.

And then, just like that, the well ran dry. Until late November Glenn was still receiving money from his overseas operations, all of which were operating under the laws of the various foreign countries with no problems at all. And then, in a single day, the governments of three foreign nations moved to shut Turner down, seizing his assets and putting all cash into escrow funds. Glenn believed that the whole thing was collusion between the American government and the countries overseas. It was hard to disagree with him.

But no matter what caused it, within weeks the pinch was felt in Jacksonville. Thus we began, bit by bit, to cut back on expenses. We didn't know it then, but it was only a matter of time before the defense would be drastically reduced, and the supporting troops a pale shadow of what they had been at the beginning of the trial.

To the credit of all the lawyers involved, no one packed up and left the minute the money tree stopped bearing fruit. Those defendants who could, made hurried arrangements to raise more money, but with the end of the trial nowhere in sight, they knew it was nothing more than a gesture. Nonetheless, the "gesture" meant the loss of savings, cars, and finally homes. One way or another, the government was putting on the screws.

Thanksgiving had passed, and soon it was Christmas, and then New Year's. There was a short break, but then the trial resumed. And again the pace was exceedingly slow.

On January 15, almost four months after the trial had begun, the government was still putting on its case. On that day it called witness number 150.

The daily transcript of the case had run to more than fifteen thousand pages. In the beginning, we were getting four copies per day. It was now down to one.

In mid-January Lynda and I went to San Diego, California, for the annual convention of the American Helicopter Association. When we got back to Jacksonville on the seventeenth, we met a demoralized crew.

The government had finally begun to put on the insider witnesses, the former company employees and consultants who could testify to a broad cross-section of events, and their impact was worse than anyone had anticipated. (One of the worst was Terrel Jones, originally a co-defendant but now a government witness with immunity.) As far as I was concerned, the evidence was nothing to worry about, and I had left Mark Kadish in complete charge. But he and I had had a few strong words about my absence from the Jacksonville scene (I had spent as little time there as possible since the holiday break). I was working on the theory that the jury would finally begin to think I must be worried about *something* if I showed up in court day after day even though no one was mentioning my name.

I did what I could to mollify a few of my fellow defendants, in particular Ben Bunting. Of all the Turner executives I had met in the time I actively represented the company, Bunting was the one man with whom I had become personally friendly. And if I liked him, Lynda loved him. Ben is a gentle-seeming man from North Carolina with what appears to be an easy-going manner. But as I had seen on several occasions, he boils underneath. And sometimes he erupts. I had watched with interest several years ago when he blew up at Glenn Turner for taking—or not taking—certain actions. Ben was one of the trio (the other two were Malcolm Julian and Clyde Cobb) who had left the company in 1971 when control of the board of directors shifted to the hard-sell, wholesale-oriented types.

Ben had not been hurt by the bulk of the government's witnesses, but in the last month there had been testimony that seriously damaged his position. It was not the kind of evidence, under normal circumstances, that couldn't be diffused on cross-examination or in the defense case. But Ben had to be concerned because of the trial's incredible length and complexity. No matter how you cut it, after a while the jury is only going to remember the high points. And the most recent high points, as far as Bunting was concerned, were not in his favor.

What bothered him more than the actual evidence, though, was the judge's reaction to it. In a bench conference out of the jury's hearing, the judge had made some startling comments about Ben Bunting and his posture in the case. Where he got the ideas from, I don't know, but he had the facts terribly messed up. At one point he said that Bunting appeared to be in "big trouble in three areas," and that "I wouldn't be surprised to see him indicted several more times after this case."

As if these remarks weren't sufficiently damaging, he added, "If I were Bunting's lawyer, I wouldn't let him take the stand anywhere in the United States." The saddest part of the whole scene, which took place while I was out of town, was that Bunting's Orlando attorney stood mute while all of this was being said.

I was upset for Ben when I heard what had happened. And I was concerned for myself, because Ben Bunting was scheduled to be my own chief "insider" witness; of all the other defendants, Ben Bunting had agreed to waive the attorney-client privilege and testify on my behalf. As he put it, "Lee, there isn't anything I could testify to that could possibly hurt you." Now, with the judge's terribly prejudicial comments as part of the record, could I ask Ben Bunting to come to my aid? It was not an easy decision.

On Monday, January 21, 1974 (four months plus four days since the trial began!), we had a hearing in the judge's chambers on the matter of his Bunting statements. Again, he sealed the record as soon as the meeting was over, but it was a hard and fruitful session. If nothing else, I let the judge know how far he had slipped from the judicial standard.

One point was clear from the meeting, and that was that the judge had no real explanation for why he had made the statements he made about Bunting. The great danger, of course, was that it indicated his "mind set," as the younger people say, and that was definitely anti-Bunting. I was buoyed by one idea, which was that the judge's misstatements would probably guarantee a severance, or separate trial, for Ben.

After the meeting, Roger Zuckerman told me he felt that there was now no way that I could be convicted in this trial. I hoped Roger was right, but the possibility of losing my own chief witness did not encourage me. The problem was whether, given the judge's attitude toward Bunting, Ben could afford to take the stand on my behalf. It was not a simple problem.

The next few weeks went by in a blur of activity. The insider witnesses hurt some of the defendants substantially, others slightly, and me hardly at all. And something very odd was happening. Every few days I received another slight hint from the judge that my days in the trial might be numbered. Of course he never came right out and said he was going to grant me a directed verdict, but he got awfully close. At one point, in regard to a witness, he said, "Don't ask him too much, and you'll be out of this case."

I wanted very much to believe the "vibes" I was getting, but there was too much history to overcome. Still, hope springs eternal and all that, and I could feel my expectations rising.

Wednesday, January 30, 1974, began as had so many other days, in an argument over admissibility of evidence, held in chambers. In fact, the jury was excused until noon. Then, to the total surprise of almost every defense lawyer, Hugh Smith stood up at five minutes to three in the afternoon and said, "The government rests."

Suddenly, there it was. After four and a half months of the government's case—and more than eighteen thousand pages of trial transcript that had cost the defense over half a million dollars— it was now our turn. Now we could put on the witnesses, the documents, the experts, and the "insiders" to counter the government's claim that the companies had been nothing more than an elaborate scheme to defraud. In one sense it should have been a heady moment, but all anyone felt was relief—and fatigue.

Two high points remained; one we expected, and the other came as a total surprise.

At the close of the government's case, Judge Tjoflat announced that he would hear motions for a judgment of acquittal on the following Tuesday.

A motion for a judgment of acquittal, or a motion for a directed verdict (as it is called in some areas), means that at the close of the government's case, a defendant can move to have the case against him settled right then and there—in his favor. Technically, the judge must consider all the direct and circumstantial evidence in the light most favorable to the government, and decide whether or not, based on that evidence, a fair-minded juror *could* decide that the defendant is guilty beyond a reasonable doubt. If in the judge's opinion a juror could not come to such a conclusion based on the evidence brought out by the government in its "case in chief" (which means its direct presentation of the evidence, as opposed to what it might offer after the defense case is finished), then he grants a judgment of acquittal, which has exactly the same weight as if the jury had so decided. In other words, the defendant walks.

Such motions are frequently made, and although they are not frequently granted, nonetheless they are not rare. I felt that I had a very good chance for a successful motion. Surprisingly, John Truman, the resident cynic, agreed with me; Mark Kadish was less optimistic, but Roger Zuckerman was convinced I would get it.

There were several reasons why I was optimistic about my chances for a directed verdict. For one thing, even though 71 of the 160 government witnesses had mentioned me (which gives some indication of government's passion to ensnare me, at the cost of losing certain other defendants against whom they could have put in devastating evidence), few if any had anything even remotely harmful to say. For another, two of the government's heavy witnesses, two state lawyers, had given very favorable testimony about my legal efforts on behalf of Turner. One of them, Scott Rawlings, an assistant attorney general from Ohio, caused Hugh Smith to flush with anger when he volunteered that I had suggested the state plant a spy in the Turner organization to see if it was on the up-and-up. The other, Harvey Tettlebaum, the Attorney General of Missouri, testified that I was actively seeking to find (and have Glenn fire) the high rollers out in the field who were causing so many of the legal problems; and that, when he told me the temporary injunction was still in effect, I said, "Good. Leave it in force. That's one state I won't have to worry about while I track down these guys." Tettlebaum had been an almost hostile witness, in his general attitude toward the defense, but he was beautiful as far as I was concerned, and his testimony certainly surprised the government.

After those witnesses, the jury would have had to believe I was the world's most inept conspirator.

As usual, it took another flat-out effort to prepare the brief in support of the motion. Not only did Kadish and Truman have to work the entire weekend without sleep, but when John Greenya, my literary collaborator, arrived in Jacksonville on Monday night, they quickly pressed him into service summarizing testimony to look for exculpatory statements that could be used in my brief. (Greenya is not a lawyer, but we needed all the warm bodies we could get. Still, he seemed to enjoy it immensely. Later I asked him how he liked the work, which had taken him until three in the morning, and he said, "I can't say I'd like to do it for a living, but I now know you weren't kidding when you told me the manpower problem was acute.")

I argued my motion for more than three hours, beginning that afternoon and ending the next morning. At several points the judge interrupted, to engage me in a discussion of the law. His manner was pleasant, much more so than it had been in a while, and I began to get the strong feeling that I was on my way out of the case. John Truman was as "up" as I'd ever seen him, though at times the old causticity crept in: He said, "If the judge denies your motion after the way he's smiling and joking with you, it will be a prime example of cruel and unusual punishment."

If our spirits were good after I argued my motion, they were even better after the government's response, which was so weak as to be almost nonexistent. The prosecution had the right to argue against my motion. Although I had talked for over three hours, Mike Kinney, who argued in opposition, took only three minutes. We were greatly surprised, and pleased. Not only was his argument so unusually brief, but he argued as if his heart were not in it. When I saw him later in the hallway, he said, "Frankly, I hope I lose."

The defense team had come to like Mike Kinney. He was a savvy guy, some fifteen or so years older than Hugh Smith, and a very successful Tampa lawyer. The word was that he was in the case for the specific purpose of cross-examining me when the time came for me to put on my defense. At first he was very close-mouthed, but after the first two months he began to loosen up, and after the Zoufaly affair he was openly friendly. I got the feeling that he did not feel particularly at home with Hugh Smith and the Katzenjammer Kids (Leventhal, Jay Johnson, and Wolinsky, the young SEC man who was monitoring the trial, and who was upset that Judge Tjoflat made him sit in the spectators' section.)

Several other lawyers had moved for judgments of acquittal for their clients, too, so that night we all gathered in our apartment for a well-earned drink. The mood was very positive.

On Saturday, February 9, the judge announced his decision: all motions for a judgment of acquittal were denied.

Under the federal court rules, the judge does not have to explain his reasons for denying the motions, and Judge Tjoflat did not do so. Kadish had warned weeks ago that the government wanted me in the case until the bitter end, and that it would probably have its way. He was dead right.

The second—and last—highlight did not occur until two and a half months later. Again, it centered around an action of the judge's, but this time his decision was a surprise to everyone.

By late March only two of the defense lawyers had finished putting on their cases. Kenny Robinson, the irrepressible young Washington, D.C., attorney from Jerris Leonard's firm, had presented the defense of the three corporations (Koscot, Dare To Be Great, and Glenn W. Turner Enterprises). It was, by all accounts, a slow process that threatened to bore the jury all over again. But it had to be done. The government had contended that the companies were in reality nothing more than a sham, so Robinson literally trucked in huge file cabinets filled with pertinent records to prove that there had indeed been product, training schools, and national advertising.

Kenny, whose quick temper and offbeat sense of humor had marked him from the beginning as the Peck's Bad Boy of the defense team, had never gotten on with Judge Tjoflat. The necessarily labored presentation of the corporations' defense did nothing to change that situation, and Robinson took a pretty good bouncing around from the judge and the prosecutors on matters of procedure. But he stuck with it, got his case in, and—most important—maintained what everyone else agreed was his popularity with the jury. On April 17, he finished with his documents and his "antivictim witnesses" (people who had good experiences with the various companies, as opposed to those government witnesses who testified that they had lost money).

One week later, Roger Zuckerman concluded his two-day defense of Harry Atkinson and Jess Hickman. It was, from the reports I received, a thorough, completely professional job. Roger's clients had been relatively low profile for the majority of the government's case, and he had no intention of raising it by putting on a lengthy defense.

Because the indictment's alphabetical order was being followed, it was now time for the case of "the defendant Bailey." The trial was in its eighth month, and in the period of time from September to April my wife's health had suffered, my financial situation had changed from black to bright red, and my law practice had all but disappeared. Finally, after all of that, I was about to confront the charges against me.

Then, as had happened in smaller ways so many times before, fate stepped in and turned the whole picture upside down. For more than two months the problems of the judge's intemperate remarks about Ben Bunting had simmered on the farthest of the back burners. Suddenly it boiled over.

It happened because we had finally come to the hard question—could Ben be called to take the stand on my behalf?

What made the question so hard was, itself, rather simple. As a co-defendant, Bunting could not be forced to take the stand as a witness for any other defendant, but—even though he had rested his own case at the conclusion of the government's—he was willing to take the stand and testify for me. However, given the judge's inaccurate on-the-record comments about Ben's "guilt," could he afford to do so?

My opinion was that Judge Tjoflat had finally realized he'd painted himself into a corner, but had no idea what to do about it. So I forced the issue by renewing a motion first made in January that he cut Ben loose by granting him a separate trial.

Beginning at 1:00 P.M. on Tuesday, April 23, we hashed out the problem, and we didn't finish until Thursday morning. Not only did the jury never get seated during all that time, but the people I'd brought to town as my first defense witnesses never got unseated. They cooled their heels in the defense room, where the same tired old magazines got still another workout.

Tuesday's argument was complicated and at times sharp. At one point the judge agreed that he would have to grant Bunting a severance, after I had made a statement (proffer) to the court that revealed the main areas of Bunting's potential testimony on my behalf. For a while I thought things were going my way—at last.

The next morning Judge Tjoflat surprised everyone by handing us a draft of a two-page order he had been working on for several hours (apparently he got up at 4:00 A.M., came down to the courthouse, and typed it out himself). I wasn't too pleased to read, on the first page, that Bunting would be required to turn over his documents to the government if he expected to get severed out, but it wasn't a total surprise. When I read the second page, I was stunned. The last "condition" of the severance read:

> Bunting similarly understands and consents that a severance pursuant to this order operates as an abandonment of all motions for mistrial made or joined in by him during the proceedings of this case and an abandonment of any complaint he may have with regard to the conduct of this case or rulings made therein, and such conduct or rulings do not taint the voluntariness of the consent embodied herein.

It was incredible. All the judge wanted Bunting to do was agree to whitewash the judge, by absolving him of all prior misconduct, in return for a severance. The right to a separate trial is exactly that, a right, and should never be the subject of an under-the-bench trade. But that's what the judge's order amounted to—and no one was buying it. As much as I needed Ben's testimony, I couldn't ask him to pay *that* price.

At this point the fur really began to fly. The judge agreed to redraft the order, and he came up with:

> Bunting similarly understands and consents that the Court holds that the severance pursuant to this order operates as an abandonment of all motions for a mistrial made or joined in by him during the proceedings of this case, and an abandonment of any complaint he may have with regard to the conduct of the case or the rulings made therein. Absent such a holding the Court would not grant severance. Bunting further represents to the Court that prior rulings of the Court on motions for a mistrial made or joined in by him or on his own Rule 29(a) motion have in no way caused him to consent to his severance from this trial, and that absent such representations, his severance would not be granted. On the basis of Bunting's acknowledgements and representations, the Court finds that his execution of the consent to the entry of this order is free, intelligent, and voluntary.

If he thought that was an improvement, I'd hate to see how he would have toughened it!

After several more hours of argument, during which the judge posed any number of hypothetical situations, referred to other cases that he thought were similar, and listened to the defense lawyers (and the prosecutors) explain how they viewed the problem at hand, Roger Zuckerman put the issue right on the line: ". . . Mr. Bunting is willing to [testify] without regard for the variety of alleged errors that he has spoken to in the past. However, he does not wish to waive those errors should he be brought before a judge for a second trial."

Judge Tjoflat was convinced that my motion for a severance of Ben Bunting was actually, or as he put it so many times, "intellectually," a Bunting motion for mistrial. As the afternoon wore on, we got closer and closer to the nub. At one point Jay Cohen (who was standing in for his partner, Mike Sigman, Bunting's lawyer of record), said to the judge, almost wearily, "Judge, I am lost in the analogies." Judge Tjoflat responded, "Where we are, Mr. Cohen, is that I am not willing to let Mr. Bunting out under what I consider to be mistrial circumstances."

And that, really, was it. Tjoflat had gotten himself around to the position where he firmly believed that if he granted a severance for Bunting he would in effect be granting him a mistrial.

Earlier, someone had used the phrase, "between a rock and a hard place." It stayed in the air, an all-too-accurate description of the bind we were in. Finally, Jay Cohen, who deserved a lot of credit for the quickness with which he had grasped a most complicated situation, told the judge that Bunting was not only willing to testify on my behalf, but also anxious, but he could not do so under the conditions the judge had laid down.

Then, suddenly, Judge Tjoflat turned the corner; he suggested that the only way out of the whole mess was for him to grant *me* a severance.

I was stunned. Severance was what I had moved for back at the very beginning. Almost a year ago. Now, after I had been stuck in this miserable trial for eight months, the judge was *offering* me a severance.

Somehow, I got my jaw back in place. I told the judge that the idea of severance was something I would most definitely have to sleep on. I asked that we recess until morning. Judge Tjoflat agreed, and I hurried back to the Villa Granada.

*        *        *

At seven that evening, I called a general strategy meeting of most of the defense lawyers, especially those whose own clients might have a stake in the issue of my severance. At first I had been bitterly opposed to the idea of severance at such a late date. But the swift consensus of the others, plus my friend and legal associate Al Johnson, was that I would be foolish to pass it up.

Ed Garland shook his head. "It's really ironic. It's as if they said to you, 'Bailey, we'll put you through an unconstitutional case, and then when it's almost over we'll grant you a severance'!"

Frank Martin, who was also urging me to take the severance offer, said, "I don't think you could ever be convicted in a separate trial. In fact, the only reason you've been kept in this case so long is because of what spilled over on your shoes from the other defendants."

After quite some time, Al Johnson looked at me and said, "Lee, there's one question that hasn't been asked yet, probably because it's so obvious. The question is: Would *you* advise a client in your own circumstances to take a severance at this point in the trial?"

It didn't take me long to answer, "Yes, I would."

As the gathering was breaking up, Ed Garland said, "The point of it all is that this gives you, in effect, two bites of the apple."

"Ed, I appreciate everything you've said tonight. And I know the truth of your last remark. But one thing bothers me just a little bit. One other person today mentioned that the severance would give me two bites of the apple."

"Who was that?"

" 'That' was His Honor, Gerald Bard Tjoflat."

Ed grinned. "I see what you mean."

At 9:02 A.M., on Thursday, April 25, 1974, I stood and said, "After consultation and after considerable reflection, . . . I move for severance."

For a second I thought the judge was going to grant the motion on the spot, but he remembered he had to ask the government if it opposed the motion. After a brief, lackluster argument by Hugh Smith, Judge Tjoflat cut me out of the case.

Back in the defense room, all hell broke loose. I don't remember who first suggested it, but suddenly the air was electric, exciting, and for one reason—the remaining defendants, everyone from LeRoy Beale all the way down the alphabetical order to Glenn W. Turner, wanted to rest his case without putting on a defense. This meant that every single remaining defendant, some of whom had been badly hurt by the evidence, was willing to go along with a "mass rest," and put the full burden of proof squarely on the government's case.

Ed Garland used a makeshift gavel to bring the room to order, and one by one he ticked off the opinions. The lawyers were far more cautious than their clients, which is really not the way it should have been, since none of the defense lawyers (with one exception) was worried about going to jail. The idea was catching on, especially among the Turnerites. At one point Hobart Wilder, who had always been the quietest man in the defense room, said, "You are all lawyers, but there is a saying among salesmen, and that is, 'A good salesman knows when to close a deal,' and I say that time is *now*. I say, let's all rest right this afternoon."

There were strong murmurs of approval from most of the other defendants. Ed looked to Ben Bunting, one of the few former Koscoters not given to shouting, "Ben, how do you feel?"

Ben looked steadily at Garland, and then said, "Back in North Carolina, we used to have a saying, too. It went like this: 'When the dog grabs your biscuit, it's time to quit sopping.' "

I could tell from looking at the lawyers that they had to think about that one for a while, but all of Glenn's people got the message right away (it was the kind of country talk they understood instinctively): let's do it together and do it right now.

That same afternoon, in what I thought was the single most dramatic scene of the entire trial, we played the script as just written. Because I had accepted the severance, the judge moved on to the next defendant. "Mr. Martin, are you ready with the defense of Mr. Beale?"

Frank Martin stood almost all the way up, and said, in his quiet, authoritative way, "Your Honor, the defendant Beale rests."

Heads spun around. The tableful of prosecutors stared in surprise. And they kept staring as the judge moved down the line. One after another, the lawyers got up to say that their clients were resting. There would be no defense case.

Finally, the judge got to Ed Garland, who looked both grim and pleased as he said, "The defendant Turner rests."

That night, back at the apartment, there was general whooping and hollering. Lynda was flushed with excitement, and looked as if she had never had any discomfort during the entire trial. Al Johnson was stuck to the phone, calling my character witnesses to tell them that they could stay home.

Mark Kadish wandered around the room, stuffing one ice cream sandwich after another into his mouth. John Truman sat on the couch, looking pleased, and for the first time in two weeks not chain-smoking. Greenya, who professed a desire to record the event, finally announced he would take no more notes, and joined in the general fun. I sat, with Lynda on my lap, and enjoyed.

Just before the news came on television, I told everyone on our team to begin "preparations to decamp," and there was a general cheer. Then, someone, probably Al Johnson, yelled for quiet—the television newscaster was about to comment on the day's events in the trial. I watched what I hoped would be the last broadcast I would ever see in Jacksonville, Florida—as a criminal defendant—and heard the announcer say, "Today, in Federal Court here in Jacksonville, in the trial of promoter Glenn W. Turner, Boston criminal lawyer F. Lee Bailey won a new trial."

From beginning to end, the press coverage of the trial had been mediocre at best. There was a noticeable lack of interest in the trial on the part of the national news people—for one thing, the facts in the case were terribly complicated, and for another, it was the Year of Watergate. When national reporters did cover the trial, they weren't on the scene long enough to grasp the full import of what was happening, and the local people were too worried about offending Judge Tjoflat.

But it bothered me that someone could say, after all those months in Jacksonville, that I had *won* anything at all.

Late in the afternoon of May 23, 1974, the U.S. marshal hung a small, gold-lettered sign on the locked door of Judge Tjoflat's court-room. It read: "No admittance. Judge charging jury." At 4:18 P.M., the case of *U.S.* v. *Koscot et al.* went to the jury.

The physical and emotional strain of the long, long case was no-where more apparent than in the final makeup of the jury. We had begun the case with eighteen jurors, twelve regulars and the six alternates. By the time the jury got the case, there were twelve regular panelists—and no more alternates. Three left for medical reasons, two left because they "overindulged in spirits" and made public comments about their opinions in the case, and the final juror was removed because it was learned that one of her relatives was dating a man who worked for Turner.

Finally, with no replacements left, there was a flap over public comments made by still another juror, but the judge allowed him to remain on the panel.

As in any other trial, the jury, both collectively and as individuals, had been the subject of countless hours of speculation. Now it was all academic. The imagined signs of encouragement and disfavor were all in the past. It was time for this oh-so-tired jury to fulfill its historic role.

The defense of course hoped for a quick result, because it would take far less time to decide "not guilty," if that was the way the jury felt, than it would to go through the entire indictment matching various defendants with various counts in order to find at least some, if not all, "guilty." There was no word from the jury the first day until late in the afternoon, when the foreman sent a note requesting that the testimony of one of the witnesses be read to it.

Again the guessing game started. As the jury filed in, and after listening to the lengthy testimony, filed out, everyone had an opinion based on the age-old practice of reading faces. It was about as scientific a practice as phrenology, which holds that you can determine a person's mental ability by the shape of his or her skull.

By the second day it was apparent that there would be no "quick" decision. For the next three days there was a flurry of notes between the jury and Judge Tjoflat, and one thing did become apparent: the jury was not deliberating calmly.

All aspects of the jury's actual deliberation are totally secret, but the notes that pass between judge and jury can be released by the judge if he sees fit. Judge Tjoflat decided (after the trial) that he would release them. They tell a fascinating story.

On the last day, one juror wanted to know if they had to "compromise," or if they were "in here to do as we individuals feel just?" Another juror complained of having to listen to the foreman's "life history," and wrote to the judge, "He is not on trial." And then there was a very disturbing note to the judge from a juror who asked if other jurors were "supposed to get mad" and say "bad words . . . I want to know, am I supposed to take this because I am black, or do I have my rights just like anyone else? Please answer."

At one point, on information from the marshal that "order is not being kept in the jury room," Judge Tjoflat ordered the jury "to stop deliberating immediately and to remain quiet until further order of the court."

In the afternoon of Tuesday, May 28, 1974, the foreman sent a note that read, "Jury hopelessly deadlocked." Within the hour, the judge officially declared a mistrial, and dismissed the jury. Judge Tjoflat did not look at all pleased. The jury, on the other hand, all but ran from the courthouse.

All defense lawyers hear leaks when a case is over. We were no different. The scuttlebutt was that the deadlock broke down to a 9 to 3 (or, said one source, 10 to 2) vote for acquittal.

The final month of trial had worn everyone down, not just physically but also financially. The lawyers had not been paid for months, and clients owed various sums to their attorneys, ranging from a low of twenty-five thousand dollars to a high of well over a hundred thousand. Although there was a momentary flush of good feeling over the outcome of the trial—after all, it could have been so very much worse —it didn't take long for reality to seep back in. Defense lawyers only cheer a mistrial result when it is clear that there will not be a second trial. But when Judge Tjoflat declared the mistrial, he announced that the retrial of the case would begin on August 5, 1974. Within days, some of the lawyers began drafting motions to withdraw from the case.

I can't say I blamed them in the least. The prospect of another six- to nine-month trial in which the defendants had no funds was simply suicidal, financially speaking.

As for me, I was going from one monetary crisis to another, on an almost daily basis, trying to repair the heavy damage of the last year. My only salvation lay in getting the case against me disposed of as soon as possible, either by trial or dismissal.

On June 4, I had a meeting with Henry Petersen, the head of the Criminal Division of the Department of Justice, and his first assistant, Mr. John Keeney. I had asked for the meeting as a way of speeding up my own case. I told Henry Petersen that I felt, as Judge Young had suggested over a year ago, that the length of the trial prior to my severance was tantamount to jeopardy, and that I therefore could not be tried a second time. I said that if the government did not agree, I would greatly appreciate a ruling on the jeopardy question as soon as possible and a retrial, if necessary, with no delay.

Petersen said he would let me know the department's decision in thirty days, after he had "debriefed" the prosecutors.

Thirty days came and went and there was no answer. On July 10 I had a friend in Washington contact Henry Petersen's office to find out if they had made up their mind yet. Mr. Keeney said there would be a decision by Monday, July 15. I went to Washington that day, and was told that the prosecution would seek a retrial of all defendants—together.

My immediate next step was to file motions to dismiss and in the alternative for a speedy trial with Judge Tjoflat in Jacksonville (who, it turned out, had just left for a much-needed vacation) and asked that the judge hear my motions on August 1.

On July 23, Judge Tjoflat's clerk informed me that the judge had decided I should wait to be heard until all the other defendants had filed their motions—apparently, the deadline for the filing of these motions had been extended, *twice*, without anyone bothering to inform me. The whole thing was very odd. As I read the rules of the Fifth Circuit, a retrial must be held within ninety days of the date of mistrial; and the court had set trial for August 5, 1974; but no one seemed to be paying any attention to that date except me.

On July 27 I sat down and wrote a long letter to Judge Tjoflat setting out every legal, professional, and personal grievance that had any bearing on my request for a clear answer to my situation. I closed the letter by saying:

> I ask no favors of the Court, but I am understandably and justifiably sick to death of being slowly strangled by "due process" as it has emerged to date. I would very much appreciate reconsideration of your decision to delay entertaining my motions, and ask a personal conference with the Court at the earliest convenient date.

I have never received an answer to that letter.

On August 29, 1974, Judge Tjoflat finally heard all of the motions of all the defendants—and the motions of all the original lawyers in the case to withdraw.

On August 30 the judge granted all the motions of counsel to withdraw, and denied all other motions. He set a new trial date for January 13, 1975—nineteen months after the date of the original indictment in the case. Although the government now talks as if I am back in the case with all the other defendants, the judge made no statement or ruling to that effect.

On September 15, 1974, I filed an appeal to the United States Court of Appeals for the Fifth Circuit, asking for an expedited appeal of Judge Tjoflat's denial, in August, of my motion to dismiss or for a speedy trial.

I included as part of my appeal brief an affidavit that set out, in embarrassing detail, a number of facts that described my personal situation. I ended it with the following paragraphs:

> . . . At present, the undersigned has no effective trial date, and no way of estimating what the future may hold. The action of

the Court has left the undersigned in the classic position of "twisting slowly, slowly in the wind."

The members of my firm who remained after the trial began continued to remain, in most cases, without compensation, up until the last ruling of the Court on August 30, 1974. Despite great financial suffering and continuing anxiety attending upon repeatedly delayed disposition of this case, these lawyers and other employees endured sixteen months of uncertainty before deciding, in view of the fact that no termination is in sight, that they would have to leave. The former "firm" [which at the time of my indictment consisted of: 11 lawyers; 2 legal interns; an office administrator; a financial manager; 8 legal secretaries; a bookkeeper; and one chief investigator plus one part-time investigator] is now reduced to one lawyer—myself—one secretary, one legal intern and one investigator, who is leaving shortly.

All during these proceedings, various state and federal trial judges have attempted to accommodate me by repeatedly continuing cases which I have been prepared to try. I am now in a position where I cannot commit myself to court appearances with any degree of assurance that these commitments will be kept. I have been forced to withdraw from some cases [such as the second trial of Billy Phillips], have been discharged in others because of the continuing cloud of indictment, and have been informed by other past clients that they have taken their business elsewhere because of my questionable availability.

The financial drain which this proceeding has caused has been severe, and has limited my ability to provide the costs (not including counsel fees) of a full and fair future defense. This problem is being aggravated on a daily basis.

My wife suffers from an untreatable and painful disease which is aggravated by anxiety, and has suffered immeasurably because of the continuing threat this case will go on indefinitely.

My family and friends, as well as myself, have suffered continuing anxiety and obloquy as a result of the scurrilous accusation of the indictment, which seemingly defies resolution.

As of early December 1974, the Court of Appeals still had not ruled on my appeal. For what it is worth, however, the signs were favorable that my long ordeal would soon come to an end.

With all the defense lawyers out of the case, and no court-appointed attorneys yet assigned, and the new trial looming ever closer—and less likely—there came yet another change in the cast. And this time it was a major figure.

With the retrial date less than six weeks away, Judge Tjoflat inherited a full calendar of cases from another judge who had become ill. The addition of those cases to his own calendar made it impossible for him to preside over the matter of *U.S.* v. *Koscot et al.* And not only did he remove himself from the case, but he granted the government's motion for a change of venue. The case was moved from Jacksonville, whose chamber of commerce calls it, "The Bold New City," to a truly beautiful spot—Tampa, on Florida's west coast.

With that stroke, all links with Jacksonville were cut. For all any of the defense team ever found out, Jacksonville may well have been a wonderful city. However, under the circumstances we would not remember it with fondness. Unfortunately, we would never be able to forget it.

The epic uncertainty of my own case continues. The Court of Appeals, in early 1975, granted my motion for an accelerated appeal, and postponed the retrial for another six months!

What, finally, did it all mean? In one sense I don't know; and in another I know all too well. Stripping it down to the bare bones, I think that I got indicted for two reasons: one, the postals convinced the U.S. Attorneys in Jacksonville that I had been, or pretended to be, an officer or director or owner of the companies involved; and, two, several eager-beaver young prosecutors not only bought that false story, but saw in the case a chance to make headlines as the lawyers who put both Glenn W. Turner and F. Lee Bailey in the can.

I believe that as far as the case against me was concerned, it was a classic example of indict first and investigate later. And to protect against *that,* there truly ought to be a law.

# The Re-Education of Sonny Carson

*I participated in a few demonstrations, got locked up once (in Mississippi—Greensville) and was bailed out by the legal defense commitee of CORE, when one day I received a telegram that Claire is . . . uh . . . in the hospital and that I should come immediately.*

*That was January, 1964, and I had spent three months there, so I immediately caught a bus to Montgomery, Alabama, and took a plane to Idlewild and then took a taxi to my Mom's, where I found out that Claire had had complications at the birth of my second son, and after being in the hospital for two weeks after giving birth to him, she had passed.*

*. . . So there I was, father of two sons . . . And I had to make a decision again as to whether to stay home and get maybe another mother for my two kids and two more fucking in-the-system jobs and all those same old complaints again that had just sent me South in the first place. Or whether to devote the rest of my life to more than my own kids; to all the beautiful black children plagued by poison paint and rats and garbage, by rotten homes and rottener schools, and by a system that says it loves kids and people and keeps proving how much it hates them when they happen to be black.**

* Mwlina Imiri Abubadika (Sonny Carson), *The Education of Sonny Carson* (New York: W. W. Norton & Co., 1972), p. 107.

I n January of 1964 Sonny Carson was thirty-one years old. He'd been around and he had seen a lot—from privation to prison—and he wanted something different. For himself, and most of all for his people, black people.

Born in South Carolina and raised in Brooklyn, Robert "Sonny" Carson had been an unusually promising student, but he got side-tracked halfway through high school. First, there was involvement with the street gangs, then small crime that led to bigger crime, and finally there was the reformatory. He was all of nineteen when he got out, after serving more than two years for stealing ninety-seven dollars from a Western Union messenger, and it didn't take him too long to get back into the swing of street things.

After that the service, where he deserted as often as he could, but finally he qualified for an elite paratroopers' corps, and was shipped to Korea. His first battle brought him his first and only wound, and he was soon out of the Army. As he wrote, almost twenty years later, "So here I was, 21 years old, $400 dollars in my pocket, a veteran who had spent four and one-half of my last five years away from home, now faced with facing whatever the world had to offer. Free again, until the next time."

But something had changed; Sonny Carson was not the same person who had been sent to reform school at seventeen. Together with his brothers and sisters, Sonny paid the lion's share of the down payment on a real home for his parents, a house in Queens. And when the family was settled, Sonny took up residence in the basement and went to school at night. Having earned his high school equivalency certificate in the service, plus a few basic college credits, he enrolled in a small college in downtown Brooklyn and began to study accounting. His friends in the old neighborhood hardly recognized him.

Normally, the next step for such an obviously ambitious young man would be marriage. And that is just what happened to Sonny Carson. Once married, and living in a small apartment in Queens, his life fell into a pattern that eventually included two full-time jobs. Everything, it seemed, was settling neatly into place. A typical American success style, or as Sonny later put it, "a regular black Horatio Alger."

But it wasn't all that it appeared to be. On the outside Sonny was the epitome of the Achiever—America's living proof that blacks can "make it in the System"—but on the inside he was chafing badly. And what bothered him most was the very system that he was, seemingly, so much a part of.

Soon it was the early sixties, and Sonny was hearing different voices, voices like Malcolm X, the man who did so much to awaken black people to their potential. It was almost ironic: life in the suburbs was what everyone was supposed to want, but Sonny Carson was feeling the first small tugs of what would become a strong pull *back* to the ghetto. As he described it, in 1972:

> Meanwhile, things were "getting better"? Shit. Just because I had a job—two of 'em—didn't mean that things were getting better. Getting better means perceiving a society where people do not have to work beyond human reason to survive. Getting better means people exchanging their talents to bring about the essentials that are needed for survival. That's all. Not some honky standing up telling me that to be a recognized part of society, I have to maintain a good job, good credit, and be good and responsible in My Community.

The problem, though, was even more complicated than Sonny's own push-pull circuitry; he wanted to leave the suburbs, but his wife Claire did not. Finally, after much discussion, they agreed on a compromise plan: he would go South and take part in the voter registration drives that were the legacy of the Freedom Rides and the Sit-ins, and when he got back they would put all their personal cards on the table and see what kind of hand they dealt one another.

And then, in 1964, while Sonny was down South, Claire died in childbirth. When he got back, "Everybody was looking at me strangely, because I'd even missed the funeral."

The next years were a blur. With Claire's parents taking care of his two sons, Sonny Carson threw himself into community organization with the zeal of a convert. Soon he was the community relations director of the Brooklyn chapter of CORE, the Congress of Racial Equality. First there were demonstrations calling for a youth program, and then, as the relations between the community and the entrenched powers worsened, there was the long, bitter confrontation in the Ocean Hill–Brownsville section that kept the schools closed for weeks and weeks in 1967 over the question of community participation in the education of its own children.

By 1968, whether he wanted to or not, Sonny Carson had become an acknowledged leader. He lived and worked in the ghetto—and he was dedicated to its improvement. Through the work of Sonny and other area leaders, the community began to show new signs of life—black life. A complex of several hotels became the focal point of Sonny's neighborhood, and the changes in the street were in marked contrast to other, similar areas of New York. For one thing, drug pushers were no longer tolerated; the mob was no longer welcome; and a number of people began to take Muslim names in keeping with the spirit of pride engendered by the teaching of the Honorable Elijah Muhammad.

The Landmark Hotel, a neighborhood relic, became the center for all that was new and good, and a set of rooms was parceled off and designated as the Swahili Room. African art was featured, and young black school children were able to gain a first-hand understanding of their own heritage. Sonny Carson had come home—with a vengeance —and he was making a difference.

There were still gangs in Sonny's old neighborhood, but in 1972 the gangs were different. Instead of the old fighting gangs that had used zip guns, the new gangs studied karate, as a defensive skill and a path to pride that had been unknown when Sonny Carson was a young teen-ager.

Finally, Sonny did something that he had been wanting to do for a long time—he sat down and wrote a book about the way his life had worked out. He called it *The Education of Sonny Carson*, and shortly after it was published, Paramount Pictures bought the story and turned it into a major motion picture. The critics liked it. For one thing, it was most definitely not a "black-exploitation film"; in fact, it was just the opposite. Sonny Carson had arrived, he was known, and even more organizations asked him to serve on their boards of directors. From all the outward appearances, the education of Sonny Carson was complete.

Then, in the late spring of 1973, Sonny Carson and six of the young men who were deeply involved in what he stood for, were arrested and charged with murder, conspiracy to murder, and kidnapping.

The "re-education of Sonny Carson" was about to begin.

The call came into my Boston office with the blunt explanation that the defendants could not pay my usual fee. Bill Manning, my office administrator, was in the midst of juggling numerous cases because I was myself on trial, but he noted the urgency of what he called, from the beginning, "the Sonny Carson case." After I had read his memo, I asked Billy to give me some more information on the case before I decided whether or not to accept it.

The more he told me about the case, the more it intrigued me. And the more he told me about Sonny Carson, the less it sounded like he was guilty. I told Bill to ask Mr. Carson to come up to the office for a talk.

He came, and I met a stocky, aggressive, yet—in his own way— gentle man. Sonny Carson was then thirty-six years old, and sported a slight paunch. But that was the only hint of physical softness. Everything else, from his handshake to his gaze, was firm. He had barely sat down when he began to spill out his story. After a few minutes the initial nervousness disappeared, and the words tumbled out, punctuated by the anger that had been building up for months.

The basic story was simple—the government was totally confused and mistaken—but the number of supporting players and their movements made it all sound elaborate and very complicated. I asked Sonny a few questions, which caused him to go back over certain points, and finally the story emerged.

Almost all of the principal characters either work or live at the Plaza North Hotel, which is adjacent to the Landmark, and is an essential part of the revitalized Brooklyn neighborhood where Sonny Carson lives and works. With one or two obvious exceptions, the people involved all looked to Sonny Carson as their leader, and, clearly, he was in charge of the group on the night when the chain of events that caused the indictment took place.

For several weeks, in early spring of 1973, the Plaza North Hotel had been plagued with a series of robberies. What so bothered Carson and the others was that the crimes had been committed by other blacks, people who should have been acting like brothers, but obviously were not. Another very sore point was that the Helio Museum, which contained African art, had been burglarized. There was a great deal of strong feeling, and Carson put out the word that he wanted to find out who did it. He wasn't interested in turning over another black man to the police unless it was absolutely necessary, but he was determined to get the art objects and the stolen furniture back. Above all, he wanted action.

On May 22, 1973, he got his wish. Unfortunately he got more action than he had bargained for. By the time the evening was over, one man was dead and another had been shot and left to die.

The evening began quietly enough. Carson had learned that John Brown, a young maintenance man who worked at the Plaza North Hotel, supposedly knew something about the robberies.

Carson and a young man named Ali Lamont went to the Plaza North Hotel and told Brown they wanted to talk to him. They drove him over to the Landmark Hotel in a green Jeep station wagon. At the Landmark, several other people were waiting, people who also worked with Carson and wanted to help solve the crimes. Johnny Brown had a very close friend, by the name of Phil Williams, who was a prime suspect, and when Brown arrived the group began to question him about whether Williams was involved. But first Ali Lamont asked Brown, "Do you have any 'stuff' on you?" Lamont was referring to marijuana. When Brown didn't answer, several people in the group asked him to empty his pockets. Finding himself in the middle of a ring of young men, almost all of whom were known to be more than adept at karate, and who also frowned heavily on the use of any drugs in and around the neighborhood, Brown became very frightened.

Seeing this, Carson interceded, told the others that they were "taking Brown's manhood away from him" by forcing him to empty his pockets. He then told the others to step outside so he could talk to Johnny Brown alone.

They talked about the robberies and the thefts. Brown implicated his close friend Phil Williams, and he said that he could lead Carson and the others to where some of the art treasures could be found. He promised to help recover them. Carson then took Brown into a meeting that was going on in the hotel, a meeting where general neighborhood problems were being discussed, and told the group of some fifteen to twenty people that he had "a brother who can tell us about our stolen paintings and who is going to help us get them back." Carson pointed to Brown, who nodded his assent.

A few minute later, Carson got a phone call from the receptionist at the Plaza North Hotel, informing him that someone was in the Helio Museum at that very moment—and as the museum was officially closed, she was sure it was the robbers again. A group of men rushed over there, but they could not find anyone, nor any evidence of a theft.

At this point everyone felt that the whole business was getting out of hand, and that they should immediately act on Johnny Brown's offer to help recover at least some of the stolen articles. Carson, the acknowledged leader, asked for volunteers, and eleven men, including John Brown, got into two cars. Brown led the way to the apartment of a man named Henry Manley, where Brown said they would find Phil Williams.

It was close to midnight as the green Jeep station wagon and the other car, a red Dodge Charger, pulled up in front of an apartment building located at 235 Rochester Avenue in Brooklyn. All but two men left the cars and went up to the second-floor apartment. Carson was not the first one into the apartment, and when he walked through the door he saw Raymond Chunn (known to everyone simply as Sharif) who was one of the volunteers, holding Henry Manley by the front of his T-shirt.

Manley was taken into the kitchen, where the questioning began, while a few of the other men searched the apartment. Thinking that some of the stolen goods might be hidden in the bedroom, Jackie Lamont went in to search it. He didn't find any of the objects, but he did find a pistol, all taped up, which he gave to one of the other volunteers in the living room.

Back in the kitchen, Manley was talking. He admitted that he and Phil Williams had been involved in the robberies, but he said he had none of the goods that were taken, and since he had not done it alone, he had no desire to "take all the weight." He agreed to lead the group to Phil Williams, and also to help them get the goods back.

Once he heard the confession, Carson decided that he had enough information to make what he understood to be a citizen's arrest. He told Sharif to take Manley back to the Plaza North Hotel. (Carson later admitted to me that if he had had more time to think, or if he had not been so angry when he heard Manley admit the thefts, he would probably have chosen someone else to take Manley back to the hotel. Sharif, alone of all the volunteers, had a reputation as a hothead who at times resorted to violence.)

The citizen's arrest idea was in Carson's mind because he felt they would need all the evidence they could get before turning Manley over to the police, because the police had—in Sonny's opinion—less than enthusiastically investigated the original crimes. Carson wanted to get Manley to the hotel so the receptionist could identify him, and then get Manley to sign a written statement admitting the crimes. As a final device for ensuring police action, Carson planned to call the press and have a reporter present at the confrontation.

After telling Sharif to bring Manley back to the Plaza North Hotel, Carson got in the second car, a red Dodge Charger, along with several other people. In the car with Carson were the Lamont brothers, Jackie and Ali, Johnny Brown, and another man, who drove. They took off for the hotel.

It was at this point that the best laid plans of Sonny Carson began to go astray.

After a few blocks, one of the occupants of the car looked back and said, "Hey, the station wagon isn't following us." And, indeed, it wasn't.

After making a few turns to retrace their route, Johnny Brown suggested that they drive over to Phil Williams's apartment. Actually, the apartment was rented to Williams's girl friend, Patricia Chance, but Williams lived there. When they arrived in front of her building, at 265 Rochester Avenue, they found the green station wagon, and upstairs, standing in front of the apartment door, the rest of their group plus Henry Manley.

By this time the original number of volunteers was down to nine; William Hampton and a man known only as Damu had stayed too long at the first apartment (Manley's) and lost their ride. They eventually took a cab back to the hotel, and had nothing further to do with the events of the rest of the night.

Even though she knew Manley, Pat Chance would not open the door to her apartment for him. But when she heard Johnny Brown's voice, she did. Not everyone entered the apartment: Sharif, Ala Mathematics, and Jackie Lamont went in; Carson, Manley, and Johnny Brown stayed in the hall; and Carlvin Smith, Ali Lamont, and another man waited outside the building.

The three men who went into the apartment did find a pair of lamps that had been stolen from the museum, but little else. Someone yelled, "Come on," and they left. As Jackie Lamont walked to the door, he noticed that Phil Williams was doubled over, as if he had been hit in the stomach. He thought Williams had probably given someone some lip, and that he was either punched, or hit with a *chukka* stick (two wooden sticks, twelve to eighteen inches long, and tied together by a piece of leather or a small chain. With proper training, a karate student can learn to use the sticks as a most effective offensive or defensive weapon).

Down on the street, in front of the building, Carson asked Jackie Lamont, "Where is Phil?" and Jackie said, "We left him," or words to that effect.

Again the red car drove off, with Carson in it, expecting the station wagon to follow. By this time Sonny was getting annoyed with all the delays and wanted to get back to the Plaza North Hotel and set the machinery in motion for clearing up the thefts and robberies, now that they had at least one of the guilty parties, Henry Manley.

When they got back to the hotel, Carson sat down with Ali Lamont, while waiting for the green station wagon to arrive, and discussed calling the press and having reporters meet them at the office of the District Attorney for Brooklyn, Victor Gold, so that Manley's arrest would not go unnoticed.

Again the green station wagon did not arrive on time. Earlier it had gone to the Chance apartment because Manley promised to find Phil Williams for them, and this time it didn't return because Manley said he could locate some of the stolen paintings.

When the wagon finally arrived at 3:00 A.M., Sonny Carson was in an angry mood. He had already sent Earl Ferguson (known also as Atiim) and Timmy Vincent (a popular neighborhood figure who used to play for the Harlem Globetrotters) to see if they could find the others. They had driven past the Seventy-seventh Precinct, because Carson thought perhaps the group in the green car had misunderstood his orders and taken Manley to the police, and also went past the Chance apartment, but saw no sign of the other car.

When it finally arrived, Sharif got out and tried to explain to Carson what had happened. By this time, Sonny had received several brief phone calls from Carlvin Smith, who had explained the delay as best he could. All Carson saw, when the group returned, was that Manley was no longer with them. Sonny was so mad that he said to Sharif, "I don't even want to talk to you."

What had happened was this: Ala Mathematics, Sharif, Carlvin Smith, and a man known only as Machuma were in the green station wagon with Henry Manley. When the search of the Williams–Pat Chance apartment revealed only two lamps, Manley became more and more worried that he would get the major share of the blame for all the robberies and thefts. He began "crying," which is the way the younger men in the car referred to excessive complaining, said that he was a "junkie" (which he was), and that if they would only listen to him he could lead them to where the bulk of the stolen goods were stored. They listened, knowing that Sonny Carson and the others would be very pleased if they returned with the paintings and other objects.

Manley told them the stuff was stored in a house in Hempstead, Long Island, out in Nassau County. This was a long way from the ghetto, both geographically and socially, but they believed Manley and set out for Hempstead.

By this time it was after midnight, and Smith and Ala Mathematics wondered if they should call Carson, but Sharif said no. So Smith drove on, and when they reached the city, Manley had difficulty finding the right street because it was so dark. Finally, after thirty minutes, Carlvin Smith became very concerned about having disobeyed Sonny Carson's instructions, and decided to stop and call him.

He went to the house of Earl Ferguson, Sr., the father of Smith's friend, Atiim. Smith had lived in the house for a while when he was working in Nassau County, and still had his own key. He used it to get in, and went to a small room on the first floor to call Sonny. The others, including Manley, went down to a recreation room in the basement.

After just a few minutes Earl Ferguson, Sr., heard the noise and came downstairs in his pajamas and robe to investigate. Carl Smith, who had gotten a busy signal when he first tried the Plaza North Hotel, explained to Mr. Ferguson that everything was all right, and then he tried to call Sonny again.

Ala Mathematics, who was also familiar with the house, went up to the kitchen and got some cold cuts, bread, and a bottle of wine out of the refrigerator. He went downstairs and the group made sandwiches. Someone had turned on the hi-fi, and with the food everyone relaxed a bit. After a while, Henry Manley looked at Sharif and said, "You know, I'm sure I know you from somewhere."

After he had repeated this once or twice, Sharif became visibly upset. A few minutes later he said to Manley, "Come on outside." He told the others that they would wait for them in the car. Moments later they heard the car start up, which was quite a recognizable sound because the muffler had dropped off as they passed through a toll gate on the way to Nassau County. (Smith had stopped the car, retrieved the muffler, and thrown it in the trunk.) They did not, however, hear the car drive away. Apparently, Sharif was simply warming it up, in the driveway, for the ride home.

When the others got to the car, neither Sharif nor Manley was anywhere around. Smith finally decided they would have to leave them, and drove off. When he turned the corner, Sharif stepped out, into the glare of the headlights, and flagged the car down. As he got in, alone, he was asked where Henry Manley was. He said only, "He got away. He took off."

No one questioned Sharif about Manley, and they all drove back to the hotel—where Sonny Carson was less than pleased to see them without the prize catch of the evening. When Carson refused to talk to Sharif, Sharif walked away. No one has seen him since.

Henry Manley, however, had not "taken off," nor had he "gotten away." He had been shot and left for dead.

But he wasn't dead. He crawled to a house not far from that of

Earl Ferguson, Sr., and collapsed at the door. As fate would have it, the house was that of a policeman.

At 1:35 A.M. May 23, Henry Manley was questioned by the police in his hospital room. He told them that he had been walking along a street in Nassau County, that a strange car had stopped and given him a ride, and that after he had driven around with its occupants for a while, one of them shot him and dumped him out of the car. (Junkie thieves who suddenly find themselves in very strange and uncomfortable surroundings usually do not make up good stories.) Although Carson and his followers didn't know it, Manley was under indictment for still another armed robbery—and had jumped bail, which made him a fugitive.

Later the same day the police paid Manley a second visit. This time the officers told him they knew all about what had happened in Brooklyn; and this time he told them a story that was much closer to the truth, naming some of the participants and failing to name others. What undoubtedly changed Henry Manley's mind was that the police mentioned the death of one Phil Williams. He had been found dead in Pat Chance's apartment, moments after Manley and the others had left, the night before.

It was then only a short time until a grand jury in Brooklyn handed down a number of indictments, charging Sonny Carson and six of his followers with murder, conspiracy to murder, and kidnaping.

Then, as somewhat of a surprise, the Brooklyn indictment was followed by one in Nassau County, citing the same charges, and naming Robert "Sonny" Carson, Ali and Jackie Lamont, William Hampton, Earl Ferguson, Jr. (Atiim), Carlvin Smith, and Wallace Hammond (Ala Mathematics).

Also indicted was Ray Chunn, better known as Sharif, who was nowhere to be found.

Sonny Carson, Ali Lamont, Jackie Lamont, William Hampton, and Atiim were never in Nassau County on the night in question— they were included in the indictment under the elastic limits of the conspiracy charge. Three other men, whose involvement was also peripheral but equal to that of the five men named above, were not indicted.

Sonny Carson was beginning his "re-education."

At the time I accepted the Carson case, the curtain had not gone up in Jacksonville, and I still believed that my involvement in *U.S.* v. *Koscot et al.* would end prior to trial. When the show opened and proved to have a disastrously long run, I was forced to postpone the case time and time again.

As the indictment in Brooklyn was second in line, so to speak, there was increasing pressure from all sides to go to trial. The only reason I was not forced to withdraw from the case because of the circumstances (as I had to do in the second trial of Billy Phillips, although I was fortunate enough to talk Henry Rothblatt into taking on Billy's defense) was the desire of the defendants to have me represent them, and the continuing good will of the trial judge, an absolute prince of a man by the name of Bernard Tomson.

Finally, in the fall of 1974, we went to trial. For Sonny Carson— and especially for several of the defendants who had spent months in jail, and the single defendant, Atiim, who was *still* in jail—it was probably the most important moment in their lives, considering what they had riding on the outcome. For me it was also something special. It was the first criminal case I would try since my own indictment. I was more than anxious.

A trial lawyer out of trial is very much like a fish out of water, and I was eager to try this case. For one thing, Sonny Carson and the six men on trial with him struck me as unusually candid and direct people. Their pride in themselves and in what they had accomplished was apparent, but they never flaunted it. I had the same feeling about them as a group as I did about Sam Sheppard as an individual—they were not the murdering type.

For another thing, I was eager to work before a jury again without the incredible albatross of being (myself) a criminal defendant. When you've spent your entire adult life arguing before a jury on behalf of someone else, it is very, very difficult to suddenly appear before one on your own behalf. I had never before had jurors look at me the way the jurors did in Jacksonville. It was not a good feeling.

I was anxious to go before the jury and tell the story of Sonny Carson and the other defendants, a story of hard work and pride overcoming huge odds, a story of a neighborhood reborn out of dedication and self-esteem—a story of anything but murder.

Yet, as we moved through pretrial and got closer to the day when we would be picking the jury, I had to admit that no matter how eager I might be, my clients were looking very nervous.

Finally, I sat down with Sonny and a few of the others. Lynda was with me, and we all talked as informally as possible. After a few moments, I knew what the problem was—the defendants were just plain scared about being tried by an all-white jury in Nassau County,

Long Island, New York. It was just not the same as downtown Brooklyn.

Sonny Carson, being the oldest, was the most conservative-looking person in the group. But even he was hardly what you would call "square." The others liked bold, stylish clothes, in the latest cuts and the warmest colors. Some favored a single earring, and others disdained jewelry for the neatness of a dashiki and an Afro hair style.

Their dress would set them apart, as would their size. And when a jury learned that almost all of them were skilled at karate, it would undoubtedly scare the daylights out of your average up-tight bigot. I could see what they meant.

I had to face the simple fact that these defendants did not want to be tried by a Nassau County jury. I don't mean to picture Nassau County as a hotbed of reactionaries, but it *is* the same county where Richard Nixon received the most vocal public support of his entire 1972 campaign. In fact, one reporter who used to cover politics in the South said the Nixon rally in Nassau County was the closet thing he had seen to a Wallace rally.

After weighing all the possibilities, I agreed to a nonjury trial.

The clincher was the presence of Judge Bernard Tomson. I had heard that he was a good one, but when I began to work through the pretrial phase, I learned for myself. He was indeed a good one.

A tall, balding man with a long, pleasant face hidden by thick, dark-rimmed glasses, Judge Tomson had a disarming sense of humor that crept in from time to time. Later I learned its source—the judge's father was Boris Tomashefsky, one of the greatest Yiddish comedians of all time. (It also intrigued me to learn that one of the judge's nephews, and one of Boris's grandsons, is Michael Tilson Thomas, the youthful conductor of the Buffalo Philharmonic Orchestra.)

If we had to go to trial before a judge as both judge and jury, we could not have asked for a better one than Bernard Tomson.

Whatever fates arranged it I do not know, but we were blessed by having a prosecutor who seemed to miss the presence of the jury even more than I did. Michael Premisler, a pleasant, rather non-descript young man, represented the people of the state of New York. From the moment the first witness took the stand until the moment the last one had left, Mr. Premisler conducted his examinations and his cross-examinations as if some phantom jury were hanging on his every word. We could not have hoped for a better break.

Still, with a jurist of Judge Tomson's stature, we could expect to gain only so much from the prosecution's emotional approach to this nonjury trial. Our main concern was the strength or weakness of the government's case, as brought out by its witnesses. Here, too, things seemed to be in our favor. At least that's what we thought until the witnesses took the stand.

Johnny Brown, maintenance man and one-time closest of friends to the late Phillip Williams, told a quite different story than the defendants had thought he would. He testified that on the afternoon of May 22, 1973, two of Sonny Carson's boys (Mathematics and Atiim) had picked him up and questioned him about the robberies and thefts from the Helio Museum.

This was true, but he claimed that they picked him up at two o'clock in the afternoon and drove him around for *eight* hours, without speaking to him and stopping only once for food. (He said they forced him to stay in the car, "a red Mustang," but that they bought him "three hamburgers and a milkshake.")

Brown testified further that when the group took him to Henry Manley's apartment about ten or ten-thirty that night, all of the men entering the apartment had guns, and that when Manley opened the door Sharif immediately spread-eagled him on the floor and stuck a gun in his neck.

Brown also said that on the "eight-hour ride" Mathematics and Atiim spoke to him once, saying they thought he was mixed up in the robberies and burglaries with Phil Williams, and that if he didn't confess they were going to "hurt me or my brother Phil." In addition, he said, on the ride back to the hotel that night, Sonny Carson told him, "If you feel any animosity toward us, you better not, or you will get the same thing that Phil and Henry Manley got." And to drive the nail deeper, Brown testified that Carson repeated the same thing to him the next day, at work.

On cross-examination, I questioned Brown about his story, especially about the eight-hour car ride, and although he stuck to it in most of the details, I got the feeling that Judge Tomson was looking at the witness a bit askance. Also, I introduced Johnny Brown's time cards from the hotel on the day he said Sonny Carson had repeated the threat—and they showed that he did not work that day.

The next witness for the government was Henry Manley, the almost victim. He said he had never been in either of the hotels, had never seen any of the defendants before May 22, 1973, but that he might have seen the missing Sharif once or twice on the street. He backed up Brown's story about being thrown down and having a gun pressed in his neck by Sharif, but he contradicted Brown by saying that he had never admitted to taking part in the robberies or the thefts. He did admit that he was a heroin user, but said he was not high on the night the men entered his apartment.

Manley described the ride to Nassau County, but he said he had no idea why he was taken there. Then he said that after the men had discussed what to do with him (at one point someone suggested he be made to walk home to Brooklyn), and after one had said, "Perhaps we ought to get rid of the guns before we let him off," they stopped the car. Then, he testified, Sharif made him lie down on the sidewalk and shot him, wounding him in the cheek.

So both Brown and Manley (and later Patricia Chance) said that the men entered the apartments armed. But, interestingly, neither Brown nor Manley testified that he had heard any shots at the Chance apartment—where Williams was, undeniably, killed.

Pat Chance was the government's third and last big witness. She said that at around midnight on May 22 there was a knock on her door, and she heard Henry Manley, whom she knew, ask to come in. She refused, but a few minutes later, when she heard the voice of Johnny Brown, she opened the door.

She testified that several armed men rushed in, among them Jackie Lamont. She said that one of the men took Williams, who was wearing only shorts, into the living room. She was taken back to the bedroom by Jackie Lamont, who, she said, noticed a five-dollar bill on the floor, and picked it up and handed it to her. (I thought I saw the judge's eyes blink at this.)

Then, she testified, she heard a couple of gun shots, and someone yelled "Come on," and everyone left. She went out to the corridor in front of her apartment and there she found Phil Williams lying on the floor, bleeding. She said she dragged him inside the apartment, and then called the police.

I didn't get Pat Chance to alter her testimony much on cross, but she did add something that was very interesting. She said that some weeks before she had heard Phil and Henry Manley planning the robbery of the hotel, and that later she saw them dividing the money. That testimony put her squarely against the story told, under oath, by Mr. Manley, that he was innocent of those charges, and cast some doubt on his statement that he had never told the defendants he was one of the robbers.

And that, as they say, was the case for the people.

＊     ＊     ＊

In answer to the government's case, I put every defendant on the stand. Every defendant, that is, except William Hampton, who had given a statement to the police that even the prosecutor seemed to accept.

I doubt if the venerable halls of the courthouse in Mineola, New York (Nassau County), had ever before contained the likes of these six proud black men. As defense witnesses go, especially defendants as witnesses, they were excellent.

Mr. Premisler had trouble from the very beginning. He clearly did not speak their language. At one point he asked Carlvin Smith about Henry Manley's "crying," and asked him why the man was shedding tears.

Carlvin is a big man, actually a former college football player, but he has a distinct gentleness about him. When the prosecutor asked the question, Carlvin shook his head slowly, and said, "Mr. Premisler [which in itself is unusual for a defendant to do. Usually they are far too scared to address the prosecutor by name], I don't think you understand the term. It does not mean 'shedding tears.' It is a black expression for someone who complains all the time, nonstop. We say he or she is 'crying.' But we don't mean it in the sense that you do."

Mike Premisler looked discomfited. He was by no means a bad egg; he was simply out of his element. It is most unusual for a criminal defendant to lecture the prosecutor on anything, much less semantics.

But if the prosecutor was having trouble with the witnesses, it was nothing compared to the problem he was having with the judge. With increasing frequency, Judge Tomson was having to say, "I don't see any relevancy in that line of questioning. Would you please move along?" And, even, "I don't see this approach as useful at all. Either change to a different line of questioning or drop it." And, finally, several times, "Mr. Premisler, there is no jury here to impress."

If I was pleased to see how well each defendant was doing on the stand, Lynda was beside herself. The case was a new and valuable experience for Lynda. In the section of New Zealand where she'd grown up, there was both mixture and equality of the races. Racial prejudice was something she had read about, but rarely if ever experienced; and yet, like so many Americans from the North, she had never known many black people.

She and the defendants had gotten on famously, if somewhat tentatively at first. Ala Mathematics, with his quick, shy smile, and the Lamont brothers (especially Ali), with their openness, had been her first friends. By the last days she was simply one of the group—no more or less accepted than, say, Mathematics's mother, who was also there every day. There is a fraternity that develops in the spectators' benches in every trial—and the lawyers seldom know its depth.

When Sonny Carson took the stand, the case was almost finished. His first set-to with the prosecutor was a draw. I knew the frustrations that Sonny must have been feeling. He wanted to get on that stand and set everything right—"no more of this legal horseshit." But it is never that easily done, not on the stand, when all the eyes in the courtroom are fixed on you and you alone.

The next time, days later, when his cross-examination continued, he was much better.

For one thing, he could never quite say "Premisler," and instead kept addressing the prosecutor as "Mr. Preminger." I didn't think it was purposeful, but it was nonetheless effective. The more Sonny talked, the more rope he was given—but it wasn't the kind you hang yourself with; it was the kind you use to save your life.

Sonny gave his idea of what a "citizen's arrest" meant, and then, given the chance, he explained that this wasn't just his own idea.

"Oh, did you talk to anyone else about this?"

"Yes, I did."

"Who did you talk to?"

"Well, one of the people was a judge in New York City, and another was . . ."

After that it got even better. Sonny explained how he made his living—in answer to one of the questions—and gave a moving account of how his earnings were turned back into the common good of the community. By the end of his testimony it sounded as if the prosecution had asked Sonny Carson to give an ad in his own behalf.

When Sonny left the stand, I put on most of the members of Johnny Brown's immediate family. Andy Tuney, who had been working on the case for several weeks, had found that there was good reason to doubt Brown's testimony that he had gone to work on the day after the murder, the day he said he had been threatened by Sonny Carson. The reason was that Johnny Brown did not go to work that day.

One by one, his mother and sisters took the stand and testified that Johnny had never left the house on the day in question.

The defense of Carson, et al, concluded with one implication:

Sharif, for reasons unknown, had killed Williams and almost killed Manley.

One thing was certain, though, Sharif did have a temper, and at times it exploded violently. Also, he was considered to be one of the most skilled karate practitioners in the group. Carlvin Smith, no slouch himself, testified that although Sharif weighed only 150 pounds, "he hit like 300."

My own theory was that Sharif had shot Williams, using a gun that he had concealed from the others (all the defendants testified that the only gun they saw all evening was the taped-up .22-caliber pistol found in Manley's apartment), and that Manley may have seen him do it. When Manley started to question Sharif (in the basement of Earl Ferguson, Sr.'s, house) Sharif got upset because he thought no one knew he had shot Williams. The more Manley pressed him, the more aggitated he became. Finally, he attempted to solve the problem by eliminating Henry Manley. This time, however, he succeeded only in wounding his victim.

All of this was why, in my opinion, Sharif had disappeared.

At the end of the case, the defense was in the position of having cast a good bit of doubt on the government's theory of what had happened. To add to the state's discomfort, I moved for "a view." This is the legal term for having the jury—in this case the judge— go to the scene of the alleged crime and view the physical premises that had been mentioned in the testimony. It is a free moment—the law insists that the lawyers cannot speak.

To the consternation of the prosecutor, Judge Tomson agreed. I did not go on the view, but I heard that it was a most interesting morning, with Judge Tomson moving slowly through the ghetto streets, taking in all the sights.

Even though a case is heard without a jury, there is still a need for final argument.

Normally, final argument is the time when the reporters who have been covering the trial, off and on, reappear, hoping to pick up quotable phrases born of the moments' need. It is usually one of the two or three most exciting episodes in any trial.

Without a jury, everything changes, except the fact that someone's life or freedom is at stake.

Final arguments were to be made after the briefs for both sides had been filed and digested. But the prosecutor asked Judge Tomson if we could make the final, oral, argument on the same day that we filed the briefs. The judge looked at Mr. Premisler as if he had not heard right. As a former trial lawyer of no small repute, he knew that it was always best to see what was in the opposition's brief before making that last argument to the court.

"Mr. Premisler," he said, wearily, "Mr. Bailey is not exactly a 'tyro.' Don't you want to at least read his brief before you argue?"

The prosecutor thought for a moment and finally said, "Yes, Your Honor, I guess that would be best."

Everyone was "up" for the final arguments. Everyone, that is, except for Sonny Carson, who was most decidedly down.

On the morning in late November when I arrived in court expecting to see the eager faces of all seven of my clients, Sonny was not there. He was in the hospital.

The pressure of the trial had aggravated an old injury, and on the day I was to make his final argument, Robert "Sonny" Carson was flat on his back in a bed in the Brooklyn VA hospital.

Judge Tomson—after a farce-like runaround from the Veterans' Hospital, which kept denying Carson's presence because it was not as yet on the official list—suggested that it would speed things up if we would make final argument in regard to the six defendants who were present. No one objected, so we went ahead.

I led off, purposely skipping the dramatics, which would only have been wasted on Judge Tomson, and weighed in heavily on the credibility and questionable testimony of the government's witnesses. I pointed up the implausibility of Johnny Brown's story of his frightening eight-hour ride, plus his family's statements that he had never left the house on the day when Carson allegedly threatened him.

Judge Tomson interrupted me several times with incisive questions, and when I finished I felt the six defendants in the courtroom had little to worry about on the murder or conspiracy to murder charge. But I was a bit concerned that the judge might be leaning toward a guilty verdict on the kidnaping charge. But I had given it my best shot, and the defendants seemed pleased.

Later someone reported to me that they overheard Premisler say, "I thought Bailey's argument was excellent—but he seemed to be directing it entirely to the judge."

There was a certain emotional letdown because of Sonny's absence, but as soon as the remaining defendants heard the prosecutor describe them, in rotund oratorical tones, as murderers, the adrenalin started flowing immediately, and soon they were on the edges of their chairs, following every word.

The prosecutor, predictably, spoke as if his phantom jury were right there in the empty jury box. He rolled on and on about the clarity of the defendants' guilt based on the testimony of his sterling witnesses. More than once he was interrupted by the judge, who said firmly, "I can't follow you. Go on to something else." He closed, after less than an hour, with a dramatic appeal for the conviction of these dastardly killers.

Judge Tomson reserved his judgment on the fate of the present defendants until we had made the final argument on behalf of Sonny.

After it had been postponed several times—Sonny kept checking out of the hospital sooner than he should have—it was decided that the argument would be made on Monday, December 9, 1974.

On the appointed day, we were all milling around the courthouse lobby waiting to get in the courtroom. But the mood was not particularly happy. For some reason, the police had decided that every defendant, plus anyone apparently associated with the defense, should be checked for weapons. Every defendant, all of whom had behaved perfectly throughout the entire trial, had to stop while an officer used an electronic frisking device to check for guns. And if that was not bad enough, we learned that the police had set up a riot squad, on call outside the building, in case the defendants reacted violently to whatever verdicts came down.

There was another problem. Sonny Carson was again absent. He was still in the hospital.

When Judge Tomson learned that Carson was not present, he was visibly upset. He issued a bench warrant ordering Sonny to appear immediately. "Immediately" took place at two o'clock that afternoon, when Sonny Carson walked into the courtroom wearing pajamas, a dark blue VA hospital-issue robe, and slippers.

A supporter leaned over the rail and whispered, "Sonny, I love your outfit."

He grinned, "Thanks, baby. When you've got class, you can wear anything."

The final arguments were brief and to the point. Even Mike Premisler seemed anxious to wrap it up. When we'd finished, Judge Tomson said he would render his decision "shortly."

One hour later the bailiff announced that "this honorable court is in session," and we rose as Judge Tomson moved swiftly to the bench.

As he read the verdicts, I noticed that most of the pages were typed, which meant he had already made up his mind about the guilt or innocence of every one other than Carson, and pretty well knew what he would need to hear in order to decide as to Sonny. That's the way the case had developed.

All defendants had been charged with five counts: conspiracy to murder, assault with a dangerous weapon, attempted murder, kidnaping, and possession of a firearm. In all, there were thirty-five individual verdicts to be returned.

Carlvin Smith and Wallace Hammond (Ala Mathematics), who were in the car when it got to Nassau County, were convicted of attempted murder, kidnaping, and possession of a firearm.

Sonny Carson, Ali Lamont, and Jackie Lamont were convicted of kidnaping.

William Hampton and Earl Ferguson, Jr. (Atiim), who had spent a year in prison on high bail, were acquitted of all charges.

Sonny Carson was convicted of kidnaping on the theory that he had set the act in motion. I could see how the judge had reasoned to that conclusion. What I couldn't see was how he figured Carlvin Smith and Mathematics were guilty of attempted murder. I thought that was harsh, and I told him so.

Judge Tomson said he would allow me, at a date in the near future, to argue to set aside the verdict. Again, he was being characteristically fair.

The defendants took the verdicts pretty well. (Their stoic reaction made it clear that there was no need for a "riot squad.") Hampton and Atiim, the two cleared of all charges, seemed almost embarrassed that they were totally free. The general feeling was that the judge had gone too far in finding Smith and Mathematics guilty of attempted murder and possession of the gun that was obviously Sharif's, and that in including Carson and the Lamont brothers in kidnaping the judge was "stretching."

But Judge Tomson had agreed to provide me with a written finding of fact, showing how he had evaluated the evidence, and that would be most helpful in any attempt I would make to set aside the verdict.

One thing that all defendants were agreed on was that they would appeal right away.

Judge Tomson let bail stand for all the defendants, over the argument of the prosecutor, who wanted them all remanded immediately. (So that they could spend Christmas in the can!) When the judge wouldn't agree, Premisler tried to have the bail raised, but the judge wouldn't do that either.

There was one point of total agreement among the defense group: we had made the right decision in waiving a jury.

The "re-education of Sonny Carson" was accelerating. He shed no tears at the verdict, nor did he rail at the judge, he simply began to talk about his appeal. For the moment he was out on bail, and, as he'd put it in his book, "free . . . until next time."

# EPILOGUE

## The State of the Law, Revisited

It is often said that the biggest fool is the man who fools himself. I believe that we as a nation fool ourselves on a daily basis.

Americans generally like to boast that ours is the finest system of justice in the world, and most of us probably believe it. Those with actual experience in the system know better. Guilty or innocent, convicted or acquitted, they have learned at first hand the cold fear associated with being a defendant in an American court.

The elements of this fear are many, and very real. To begin with, the financial burdens of a first-class defense are crippling to all but a favored few. Even when top fees can be paid, a defendant has precious little protection against getting a lawyer of less skill than he paid for. There is no special license, no badge or certification of any kind that marks the true professional defense lawyer. Many a defendant has learned when it was far too late that his advocate wasn't equal to the responsibilities he assumed.

Innocent people, in particular, are frequently the unwary victims of a peculiar syndrome that lands them in jail. It goes this way:

An ordinary citizen, with no criminal background, gets indicted for a serious crime. It may be a businessman accused of some financial fraud or "white-collar crime." It may be an auto mechanic accused of rape, the victim of a wrongful identification by the victim. Because he knows in his heart of hearts he is innocent, he is complacent about the risks involved. He believes that the truth will out, that justice will be done, that the courts will protect him. He hires a local lawyer, perhaps a general practitioner with modest experience in criminal matters, for two reasons: first, he wants to keep the costs down since he has done nothing to deserve them; and second, he is afraid that if he hires a known criminal lawyer his friends—and perhaps the jury—will think he is guilty.

His case is not well prepared. The cross-examination falters on a few key points. The summation fails to establish a reasonable doubt. The jury convicts. The defendant is stunned. So are his family and friends, some of whom may have been his alibi witnesses. Suddenly the matter is indeed serious. A collection is taken up, the house is mortgaged, and the record is brought to a specialist in criminal work, with an agonizing plea for some legal wizardry.

This has been the posture of too many cases that have walked into my office in sad lament. Appeal at once, I am urged, and right this miscarriage. Cost is no object. The family, perhaps the neighborhood, will raise the necessary funds.

Then comes the bad news. Unfortunately, the jury has believed the wrong witness, or drawn the wrong inference from circumstantial evidence. How the jurors went about it we will never know, since their deliberations are the one part of the trial that is never recorded. And from their mistakes there are no appeals.

If the trial judge had made a mistake in one of his rulings—a serious mistake—there may be a chance of a new trial, even though that mistake had no bearing whatever on the jury's decision. Oh-oh! More bad news. This particular trial judge is one of the brightest and fairest on the bench. The chances of a reversible error are just about nil.

What do we do now? We comb the trial record, look for new evidence, we even consider the unlikely prospect of executive clemency. But our defendant, despite all these and other efforts, is most likely going to remain in jail. The system has misfired; and there is no effective remedy.

It happens every day. And the only ones who are really aware that it happens are the victims of the system, their heartbroken loved ones, and the lawyers.

If this were some sort of insoluble flaw, one that simply had to be suffered as a necessary evil generic to the jury system, it would be more tolerable. But it is not necessary, not necessary at all. Convicting the innocent is a "flaw" that continues year after year, in case after case. It happens because most people don't believe that it does happen, and of those who know better, not enough really care. If this is a sad commentary on American jurisprudence, it is nonetheless one that is statistically defensible by any of us who can really speak from experience.

Of course, this isn't a one-way street. As a defense lawyer I am infinitely more offended and horrified by the conviction of an innocent man than by the acquittal of one who is guilty. Society can far better tolerate the consequences of a legal error than any citizen can, but an ideal system would reach a truthful result in all cases. Although not all crimes—especially those triggered by overheated passion—can be deterred by the threat of conviction and punishment, most of those carried out for monetary gain can. If the prospective felon could fairly bet that he would be discovered, prosecuted, convicted, and jailed, the crime rate would drop dramatically.

After more than twenty years of watching and working with the criminal law, and repeatedly feeling the frustration of its shortcomings, I come back again and again to what I must consider the basic fault—the *people* in the system, the ones who run it, or are supposed to.

Every day, in this country and abroad, millions of people board commercial airliners and entrust their lives to the men in the cockpit for safe passage. All but a handful land safely somewhere, and go about their business. In the rare case where mistakes are made and a crash occurs, the event is so extraordinary that it becomes worldwide news. Statistically, these mistakes are few and far between.

But airline pilots are superbly skilled and trained people, who must demonstrate their proficiency on a current basis or their special license is removed. In addition to being highly professional, they are very much involved in what they do; after all, in any crash the cockpit goes too, and usually first.

As one who has been an active flier longer than an active lawyer, it has long puzzled me that affairs of human liberty are so much less rigidly guarded, for certainly next to life itself liberty must be the most precious thing man owns. It would seem quite reasonable for society to require a competitive degree of expertise, high professional standards, and dedication from those who command the cockpits of the law—to require that, like the air traveler, the price of a ticket fairly guarantees the best and safest service that human endeavor can furnish.

Sadly, however, nearly the reverse is true. There are no special training places, no periodic tests of skill, no four-striped jackets signifying command rank.

Worse yet, there is no requirement that one spend thousands of hours in the co-pilot's seat, learning, polishing, and quickening under the supervision of the master.

In truth, a good many of our trial lawyers are trial lawyers because they say that they are. If you ask for their special licenses, they have none. If you probe their special training in the vital arts of investigation, preparation, examination and cross-examination, summation and appellate argument, you are apt to find very little, and none of it very formal. There seems to be some notion floating about that these talents develop spontaneously, merely by accepting a case and stepping into a courtroom. This notion is as false as it is absurd. Trial lawyers in America range from very very good to simply awful, and clients frequently cannot tell the difference until after the trial is over, or beyond repair.

During the last six months, I have often been asked by lecture audiences to comment on the meaning of the Watergate scandal in relation to the legal profession. By this time I would have thought that everyone would feel thoroughly Water(gate)logged, but apparently that is not so in regard to this particular question. Nonetheless, I will limit my observation to this point: if the lawyers involved in the Watergate matter had truly acted like lawyers, there would have been no need for a cover-up because there would have been nothing to cover up.

According to the public record, a lawyer suggested the break-in and several other lawyers approved it; and when the plan misfired, a virtual gaggle of lawyers tried to cover it up. Most shocking of all was that another lawyer, who happened to be the President of the United States, felt that he could *fix* the case, and that he could so do "in the national interest."

My point is this: there is a huge flaw somewhere in our system if these lawyers felt, as they apparently did, that there was a *good chance* they could pull off the fix. And the reason the President and his men thought they could get away with it was because they thought they could control and handle the lawyers. What followed is a nasty part of history that need not be repeated, but which landed many lawyers in jail. And that cost the nation dearly.

I sincerely doubt that, if we had some system under which lawyers were properly categorized and ticketed as to special skills, the Watergate scandal would ever have occurred. We have got to stop pretending that all lawyers are equal simply because they have a law school diploma and a certificate from the bar examiners. Such thinking flies in the face of reason.

The British faced this problem centuries ago. In England there are solicitors and barristers; the former prepare cases and the latter try them. And everyone is better served by it.

What's more, and even better, a barrister is not forced by the system to be either a prosecutor or a defense attorney. He may be one on Friday and the other on Monday. The wisdom of this practice is that it keeps trial lawyers from developing a narrow point of view, as happens all too frequently in this country.

We need to restructure the system so that the best trial lawyers do the courtroom work, and do it without concern for which "side" they are on. To be a trial lawyer means to be an advocate, which in turn means to argue on behalf of someone else (with no reference to "defense" or "prosecution"), and it is not good, over the long haul, for someone like myself to think of himself solely as a defense lawyer. Granted, I like being a defense lawyer, but it is the system that has forced me to chose one side over the other.

The view I'm pushing is not without historical precedence: back at the turn of this century there was a magnificent criminal lawyer by the name of Earl Rogers. When the Los Angeles Times building was dynamited—at the height of a bitter struggle between labor and management—Rogers was named as the special prosecutor. He worked day and night for months until the grand jury returned its indictments. Then, months later, a lawyer who represented the two brothers charged with the dynamiting was indicted for allegedly bribing several jurors. The lawyer hired Earl Rogers to mastermind his defense. When the jury got the case it took only minutes to acquit. (By the way, the name of the lawyer who hired Earl Rogers was Clarence Darrow.)

Today, such a feat of switch-hitting would probably be prohibited as a clear case of conflict of interest. But my point is that it's very healthy for trial lawyers to work both sides of the courtroom. There should be no conflict in that.

I think it is high time we take several more pages from the British book.

A final point: Late one night in the middle of my own trial in Jacksonville, Lynda and I were bushed after an especially emotional day in court. But instead of falling asleep, we stayed up half the night because she asked me one simple question.

"Lee, if we woke up tomorrow and this whole ugly business was over and done with, and you had enough money to do just what you wanted to do, what would it be?"

Oddly enough, I hardly had to think about it. I said, "I'd start my own school for trial lawyers."

If there were money and time enough, I'd set up the most intensive educational environment any lawyer had ever seen. I'd take only a small group, say twelve at a time, and keep them at it for at least a year—with no time off. It would be a live-in school (in my own home, if necessary) and the student-lawyers could kiss their wives or husbands or friends good-bye until they got out. They could make love to the law.

I'd put them through all the wringers I know and invent new ones if I had to. There'd be training—and testing—in trial preparation, in the proper way to interview witnesses, in the many excellent methods that are available for paring a case down *before* trial, in the art (and that is exactly what it is) of cross-examination, in scientific tools such as the polygraph, and in a myriad of other important elements.

The school would be hard to get into—not financially, but on a merit basis—and there would be no token diploma at the end. If a student didn't earn it, he or she wouldn't get it. And they'd all know that up front.

The whole thing would be made to be as practical as it could possibly be. There'd be little or no similarity between my school and any class in law school (where they always go entirely by the rules).

A good trial lawyer has to know what to do when the other side suddenly slips off the gloves and hits below the belt. If need be, I'd turn student against student, and the mock trials would be more like war games.

The students would probably hate the school—on a day-to-day basis. But they would never regret it.

Lynda and I haven't talked much about "my school" since then, but it comes to mind occasionally. I usually think of it during a trial when the other side tries a fast one, and Lynda asks me, later, "Was that fair?"

If there were more trial lawyers around who'd been properly trained, there would be fewer "fast ones" and more examples of truly fair trials. If the idea of giving trial lawyers solid training ever caught on, who knows what might happen? We might even get back to talking about justice.

One morning toward the end of the Carson trial, Lynda and I were stumbling through the cafeteria line at the courthouse. It was eight-thirty, but we'd already been up for three hours because we'd flown down from Marshfield to Hempstead, Long Island, and driven a rental car through rush-hour traffic for almost an hour to get to Mineola.

I wanted hot coffee and no conversation, but I noticed a large, friendly-looking woman bearing down on us. "Excuse me," she said, "but aren't you F. Lee Bailey?"

I answered, somewhat tiredly, "More or less."

Fortunately, the woman wasn't offended, even though it must have sounded like a flippant response. But it was the truth.

As I said in my first book, I like being F. Lee Bailey. But ever since the government indicted me, I'd felt less and less like myself. But as each day and week passed the memory of Jacksonville faded just a little bit more. And I felt more like myself.

What I needed more than anything else was to get back "in the pit." Most experienced trial lawyers begin to get antzy when they are not trying cases. The Carson case was helping, and I was quite pleased that more cases were coming into my (noticeably smaller) law firm every day. One of them did wonders for my spirits.

In mid-November I was asked to seek a new trial for a client who'd been convicted of rape. I'm not fond of rape cases, and if a defendant tells me, "Yes, I did it, but I want a good lawyer who can get me off," I send him elsewhere. This defendant, however, swore he was innocent. And when I learned that the man who had contacted me on behalf of the potential client was the man's employer, my ears perked up a bit. I learned that the case had turned on eyewitness testimony, and I've always been sympathetic to people who find themselves in that situation.

I asked if the young man would be able to pay the kind of fee that would enable me to prepare a first-class appeal. The caller hesitated a bit, and then said, "Mr. Bailey, he's really just a kid, but me and some of the other boys in the shop have taken up a collection, and we hope it'll be enough to pay your fee. Myself, I put up a grand, and so did the fourteen other guys. Will that be enough?"

I had no idea if it would or not, but I was so intrigued by the prospect of defending a man who had fifteen less-than-wealthy friends who were willing to put up a thousand dollars apiece because they believed in him that I answered right away.

I said, "Certainly."

Two weeks later, I got the results of the polygraph examination. My new client had passed with flying colors. As I write this, the defendant is anxiously awaiting his new day in court—and so am I.

# INDEX